DEDUCTIVE FORMS

Harper & Row, Publishers

New York, Evanston and London

ROBERT NEIDORF

State University of New York at Binghamton

DEDUCTIVE FORMS

An Elementary Logic

To Mary

Contents

**Chapter 3 • Natural Deduction for
Propositional Arguments   121**

Chapter 4 • Generalizations and Normal Forms   195

Preface

In this century, certain methods of logical analysis have been developed that employ numerous specialized concepts and symbols. These have become so widely used that they now form the basis of a technical language commonly utilized by philosophers, logicians, mathematicians, and many others. This book endeavors to set forth those concepts and symbols as intuitively plausible aids for the evaluation and construction of ordinary verbal arguments, without prejudice to the latter.

The aim of the book contributes to its length. Many of the conventions and techniques expounded in it could be defined and explained in short order were they treated as parts of an autonomous symbolic system; but they are not so treated here. In particular, the system of inference rules that emerges in the text is not systematically developed from a slender set of postulates or axioms. That mode of development (axiomatization) permits a brief exposition and facilitates the study of the system itself, but it also tends to overshadow the relations between formal rules and verbal contexts. I have generally proceeded by the examination of simple arguments, the validity (or invalidity) of which appear self-evident. Reflection on these leads to problems of interpretation, but eventually to the identification of logical forms and general criteria. New methods are added as new problems or new types of arguments come into view. The result is an unfolding series of interrelated techniques. For the most part, the systematic coherence of their relations to each other is evident; where not, it is discussed or (when feasible) demonstrated.

The text is organized around two questions: (i) How can one decide whether or not a given argument is valid? (ii) How can one go about constructing exclusively valid arguments? Answering the first question facilitates discussion of the second; hence, where possible they are taken in the order listed. In Chapters 2 and 5 the first question is answered, at different levels of complexity, and in Chapters 3 and 6 the second question is answered at the corresponding levels. In Chapter 8 the methods of Chapter 6 are extended into an area in which no general answer to the first question is available. Chapters 1 and 4 are essentially transitional, and Chapter 7 is a digression.

(Chapters 6 and 8 contain what is sometimes called a natural deduction system for the restricted predicate calculus. This topic has become a classic stumbling-block because of the somewhat complex series of qualifications that have to be attached to its primary inference rules. In accordance with the aim of the text, I have adopted a symbolism that permits those qualifications to be understood as symbolic versions of prosaic restrictions that might be made by any alert arguer if he were discussing, wholly in prose, certain logical relations between sets of objects. For this purpose a device referred to as a particulate variable is introduced in Chapter 6 and retained thereafter; it represents the only substantial departure from currently standard symbolic usage.)

Academic needs and tastes vary widely, and justifiably so. This fact must qualify any specification of the book's possible place in college curricula. Generally, it is intended for use in connection with a first introduction to logic, provided a good deal of formal analysis is part of the purpose of such a course. However, for this use not all of the material may be wanted, and the following portions are suited to summary treatment, abridgement, or omission: Chapter 3, Sections 3 and 5; Chapter 4, Sections 2–7; Chapter 5, Sections 8–14; Chapter 6, Section 5; and all of Chapter 8. Where a first course in symbolic logic is customarily offered independently of an introduction to general logic, the entire book is more likely to be appropriate.

Like all textbook writers I have tried to make the book independently readable, but with special regard for those who desire an acquaintance with modern deductive methods that is neither casual nor credulous, and who cannot for whatever reason submit to the formalities of "taking a course." Hence, no technical background is presupposed, and in addition to the generally deliberate pace of the text there are substantial digressions on traditionally vexing topics (such as material implication, necessary and sufficient conditions, and vacuous truths). There are also numerous exercises. Usually, these call for an application of the methods developed in immediately preceding pages, or supplement discussions and demonstrations given in the main text, or anticipate further developments; rarely do they demand symbolic manipulation for its own sake.

The entire book presupposes that deductive inferences can be illuminated by isolating, within a nexus of argument, certain contained elements that may occur more than once and a form or structure in which those elements are arranged. It is then a logical step to employ special symbols in order to focus attention on the form. The methods developed in the sequel are, it is claimed, natural and useful; it does not follow that they are unique, or uniquely good, or entirely free from philosophically contestable assumptions.

Whatever is correct in the book derives from the inspiration, instruction, or assistance of more persons than I could possibly enumerate. These include teachers and authors, colleagues and critics, editors and friends; among the teachers I also count many who were officially my students. I owe to Mrs. Iva Weaver a special debt of gratitude for her patient and accurate creation of a readable typescript. Those parts of the book that are incorrect or otherwise misconceived can only be attributed to my own oversights, or failures of insight.

ROBERT NEIDORF

Binghamton, New York

Everyone should firmly persuade himself that none of the sciences, however abstruse, is to be deduced from lofty and obscure matters, but that they all proceed only from what is . . . easily understood.

—René Descartes

The sole object of Logic is the guidance of one's own thoughts.

—John Stuart Mill

A centipede was happy quite
Until a frog in fun
Said, "Pray which leg comes after which?"
This raised her mind to such a pitch,
She lay distracted in a ditch,
Considering how to run.

—Anonymous

CHAPTER 1

Preliminary Ideas
and Methods

ABSTRACT: Four programs are carried out: First, the subject matter is identified and (in a rough way) defined by means of a series of narrowing distinctions; the distinctions themselves provide the beginnings of a technical vocabulary. Secondly, an extended search is made for some adequate formulation of the idea of a *valid deductive argument;* eventually, the search ends and a definition is offered. Thirdly, the concept of *logical form* is introduced and developed, largely by confrontation with numerous examples. Fourthly, four rudimentary techniques are stated, techniques that may be used to show that given deductive arguments are valid or invalid. The first program occupies Sections 1–4; the others are carried on concurrently in the remainder of the chapter.

1 • LOGICAL INFERENCE

Most of the things we claim to know *are* known by us because they are related in some way to *other* things we know. We then say that the former are *inferred* from the latter. We might, for example, claim to know that "democracy is better than tyranny," or that "aromatic hydrocarbons sometimes cause cancer." Were we asked to state the reasons or justifications for these beliefs we could be expected to refer to other beliefs or items of knowledge: Perhaps convictions about the nature of men and governments; perhaps records of laboratory experiments. In any case, we usually find that a given item of knowledge (or belief) is connected to others and *depends* upon them in the sense that it is justified by reference *to* them.

Of course there must be some items of knowledge that are known independently, without being inferred in any ordinary sense from other items; for if all bits of knowledge depended upon other bits, none of our knowledge would be well founded finally. Sometimes we claim to know things directly without inference by observation; for example, "John is tall." Again, we sometimes say that certain things are known directly without inference because of their intuitive obviousness; for example, "The whole is no smaller than the sum of its parts." The attempt to discover and enumerate such items of knowledge is a possible and important project: It is the task (perhaps endless) of finding and justifying the fundamental principles and pieces of knowledge upon which all the rest of our knowledge ultimately rests. But this book is primarily unconcerned with that project; we shall concentrate instead on certain *relations* between items of knowledge and belief that enable us to justify some by reference to others.

These relations may be of several kinds, not equally respectable nor equally persuasive. We often observe attempts to justify beliefs on the basis of other beliefs where the connection is established, or at least urged, by an appeal to emotions or esthetic preferences. Alternatively, the connection is sometimes established, or urged, by an appeal to what might be called reason, or the sense of logic. It is often supposed that appeals of the former sort are one and all deceptive and disreputable; but they are sometimes quite appropriate and desirable, particularly when combined, as they usually are, with the latter species. The study of the art of persuasion of all kinds is usually called *rhetoric*. Our purpose here will be to study only those kinds of connections between beliefs that obtain their persuasive force by appealing to what we think of as the reasoning power in us. It is this study that is ordinarily called *logic*.

Hence it is *logical inference* that we will analyze. By logical inference we mean a mental or intellectual process in which some things are recognized as knowable in virtue of a relation to other items of knowledge, the whole process being effected by our reasoning powers. This definition is perhaps circular, because if we were asked to state what is meant by our reasoning powers we might end by talking about the ability to make logical inferences. Nevertheless, the definition serves to indicate the area of the study that follows and to separate it from other mental phenomena.

Two additional qualifications must be made: First, it must not be supposed that the study of logical inference is merely a branch of psychology, or an attempt to describe the way the human mind happens to work. Logic is at least partly a normative discipline. That is, we shall try to find criteria for making and discovering *reliable* inferences; hence, logical rules are in a sense prescriptions for how the mind *ought* to work. Put differently, logic seeks to unfold the forms, not merely of inference, but of *correct* inference. Just how we come to recognize the difference between correct and incorrect inference, between logical and illogical thinking, is a psychological and philosophical problem beyond the scope of this treatment. For the present, we will simply assume that such recognition is possible.

Secondly, it must not be supposed that our possession of a certain item of knowledge is necessarily based on the fact that it can be properly inferred from other items. A man's knowledge that the planets do not twinkle might be based, in his own mind, on direct observation, even though he may be aware that it could be inferred from other items. It was for this reason that we defined logical inference as a process in which things are recognized *as knowable* in virtue of a relation to other items; we did not say that the beliefs in question are necessarily known or held primarily *because* of this relation. As we shall see in due course, it is sometimes important to know that some possible belief could be inferred from other possible beliefs, even if the latter or the former or both are actually thought to be false.

Our focus will always be on the (logical) relation between possible beliefs or items of knowledge, not on the beliefs themselves, and not on the psychological processes that are involved when we think and reason. The reader who is dissatisfied with this somewhat vague account of the subject is asked to be patient: It will become clear when the actual technical manipulation of logical forms begins.

2 • ARGUMENTS, PROPOSITIONS, AND SENTENCES

Inferences, good and bad, are expressed in words; and it is only through the medium of words that we can analyze and manipulate inferences. Consequently, we have to distinguish between inferences and the verbal structures in which they are expressed: The former are mental or intellectual acts; the latter are purely physical entities, ink shapes on paper or sound vibrations in the air. We shall use the term *argument* to refer to a series of words that expresses or purports to express an inference. This is a technical meaning of argument, and its ordinary meaning, "a fight with words," should be left behind. The verbal clue to the presence of an argument is the word *therefore* or some equivalent, such as *hence, so, thus,* and so on. These terms usually signify that what follows is intended to be logically justified by what precedes; the shopworn example is

All men are mortal and Socrates is a man; therefore, Socrates is mortal.

The materials of inference are items of possible belief or knowledge, that is, things that are believed or may be proposed for belief. They are reasonably called *propositions* and are expressed in declarative sentences. Roughly, a proposition is what a declarative sentence means. The distinction between proposition and sentence must be drawn, because two or more sentences (in the same language or in different languages) may have the same meaning; in such cases we say that the different sentences express the same proposition. A proposition is in some way an intellectual or mental entity; a sentence is a physical artifact.[1]

---

[1] Although not needed for our purposes, it is possible to draw a further distinction between sentences and the *individual* physical entities with which they are associated. Consider (i) *John runs,* (ii) *John runs,* and (iii) *John is running.* Take

Obviously, the structures of inferences and propositions are intimately related to the structures of the arguments and sentences by which they are expressed. Consequently it is not always necessary or desirable to attend to these distinctions; frequently, *argument* and *inference, sentence* and *proposition,* are conveniently used interchangeably and without confusion.[2] In this text we generally use *argument* rather than *inference* in order to draw attention to the visible structure that inferences exhibit when expressed as written arguments; for (as will be seen) it is this structure that is the most prominent factor in the analysis of inferences. On the other hand, we usually use *proposition* rather than *sentence* in order to draw attention to the meanings of the sentences ingredient in an argument. English and most natural languages require that propositions be repeated with slight variations in the structure and vocabulary of the corresponding sentences, and (as will be seen) these minor variations must be routinely ignored if one is to grasp the structure of an underlying inference.

It is characteristic of propositions that they may be true or false, and they must be one or the other. This does not imply that we necessarily know or can know whether or not a given proposition is true. There is probably no way of finding out whether the proposition (expressed by) "One of the the great-grandfathers of Eric the Red was bald" is true; it remains a proposition still. Also, many propositions lack a clear significance unless a context is understood. "I am sitting" may be true at one time, false at another; but any given assertion that "I am sitting" is assumed to refer to some specifiable "I" and some specifiable time, and when so understood it will be true or false, not both.

---

these as three distinct physical objects. As such, (i) and (ii) are distinct, but they can be regarded as instances of just *one* sentence. In this spirit one could identify a single sentence as a certain class of physical entities that are all alike in some way. (Just *what* way may be hard to specify.) Of course, (iii) is distinct from the others both as a physical object and as a sentence, but it expresses the same proposition. A similar series of distinctions could be made for arguments, and for words or phrases.

[2] The ability to use a language implies, among other things, the ability to pass from words to their meanings and conversely with little or no conscious effort; hence, we habitually ignore these distinctions. We must here ignore the complex and difficult philosophical question, "What *are* meanings?"

Consider some examples. Which of the following express propositions?

1. John runs.
2. Plato is wrong.
3. Honesty is the best policy.
4. Man is a rational animal.
5. Beryllium oxide is purple.
6. The sun rises in the east.
7. The sun rises in the west.
8. He it book tree.
9. Quadruplicity drinks blue.
10. John runs and Mary runs.
11. John runs or.
12. It is not true that houses.
13. If Mary goes, John goes.
14. Only if Mary goes, John goes.
15. If Mary and John go, Plato is wrong.

All except 8, 9, 11, and 12 express propositions. Number 9 is an example of a series of words that obeys the laws of grammar but lacks any meaning; it therefore does not express a proposition, and for our purposes it should not be regarded as a sentence.

When an argument is written out in full, the propositions of which it is made fall into two groups: One group consists of those propositions that fall before the word *therefore* or its equivalent. This group is called the *premise-set*, and the individual propositions in the group are called *premises*. The other group, which usually contains only one proposition, falls after the word *therefore* or its equivalent and is called the *conclusion*. Obviously, the premises form the justification on the basis of which the conclusion is inferred. An example is

All men are mortal.	Premise ⎱ Premise-set
Socrates is a man.	Premise ⎰
Therefore, Socrates is mortal.	Conclusion

In idiomatic English discourse we do not always put the conclusion last. It is perfectly proper, for instance, to say, "Socrates is a man and hence mortal, for all men are." It is clear that this argument is equivalent to the preceding example, except that the first premise has been placed after the conclusion; such premises are customarily introduced by words like *for, since,* or *because.* In practice one encounters very little difficulty in distinguishing premises from conclusions. When subjecting arguments to formal analysis, we shall generally write them with the conclusion last.

3 • INDUCTION AND DEDUCTION

Logical inferences are divisible into two broad types that we shall illustrate with examples. Consider first the following argument:

> All swans I have seen are white.
> I have seen a great many swans.
> Therefore, all swans are white.

Everyone would admit that this *is* an argument, and a fairly good one, for the premises do provide some justification for the conclusion. Yet it remains possible, admitting the premises, that there could be some swans that are not white. Unlikely perhaps, particularly if "I" have seen a great many swans, but still possible. That is, admitting that the premises are true, we would infer that the conclusion is probably right but possibly wrong. The inference from premises to conclusion is a probable inference only; we shall call such inferences *inductions.* The above is thus one example of an *inductive argument,* which embodies an *inductive inference.*

In contrast to this situation consider again our ancient example:

> All men are mortal.
> Socrates is a man.
> Therefore, Socrates is mortal.

In this case, admitting the premises, it is clear that the conclusion is *certainly* true, for there remains no conceivable possibility that Socrates could be immortal. Or to put it differently, in this example the inference from premises to conclusion is absolutely certain, not merely probable. We shall call such inferences *deductions.* Hence, the preceding is an example of a *deductive argument,* which embodies a *deductive inference.* Here are two more examples of deductive arguments.

> If the radio is turned on, then someone is listening.
> The radio is turned on.
> Therefore, someone is listening.

> Either calcium or sodium raises the blood pressure.
> Calcium does not.
> Therefore, sodium does.

To summarize then, in inductive arguments the conclusions probably follow from the premises. In deductive arguments the conclusions certainly follow from the premises (unless the arguments are fallacious: a difficulty we shall face shortly). In deductive arguments, or at any rate in good ones, it is customary to say that the conclusion *follows from* the premises, or that the premises *imply* the conclusion.

Note that the distinction between induction and deduction depends upon the character of the logical *relation* between premises and conclusion, not upon the *content* of the propositions themselves. Hence, a proposition stating that something is probable or possible may itself be part of a *deductive* argument. Example:

> If everyone gets an A then it is probable that everyone understands the work.
> Everyone does get an A.
> Therefore it is probable that everyone understands the work.

Here the conclusion states a probability only. But it is obvious that in this argument, assuming the premises are true, the conclusion is certainly true; hence, the argument is deductive.

As its title indicates, this book will concern itself solely with deductive inferences. The treatment of inductive inference is an extraordinarily important topic belonging partly to logic, partly to philosophy of science, and partly to the theory of statistics. Its thorough development presupposes, however, an adequate science of deductive inference, and it is this latter that will engage our attention hereafter.

One further remark should be made: When, later, we begin to distinguish between good and bad deductive arguments, or proper and improper ones, the possibility arises that an argument failing as a *de*duction may yet have some perfectly valid force as an *in*duction. Hence, in some cases it may be impossible to decide merely from inspection of an offered argument whether it is intended as an induction or a deduction; some knowledge of the context is then required. In all of our subsequent discussions we will take it for granted that the arguments studied are intended as deductions.

Exercises

Decide which of the following arguments are inductive, which deductive. Here and hereafter, the asterisk (*) indicates an exercise of more than ordinary difficulty.

1. Swan number 1 is white. Swan number 2 is white. Swan number 3 is white. Therefore, all swans are white.

2. If this bird is white, then this bird is a swan. This bird is white. Therefore, this bird is a swan.

3. If all the swans I have seen are white, then all swans are white. All the swans I have seen are white. Therefore, all swans are white.

4. All long-necked birds are white. All swans are long-necked. Therefore, all swans are white.

*5. All long-necked birds are swans. All long-necked birds are white. Therefore, all swans are white.

6. If all kangaroos I have seen are gray, then probably all kangaroos are gray. All kangaroos I have seen are gray. Therefore, probably all kangaroos are gray.

4 • VALIDITY AND SOUNDNESS

We must now try to understand the difference between good or correct deductive arguments and bad or fallacious ones. All the examples of deductive arguments that have been given in the main text up to this point have been good arguments, in the sense that their conclusions do indeed follow certainly from their premises. But it is notoriouly true that this need not always be the case. Consider this example:

All Communists favor labor.
All Socialists favor labor.
Therefore, all Socialists are Communists.

Is this a good argument? Take another example:

> If Einstein is right, Mercury will appear at location L on the photograph.
> Mercury does appear at location L on the photograph.
> Therefore, Einstein is right.

We may be in doubt about these and similar arguments. But no one would be in doubt about the following examples, which are clearly bad arguments:

> All horses are animals.
> All men are animals.
> Therefore, all men are horses.

> If an evil demon possesses Percy, then Percy will behave cruelly.
> Percy behaves cruelly.
> Therefore, an evil demon possesses Percy.

Again, we have to ask just what is the difference between good deductions and bad ones, and what are the criteria that will enable us to decide doubtful cases? In a certain sense, the balance of this book will be devoted to the development of criteria for distinguishing between good and bad arguments and the development of techniques for the construction of exclusively good ones. But for the present we must try to formulate in a preliminary way what it is that we mean when we say in some cases that the conclusion clearly follows from the premises, and in others that it clearly does not. Putting it differently, we wish to know what it is that we are recognizing when we realize in some cases that a deductive inference is right and in other cases that it is not. Only when we have an answer to this question can we know how to approach doubtful cases. Only when we have an answer to this question can we develop systematic rules and techniques for the construction of exclusively correct arguments.

Let us begin by giving a *wrong* answer, a wrong answer that is frequently and repeatedly given. It is often said that a good or correct deductive argument is one in which the premises and conclusion are one and all *true*. It can be shown in several ways that this formulation, tempting as it may appear at first glance, is absolutely and unequivocally incorrect.

In the first place, take this argument:

> If Troy is a mythical city, then the *Iliad* is an entirely imaginary work.
> Troy is a mythical city.
> Therefore, the *Iliad* is an entirely imaginary work.

It should be clear at a glance that this is a perfectly good argument, for if the premises are true the conclusion certainly follows. At one time it was thought that the premises *were* true and, hence, the conclusion as well. It is now known that one of the premises (the second) is false and so is the conclusion. But the argument itself, as an example of a good deduction, is not altered in quality because we happen to have found out that some of its constituent propositions, once thought to be true, are really false. For if we focus our attention on the logical quality of the argument as such, that quality depends only upon the fact that, *were* the premises true, the conclusion would be true as well. That is, the logical quality of the argument has to do only with some kind of *relation* between the premises and the conclusion, not with their *content*. And even though the second premise and the conclusion are in reality false, it remains as true as ever that if the premises *were* true, the conclusion would also be true. That is to say, the premises do imply the conclusion, and we have here an example of a perfectly good deductive argument in which premises and conclusion are *not* one and all true.

Secondly, consider this case:

> Los Angeles is in California.
> All whales are mammals.
> Therefore, gold is yellow.

As an example of a deductive argument this is a bad joke. Yet the premises and conclusion are one and all true. Here we have the reverse of the previous case: an argument that is clearly bad as a deduction, in which premises and conclusion are all true.

Lastly, consider one of the uses of logical deduction: In the process of scientific inquiry, for example, a certain hypothesis about the nature or behavior of an object may be investigated by deducing, from the hypothesis, consequences that can be checked by observation in the laboratory. That is, we take certain propositions (hypotheses) as premises for deductive arguments and then infer conclusions from them; and we do this *not knowing* whether or not the premises are true, but in order to facilitate an inquiry *into* their truth. This procedure, which is a commonplace of science and common sense, would be entirely without foundation unless there were some meaning for the concept of a good deduction entirely independent of the actual truth or falsity of the constituent propositions. So we can *not* answer our original question by saying that a good deduction is one in which all the constituent propositions are true.

Yet we prefer when possible to argue from true premises; it must be admitted that, if two arguments are equally correct as deductions and one of them has true premises, one enjoys a desirable property that the other lacks. We shall mark this distinction hereafter by using the word *valid* to refer to a good or correct deduction without regard to the truth or falsity of its constituent propositions; that is, we shall say that a deductive argument is valid when the conclusion does indeed follow from the premises (although we have not yet found out what that means). If, in addition to being valid, an argument has true premises, we shall say that it is *sound. Hence, all sound arguments are valid as well; but some valid arguments are sound, some unsound.*

From now on we shall not speak of arguments as good and bad, correct and incorrect, and so on; instead, we w'll speak only of validity and invalidity, soundness and unsoundness. The primary concern of logic is with the validity of arguments, and it is on the question of validity that our attention will hereafter be focused. Soundness of arguments will be a matter of only subsidiary interest, because soundness depends upon more than purely logical considerations. Also, it should be clear that validity is a necessary (but not sufficient) condition for soundness.

Exercises

1. Run through the examples of deductive arguments that have appeared in the preceding pages. Choose the ones you think are valid, and among those decide which are sound.

2. Could an unsound argument be valid?

3. Could an invalid argument be sound?

4. Could a valid argument have a false conclusion?

5. Could a sound argument have a false conclusion?

6. A given argument has false premises and a true conclusion. Could it be valid? Could it be sound? If the answer to either question is "Yes," give an example.

7. A given argument has true premises and a false conclusion. Could it be valid? Could it be sound? If the answer to either question is "Yes," give an example.

5 • MEANING OF VALIDITY: VALID FORMS

As a result of introducing the technical terms *validity* and *soundness*, we must now rephrase the question we originally set out to answer. We are trying to find out what is meant by saying that an argument is *valid* or *invalid*. *Or*, we want to find out what it is that we recognize when we realize that a certain argument is or is not *valid*. And we have seen that a valid argument need not have true premises and a true conclusion. What then?

To make further progress we shall have to examine a rather long list of sample arguments and decide with regard to each one whether it is valid or invalid. In the process there will emerge some very rudimentary techniques for the analysis of arguments and some important properties of deductive inference.

First consider this old friend:

> **Sample 1:** All men are mortal.
> Socrates is a man.
> Therefore, Socrates is mortal.

There seems to be no doubt whatever that this is a valid argument. It is so obviously valid, in fact, that we could confidently reject any proposed criterion of validity under which *this* argument would be *in*valid. Hence, we shall say that this argument is obviously valid and is intuitively known to be so.

Next, consider

> **Sample 2:** All angels are Greek.
> Socrates is an angel.
> Therefore, Socrates is Greek.

Is this valid? Here the answer is not so immediately obvious, but a moment's thought will probably convince anyone that it is. We perhaps tend to be uneasy in the presence of this argument because its premises are so patently false. But let us compare it with Sample 1. To facilitate the comparison we place them side by side:

All men are mortal.   All angels are Greek.
Socrates is a man.   Socrates is an angel.
Therefore, Socrates is mortal.   Therefore, Socrates is Greek.

Evidently these arguments are similar. They are in fact identical except that the terms *man* and *mortal* in Sample 1 have been replaced by the terms *angel* and *Greek* in Sample 2. This similarity, once grasped, should help to strengthen one's conviction that Sample 2 is just as valid as Sample 1; although the premises in Sample 2 are false, the conclusion in Sample 2 follows from its premises just as surely as the conclusion in Sample 1 follows from *its* premises.

A further example is

Sample 3: All horses are Persian.
Socrates is a horse.
Therefore, Socrates is Persian.

By now it should be clear that this argument is just as valid as the preceding ones. In fact, it bears the same resemblance to Sample 1 that Sample 2 does. And if nothing else convinces us of its validity, we should certainly be convinced when we see the resemblance displayed clearly before us:

All *men* are *mortal*.   All *horses* are *Persian*.
Socrates is a *man*.   *Socrates* is a *horse*.
Therefore, *Socrates* is *mortal*.   Therefore, *Socrates* is *Persian*.

The right side is identical with the left, except that *man* and *mortal* are replaced by *horse* and *Persian*.

We can summarize the resemblance between all three samples by noting that they all have the same *form* or *structure*. Schematically, they all have the form,

All X's are Y.
Socrates is an X.
Therefore, Socrates is Y.

Clearly the same arguments would be valid with regard to any individual other than Socrates, and we could just as well have changed from Socrates to some other person in moving from one Sample to another. Hence, a complete schematic or symbolic representation of the *form* of Samples 1, 2, and 3 would be the following:

All X's are Y.
Z is an X.
Therefore, Z is Y.

We can now claim with some confidence that *any* argument having this form is valid. Anyone skeptical of that claim should try substituting various terms in place of the symbols X, Y, and Z, and convincing himself that the resulting arguments are indeed one and all valid.[3]

It is useful at this point to define a technical term, *substitution instance*. We shall say that any particular argument obtained from a symbolic form by substituting appropriate terms or phrases for the symbols in the symbolic form is a *substitution instance* of that form. Hence, Samples 1, 2, and 3 are all substitution instances of the form displayed here.

Two important results are implicit in our discussion so far. First, it has become apparent that the validity of an argument is in some way bound up with its form or structure; and we might very well suspect that invalidity will be related to form as well. Secondly, we have found a method for proving the validity of an argument that is not itself obviously valid. The method is this: *Show that the argument has the same form as an argument that is obviously valid.*

As a technique this will not carry us very far for reasons that will emerge shortly. But however rudimentary, it is our first technical device and we must make the most of it. Let us first try it out in a different context:

No large bushes are toxicondrons.
All shrubs are large bushes.
Therefore, no shrubs are toxicondrons.

Here the unfamiliarity of a term may obscure one's attempt to think through the argument directly. But assuming that toxicondron

---

[3] Naturally the substitutions must be of such a nature that *propositions* result.

is meaningfully used in this context, we may exhibit the form as

> No X's are Y's.
> All Z's are X's.
> Therefore, no Z's are Y's.

Another substitution instance of this is

> No men are angels.
> All sailors are men.
> Therefore, no sailors are angels.

which is evidently valid; hence, the former is also valid.

Again,

> Either the sun is a star or Newton is wrong.
> It is not true that the sun is a star.
> Therefore, Newton is wrong.

Here the attempt to decide intuitively and immediately about the argument may be obscured by the evident falsity of the second premise. But the following is clearly valid:

> Either Mary is going or John is lying.
> It is not true that Mary is going.
> Therefore, John is lying.

Both are substitution instances of

> Either W is X or Y is Z.
> It is not true that W is X.
> Therefore, Y is Z.

It follows that both are valid. Note that in the formal schema, W *is* X and Y *is* Z repeat as unaltered units, and it would be sufficient to capture the logical structure of the argument if we used single symbols, such as P and Q, in their place. Then as the most economical symbolic representation we would have

> Either P or Q.
> It is not true that P.
> Therefore, Q.

Any substitution instance of this form (with whole propositions in place of the letters) would itself be a valid deductive argument.

The possibility of symbolizing forms in greater or less detail brings us to an objection against our method for proving validity. Consider the form

All X's are Y's.
Therefore, all X's are Z's.

and then compare two arguments, both substitution instances of it:

All men are omnivores and vertebrates.
Therefore, all men are vertebrates.

All birds are warm-blooded.
Therefore, all birds are egg-layers.

Someone might contend that the second argument is valid because the first one clearly is, and they both have the same form. The difficulty rests on the fact that in the first argument a logically complex term (*omivore and vertebrate*) corresponds to a symbolically simple term (Y) in the formal schema; this just happens to obscure a relevant structural feature of the argument, because *part* of the verbal correlate of the symbol (*vertebrate*) turns up again later in the argument. If we had taken the form of the first argument as

All X's are V's and W's.
Therefore, all X's are W's.

there would have been no difficulty.

Similarly, one might think of Sample 1 as having the form P, Q, *therefore R*, where the letters stand for propositions. But it is clearly wrong to infer that because Sample 1 is valid, so is any argument having two premises. Again we see that P, Q, *therefore R* fails to exhibit enough structural detail, when taken as the form of Sample 1.

We could evade these difficulties by agreeing to symbolize the forms of arguments with as much detail as possible, always. But this is inconvenient and really negates one of the main purposes of symbolic representation. A less radical cure is possible. It is apparent from the few examples we have scrutinized that valid arguments get to *be* valid because certain terms or groups of terms appear more than once within them, and arranged in certain ways. Thus, to be sure that a symbolic representation of the form of an argument does not obscure vital detail, we need only adopt this rule: *Repetition of terms within a verbal argument must be reflected by repetition of the corresponding symbols in any formal schema assigned to the argument.* This forbids using *Y* for *omivore and vertebrate* and, later in the same context, using *Z* for *vertebrate*. It also forbids using *P* for "Socrates is a *man*" and later in the same context using *Q* for "All *men* are mortal." When generating substitution instances from a given symbolic form, this rule implies that distinct symbols must be replaced by wholly distinct terms or groups of terms.[4]

We shall call this rule the *principle of symbolic uniqueness*. Strict adherence is not really required in practice; the possibility of making harmless exceptions (and the reasons why they are harmless) will occur to the reader eventually. For the present we adopt the principle as an implicit ingredient in the formulation of techniques for proving validity and (shortly) invalidity; that is, whenever speaking of the form of an argument, we mean some symbolic schema that satisfies the symbolic uniqueness principle.

Exercises

1. In the following three arguments, the first is intended to be obviously valid. Express its form symbolically and then decide which of the other two arguments has the same form (only one has). State explicitly which words, phrases, or propositions correspond to which symbols. Lastly, show how the form of the remaining argument differs from the other two.

   a. All mammals are warm-blooded.
      All whales are mammals.
      Therefore, all whales are warm-blooded.

   b. All real craftsmen are wise.
      All patient men are wise.
      Therefore, all patient men are real craftsmen.

---

[4] In speaking of terms in this connection we mean words indicating what a proposition is about: names of things, properties, activities, classes, events. Words that merely serve to indicate connections and formal relations between the contents of a proposition, such as *is*, *or*, *not*, are not counted as terms. Thus, *P* could stand for "Newton is right," and in the same context *Q* could stand for "Aristotle is Greek," without violating the rule; for *is* does not count as one of the substantive terms of the statements.

   c. All planets are stars.
     All stars are icy.
     Therefore, all planets are icy.

2. Do the same with the following arguments.

   a. If the army has been called out, then the town can be defended.
     The army has been called out.
     Therefore, the town can be defended.

   b. If 2.9 is a solution for that equation, then 2.9 is the answer to this
     problem.
     2.9 is the answer to this problem.
     Therefore, 2.9 is a solution for that equation.

   c. If the moon is made of green cheese, then all the merchants have
     sold out.
     The moon is made of green cheese.
     Therefore, all the merchants have sold out.

3. Is the order in which the premises are stated a relevant feature of the logical form of an argument? Explain, with examples.

*4. Following are *two lists*, one of arguments and one of proposed symbolic forms. Each argument can be correlated with one or two of the forms (while satisfying the symbolic uniqueness principle). Match them accordingly.

   a. Either all trolls are crafty or some witches are clever.
     It is not true that all trolls are crafty.
     Therefore, some witches are clever.

   b. All trolls are crafty and some witches are clever.
     All gnomes are trolls.
     Therefore, all gnomes are crafty.

   c. All trolls are crafty and some witches are crafty.
     It is not true that all trolls are crafty.
     Therefore, some witches are crafty.

   a. All X's are Y and some Z's are W.
     All V's are X's.
     Therefore, all V's are Y.

   b. Either P or Q.
     It is not true that P.
     Therefore, Q.

c. P.
   Q.
   Therefore, R.

d. All X's are Y and some Z's are Y.
   It is not true that all X's are Y.
   Therefore, some Z's are Y.

e. Either all X's are Y or some Z's are W.
   It is not true that all X's are Y.
   Therefore, some Z's are W.

f. P and Q.
   It is not true that P.
   Therefore, Q.

g. P and Q.
   R.
   Therefore, S.

6 • MEANING OF VALIDITY: PROVING INVALIDITY

In searching for the meaning of validity, we have stumbled upon one quite limited method for proving the validity of given arguments and turned our attention to that technique. What are the limitations or objections to that technique?

First, the technique requires us to show that a given argument whose validity we wish to demonstrate is structurally or formally identical with some obviously valid argument. But there are many obviously valid arguments hav'ng the same form. We naturally desire to cut down the endless proliferation of obviously valid arguments to which appeal is to be made. We could accomplish this by referring to some structure, say

All X's are Y.
Z is an X.
Therefore, Z is Y.

as an obviously valid *form*, and agreeing to justify all substitution instances of it merely by showing that they are indeed substitution instances. (In fact some people seem to find abstract forms more obviously valid than substitution instances.) Following this line, we then restate our technique for proving validity as follows: *To prove an argument valid, show that it has an obviously valid form.* Or we could say, *To prove an argument valid, show that it is a substitution instance of an obviously valid form.* This takes care of the first objection, and the alternative formulations of the technique may be helpful.

But now we come to more serious objections. Appeal to obviously valid forms for justification is feasible so long as the number of such forms is small, and each of them is simple enough to render plausible the notion that its validity is intuitively evident. The obviously valid forms would then play a role akin to the function of axioms or postulates in Euclid's geometry. But, as we shall soon see, the forms of valid argument are literally endless and sometimes quite complex. We shall then be faced with two necessities, equally repugnant. First we shall have to expand the list of fundamental obviously valid forms endlessly, and we will never have any confidence that we have included all the possible cases or even the most important ones. Secondly, we shall have to claim that some quite long and complex forms are obviously valid; whereas, for ordinary mortals, the great majority of valid forms are not *obviously* valid at all. For instance, who will claim that the following form is obviously valid?

Either P is false or Q is true.
If R is false, then Q is false.
P and S are true.
Therefore, if T is false, then R is true.

Yet, where the letters stand for propositions, this is a genuinely valid form.

So we must find other, more refined techniques. But it is not clear how to make progress in this direction without first providing some answer to our original question, "What does it mean to say that an argument is valid?" Consequently, we shall have to defer the search for more elegant or systematic techniques of proving validity and return instead to the problem of the meaning of valid argument.

Our first three samples were all valid arguments. We shall now examine a few invalid arguments, in hopes that some critical contrast will suggest itself. Consider the following, which we have seen before.

Sample 4: All horses are animals.
All men are animals.
Therefore, all men are horses.

This is clearly invalid. How do we know? We might make the same sort of claim that we made in reference to Sample 1, and say simply that it is obviously invalid. But in this case we can note a feature of the argument that is more definite than its obvious (?) invalidity. Namely, *the premises are true and the conclusion false.* This being so, it is clear at once that the conclusion cannot follow from the premises, and the premises cannot imply the conclusion. In fact, it is the evident truth of the premises and falsehood of the conclusion that make the invalidity of the argument so obvious.

Next, consider

Sample 5: All mammals are animals.
All whales are animals.
Therefore, all whales are mammals.

This argument is likewise invalid, although all its propositions are true. How can we show this? First let us imagine that the conclusion is false. That is, let us conceive of a world in which there are large marine animals called whales that lack mammalian characteristics. (This is relatively easy to conceive, because the identification of a whale as a mammal is a somewhat sophisticated biological notion.) In such a world, it would still be true that whales are animals, and it could still be true that all mammals (not any of which are whales) are animals. Hence, we can conceive of a possible (although not actual) state of affairs in which the premises of Sample 5 could be true and the conclusion false. But we know that in a valid argument if the premises are true the conclusion *has* to be true. This shows that Sample 5 is invalid, for it is conceivable or imaginable that the premises could be true and the conclusion not. Or, to put it differently, we see that the conclusion, although factually true in our world, does not *have* to be true just because the premises are.

We have now developed, actually, a method for showing that a given argument is invalid: *To prove that an argument is invalid, describe a possible state of affairs in which the premises are true and the conclusion false.*

Let us try this method on another example:

Sample 6: All mammals are white.
All whales are white.
Therefore, all whales are mammals.

Again, suppose whales are really fishes rather than mammals. And we could also suppose that all mammals (not any of which are whales) are white, and that all whales (all of which are fishes) are also white. Under these possible circumstances, the premises of Sample 6 are true and the conclusion false. Hence, Sample 6 is invalid.

Thus, while seeking to specify the *meaning* of valid (or invalid) argument, we have stumbled instead upon a useful *technique* for showing that arguments are invalid. Like our earlier technique for proving validity, the present method suffers from severe limitations that will be discussed in the sequel. We have not yet found the meaning of validity.

Exercises

(Evaluation of arguments given as exercises in this introductory chapter will not necessarily be easy. The techniques for evaluation stated in this chapter are basic, but in order to apply them routinely or rapidly they must be combined with a survey, analysis, and classification of the common types of propositions and arguments; this begins in Chapter 2.)

1. The following arguments are invalid. Show this by specifying circumstances under which the premises are true and the conclusion false.

   a. All aromatics are carcinogens.
      Some aliphatics are not aromatics.
      Therefore, some aliphatics are carcinogens.

   b. Launcelot is not happy, or he is in love with Guinevere.
      Launcelot is not happy.
      Therefore, he is not in love with Guinevere.

2. Are the following arguments valid or invalid? Prove your result by the technique for proving invalidity developed in this section, or the technique for proving validity developed in the previous section.

    a. Some rotten apples are sour.
      All apples are rotten apples.
      Therefore, all apples are sour.

    b. Launcelot is happy, or he is in love with Guinevere.
      He is in love with Guinevere.
      Therefore, he is happy.

    c. All species of sumac are toxicondrons.
      No toxicondrons are poisonous.
      Therefore, no species of sumac are poisonous.

    d. No toxicondrons are poisonous.
      No sumacs are toxicondrons.
      Therefore, no sumacs are poisonous.

  *e. No invertebrates are mammalian.
      Some mammalians are bipedal.
      Therefore, some invertebrates are not bipedal.

  *f. No mammalians are invertebrate.
      Some mammalians are bipedal.
      Therefore, some bipedals are not invertebrate.

7 • MEANING OF VALIDITY: INVALID FORMS

Our technique for showing invalidity is very useful but is also subject to severe limitations. For one thing it may involve us in a great deal of work and put a large strain on our ingenuity, for it is not always easy to conjure up a possible state of affairs under which the premises would be true and the conclusion false. (And for all we know at present, there might be invalid arguments in which it is not even *possible* to do so.) Furthermore, it is not always clear what constitutes a possible state of affairs; particularly in complex cases, some people will argue that a described set of facts is possible or conceivable, others that it is not. Hence, our first method for showing invalidity is sorely limited, but another is close at hand. We shall develop it before turning again to the problem of the *meaning* of validity.

    Sample 7: All animals are impalpable.
               All material objects are impalpable.
               Therefore, all material objects are animals.

Like Samples 4, 5, and 6, this one is invalid. But we might be hard pressed to demonstrate its invalidity by imagining a situation in which the premises are true and the conclusion false, for some might contend that the premises cannot be imagined to be true. What other technique can we turn to?

Let us place Samples 4 and 7 side by side:

All horses are animals.	All animals are impalpable.
All men are animals.	All material objects are impalpable.
Therefore, all men are horses.	Therefore, all material objects are animals.

It emerges at once that both arguments have the same form. The key terms, *horses*, *animals*, and *men*, on the left are replaced respectively by *animals*, *impalpable*, and *material objects* on the right. Symbolically, both arguments are substitution instances of the form

All X's are Y's.
All Z's are Y's.
Therefore, all Z's are X's.

How does this help to demonstrate the invalidity of Sample 7? In our earlier method for showing *validity* we agreed that any argument having the same form as a valid argument is itself valid. The principle that now suggests itself is that any argument having the same form as an argument known to be *in*valid is itself *in*valid. In fact we can verify this principle independently. Consider Samples 4 and 7. We already know that Sample 4 is invalid. Sample 7 is either valid or not. *Suppose Sample 7 is valid.* Then any argument having the same form is likewise valid. Therefore, Sample 4 is also valid. But we have also established that Sample 4 is not valid. This creates a contradiction that can be avoided only if we agree that Sample 7 is in fact not valid.

The same line of reasoning can be applied to any two arguments A and B that have the same form, when A is known to be invalid and we are trying to decide about the validity of B. For if B were valid, A would also be valid; and because A is known to be invalid, B must be invalid also. So we have a new method: *To prove that a given argument is invalid, show that it has the same form as another argument known to be invalid.* The other argument could be known to be invalid either because it is "obviously" so, or by means of the *other* technique for showing invalidity. Also, it should now be clear that the *form* of any argument known to be invalid would generate other invalid arguments when other substitution instances of it are designated. Hence, we could develop a list of invalid forms and rephrase our present technique as follows: *To prove that a given argument is invalid, show that it has an invalid form; or, to prove that a given argument is invalid, show that it is a substitution instance of an invalid form.*

Of course this new method, which is actually quite powerful, is still limited. For in order to use it we must first grasp *by other means* that some argument or form is invalid. Insofar as those other means involve appeal to intuitive obviousness, we still have the usual difficulties attending such appeals: How many obviously invalid arguments are there, and who is to decide what is obvious? Insofar as those other means involve an appeal to the method of describing situations wherein the premises are true and the conclusion false, we are still burdened with the limitations of that method, which have already been discussed.

To sum up, we have discovered that the validity or invalidity of argument is a matter closely connected with the form or structure of the constituent propositions, rather than the content. Furthermore, we have developed three somewhat limited techniques for proving validity or invalidity in nonobvious cases. We shall now give each of them a final formulation and a label:

Tech 1: An argument suspected to be valid may be proved to be so by showing that it has the same form as another argument already known to be valid. The other argument could already be known to be valid only by some appeal to immediate obviousness. The form of an argument already known to be valid may be taken as a valid form. In that case an argument suspected to be valid may be proved to be so by showing that it is a substitution instance of a valid form.

Tech 2: An argument suspected to be invalid may be proved to be so by describing actual or possible circumstances under which the premises would be true and the conclusion false.

Tech 3: An argument suspected to be invalid may be proved to be so by showing that it has the same form as another argument already known to be invalid. The other argument could already be known to be invalid through Tech 2, or through some appeal to immediate obviousness. The form of an argument already known to be invalid may be taken as an invalid form. In that case an argument suspected to be invalid may be proved to be so by showing that it is a substitution instance of an invalid form.

Tech 1 and Tech 3 are subject to the understanding that the principle of symbolic uniqueness has to be satisfied in exhibiting identity of form.

It should be observed that we have not yet answered our main question as to the meaning of validity.

Exercises

1. Refer to the following arguments in the exercises at the end of Section 6: 1a, 1b, 2a, 2b, 2d, 2e. Show that each one is invalid by inventing another argument having the same form in which the premises are actually true and the conclusion actually false.

2. You are to determine which of the following arguments are valid, which invalid. Prove your results by employing any one of the techniques developed so far in this chapter.

   a. If the switch is closed, then the train is late.
      If the switch is closed, then the connection cannot be made.
      Therefore, if the train is late, then the connection cannot be made.

   b. Either the switch is closed or the train is late.
      The switch is closed or the connection cannot be made.
      Therefore, the train is late and the connection cannot be made.

   c. If the train is late, then the connection cannot be made.
      If the switch is closed, then the train is late.
      Therefore, if the switch is closed, then the connection cannot be made.

   d. All saints are merciful men.
      Some merciful men are not pious.
      Therefore, some saints are not pious.

   e. All merciful men are saints.
      Some merciful men are not pious.
      Therefore, some saints are not pious.

   f. All merciful men are saints.
       Some pious men are not merciful men.
       Therefore, some pious men are not saints.

8 • DEFINITION OF VALIDITY

We are now on the verge of an answer to our main question, "What is the meaning of validity? Suppose we are confronted with this rather puzzling argument, and we suspect it is invalid:

Ewing-Smythe is not fastidious.
All tobacco chewers are fastidious.
Hence, Ewing-Smythe is not a tobacco chewer.

We shall attempt to prove that it is *in*valid by the use of Tech 2. We must therefore try to show that it is possible for the premises to be (all) true and the conclusion false. We begin by supposing that the conclusion is false; that is, we assume it is true that

    (i) Ewing-Smythe is a tobacco chewer.

Now if we are also to assume that both premises are true, we must assume in particular that the second premise is true; that is, it would have to be true that

    (ii) All tobacco chewers are fastidious.

But from (i) and (ii) together, as premises of an argument, it follows that

    (iii) Ewing-Smythe is fastidious.

Indeed, the argument with (i) and (ii) as premises and (iii) as conclusion (which is not to be confused with the argument we started with) is obviously valid and has the same form as Sample 1 ("All men are mortal . . ."). *But proposition (iii) is in direct contradiction to one of the premises of the original argument.* That is, if the conclusion and the second premise of the original argument are true, the first premise cannot be true. This shows that it is in no way possible for the conclusion to be false while all the premises are true. Therefore, the original argument can never be proved to be invalid by Tech 2. Should we then conclude that it is *valid*?

The answer is, *Of course we should.* For if it is not possible for the premises to be true while the conclusion is false, it must be the case that if the premises are true, the conclusion follows. Thus, contrary to our original suspicion, it turns out that the Ewing-Smythe argument is val d. And we are convinced of its validity when we see (in this case by means of an auxiliary argument) that it is not possible for the premises to be true while the conclusion is false. This suggests that the impossibility of that combination—true premises with false conclusion—strikes very close to the essential nature of what it is to be a valid argument. We shall now confirm this suggestion from another direction.

In every argument the conclusion is either true or false, and either all of the premises are true or one (or more) false. This gives four possible cases:

	Premises	Conclusion
Case I	All true	True
Case II	All true	False
Case III	Not all true	True
Case IV	Not all true	False

Now let us review the seven arguments that have been labeled Samples in this chapter and ask under which case each argument falls. For convenience of reference, the seven samples are reproduced below:

Sample 1: All men are mortal.
Socrates is a man.
Therefore, Socrates is mortal.

Sample 2: All angels are Greek.
Socrates is an angel.
Therefore, Socrates is Greek.

Sample 3: All horses are Persian.
Socrates is a horse.
Therefore, Socrates is Persian.

Sample 4: All horses are animals.
All men are animals.
Therefore, all men are horses.

Sample 5: All mammals are animals.
All whales are animals.
Therefore, all whales are mammals.

Sample 6: All mammals are white.
All whales are white.
Therefore, all whales are mammals.

Sample 7: All animals are impalpable.
All material objects are impalpable.
Therefore, all material objects are animals.

We can now line up the samples in a column corresponding to the four possible Cases in the table:

	Premises	Conclusion	Arguments
Case I	All true	True	Samples 1 and 5
Case II	All true	False	Sample 4
Case III	Not all true	True	Samples 2 and 6
Case IV	Not all true	False	Samples 3 and 7

Recalling that the first three samples are all valid and the remaining ones invalid, we see that there are both valid and invalid arguments corresponding to each case, *save one*. In Case II, we have a corresponding invalid argument, but no valid one. That is, there is no sample of a valid argument with true premises and a false conclusion. No such combination is *possible* in a valid argument: In a certain sense we have really known that all along; anyone skeptical of the fact is invited to invest an hour or two trying to invent a counterexample. In fact, may we not take this impossibility as defining the very nature or meaning of validity? That is, we now propose to answer our original question as to the meaning of validity in the following way:

> A valid argument is one in which it is impossible for the premises to be true and the conclusion false.

It should be understood that the impossibility referred to in this definition is meant to rule out a *simultaneous* condition of true-premises-with-false-conclusion. There may be one set of circumstances under which the premises of a valid argument are true, and some other (different) set of circumstances under which the conclusion of the same valid argument is false; but there is no *single* set of circumstances under which the premises are true and the conclusion simultaneously false.

We can now define invalidity in a similar way:

> An invalid argument is one in which it is possible for the premises to be true and the conclusion false.

Here again, it is understood that the premises of an invalid argument can be true and the conclusion false *simultaneously*, that is, under a single set of circumstances. We have already used this principle as a method (Tech 2) for proving invalidity.

We have now answered our question concerning validity. Presumably, when we recognize an argument as valid we are recognizing in some way the impossibility of the premises being true while the conclusion is false; and when we recognize an argument as invalid we are recognizing the possibility of that combination.

It may be felt that these answers to our earlier questions are trivial, particularly because the formulations are so close to earlier assertions about valid argument and invalid argument. We have said a dozen times that a valid argument is one in which, *if* the premises are true, *then* it is impossible for the conclusion to be false. But *that* formulation embodies the expression "if . . . then, " which is in turn somewhat puzzling in meaning and closely related to the meaning of logical deduction itself. The present formulation in the text is devoid of the "if . . . then" idea, and hence somewhat simpler and clearer. With its aid we shall be able to develop some systematic and powerful techniques. With its aid, also, at a later stage we shall be able to give a clear account of the various significances of the English connective, "if . . . then."

There remain some legitimate questions about the term *possibility* as we have used it in this logical context. What does it mean? And how do we recognize it? But these are properly philosophical inquiries lying outside our purview. There are surely elementary cases in which we *do* recognize, with immeasurable confidence, logical possibilities and impossibilities. Our task here is to accept these as given foundations, and to erect a reliable structure of techniques and criteria upon them.

Exercises

1. "In a sound argument, the conclusion must be true." Is this correct?

2. "A sound argument is one in which it is impossible for the premises to be true and the conclusion false, and the conclusion is true." Is this correct?

3. Construct seven sample arguments analogous to Samples 1–7 in this chapter, but of such a nature that they are appropriately symbolized using letters for whole propositions.

*4. Can an argument be both valid and invalid? Can you construct an argument supporting your answer?

*5. Can an argument be neither valid nor invalid? Can you construct an argument supporting your answer?

9 • INDIRECT PROOF

Before we undertake the systematic examination of logical forms and methods, we must not fail to notice a new technique for proving validity that was, in effect, employed in the discussion of the Ewing-Smythe argument of Section 8. We can formulate the new method as follows:

> *Tech 4:* An argument suspected to be valid may be proved to be so by assuming that the conclusion is false, and then showing by means of some other valid argument(s) that the premises cannot all be true.

In the Ewing-Smythe case, we assumed that the conclusion was false and the second premise true. We then deduced a proposition that contradicted the first premise, hence showing that not all the premises could be true (when the conclusion was false).

Tech 4 really follows immediately from our definition of validity. For if we assume that the conclusion of an argument is false and prove under that assumption that not all the premises can be true, we show in effect that it is *impossible* for the premises to be (all) true and the conclusion false: This is just the condition that makes an argument valid. Thus, Tech 4 is related to the definition of validity in the same way that Tech 2 is related to the definition of invalidity.

Tech 4 is known as the method of *indirect proof*, and it will play a prominent role in later chapters. For the present, its value is just as limited as the other three techniques. For in order to use it we must be able to construct, easily and quickly, other valid arguments; and as yet we have no systematic guide lines whatever for doing so. In fact we have concentrated exclusively on formulating the meaning of validity and invalidity, and stating some preliminary methods for showing that *given* arguments are valid or invalid; but we have not even approached the problem of finding rules for the construction of valid arguments: That topic will be first treated in Chapter 3.

Here is another example of the use of Tech 4:

> If the train is on time, then the conductor is relaxed.
> The conductor is not relaxed.
> If the track is fixed, then the train is on time.
> Therefore, the track is not fixed.

We show that this argument is valid by first assuming that the conclusion is false; that is, we assume that

> (i) The track is fixed.

We can combine (i), as a premise, with the third premise of the original argument:

> (ii) If the track is fixed, then the train is on time.

It is clear that (i) and (ii) together imply as a conclusion:

> (iii) The train is on time.

Next we combine (iii), as a premise, with the first premise of the original argument:

> (iv) If the train is on time, then the conductor is relaxed.

And again it is evident that (iii) and (iv) together imply that

> (v) The conductor is relaxed.

But this contradicts the second premise of the original argument. Therefore, assuming that the conclusion (of the original argument) is false and the first and third premises true, we have shown that the second premise cannot be true. Hence, the argument is valid by Tech 4. Note that we here employed *two* auxiliary arguments, both having the obviously valid form

> If *P*, then *Q*.
> *P*.
> Therefore, *Q*.

Exercises

1. For each of the following arguments, you are to find out whether it is valid or invalid. If valid, prove that it is so by Tech 4. If invalid, prove it by Tech 2. In constructing auxiliary arguments for Tech 4, try to confine yourself to simple (valid) arguments whose forms have already been exemplified and discussed in this chapter.

   a. If the murder was unplanned, then clemency should be recommended.
   Clemency should not be recommended.
   Therefore, the murder was not unplanned.

   *b. If the murder was unplanned, then clemency should be recommended.
   Clemency should be recommended.
   Therefore, the murder was unplanned.

   c. No apple-growers are cherry-growers.
   All peach-growers are cherry-growers (too).
   Hence, no apple-growers are peach-growers.

   d. No apple-growers are cherry-growers.
   No peach-growers are apple-growers.
   Therefore, all peach-growers are cherry-growers.

   e. Not all apple-growers are peach-growers.
   All peach-growers are cherry-growers.
   Therefore, not all cherry-growers are apple-growers.

   *f. Mary is kind.
   Therefore, either Mary is kind or nothing is certain.

2. Which, if any, of the arguments in Exercise 1 have the same form as one of the arguments in Samples 1–7?

3. Which, if any, of the auxiliary arguments you used in analyzing the problems of Exercise 1 has the same form as one of the arguments in Samples 1–7?

CHAPTER 2

Truth-Functional Molecules and Propositional Arguments

ABSTRACT: An exhaustive study of truth-functional molecular propositions and those deductive arguments whose logical force depends solely on the truth-functional relations of their constituent propositions is presented. Sections 1–8 are restricted to treatment of the connectives *and, or,* and *not.* A series of symbolic techniques based on truth tables is evolved, facilitating the logical analysis of molecular propositions built around these three terms and issuing finally in a routine and foolproof method for the evaluation of arguments containing just such propositions. In Sections 9–13 the connective "If . . . then" is subjected to extensive scrutiny, and the techniques for logical analysis are then broadened to include it. This permits the method for evaluating arguments to be restated in a more fruitful way and to be reworked finally to provide far greater speed and facility in actual employment. Finally, in Sections 14–18 a wide variety of English truth-functional expressions is discussed and brought within the scope of the methods previously developed.

1 • PROPOSITIONAL ARGUMENTS: ATOMS AND MOLECULES

The deductive arguments used as examples in the preceding chapter may be divided into two types, depending upon the extent to which details of structure are relevant in the determination of validity or invalidity. Consider

> Socrates is bald and Plato is mortal.
> Therefore, Socrates is bald.

To symbolize the structure of this argument it is evidently sufficient to use letters in place of entire propositions. Hence, letting P stand for "Socrates is bald," and Q for "Plato is mortal," we have

> P and Q.
> Therefore, P.

which is obviously valid. The main point here is that the structural aspects that make it valid appear to be adequately represented by using symbols for whole propositions. We *could* use symbols for words or phrases instead. Certainly no harm would come of it—but no gain, either. In contrast to this, the samples of Chapter 1 require a more detailed use of symbols (in place of words or phrases) if we seek to capture their relevant form. Arguments of the former type, in which no investigation into groups of words smaller than those expressing propositions appears to be needed, will be called *propositional arguments*. In the sequel we shall speak of analyzing arguments *at the propositional level*, by which is meant the assignment of letters to whole propositions rather than to words or phrases.

Next, consider this closely related argument:

> Socrates is bald and Plato is bald.
> Therefore, Socrates is bald.

We are tempted to symbolize as before, with P for "Socrates is bald," and Q for "Plato is bald." But our commitment to the principle of symbolic uniqueness (Chapter 1, Section 5) forbids this, because P and Q would conceal a repetition of a substantive term (bald). Thus it seems that, to expose the structure of this argument, a more detailed symbolic treatment is required. Still, one may object that further structural details can only obscure rather than illuminate the structural aspects that make *this* argument valid. Differently said, the form *P and Q; therefore, P* is obviously valid, regardless of further details of structure that may be concealed by the symbols. Hence, we are moved to discard the symbolic uniqueness rule and admit this form as a legitimate and adequate representation of the structure of the argument concerned. In the same vein, the argument

> The baby is a boy or the baby is a girl.
> It is not true that the baby is a boy.
> Therefore, the baby is a girl.

is adequately represented by

> *P* or *Q*.
> It is not true that *P*.
> Therefore, *Q*.

despite the concealed repetition of "the baby."

What harm can come of this? We have seen that validity of an argument depends upon the repetition of certain elements. If we symbolize in a way that conceals repetitions, two kinds of dangers result.

In the first place, we might err when trying to evaluate an argument by comparing it to another of known validity or invalidity which has the "same" form. For instance, suppose we assign *P, Q; therefore R* as the common form of Sample 1 and Sample 4 (in Chapter 1). Suppose also that we have decided by some direct examination of its verbal formulation that Sample 1 is valid; we might then infer (wrongly) that Sample 4 is also valid. Or, if we have already decided that Sample 4 is invalid, we might infer (wrongly) that Sample 1 is also invalid.

When evaluating arguments in this way we depend upon a prior evaluation of some other particular argument. But the methods developed in the balance of this book mainly follow a different order. They will provide, in effect, an initial evaluation of symbolic forms themselves, and then use those evaluations as a basis for estimating the validity or invalidity of corresponding arguments. Consequently, as will be seen, we can ignore this particular kind of danger.

Even so, a second kind of danger remains if we abandon symbolic uniqueness. We could easily decide that a valid argument is *in*valid if the symbolic form assigned to it appears to be an invalid form but conceals essential repetition. This is what would happen if we took *P, Q; therefore R* as the form of Sample 1 and inferred that Sample 1 is invalid becase its form is. This difficulty is irreducible; it means that judgments of *in*validity arrived at through evaluation of an argument's apparent form have to be understood as provisional, unless the symbolic uniqueness rule happens to be satisfied.

In practice, this kind of danger is a very small threat, and it is usually easy to tell at a glance whether or not essential repetitions are concealed. Consequently, for reasons of convenience, *we shall now abandon the symbolic uniqueness principle.* (But we shall never knowingly let different symbols stand for *exactly* the same thing, except in some special contexts that arise in Chapter 8.) As a further consequence, we must now admit that judgments of *in*validity arrived at through symbolic analyses *at the propositional level* are theoretically provisional (unless symbolic uniqueness happens to hold). What such judgments show is that an analysis at the propositional level is *in*-sufficient to establish *validity;* further examination of details may yet do so. Clearly the converse does not hold; that is, if an analysis of an argument's form at the propositional level suggests that the argument is valid, then the repetitions needed for validity are already present, and no scrutiny of finer details could overturn that judgment.

It is now helpful to appeal to a chemical analogy for the sake of a terminology. Consider the propositions,

> Socrates is bald and Plato is bald;
> Socrates is bald.

The second proposition is clearly imbedded in the first, yet the first is also a single proposition in its own right. The difference between the two may be formulated thus: The first proposition has (constituent) propositions among its parts; the second does not. The first is analogous to a chemical *molecule,* which has (constituent) *atoms* among its parts; the second is analogous to a chemical *atom,* which does not have other atoms among its parts. We shall call the first a *molecular proposition,* or simply a molecule; we shall call the second an *atomic proposition,* or simply an atom. It will be found that all valid propositional arguments contain at least one molecule. (The chemical analogy cannot be relied on to extremes; we shall shortly discover molecular propositions containing only one atom.)

Exercises

1. Which of the arguments discussed in the text and exercises of Chapter 1 are propositional?

2. Decide whether the following are atoms or molecules. For each molecule, identify the constituent atoms.

    a. The weather will be fair.

    b. The weather will be clear.

    c. The weather will be fair and the weather will be clear.

    d. The weather will be fair and clear.

    e. Either the weather will be fair or it will be rainy.

    f. Either the weather will be fair or rainy, or it will snow and hail.

    g. Mary is clever.

    h. It is not the case that Mary is clever.

    i. Mary is not clever.

    j. It is false that Mary is clever.

    k. It is true that Mary is clever.

    l. It is false that Mary is not clever.

    m. Marilyn is frosty and George is gallant; also, Harry is crude or George is gallant.

    n. It is not the case that cigarettes cause cancer and industrial waste does not cause cancer, *or*, it *is* the case that cigarettes do not cause cancer and automobile exhaust does.

    o. Either, on the one hand, this coal burns well, or, on the other hand, it is easy to mine and either cheap to ship or abundantly available.

2 • TRUTH-FUNCTIONAL MOLECULES

We begin the discussion of propositional arguments by analyzing some simple examples. Take first:

> Harry is proud and his son is downright arrogant.
> Therefore, Harry is proud.

Probably everyone recognizes this somewhat trivial argument as valid. The premise is a form of sentence usually called *compound*; it is general y understood that the word *and* used as a conjunction connotes the joint assertion of the two subsentences so conjoined. In our terminology we will say that the premise is a molecule of the form *P and Q*; it is understood that this proposition, if true, connotes the truth of both of its constituent atoms. Thus, we see at once that the conclusion, which is merely one of those atoms, must be true as well. The argument is therefore clearly valid.

The nerve of our recognition of validity in this case rests on our grasp of the meaning of the molecule *P and Q*. To illustrate in another way the crucial role of the molecule and our understanding of it, let us show that the argument is valid through Tech 4. The argument has the form

> *P* and *Q*.
> Therefore, *P*.

Suppose the conclusion *P* is false. Then the premise, which states that *P* and *Q* are both true, must also be false. Hence, it is impossible for the premise to be true while the conclusion is false, and the argument is valid, still.

Again we see that the analysis rests on an understanding of the meaning of the molecule *P and Q*. Specifically, the critical fact is that the molecule *P and Q* is true if both of its atoms are true, and otherwise not. That is, the truth or falsity of the proposition *P or Q* is *a function of* the truth or falsity of its constituent atoms. We give a name to this situation by saying that *P and Q* is *truth-functional*. In general, a truth-functional proposition is a molecular proposition whose truth or falsity is determined solely by the truth or falsity of its constituent atoms.

Consider another example:

> John is going or Mary is going.
> John is going.
> Therefore, Mary is going.

This argument is not valid, as can be shown by Tech 2. The first premise is a molecular proposition which, if true, connotes that one or the other of its constituent atoms is true, but it does not assert that *both* are true. Perhaps it does not in its meaning exclude the possibility that both are true; but in any case it does not insist that they are. In brief, the molecule *P or Q*, unlike the molecule *P and Q*, means that at least one of its atoms is true. Our argument has the form:

> *P* or *Q*.
> *P*.
> Therefore, *Q*.

Now we can suppose that the conclusion *Q* is false, while the second premise, *P*, is true. In this case it is also possible for the first premise, *P or Q*, to be true as well, so the argument is invalid. In concrete terms, we can suppose that Mary is *not* going and John *is*. Then the premises would both be true and the conclusion false.

The key to this example is of course the molecule *P or Q*. It is truth-functional like *P and Q*, and it is true if at least one of its constituent atoms is true, otherwise false. (We shall see later that the word *or* is ambiguous in English and can have another meaning that is also truth-functional.)

Here is a last example, more complex than the others:

> It is not the case that: The bank president is a fraud and the examiners are corrupt.
> But the bank president is a fraud.
> Therefore, the examiners are not corrupt.

Here we will be helped if we first extract the form. The first premise is a denial of a molecular proposition that itself contains two atoms. It can be symbolized as

> Not − (*P* and *Q*)

where *P* means "The bank president is a fraud" and *Q* means "The examiners are corrupt." The whole argument then has the form:

> Not − (*P* and *Q*).
> *P*.
> Therefore, not − *Q*.

We will show by Tech 4 that this is valid. Suppose first that the conclusion is false. If *not − Q* is false, then *Q* must be true; in words, if "The examiners are *not* corrupt" is false, then "The examiners *are* corrupt" is true. Next we will further suppose that the second premise, P, is true. Thus we have it that P and Q are both true, which means that the molecular proposition P *and* Q is likewise true. But the first premise is a denial of the molecule P *and* Q. Therefore, it is not possible for all the premises to be true while the conclusion is false, so the argument is valid.

In this discussion we have in effect introduced a third kind of truth-functional proposition, having the form $not - P$. Equivalent formulations are P *is false*, or *It is not the case that* P. Such a proposition is evidently true if its constituent atom is false, and false if its constituent atom is true. Hence, $not - P$ is the promised truth-functional molecule having only one constituent atom.

Exercises

1. Show that this argument is valid by Tech 4.

Either all men are mortal or some men die.
It is not true that all men are mortal.
Therefore, some men die.

2. Show that this argument is invalid by Tech 2.

Whales or sharks are fishes.
Whales are not fishes.
Therefore, sharks are not fishes.

3. Determine the validity or invalidity of the following argument and prove your result in some appropriate way:

The old man is dying or very ill.
Either the old man is not dying or his sons will soon be rich.
Either the old man's doctor will soon be rich or the old man is not very ill.
Therefore, either the old man's sons will soon be rich or his doctor will.

4. Determine the validity or invalidity of the following argument and prove the result:

The report is false.
It is false that the agent lied and, at the same time, treated us well.
Either the agent treated us well or the report is false.
Therefore, the agent lied.

3 • TRUTH TABLES

It is expedient at this point to formalize and tabulate the results of the discussion so far. First, we have discovered that *A and B* (where *A* and *B* stand for propositions) is a truth-functional proposition that is true only when both of its constituents are. Each of the constituents, *A* and *B*, can itself be true or false. There are therefore four possible cases: Either *A* and *B* are both true, or *A* is true and *B* false, or vice versa, or they are both false. In the first case the molecule *A and B* is also true; in all the other cases it is false. We gather these results into the following table:

A	B	A and B
True	True	True
True	False	False
False	True	False
False	False	False

To facilitate the presentation of this table and others like it, we adopt some further symbolic conveniences. In place of the word *and* we shall use a dot, · ; in place of the word *true*, the numeral 1; and in place of the word *false*, the numeral 0. Then the table, which we want to call *Truth Table 1* or *TT1* for short, is conveniently written thus:

TT1:	A	B	A · B
	1	1	1
	1	0	0
	0	1	0
	0	0	0

Before plunging into the development of methods based on this table (and others to follow) it is necessary to discuss the significance of the capital letters *A*, *B*, *P*, *Q*, and so on, that we have been using. In the previous sentence the letter *A* has been italicized in order to emphasize that we were talking *about* it rather than *using* it to express a word or to stand for some proposition; the same holds for *B*, *P*, and *Q*. The distinction between *use* and *mention* of letters, words, or other symbols occurs in ordinary language and often has to be marked out by italics, quotation marks, or other devices. For example, if we see the sentence, "That is a verb," we might wonder what it refers to. But if we see, *"That* is a verb," or " 'That' is a verb," we know that it refers to the word *that* and expresses a false proposition. Usually it is clear from the context whether symbols of any type are being used or mentioned. In this text, letters that are used as artificial symbols are italicized in both types of occurrence.

Precisely what do the letter symbols stand for? Earlier we used P and Q (and R) to stand for specified propositions, such as "Socrates is bald"; that is, the letters were utilized as arbitrary abbreviations for specified propositions. In such usage it is convenient to refer to the letters P and Q (and others used similarly) as *constants*. In other contexts, however, we have spoken of propositions having the form P *and* Q where the individual letters refer to *un*specified propositions. In this usage, P and Q are understood as *variables*; that is, symbols of unspecified meaning that stand for any proposition at all. We have used A and B instead of P and Q in TT1 to emphasize the fact that they (that is, A and B) do not stand for certain specified propositions. But again, it is usually clear from context whether a given letter is intended as a variable or a constant, so we shall *not* endeavor to mark the distinction systematically by always using different classes of symbols.

Let us now return to our truth table, TT1. It exhibits the meaning of the word *and* when used as a connective between propositions. Because *and*, when so used, produces a truth-functional molecule, we shall say that *and* is a *truth-functional connective*. Also, it is convenient to call the molecule of the form $P \cdot Q$ a *conjunction* and its two component parts *conjuncts*. It is clear that the conjuncts may themselves be molecules (although they need not be), and in particular they may themselves be conjunctions.

A table similar to TT1 can now be constructed for the connective *or*. We will introduce the sign v to stand for the word *or*. Because any proposition A v B is true if at least one of the components A and B is true, the meaning of v can be displayed as follows:

TT2:	A	B	A v B
	1	1	1
	1	0	1
	0	1	1
	0	0	0

We see that *or* when used in this way is likewise a truth-functional connective. We shall say that a proposition of the form *P* v *Q* is a *disjunction*, and its component parts are *disjuncts*.

A third such table can be made for negation. We use the sign ~ to stand for *not*. Because ~*A* (read *not* − *A*) is true when *A* is false and false when *A* is true, we have

TT3:

A	~A
1	0
0	1

A prosposition of the form ~*A* will be called a *negation* or *denial*.

These truth tables exhibit in convenient form the way in which a molecule becomes true or false depending on the combinations of truth and falsity taken on by its constituent parts. For ease of expression, we shall say that a true proposition has the truth-value *true* and a false proposition has the truth-value *false*. Hence, the tables show how the truth-values of certain types of truth-functional molecules vary with the truth-values of their parts.

The construction of truth tables can be carried out for quite complex propositions, and we will show eventually that such procedures lead to a systematic method for determining the validity or invalidity of propositional arguments. For the moment, we shall see how truth tables for complex propositions are made. For example, let us consider:

> It is not the case that: The bank president is a fraud and the examiners corrupt.

As we have seen, it has the form *not* − (*P and Q*); or, in briefer symbols, ~ (*P·Q*). Now suppose we wish to know under what circumstances it will be true, what false. We first arrange a list of all the possible combinations of truth and falsity of its atoms, as follows:[5]

1	2
P	Q
1	1
1	0
0	1
0	0

---

[5] The columns are numbered only to facilitate reference to them; the numbers are not an essential or logically relevant feature of truth tables.

Next, recalling TT1, we place in an adjacent column the corresponding truth-values for the proposition $P \cdot Q$.

1	2	3
P	Q	P·Q
1	1	1
1	0	0
0	1	0
0	0	0

We now need to refer to TT3; that table displays the fact that a proposition of the form $\sim A$ has truth-value 0 when A has truth-value 1, and conversely. Now, however, we wish to determine the truth-values for a proposition of the form $\sim(P \cdot Q)$. Because A in TT3 stands for any proposition atomic or molecular, we can now think of $(P \cdot Q)$ as playing the role of A. Hence, $\sim(P \cdot Q)$ will have the value 0 when $(P \cdot Q)$ has the value 1, and conversely. This enables us to fill in a fourth column, as follows:

1	2	3	4
P	Q	P·Q	∼(P·Q)
1	1	1	0
1	0	0	1
0	1	0	1
0	0	0	1

Thus we see that the proposition we started with is false if the bank president *is* a fraud and the examiners *are* corrupt, and otherwise true. The third column in the completed table was constructed by reference to columns 1 and 2, and TT1; the last column was constructed by reference to column 3, and TT3.

Here is a more complicated example:

> Either the weather will be fair and the game will be played, or we will end up at the movies and the game will not be played.

In rendering long propositions into symbolic form it is often advisable to avoid confusion by writing out an explicit dictionary indicating the assignment of symbols to propositions:

P: The weather will be fair.
Q: The game will be played.
R: We will end up at the movies.

In symbols, then, the whole proposition is

$(P \cdot Q) \lor (R \cdot \sim Q)$.

Its full truth table is:

1	2	3	4	5	6	7
P	Q	R	P·Q	~Q	R·~Q	(P·Q) v (R·~Q)
1	1	1	1	0	0	1
1	1	0	1	0	0	1
1	0	1	0	1	1	1
1	0	0	0	1	0	0
0	1	1	0	0	0	0
0	1	0	0	0	0	0
0	0	1	0	1	1	1
0	0	0	0	1	0	0

Thus, the full proposition is true if its first two atoms are true (compare the first and second rows—not columns), or if the third atom is true and the second false (compare the third and seventh rows); otherwise, the whole proposition is false.

Exercises

1. Construct truth tables for the following propositions:

   a. *Either* the sun rises in the east or Newton is wrong, *or* Galileo is right.

   b. *Either* the sun rises in the east, *or* Newton is wrong or Galileo is right.

   c. The compass is broken, and we are lost and we will probably never be found.

   d. The compass is broken and we are lost, and we will probably never be found.

   e. It is not the case that the spring is broken, and it can be fixed.

   f. It is not the case that the spring is broken and it can be fixed.

   g. The spring is broken or the spring is not broken. (one atom)

   h. It is not the case that the spring is not broken.

    i. It is not the case that it is false that the spring is broken.

    j. It is not the case that it is false that the spring is not broken.

    k. It is false that it is not the case that it is false that the spring is broken.

    l. Either the conservatives must give ground or the liberals must compromise, and the independents had best say nothing.

    m. Either the conservatives must give ground, or the liberals must compromise and the independents had best say nothing.

2. Construct complete truth tables for the following propositions:

    a. The train is on time or I miss my connection, and, I make my connection or I lose my job. (There are only *three* different atoms here.)

    b. John is kind and Saul holy, or John is smart and Saul unholy.

    c. It is not the case that the president steals and the vice-president cheats.

    d. It is not the case that the president steals, and the vice-president cheats.

3. Make a truth table for this proposition, and note its peculiarity: "Either tobacco is profitable or the following statement is false: — Corn is easy to grow, and, tobacco is profitable or corn is not easy to grow."

4. Make a truth table for the following proposition, and note its peculiarity: "Corn is hard to grow and tobacco is not profitable, and, either corn is not hard to grow or tobacco is profitable."

5. Consider the plight of Hercules Poirot, the famous French detective. He knows that if any of the sisters of the deceased told a lie, the father is guilty. On the other hand, if the sisters all told the truth, the mother is guilty. Here is the testimony of the sisters:

Sister Mary: "The clock stopped at noon or the butler was not in the room."

Sister Grace: "It is not true that the clock stopped at noon and the butler was not in the room."

Sister Ann: "It is not true that the clock stopped at noon, and the butler was in the room."

Whom does he arrest, and why?

*6. Find a molecular proposition involving three atoms that is true when one and only one (but *any* one) of its atoms is true, and otherwise false.

*7. Find a molecular proposition involving three atoms that is false when two or more of its atoms are true, and otherwise true.

4 • LARGER TRUTH TABLES

We will sometimes want to make truth tables for propositions that contain four, five, or more atoms; the work involved will be quite tedious but in principle no different from previous cases. The only difficulty lies in the setting out of the initial columns, in which one must be sure to list all the possible truth-value combinations for the constituent atoms. To aid in this process the following rule may be helpful:

If there are n atoms in a given proposition, the number of possible truth-value combinations is 2^n (that is, $2 \times 2 \times 2 \ldots$ and so on, n times). In listing them, first divide 2^n by 2; then, in the first column under the first atom write the numeral 1 $2^n/2$ times, then write 0 the same number of times. Next take the number used in the first column and divide by 2 again, giving $2^n/4$; in the second column put the numeral 1 $2^n/4$ times, then 0 the same number of times, then 1 the same number of times again, and lastly 0 the same number of times again. Next divide by 2 again, giving $2^n/8$; for the third column put alternately $2^n/8$ ones and zeroes, and so on and on.

Here is a complete truth table for a four-atom molecule.

> Merchants are shrewd or they go out of business, and, merchants are honest or they go to jail.

> > P: Merchants are shrewd.
> > Q: Merchants go out of business.
> > R: Merchants are honest.
> > S: Merchants go to jail.

The complete symbolic translation is

$(P \text{ v } Q) \cdot (R \text{ v } S)$.

The truth table is shown on p. 52.

P	Q	R	S	P v Q	R v S	(P v Q) · (R v S)
1	1	1	1	1	1	1
1	1	1	0	1	1	1
1	1	0	1	1	1	1
1	1	0	0	1	0	0
1	0	1	1	1	1	1
1	0	1	0	1	1	1
1	0	0	1	1	1	1
1	0	0	0	1	0	0
0	1	1	1	1	1	1
0	1	1	0	1	1	1
0	1	0	1	1	1	1
0	1	0	0	1	0	0
0	0	1	1	0	1	0
0	0	1	0	0	1	0
0	0	0	1	0	1	0
0	0	0	0	0	0	0

Exercises

1. Under what circumstances will the following proposition be true? "It is not the case that trains are fast or comfortable, and, it is false that planes are slow or trains safe." (four atoms)

2. Under what circumstances will the following proposition be true? "Either it is not the case that trains are fast, or they are comfortable; *and,* either it is false that planes are slow, or trains are safe."

3. Make a truth table for the following proposition, and note its peculiarity: "On the one hand, either maturity is valued or we fail to learn from experience and should suffer in the long run; or, on the other hand, it is not the case that maturity is valued and age respected." (four atoms)

*4. Make a truth table for the following proposition and note its peculiarity: "*Either:* The roses are best and the violets next best, or the zinnias are worst; *or* it is not the case that: The zinnias are worst and the peonies first or second." (five atoms)

5. Holmes knows that if it is logically possible for all the witnesses to be telling the truth, they are all innocent. Otherwise, he must ask them to remain in the house over the week end. Following is the testimony of the witnesses.

Simon:	"The window was closed or the butler was out."
Peter:	"The window was open or the butler was in."
Paul:	"The window was closed and the heater was on; and, the maid was below stairs."
Matthew:	"The maid was not below stairs; or, the window was open and the heater was off."

What should Holmes do?

5 • SYMBOLIC AMBIGUITIES AND CONVENTIONS

As we are now beginning to use a rich set of symbols, we must be clear about their syntax (that is, rules of proper arrangement). Certain expressions carelessly formed are ambiguous. For example,

$P \text{ v } Q \cdot R$

may mean

$P \text{ v } (Q \cdot R)$, or
$(P \text{ v } Q) \cdot R$.

A moment's work with truth tables will show that these two interpretations are not equivalent, and some use of parentheses is required to specify which interpretation is intended. We can of course place parentheses within parentheses and use brackets, braces, and so on, to help indicate which are matched with which. Thus,

$P \text{ v } Q \cdot R \text{ v } S$

could mean

$P \text{ v } [(Q \cdot R) \text{ v } S]$, or
$P \text{ v } [Q \cdot (R \text{ v } S)]$, or
$(P \text{ v } Q) \cdot (R \text{ v } S)$

or two other things that are left as exercises for the reader to find. Analogies in ordinary language and in mathematics are obvious.

Some ambiguities are quite innocent. The expression $P \text{ v } Q \text{ v } R$ could be understood as $(P \text{ v } Q) \text{ v } R$, or as $P \text{ v } (Q \text{ v } R)$, but these two are equivalent. We express this briefly by saying that disjunction is *associative*; that is, three (or even more) propositions may be joined disjunctively without specifying their pair-wise groupings (or associations). A similar result holds for conjunction. Analogies are found in the arithmetical operations of addition and multiplication.

In this context it is noteworthy that disjunction and conjunction are also *commutative*. That is, propositions of the form P v Q or $P \cdot Q$ are equivalent, respectively, to Q v P or $Q \cdot P$. This permits one to reverse (commute) the order of expressions flanking disjunction or conjunction signs. A similar truth holds for addition and multiplication signs.

It is useful for later purposes to speak of the *scope* of a connective, or to say that one connective *extends over* another. In the expression P v $(Q \cdot R)$ the connective v extends over the $\cdot$ because the v joins two disjuncts one of which includes the $\cdot$ within itself; in different words, the v has greater scope than the $\cdot$. In the expression $(P \text{ v } Q) \cdot R$ the situation is reversed; the $\cdot$ extends over the v because it joins two conjuncts one of which includes the v within itself; again, the $\cdot$ has greater scope than the v. Generally speaking, then, we use parentheses, brackets, and braces to indicate the relative scope of connectives without ambiguity. In the expression P v $[(Q \cdot R) \text{ v } S]$ the first v has the greatest scope and extends over both of the other connectives; the $\cdot$ has the least scope and does not extend over any of the other connectives.

Lastly, we must consider our sign for negation, whose role is somewhat analogous to the use of the minus sign in mathematics. In arithmetic, it is our habit to interpret the minus sign as having the least scope that the structure of an expression will permit for it. Thus, we take the expression $-2 + 3$ to mean $(-2) + 3$ and not $-(2 + 3)$. Similarly, in logical symbolism it is natural to take $\sim P$ v Q as meaning $(\sim P)$ v Q and not as meaning $\sim(P \text{ v } Q)$. We *could* distinguish between the two possible meanings at every occurrence with a lavish use of parentheses, but as this becomes cumbersome it is best to have an understanding that the first interpretation will apply rather than the second. In general, we adopt the principle that the negation sign has minimal scope. To be perfectly definite, we lay down the following series of conventions:

   (i) If $\sim$ appears to the left of a letter, its scope extends only over that letter. Hence, $\sim P \cdot Q$ means $(\sim P) \cdot Q$, not $\sim(P \cdot Q)$.
   (ii) If $\sim$ appears to the left of a parenthesis, its scope extends as far

as the corresponding parenthesis. Hence, $\sim(Q$ v $R)\cdot S$ means $[\sim(Q$ v $R)]\cdot S$; not $\sim[(Q$ v $R)\cdot S]$.

(iii) If $\sim$ appears to the left of another $\sim$, its scope extends just as far as the scope of the other $\sim$. Hence, $\sim\sim P\cdot Q$ means $\sim(\sim P)\cdot Q$; not $\sim[(\sim P)\cdot Q]$.

Of course, an overgenerous use of parentheses is always permitted for the sake of clarity.

Exercises

1. List the possible interpretations of the following ambiguous expressions.

   a. $P\cdot Q$ v R

   b. $P\cdot Q$ v $R\cdot S$

   c. $\sim P\cdot R$ v Q

   d. $\sim(P$ v $Q\cdot R$ v $S)$

2. In the following expressions indicate which is the connective of the greatest scope.

   a. $\sim(P\cdot Q)$

   b. $(\sim P\cdot Q)$ v $(R\cdot S)$

   c. $\sim[P$ v $(Q\cdot R)]$

   d. $\sim\sim[(P$ v $Q)\cdot(R$ v $S)]$

6 • ABBREVIATED TRUTH TABLES

There is a way to escape some of the tedium involved in the construction of truth tables. In this section we will show how to construct abbreviated truth tables, and in all subsequent discussions and illustrations abbreviated truth tables will be employed.

Consider first a proposition of the form P v $\sim Q$. To build a regular truth table we would require four columns constructed in the following order: (i) A column of possibilities for P, containing two 1's and two 0's. (ii) A column of possibilities for Q, containing a 1 and a 0, then another 1 and 0. (iii) A column of resulting truth-values for $\sim Q$. (iv) A column of resulting truth-values for $P \text{ v} \sim Q$.

To construct an abbreviated table we will carry out the same steps in the same order but with less labor. First we write down in symbolic form the proposition we are studying, leaving plenty of room between the symbols; then we place the columns of possibilities for the atoms P and Q directly under the letters themselves:

1	2	3	4
P	v	~	Q
1			1
1			0
0			1
0			0

Next we need a column for $\sim Q$, to be constructed by reference to column 4. We will place this column directly under the connective that is applied to Q, namely, the $\sim$:

1	2	3	4
P	v	~	Q
1		0	1
1		1	0
0		0	1
0		1	0

It is understood that the numerals in column 3, because they are written under a connective, indicate the truth-values for the entire proposition that is included in the scope of the connective. Lastly, we need a column for the entire molecular proposition we started with; we construct it by reference to columns 1 and 3, and place it under the connective symbol that includes the entire proposition in its scope:

1	2	3	4
P	v	~	Q
1	1	0	1
1	1	1	0
0	0	0	1
0	1	1	0

This completes the table. Column 2 contains the truth-values for the entire proposition and corresponds to what would appear in the last column to the right in a full truth table.

Another example is

1	2	3	4
~	(P	·	Q)
0	1	1	1
1	1	0	0
1	0	0	1
1	0	0	0

Here column 3 contains the values for $(P \cdot Q)$, because the connective that heads the column extends in scope only over the P and the Q and does not include the $\sim$. Column 1 contains the values for the entire proposition, because the $\sim$ extends over the whole of it.

Here finally is a more complex example:

1	2	3	4	5	6	7	8	9	10	11	12
(P	v	~	Q)	·	~	[P	v	~	(Q	v	R)]
1	1	0	1	0	0	1	1	0	1	1	1
1	1	0	1	0	0	1	1	0	1	1	0
1	1	1	0	0	0	1	1	0	0	1	1
1	1	1	0	0	0	1	1	1	0	0	0
0	0	0	1	0	1	0	0	0	1	1	1
0	0	0	1	0	1	0	0	0	1	1	0
0	1	1	0	1	1	0	0	0	0	1	1
0	1	1	0	0	0	0	1	1	0	0	0

Column 5 contains the values for the entire proposition.

Exercises

1. Which contains more columns of numerals, a full truth table or an abbreviated truth table? In what sense is an abbreviated truth table an abbreviation?

2. Refer to Exercises 2, 3, and 4 at the end of Section 3. Construct abbreviated truth tables for the propositions listed there, and check your results for the final outcome with what you obtained at that time.

7 • LOGICAL TRUTH AND FALSEHOOD

There are some molecular propositions that must be true regardless of the truth or falsity of their constituent atoms. A simple and ancient example is the proposition, "Either there will be a sea fight tomorrow or there will not be a sea fight tomorrow." A truth table for this is

P	v	~	P
1	1	0	1
0	1	1	0

The second column shows that the whole proposition is true whether its constituent atom is true or false. Another example is, "It is not the case that: Chopin is advanced and Liszt romantic, and Chopin not advanced." The truth table is

~	[(P	·	Q)	·	~P]
1	1	1	1	0	0
1	1	0	0	0	0
1	0	0	1	0	1
1	0	0	0	0	1

The first column (obtained by reference to the fifth) shows that the whole proposition is always true. (Incidentally, note that the truth-values for P were not repeated at the extreme right in this truth table.)

In general, if the truth-value of a proposition turns up as the numeral 1 in every row, it is clear that the proposition in question cannot help but be true. Such a proposition is called a *logical truth*, or is said to be *logically true*. Logical truths, as we shall see later, are closely related to valid arguments.[6]

It is also possible for a molecular proposition to turn up false in every row. Such a proposition is called a *logical falsehood*, or is said to be *logically false*. Other terms having the same meaning are *inconsistent* and *self-contradictory*. The simplest example is a proposition of the

---

[6] Logical truths are often called *tautologies*. As this term has a pejorative connotation quite out of keeping with the importance of logical truths, it has been reserved for another use in this text.

form $P \cdot \sim P$, such as, "There will be a sea fight and there will not be a sea fight."

P	·	∼P
1	0	0
0	0	1

Most propositions are of course neither logically true nor logically false: In some cases (that is, in some rows) they turn up as true and in other cases false. And of course the determination of the truth or falsity of such propositions is more than a merely logical matter. It is convenient to have a name for these, and it is usual to refer to them simply as *consistent* propositions. However, the term *consistent* also has a wider meaning, referring both to propositions that are neither logically true nor logically false, *and* propositions that are logically true. That is, *consistent* properly refers to any proposition that is *not in*consistent. When we wish to mark the difference between consistent propositions that are not logically true and those that are, we shall call the first type *contingent*.

Exercises

1. Can a logically false proposition be contingent?

2. Are all logically true propositions consistent? Are all consistent propositions logically true?

3. Are all logically true propositions contingent? Are any?

4. Decide by truth-table analysis which of the following are logically true, which inconsistent, and which contingent.

   a. $\sim(P \cdot \sim P)$

   b. $\sim P \cdot \sim P$

   c. $\sim P \vee P$

   d. $\sim(P \vee P)$

   e. $P \vee \sim P \vee Q$

   f. P

   g. $\sim[(\sim P \vee Q) \cdot (\sim Q \vee R)] \vee (\sim P \vee R)$

   h. $\sim\{[(P \vee Q) \cdot (\sim P \vee R)] \cdot (\sim Q \vee S)\} \vee (R \vee S)$

   i. $[P \cdot \sim(P \cdot \sim Q)] \cdot \sim Q$

   j. $\sim P$

   k. $(\sim P \vee Q) \cdot (\sim Q \vee P)$

   l. $(P \vee Q) \cdot (\sim P \vee \sim Q)$

   m. $(P \cdot Q) \vee (\sim P \cdot \sim Q)$

5. Show that any argument with an inconsistent conclusion must be unsound.

*6. Is it true that any argument with inconsistent premises must be valid?

8 • PROVING VALIDITY AND INVALIDITY

We are now ready to employ our truth-table apparatus to decide on the validity or invalidity of some proposed arguments. Of course we are so far limited to arguments whose constituent molecular propositions are built solely around the connectives *and, or,* and *not*; but this restriction will be removed at later stages. We proceed at once to the discussion of a fairly complicated example. Take the argument:

> Either this port is sour or the taster is ill.
> Either the taster is not ill or the whole batch is misgraded.
> Therefore, either the whole batch is misgraded or this port is sour.

> P: This port is sour.
> Q: The taster is ill.
> R: The whole batch is misgraded.

In symbols the argument is then:

> $P \vee Q$.
> $\sim Q \vee R$.
> Therefore, $R \vee P$.

To see if it is valid or not we will write out the premises and conclusion side-by-side, putting a slash, /, between each premise and a double slash, //, before the conclusion:

> $P \vee Q / \sim Q \vee R // R \vee P$.

Next, we construct a single truth table under this entire set of three propositions. Because there are three different constituent atoms in the entire argument, we will need eight rows, and we begin by filling in the possible combinations of truth-values for the atoms:

P	v	Q	/	~Q	v	R	//	R	v	P
1		1		1		1		1		1
1		1		1		0		0		1
1		0		0		1		1		1
1		0		0		0		0		1
0		1		1		1		1		0
0		1		1		0		0		0
0		0		0		1		1		0
0		0		0		0		0		0

Next we can fill in the rows for the propositions themselves in the usual way:

P	v	Q	/	~Q		R	//	R	v	P
1	**1**	1		0	**1**	1		1	**1**	1
1	**1**	1		0	**1**	0	0	0	**1**	1
1	**1**	0		1	**0**	1	1	1	**1**	1
1	**1**	0		1	**0**	1	0	0	**1**	1
0	**1**	1		0	**1**	1	1	1	**1**	0
0	**1**	1		0	**1**	0	0	0	**0**	0
0	**0**	0		1	**0**	1	1	1	**1**	0
0	**0**	0		1	**0**	1	0	0	**0**	0

The long boxes enclose the resulting truth-values for each premise and the conclusion.

What is the use of this construction? A valid argument, according to Chapter 1, is an argument in which it is impossible for the premises to be true and the conclusion false. *Examination of the preceding table shows how such an impossibility is easily recognized in the present case.* Each horizontal row represents one possible combination of truth-values for the constituent atoms in the argument; between them, the rows exhaust all possible combinations. Examination of each row individually reveals that there is no row in which all the premises are true and the conclusion false. Hence, such a combination is not possible, and we are constrained to infer that the argument is valid.

Actually, one need not examine all the rows individually. It is sufficient to observe that there are only two cases where the conclusion is false (sixth and eighth rows); in both cases one of the premises is likewise false. Hence, there is no row with false conclusion and all true premises, so the argument is valid. It is evident that if such a row *did* turn up, we would know at once that the argument is invalid.

Another example is

It is not true that cigarettes cause cancer and car smoke does not.
Car smoke causes cancer.
Therefore, cigarettes cause cancer.

P: Cigarettes cause cancer.
Q: Car smoke causes cancer.

$\sim(P\cdot\sim Q)$.
Q.
Therefore, P.

$\sim$	(P	$\cdot$	$\sim$	Q)	/	Q	//	P
1	1	0	0	1		1		1
0	1	1	1	0		0		1
1	0	0	0	1		1		0
1	0	0	1	0		0		0

This argument is *in*valid because, as the third row shows, it *is* possible for the premises to be true and the conclusion false. The possibility arises when P is false and Q true, as we also see at once from the table. That is, the argument is invalid because it is quite conceivable that cigarettes do not cause cancer and car smoke does.

This method provides us with a systematic technique for the determination of the validity or invalidity of a given argument. In Chapter 1, we developed no less than four techniques for proving that an argument is valid or not. However, not one of them was systematic in the sense of the present method, for in no case could one be certain that a decision on the validity of a given argument would be reached after a finite number of analytical steps, or would ever be reached at all. In contrast, the truth-table method provides such a guarantee. It is accordingly called a *decision procedure*, that is, a method that guarantees arrival at a decision in a finite number of steps, and does not depend upon luck or ingenuity.

Exercises

1. Check the following arguments for validity or invalidity by the truth-table technique.

   a. It is not the case that: Helium is buoyant and hydrogen cannot be used to raise balloons.
   Helium is buoyant.
   Therefore, hydrogen can be used to raise balloons.

   b. Either the Orient Express is not on time or it is on track 3.
   The Orient Express is on time.
   Therefore, it is on track 3.

   c. It is not true that Buddha was Japanese and Confucius not Chinese.
   Either Confucius was not Chinese or Buddha was not Japanese.
   Hence, Buddha was not Japanese.

   d. Confucius was wise.
   Either Confucius was wise or Buddha was.
   Therefore, Buddha was wise.

   e. It is not true that: Becoming precedes being and being does not precede essence.
   It is likewise not true that: Being does not precede essence and necessary being exists.
   Therefore, either becoming does not precede being or necessary being exists.

   f. Either extreme preparedness for war is unwise, or the following is false:
   The enemy ·is unreasonable, and they are armed to the teeth, and negotiation is not possible.
   Extreme preparedness is wise, and the enemy is unreasonable.
   The enemy is either unreasonable or armed to the teeth.
   Therefore, negotiation is possible.

   g. John is mad and Sally is gone.
   Therefore, John is mad or Sally is gone.

   h. John is mad.
   Therefore, John is mad or Sally is gone.

   i. Death is a long sleep or a pleasant dream.
   Death is not a long sleep, or it is not terrible.
   Death is not terrible, or it is not a pleasant dream.
   Hence, death is not terrible.

j. At least one of the following is true: Death is not a long sleep or not terrible, and death is not terrible or not a pleasant dream.
Therefore, death is not terrible.

k. Holmes is not in the garden or Moriarty is.
Holmes is in the garden.
Moriarty's accomplice is in the garden or Holmes is not.
Therefore, Moriarty is in the garden and so is his accomplice.

l. Either teachers are not timid or newspapermen like a good story.
Either newspapermen like a good story or school boards are not inflexible.
Newspapermen do like a good story.
Hence, either teachers are timid or school boards inflexible.

2. The truth-table method for analyzing propositional arguments is simply a systematic application of certain of the techniques of Chapter 1. Which techniques? How are they applied?

*3. Inspector Battle knows for a fact that the victim was not killed by bullets. He also knows that either, on the one hand, the butler was in the pantry and the maid was in the parlor or the upstairs bedroom, or, on the other hand, the victim was killed by bullets and the maid was in the parlor. Two witnesses testify as follows:

Lord Epping: "The maid was in the parlor or she was in the upstairs bedroom. Also, the butler was in the pantry or the victim was killed by bullets."

Lady Epping: "The maid was in the parlor or the victim was killed by bullets. Also, either the victim was killed by bullets or the maid was in the upstairs bedroom."

Can Battle tell whether or not Lord Epping is telling the truth? What about Lady Epping?

4. A certain argument has premises P, Q, and R and conclusion C. A second argument is formed having the same conclusion but only one premise; that premise, however, is a conjunction of the three premises of the first argument, that is, $P \cdot Q \cdot R$. Show that if the first argument is valid so is the second, and conversely.

5. A certain argument has premises P, Q, and R and conclusion C. A proposition is formed consisting of a conjunction of four conjuncts, the first three

conjuncts are P, Q, and R, and the last is $\sim C$. In other words, the proposition is $P \cdot Q \cdot R \cdot \sim C$. Show that if the argument is valid the proposition is inconsistent, and conversely.

*6. Is this argument valid?

> John is white.
> John is not white.
> Therefore, Anna is the Queen of Siam.

*7. Is this argument valid?

> John is white.
> Therefore, either Anna is the Queen of Siam or
> Anna is not the Queen of Siam.

9 • THE CONNECTIVE "IF . . . THEN"

We must now discuss one of the most frequent, important, and confusing of English connectives, "If . . . then." It will be symbolized by a hook, $\supset$. In other words, we now wish to examine molecular propositions of the form, "If P, then Q"; in symbols, $P \supset Q$. To emphasize the extreme frequency of its occurrence in ordinary discourse we list at once several examples that will be employed in the subsequent discussion:

> If helium is buoyant, then hydrogen can be used to raise balloons.
> If the Orient Express is on time, then it is on Track 3.
> If Socrates is a man and men are mortal, then Socrates is mortal.
> If this herd has colts in it, then it has mares.
> If the temperature rises, then the reaction will accelerate.
> If the instructor drops the chalk, then it will hit the floor.

We shall refer to expressions of this sort as *conditional* propositions; the atom (or molecule) that follows the *if* is called the *antecedent*, and the atom (or molecule) that follows the *then* is called the *consequent*. Hence, $P \supset Q$ is a conditional proposition, where P is the antecedent and Q the consequent. In ordinary English it is common to omit the *then*, as: "If John can run, Mary can walk"; it is also common to invert the order of antecedent and consequent, in which case omission of the *then* is mandatory, as: "Mary can walk if John can run."

We must first decide whether conditional propositions are truth-functional. It will be recalled that a truth-functional proposition is one whose truth-value is determined solely by the truth-values of its constituent parts. It was fairly clear that propositions of the form $P \cdot Q$, $P \vee Q$, and $\sim P$, were truth-functional in this sense. But it is also obvious that not all molecular propositions are truth-functional.[7] For example, "John believes that Esther is beautiful," which has the form "John believes P," is a molecular proposition containing the atom P. Yet, the truth or falsity of the whole proposition does not depend solely upon the truth or falsity of P, and perhaps it does not depend upon the truth or falsity of P at all. In any case, we cannot, *merely by knowing the truth-value of P*, state at once what is the truth-value of the whole proposition. Hence, the whole proposition is not a truth-functional molecule in our present sense.

What about conditionals? We will show that conditionals are *primarily* truth-functional in nature. But as this question has been in the past a subject for enormous amounts of discussion and obscurity, we will treat it at considerable length in the pages to follow.

We begin by discussing, not a conditional, but a proposition of another sort whose nature is already familiar:

> (i) It is not the case that: Helium is buoyant and hydrogen cannot be used to raise balloons.

Using obvious symbols, it can be rendered as $\sim (P \cdot \sim Q)$; its truth table is

(i)	$\sim$	(P	$\cdot$	$\sim$	Q)
	1	1	0	0	1
	0	1	1	1	0
	1	0	0	0	1
	1	0	0	1	0

We first assume that (i) is true. Then suppose helium *is* buoyant; it would follow that hydrogen *can* be used to raise balloons, for if not

---

[7] Or if they are, they are not truth-functions of their *explicitly* constituent propositions.

we would have just the situation that is denied in (i).[8] Thus, so long as we assume (i), it follows that,

(ii)   If helium is buoyant, then hydrogen can be used to raise balloons.

We note that (ii) is a conditional, rendered symbolically as $P \supset Q$. With respect to the pair of propositions (i) and (ii), we have shown that if (i) is true, so is (ii).

Now assume that (i) is false. Then the situation denied in (i) must be true; that is, it must be the case that helium *is* buoyant and hydrogen can*not* be used to raise balloons. This is confirmed by inspection of the second row of the truth table. Next, we shift our attention to proposition (ii) and ask under what circumstances we would be constrained to admit that it is false. Surely the conditional is false if its antecedent is true and its consequent false. That is, the assertion "If helium is buoyant, then hydrogen can be used to raise balloons," is understood to be false if it is the case that helium *is* buoyant and hydrogen can*not* be used to raise balloons.[9] But these are just the circumstances that hold when (i) is assumed to be false. Hence, we have shown that when (i) is false, so is (ii).

To sum up, we see that when (i) is true so is (ii); and likewise when (i) is false so is (ii). Thus the truth-value of (ii) follows upon that of (i). Because (i) and (ii) have precisely the same atoms, and because (i) is truth-functional, the same holds for (ii).

Furthermore, because (i) and (ii) are alike true or false, we can infer that they will take on the same truth-values for each combination of truth-values of their constituent atoms. Then, knowing the truth table for (i), we can construct a corresponding table for (ii):

(i)	∼	(P	·	∼	Q)
	1	1	0	0	1
	0	1	1	1	0
	1	0	0	0	1
	1	0	0	1	0

(ii)	P	⊃	Q
	1	1	1
	1	0	0
	0	1	1
	0	1	0

[8]Compare exercise 1a at the end of Section 8.

[9]Perhaps it is false under other circumstances as well; we cannot rule out this possibility because we still lack a clear account of the meaning of propositions such as (ii). But for our present purposes it is sufficient to agree—and it could hardly be denied—that (ii) is false under the indicated circumstances.

The boxed columns are, and must be, identical.

No part of this discussion really depends upon the specific content of the propositions (i) and (ii), but only on their propositional structure. Thus, we seem to have proved that conditional propositions are truth-functional and also to have found out what their truth-function is. We will now show how the same results can be reached from a different starting point.

Consider the following proposition:

(iii)   Either the Orient Express is not on time or it is on track 3.

Using obvious symbols it can be rendered as $\sim R$ v S; its truth table is,

(iii)	$\sim$	R	v	S
	0	1	1	1
	0	1	0	0
	1	0	1	1
	1	0	1	0

We first assume that (iii) is true. Then suppose the Orient Express *is* on time; it would follow that it is on track 3.[10] Thus, so long as we assume (iii), it follows that,

(iv)   If the Orient Express is on time, then it is on track 3.

We note that (iv) is a conditional, rendered symbolically as $R \supset S$. With respect to the pair of propositions (iii) and (iv), we have shown that when (iii) is true so is (iv).

Next assume that (iii) is false. Because (iii) asserts that one of a pair of constituent disjuncts is true, to say that (iii) is false is to say that neither of the disjuncts is true. That is, saying that (iii) is false amounts to saying that the Orient Express *is* on time and is *not* on track 3. This is confirmed by inspection of the second row of the truth table. Now we note that (iv), like (ii), would be false if its antecedent were true and consequent false. That is, (iv) would be false if the Orient Express were on time and not on track 3. But those are just the circumstances that obtain when (iii) is assumed false. Thus, when (iii) is false, so is (iv).

---

[10]Compare Exercise 1b at the end of Section 8.

To sum up again, we see that when (iii) is true so is (iv); and likewise when (iii) is false so is (iv). Hence, the truth-value of (iv) follows on that of (iii). And because (iii) and (iv) have precisely the same atoms, and because (iii) is truth-functional, (iv) must also be truth-functional.

Also, as in the previous case, we can infer that (iii) and (iv) take on the same truth-values for each combination of truth-values of their atoms. Knowing the truth table for (iii), we can then construct a table for (iv):

(iii)	~	R	v	S
	0	1	1	1
	0	1	0	0
	1	0	1	1
	1	0	1	0

(iv)	R	⊃	S
	1	1	1
	1	0	0
	0	1	1
	0	1	0

The boxed columns are, and must be, identical. Note that the table constructed for (iv) is the same as the table earlier constructed for (ii). As (ii) and (iv) are structurally identical, we have arrived by a different road at the same point.

Earlier in this chapter we stated fundamental Truth Tables 1, 2, and 3, defining the meaning of the truth-functional connectives ·, v, and ~. We are now in position to add a fourth fundamental table, defining the meaning of ⊃:

TT4:	A	B	A ⊃ B
	1	1	1
	1	0	0
	0	1	1
	0	0	1

Evidently TT4 states in full truth-table form, and for *any* constituent propositions *A* and *B*, what we have already seen in connection with the abbreviated tables for (ii) and (iv). It will be noted that according to TT4 a conditional proposition is *always true* unless its antecedent is true and its consequent false. This fact leads to some further results that are at first glance surprising and perhaps repugnant; they will be discussed in detail in the following section.

Exercises

1. Determine by truth table methods which of the following arguments are valid.

  a. If fraternities are democratic, then Edgar will join.
     Fraternities are democratic.
     Therefore, Edgar will join.

  b. If fraternities are democratic, then Edgar will join.
     Edgar will join.
     Therefore, fraternities are democratic.

  c. If fraternities are democratic, then Edgar will join.
     Fraternities are not democratic.
     Therefore, Edgar will not join.

  d. If fraternities are democratic, then Edgar will join.
     Edgar will not join.
     Therefore, fraternities are not democratic.

  e. If Descartes is right, then Spinoza is right.
     Therefore, if Spinoza is right, then Descartes is right.

  f. If Descartes is right, then Spinoza is right.
     Therefore, if Descartes is wrong, then Spinoza is wrong.

  g. If Descartes is right, then Spinoza is right.
     Therefore, if Spinoza is wrong, then Descartes is wrong.

  h. If Morris is well, the medicine worked.
     If the medicine worked, the doctor was right.
     Therefore, if Morris is well, the doctor was right.

  i. If Morris is well, the medicine worked.
     If the doctor was right, the medicine worked.
     Therefore, if Morris is well, the doctor was right.

  j. If the medicine worked, Morris is well.
     If the medicine worked, the doctor was right.
     Therefore, if Morris is well, the doctor was right.

  k. If Morris is well, the medicine worked.
     If the medicine worked, the doctor was right.
     Therefore, if the doctor was not right, then Morris is not well.

l. Either the color is red or the solution is neutral.
Therefore, if the color is not red, the solution is neutral.

m. Either the color is red or the solution is neutral.
Therefore, if the color is red, the solution is not neutral.

n. It is not the case that the color is red and the solution neutral.
Therefore, if the color is not red, the solution is neutral.

o. It is not the case that the color is red and the solution neutral.
Therefore, if the color is red, the solution is not neutral.

p. If it rains today it will be clear tomorrow.
If it is not clear tomorrow, it will not rain Wednesday.
Therefore, if it rains today, it will rain Wednesday.

q. If it rains today, it will be clear tomorrow.
If it is not clear tomorrow, it will not rain Wednesday.
Therefore, if it rains today, it will not rain Wednesday.

r. If maintenance was overdue and the engine failed, then the company is liable. Therefore, if maintenance was overdue, then if the engine failed the company is liable.

s. If maintenance was overdue, then if the engine failed the company is liable. Therefore, if maintenance was overdue and the engine failed, then the company is liable.

t. The train is late and it is raining. If it is raining, I will surely catch cold. If I catch cold, I will have to cancel the interview. Therefore, I will have to cancel the interview.

u. If the train is on time and Sergei makes the connection at Athens, Roskovitch will be arrested in Istanbul. If Kelly detains the switchman the train will be on time, and Sergei will make the connection at Athens if he can escape the ambush. Sergei can escape the ambush and Kelly will detain the switchman. Hence, Roskovitch will be arrested in Istanbul.

v. If the legal minimum wage exceeds one dollar per hour it will be too high. If it is applied to all workers it will be too sweeping. But either it will exceed one dollar per hour or it will be applied to all workers. Hence, it will either be too high or too sweeping.

w. If the legal minimum wage exceeds the fair market value of labor it is dangerous. If it does not exceed the fair market value of labor it is useless. Either it exceeds the fair market value of labor or it does not. Therefore, either it is dangerous or useless.

x. If the legal minimum wage exceeds the fair market value of labor it is dangerous. If it does not exceed the fair market value of labor it is useless. Therefore, either it is dangerous or useless.

y. If the conductor is experienced, the music is good. If the hall is well built, the acoustics are good. Either the music is no good or the acoustics are bad. Thus, either the conductor is inexperienced or the hall is not well built.

z. If the train is on time, it is on track 1. And if it is quite long, it is run in two sections. The train is either late or short. Hence, it is either not on track 1 or not in two sections.

2. Determine which of the following are logical truths.

a. $[(P \supset Q) \cdot P] \supset Q$

b. $[(P \supset Q) \cdot Q] \supset P$

c. $[(P \supset Q) \cdot \sim P] \supset \sim Q$

d. $[(P \supset Q) \cdot \sim Q] \supset \sim P$

e. $(P \supset Q) \supset (Q \supset P)$

f. $(P \supset Q) \supset (\sim P \supset \sim Q)$

g. $(P \supset Q) \supset (\sim Q \supset \sim P)$

h. $[(P \supset Q) \cdot (Q \supset R)] \supset (P \supset R)$

i. $[(P \supset Q) \cdot (R \supset Q)] \supset (P \supset R)$

j. $[(Q \supset P) \cdot (Q \supset R)] \supset (P \supset R)$

k. $[(P \supset Q) \cdot (Q \supset R)] \supset (\sim R \supset \sim P)$

l. $(P \vee Q) \supset (\sim P \supset Q)$

m. $(P \vee Q) \supset (P \supset \sim Q)$

n. $\sim(P \cdot Q) \supset (\sim P \supset Q)$

o. $\sim(P \cdot Q) \supset (P \supset \sim Q)$

p. $[(P \supset Q) \cdot (\sim Q \supset \sim R)] \supset (P \supset R)$

q. $[(P \supset Q) \cdot (\sim Q \supset \sim R)] \supset (P \supset \sim R)$

r. $[(P \cdot Q) \supset R] \supset [P \supset (Q \supset R)]$

s. $[P \supset (Q \supset R)] \supset [(P \cdot Q) \supset R]$

t. $\{[(P \cdot Q) \cdot (Q \supset R)] \cdot (R \supset S)\} \supset S$

u. $\{\{[(P \cdot Q) \supset R] \cdot [(S \supset P) \cdot (T \supset Q)]\} \cdot (T \cdot S)\} \supset R$

v. $\{[(P \supset Q) \cdot (R \supset S)] \cdot (P \text{ v } R)\} \supset (Q \text{ v } S)$

w. $\{[(P \supset Q) \cdot (\sim P \supset R)] \cdot (P \text{ v } \sim P)\} \supset (Q \text{ v } R)$

x. $[(P \supset Q) \cdot (\sim P \supset R)] \supset (Q \text{ v } R)$

y. $\{[(P \supset Q) \cdot (R \supset S)] \cdot (\sim Q \text{ v } \sim S)\} \supset (\sim P \text{ v } \sim R)$

z. $\{[(P \supset Q) \cdot (R \supset S)] \cdot (\sim P \text{ v } \sim R)\} \supset (\sim Q \text{ v } \sim S)$

*3. An argument of the *form* of Exercise 1r was used in the text of this section. Where?

*4. Inspector Heladjian is a prisoner in the land of the Yacks. All Yackis are divided into two types. Those of one kind wear beards and always tell the truth. The others are clean-shaven and always lie. The inspector is in a room, blindfolded, with five Yackis. He has been promised his freedom if he can correctly identify any *two* of the five as bearded or clean-shaven. An outsider tells him, truthfully, that the Yackis will speak in the following order: first Hadji, then Nidji, then Ali, then Toril, lastly Moab. They speak as follows.

> Hadji. "Moab is clean-shaven."
> Nidji: "Hadji has a beard."
> Ali: "If Nidji has a beard Toril is clean-shaven."
> Toril: "Hadji is clean-shaven and so is Moab."
> Moab: "Nidji is clean-shaven or Ali is."

"The day is saved," says Inspector Heladjian, "for I can tell about Ali and also about Toril." *What* can he tell about them, and how?

10 • MORE ON "IF . . . THEN"

At the end of the last section it was suggested that some reasonable objections could be made to our truth-functional analysis of the meaning of the connective "If . . . then". In this section we will discuss at length three such objections.

I. Many English conditional propositions are actually freighted with a good deal more meaning than is indicated by the truth-functional interpretation. For example, one might say "If the patient fasts, then he will die." Truth-functionally this means only that the patient will not fast *and* survive (compare TT4), and this could be so simply because the patient will not survive in any case. But these words, uttered by a despairing physician to an anxious family, would mean a great deal more than that. They would also convey the notion that starvation is *causally related* to malnutrition and death, and that the demise of fasting patients is generally a predictable and certain result of their behavior in respect to food—an avoidable result if they would only eat. All this is far more than what is conveyed by the simple truth-functional meaning.

Again, one may find it written in a logic book that "If all men are mortal and Socrates is a man, then Socrates is mortal." Here part of the meaning is captured in the truth-functional notion that it is not the case that the antecedent is true while the consequent is false. But this proposition also conveys the idea of a valid deduction running from the antecedent as premise to the consequent as conclusion. Hence, it suggests that there is no *logical* possibility of the antecedent being true and the consequent false. This is clearly a stronger meaning than the bland assertion that it does not happen to be the case that the antecedent is true and the consequent false (which is all that the truth-functional meaning can give us).

In both examples, we see that the truth-functional interpretation seems to miss some essential part of the meaning. For truth-functionally, the proposition $P \supset Q$ is merely a denial of the joint truth of the antecedent and falsehood of the consequent (compare TT4, especially the second row); if the antecedent is in fact false or the consequent in fact true, the whole conditional is true. The antecedent could be false or the consequent true *independently of any relation between them*, yet we expect, in the given examples, that some sort of relation between antecedent and consequent, or between the facts or events they refer to, is implied. Thus it seems that the connective "If . . . then" is not really truth-functional after all, or at least not entirely or always so.

This objection is met by admitting it. Certainly many conditionals carry more than truth-functional meaning; this is notoriously true of other sorts of propositions as well. But one of the purposes of logical analysis is to expose covert or implicit meanings and render them explicit, so that we can be in control of the meanings of our words rather than at their mercy. And in fact the truth-functional analysis of the connective "If . . . then" will help us to do just that. Let us examine a specific case.

We shall imagine that two men, Cain and Abel, approach a herd of horses carrying on this dialogue:

> Cain: "If this herd has colts in it, then it has mares."
> Abel: "We shall go closer and see."

Approaching nearer they discover that the herd contains only stallions; the discussion then continues as follows:

> Cain: "Well, I was right."
> Abel: "No, you *may* have been right, but we cannot tell merely by observing this herd, for it has no colts at all."
> Cain: "Precisely so, for I only asserted that it would not be the case that this herd *would* have colts and *not have* mares. That is all it means to say, ' If this herd has colts, then it has mares.' "
> Abel: "Nonsense. When you claimed that if there were colts then there were mares, you also meant that this herd *would* have mares if it *did* have colts, even though it does not. That is, you implied that all herds of horses that have colts in them also have mares. And you have not proved that, nor could you, simply by observing this herd."
> Cain: "But if I had wanted to say that all herds having colts have mares as well, I would have said so. I did not, I only said something about *this* herd, and I still think I was right."

In this disagreement, we are in fact dealing with two quite different propositions:

> (1) If this herd has colts, then it has mares.
> (2) All herds that have colts have mares.

Cain claims to have stated (1) explicitly and to have implied nothing else. Abel agrees that he stated (1) but claims that (2) was meant as part of the meaning of (1). We cannot adjudicate such disagreements because we cannot read minds. But it should be clear that (1) and (2) are different propositions, and if (1) is explicitly stripped of extra connotations it is a molecular proposition having purely truth-functional significance.[11] Furthermore, it is intuitively evident that (2) logically implies (1), but not conversely.[12] For if *all* herds with colts have mares, it follows that *this* herd, if it has colts, has mares. On the other hand (1) does not logically imply (2); it may be true for whatever reason that *this* herd has mares if it has colts, and yet false that *all* herds with colts have mares.

It is often our habit to use a proposition such as (1) intending something like (2) as part of the meaning. This is perfectly reasonable usage and can scarcely be condemned as such, particularly when the context is such that no confusion or obscurity arises. But we now see that it is possible to distinguish between various parts of the meaning of a conditional utterance, and to avoid confusion thereby.

Here is another example of a somewhat different sort:

(3) If the temperature rises, then the reaction will accelerate.
(4) A rise in temperature will accelerate the reaction.

In a given context of utterance (3) might perfectly well be intended to convey (4). Yet (4) is an *atomic* proposition asserting a causal connection between temperature and reaction speed; (3) is explicitly a molecular proposition, asserting only that there will not be an increase in temperature without an accompanying rise in reaction speed; it says less than (4). And although (4) logically implies (3), (3) does not logically imply (4); for a temperature rise might be accompanied by an increase of reaction speed—making (3) true—and yet the temperature change might not be the *cause* of the change in reaction speed—making (4) false.

One further example:

(5) If John goes and Mary does not, then John goes.
(6) "John goes and Mary does not" implies (logically) that John goes.

---

[11]Propositions such as (2) are discussed in a later chapter. It will be seen that they can in a sense be thought of as molecules, and in certain restricted circumstances they can be thought of as truth-functional molecules of an ordinary sort. But in the present context we treat (2) as an atom, for it does not contain any *explicit* propositions as subparts, and there is no simple way of rewriting it so that it does.

[12]The study of such inferences also belongs to a later chapter; the argument is not propositional.

Again (5) when stated may be meant to convey the sense of (6). Yet (6), although molecular like (5), is not truth-functional. For (6) states that there is a valid argument leading from one of its constituent propositions to the other. Hence (6) is true if and only if the following argument is valid:

> John goes and Mary does not.
> Therefore, John goes.

It is trivial to observe that this argument is valid, but it is important to recall that the validity does not depend solely on the truth-values of the constituent propositions. Hence, the truth-value of (6), which depends upon the validity of the argument, does *not* depend upon the truth-values of its constituent propositions. Therefore (6) is molecular— like (5) and unlike (2) and (4)—but it is *not* truth-functional. As in the other pairs of examples, (6) logically implies (5), but not conversely.

Looking back over the examples, a pattern is discernible:

(1) If this herd has colts, then it has mares.

(2) All herds that have colts have mares.

(3) If the temperature rises, then the reaction will accelerate.

(4) A rise in temperature will accelerate the reaction.

(5) If John goes and Mary does not, then John goes.

(6) 'John goes and Mary does not' implies that John goes.

Let us interpret the odd-numbered examples as strictly truth-functional assertions, with no extra connotations. The corresponding even-numbered statements express non-truth-functional connections that *might* under some circumstances be intended as part or all of the meaning of the odd-numbered statements. Yet the even-numbered propositions all imply (logically) the corresponding odd-numbered propositions. Hence, even if the non-truth-functional meaning is intended partly or primarily in any occasion of utterance of (1), (3), or (5), we see that the strictly truth-functional meaning emerges as an unavoidable part of the intention. Thus, we can say that the truth-functional meaning of "If *P*, then *Q*," as defined in TT4, is the logical core or skeleton of meaning common in all such propositions.

In the remainder of this text we shall feel free to use the connective "If . . . then" whenever we intend to convey a truth-functional connection in accordance with TT4. When, however, something more is intended, such as universal association (2), or causal connection (4), or logical implication (6), we shall make an effort to employ some other grammatical construction, particularly if the context is such as to render an ambiguity odious. This is in any case a useful principle for the creation of logically clear English discourse.

Meanwhile, what course shall we adopt when confronted with an "If . . . then" proposition? Because the truth-functional meaning is the *minimum* meaning that such a proposition can have, and part of the meaning that it *must* have in any case, the prudent course is to assume that nothing more is meant unless the context makes it clear that some further connection is intended. Unhappily this principle will sometimes lead us astray, particularly when conditional propositions are negatively stated.[13] But no other general rules for the interpretation of conditional propositions are available that are simple enough to be practical. In the long run we must rely on our awareness of the nuances of language and on our sensitivity to the intricacies of logical form. Our ultimate concern is with deductive arguments in which conditionals play a part. Fortunately, as experience will show, even where conditionals are meant to convey non-truth-functional meanings it is usually their truth-functional aspect alone that is relevant to the validity or invalidity of the argument in which they appear. Accordingly, we shall lay it down as a principle of first approximation in the analysis of deductive arguments containing conditionals, that the conditionals be interpreted as having truth-functional significance only.

II. A second difficulty with conditionals turns directly on the fact that such propositions are taken as true whenever their antecedents are false, regardless of the truth-value of the consequent. The following propositions are, therefore, factually true:

> If the sun rises in the west, the moon is a stone.
> If the sun rises in the west, the moon is a cheese.
> If the sun rises in the west, then it rises in the east.

---

[13]This is because the denial of a truth-functional conditional implies that the antecedent *is* true and the consequent *is* false, which may be *more* than is meant if a primarily non-truth-functional meaning was intended.

This result may seem peculiar, but only because one tends to anticipate *some further asserted connection between antecedent and consequent* (that is, non-truth-functional: typically causal or logical) as
part of the intention of anyone who writes or utters such sentences.
So understood, the sentences would indeed express false propositions;
but understood truth-functionally they are true.

True conditionals with false antecedents are by no means rare:

> If Lincoln was short, a short man can be President.
> If lye is an acid, it turns litmus paper red.

In general, we employ true conditionals with false antecedents whenever we argue *soundly* in the following way:

> If P, then Q.
> But $\sim Q$.
> Therefore, $\sim P$.

This form occurs whenever a hypothesis, P, is overturned by showing
that some proposition, Q, whose truth goes along with *its* truth is in
fact false.

One further illustration: Consider the propositions

> (7) If the instructor drops the chalk today, it will hit the floor.
> (8) If the instructor drops the chalk today, it will fly out the door and up
> to the moon.

Suppose the instructor does *not* drop the chalk today. Then according
to our analysis both propositions are true. Yet we would want des-
perately to say that (7) is true and (8) not. The difficulty here rests on
the fact that (7) and (8) *both* connote more than a truth-functional
connection between antecedent and consequent. When such sentences
are uttered, particularly in juxtapposition, they are almost always
meant to be elliptical statements of general rules of physical behavior,
or natural laws; by implication, both refer to much more than the
particular situation(s) mentioned explicitly in them. Hence (7) is
true because the truth-functional part of its meaning is true (the antecedent being false), and the other more complex part of its meaning
(all dropped pieces of chalk hit the floor) is true as well. On the contrary, (8) is false because, although the truth-functional part of its
meaning is true, the other more complex part is not. Explicitly stripped

of non-truth-functional connotations, (7) and (8) are alike true under the assumed circumstances.

III. Examination of the first and third rows of TT4 shows that a conditional is true if its consequent is true, no matter what the truth value of the antecedent. Thus, the following are factually true:

> If the moon is a stone, the sun rises in the east.
> If the moon is a cheese, the sun rises in the east.
> If the sun rises in the west, then it rises in the east.

The appropriate treatment of these expressions follows the same lines as the discussion of conditionals with false antecedents and is left for the reader to supply.

In general, whenever the strictly truth-functional interpretation of a conditional sentence appears hopelessly repugnant, it is almost always the case that there is some confusion between truth-functional meanings and more complex connotations that are present or expected.

IV. A certain residue of verbal ambiguity in connection with conditional expressions is unavoidable. Confronted with a sentence of the form, "If P, then Q," one is sometimes tempted to render it as P *implies* Q without meaning to assert that P and Q are, respectively, premises and conclusion of a valid argument. In this way one may say, " 'The sun comes up' implies 'the stone gets warm.' " (It would be more usual to express this indirectly as, "The sun's rising implies the stone's warming.") Thus, *imply* can be used, and often is, in contexts where no assertion of logical deducibility is intended. In such cases the minimum meaning we can assign to "P implies Q" is the truth-functional meaning defined in TT4.

In fact, it is sometimes convenient to the point of necessity to use the word *imply* in this way. Consider for example the following rather common type of molecule:

$$[(P \supset Q) \cdot (Q \supset R)] \supset (P \supset R).$$

If we seek to read this off in words we get, "If, if P then Q and if Q then R, then, if P then R." It is far less awkward and far clearer to say, "If P implies Q and Q implies R, then P implies R."

To distinguish sharply between (i) *imply* as signifying the logical connection that obtains between premises and conclusion of a valid argument, and (ii) *imply* as signifying the truth-functional relation of TT4, it has been proposed that we say *"P formally implies Q"* or *"P logically implies Q"* for (i), and *"P materially implies Q"* for (ii). In this usage the relation defined in TT4 is known as *material implication*, whereas the relation between premises and conclusion of a valid argument is *formal implication* or *logical implication*. We will not frequently avail ourselves of this artificiality; but it is useful to note the technical terminology and the distinction it marks.[14]

Exercises

1. Which of the following completions are correct? — All propositions of the form, "If *P*, then *Q*," mean

   a. at most, *"P* materially implies *Q."*

   b. at least, *"P* materially implies *Q."*

   c. precisely, *"P* materially implies *Q."*

   d. at most, *"P* ⊃ *Q."*

   e. at least, *"P* ⊃ *Q."*

   f. precisely, *"P* ⊃ *Q."*

2. The following propositions have a truth-functional conditional as part or all of their meaning. In some cases it is clearly only a part of the meaning, in some cases clearly all of the meaning, and in some cases ambiguous. Decide which are which.

   a. If the sun comes out today the beach will warm up.

---

[14]Under pressure of the ambiguities of *imply*, many philosophers and logicians have taken to using *entails* in place of *formally implies* and *entailment* in place of *formal implication*, thus reserving *implies* and *implication* exclusively for truth-functional (or other) meanings. This usage is ideally clear when it is understood. It is not adopted in this text because it does not seem to have been adopted generally in the English language; in particular, mathematicians persistently use *implies* in the formal sense.

But technical vocabularies can be bewildering:—In the history of logic and the philosophy of mathematics it is almost impossible to overestimate the importance of A. N. Whitehead and B. Russell's *Principia Mathematica* (Cambridge: The University Press, 1925); but in that work *formal implication* refers to propositions of the type, "For any *x*, if *x* is an *F* then *x* is a *G*."

 b. If the sun comes out today it will warm up the beach.

 c. If the sun comes out today the beach will warm up, as always.

 d. "The sun comes out today" formally implies that "the beach will warm up today."

 e. If the sun comes out today, that implies formally that the beach will warm up today.

 f. The sun's coming out today materially implies that the beach will warm up today.

 g. The sun's coming out today implies that the beach will warm up today.

 h. It is not the case that the sun will come out today and the beach not warm up.

3. The following proposition could conceivably have at least three meanings. Specify them.
 "If the moon rises early, it implies that there will be a late tide."

4. Which of the following arguments are valid? Use truth-table analyses *where possible*, and interpret the *explicit* conditionals as truth-functional only.

 a. If the shield is removed, the temperature rises.
  If the temperature rises, the speed increases.
  Therefore, if the shield is removed, the speed increases.

 b. Removing the shield causes the temperature to rise.
  Rising of the temperature causes the speed to increase.
  Therefore, removing the shield causes the speed to increase.

 c. John loves Mary.
  Mary loves Jack.
  Therefore, John loves Jack.

 d. Removing the shield causes the temperature to rise.
  Rising of the temperature causes the speed to increase.
  If any one thing causes a second thing, and the second thing causes a third thing, then the first causes the third.
  Therefore, removing the shield causes the speed to increase.

 e. If the shield is removed, the temperature rises.
  Therefore, removing the shield causes the temperature to rise.

f. Removing the shield causes the temperature to rise.
Therefore, if the shield is removed the temperature rises.

g. If the shield is removed the temperature rises.
If the temperature rises the speed is increased.
Therefore, removing the shield causes the speed to increase.

h. Removing the shield causes the temperature to rise.
Rising of the temperature causes the speed to increase.
Therefore, if the shield is removed the speed is increased.

5. Which of the following arguments are valid when the conditionals are interpreted purely truth-functionally? Of those, which remain valid when the conditionals are given some additional connotations suggested by the contexts?

   a. The sun rises in the east.
   Therefore, if the moon rises in the west the sun rises in the east.

   b. The sun rises in the west.
   Therefore, the sun rises in the west if the moon rises in the west.

   c. The sun does not rise in the west.
   Therefore, if the sun rises in the west so does the moon.

   d. If Caesar did not cross the Rubicon, we can save the Republic.
   Caesar did cross the Rubicon.
   Therefore, we cannot save the Republic.

   e. If Caesar did not cross the Rubicon, we can save the Republic.
   We cannot save the Republic.
   Therefore, Caesar did cross the Rubicon.

   f. It is not the case that if you do your work you will be paid.
   Therefore, you will do your work.

   g. It is not the case that if you do your work you will be paid.
   Therefore, you will not be paid.

6. Which of the following arguments are valid? Of those, which could conceivably be sound?

   a. Chicago is west of Cleveland. If Chicago is west of Cleveland, Evanston is east of Cleveland. Evanston is not east of Cleveland. Therefore, Evanston is west of Cleveland.

   b. Chicago is west of Cleveland. If Chicago is west of Cleveland, Evanston is east of Cleveland. Evanston is not east of Cleveland. Therefore, Chicago is not west of Cleveland.

c. Chicago is west of Cleveland. If Chicago is west of Cleveland, Evanston is east of Cleveland. Evanston is not east of Cleveland. Therefore, all Persian statues are made of bronze.

d. Police are kind. Police are not kind. Therefore, Caesar did not cross the Rubicon.

e. Caesar did not cross the Rubicon. Therefore, either there will be a seafight tomorrow or there will not be a seafight tomorrow.

f. If the ship sails today, the profit is doubled. The ship does not sail today. Thus, if either the ship sails today or the profit is doubled, and the ship does not sail today, then the profit is doubled.

7. A teacher says, "It is not true that, if you pass this examination then you will pass this course." A student protests loudly that this involves a sinister prediction. What is wrong here? How could the remark be rephrased to avoid misunderstanding?

8. Given an argument whose conclusion has the form $P \supset Q$, show that to determine the validity of this argument it is sufficient to find out the truth-values of the premises when P is true and Q false.

11 • THE FUNDAMENTAL THEOREM

There is evidently a close relation between conditional propositions and deductive inferences. We have seen that a proposition of the form, "If P, then Q," sometimes suggests that P logically implies Q. And, confronted with a valid argument, it is extraordinarily common to remark that *if* the premises are true, *then* the conclusion is true. We now state precisely the nature of this relation.

Consider the following schemata:

P.
Q. $(P \cdot Q \cdot R) \supset C$
R.
Therefore, C.

On the left is an argument, on the right a conditional proposition. The premises of the argument appear, conjoined, as the antecedent of the conditional. The conclusion of the argument appears as the consequent of the conditional. If the argument is valid there is no way in which P, Q, and R can be true while C is false; but those are the *only* circumstances under which the conditional could be false. Hence, if the argument is valid the conditional is a logical truth. For equally obvious reasons, if the argument is not valid the conditional is not a logical truth. Thus, the argument is valid if and only if the conditional is logically true.

We now formalize this insight:

> **Definition:** For every argument there exists a conditional proposition, called the *corresponding conditional*, whose antecedent is a conjunction of the premises of the argument, and whose consequent is the conclusion of the argument.

Without further justification we assert the following principle, called the *fundamental theorem of deductive inference.*

> **Theorem:** An argument is valid if and only if its corresponding conditional is a logical truth.

Although this theorem has been developed and stated with respect to propositional arguments, it will be seen in later chapters that it applies to other classes of deductive argument as well.

The fundamental theorem suggests a new method for the evaluation of propositional arguments. For to test an argument for validity, we need only formulate the corresponding conditional and build an abbreviated truth table beneath it to see if it is logically true. Ob-. viously this is exactly equivalent to our former procedure of setting out premises and conclusion separated by slashes, building a common truth table beneath, and checking for rows with true premises and a false conclusion. In fact the new procedure is more cumbersome, because it requires the construction of extra truth-table columns; in practice one therefore stays with the old method, which is now understood as a shorthand way of scrutinizing an argument's corresponding conditional for logical truth. The motives for restating the procedure in this new way are largely ulterior: The new formulation is clearer and more elegant and will be extraordinarily useful for later purposes.

We are now in a position to discuss some strange and (perhaps) distressing types of arguments, examples of which appeared in the exercises attached to the last section. For example;

> P.
> $\sim P$.
> Therefore, Q.

The corresponding conditional is $(P \cdot \sim P) \supset Q$. We see at once that the antecedent is logically false, and because it can never be true, the whole conditional can never be false. Thus, the conditional is logically true and the argument valid. The same result will hold whenever the premises are inconsistent (that is, cannot all be true), no matter how subtly the inconsistency may be concealed in the structure. We thus have it that any argument whose premises are inconsistent is valid. This result should not be repugnant. For the premises of such arguments can never all be true, so we could never by appeal to them infer false conclusions from true premises. Differently said, inconsistent premises *validly* imply *any* propositions but *soundly* imply *none*.

Incidentally, it is now demonstrable that inconsistent *conclusions* can be validly inferred only from inconsistent premises. Consider a valid argument whose conclusion is logically false; its corresponding conditional is true in every row, but its consequent is false in every row; hence, the antecedent is likewise false in every row, and the premises as a group are therefore inconsistent.

Another example of a surprising argument is

> P.
> Therefore, Q v $\sim Q$.

Here the corresponding conditional is $P \supset (Q$ v $\sim Q)$. We can see by inspection that the *consequent* is a logical truth; hence, the conditional will always have a true consequent and will itself always be true, making the argument valid. The same result will hold for any argument whose conclusion is a logical truth. We thus have it that any argument whose conclusion is logically true is valid; or, logical truths can be deduced from any premises.

This result is probably not as initially puzzling as the other. One tends to feel that it would be superfluous to offer an argument on behalf of a logical truth, for the argument would be sound only if the premises were in fact true, and it would be odd to make our confidence in logical truths depend upon the factual truth of some other propositions. On the other hand, a logical truth being the sort of entity it is (that is, always true regardless of factual conditions), it is entirely reasonable that we should be able to deduce it, if we choose to deduce it at all, from any starting place.[15]

The fact that all arguments whose conclusions are logical truths are valid is related to another theorem that is sometimes useful and intuitively quite congenial: From logical truths as premises, only other logical truths can be validly deduced. Proof is left as an exercise.

Exercises

1. Prove that from logical truths as premises only other logical truths can be validly deduced.

2. Go back over the arguments of Exercise 6, Section 10, and determine which have inconsistent premises or a logically true conclusion.

3. Given an argument with one logically false premise (among others not logically false). Can it be valid? Can it be invalid?

4. Suppose we have two valid arguments, A and B. The conclusion of A is also the sole premise of B. Show by reference to the fundamental theorem that the premises of A logically imply the conclusion of B.

5. Suppose we have three valid arguments, A, B, and C. The conclusions of A and B form the premises of C. Show by reference to the fundamental theorem that the premises of A and B together logically imply the conclusion of C.

6. *Definition:* For any argument there exists a proposition, called the *corresponding conjunction*, that consists of a conjunction of all the premises with the negation of the conclusion. Show that an argument is valid if and only if its corresponding conjunction is inconsistent.

---

[15]In a later chapter it will emerge that a logical truth can be viewed as a proposition validly deducible from no premises whatever.

12 • EQUIVALENCE, CONTRADICTION, AND OTHER RELATIONS

We have seen several examples of pairs of propositions that are both true or both false under any circumstances (that is, any assignment of truth values to their constituent atoms). Examples are $\sim(P \cdot \sim Q)$ and $P \supset Q$, or $\sim(P \text{ v } Q)$ and $\sim P \cdot \sim Q$. Whenever such a situation obtains between a pair of propositions we shall say that they are *equivalent*. Clearly, truth tables will show whether or not any given pair is equivalent.

Because equivalent propositions always have the same truth value, it will be impossible for one to be true and the other false; hence, using either one as a premise, the other is validly deduced as a conclusion. Conversely, if two propositions each imply the other, it will never be possible for them to take on different truth-values, and hence they will be equivalent.

We can have a situation that stands at the opposite extreme from equivalence. Two propositions may be so related that they *never* take on the same truth-values, so that if one is true the other is false, and if one false the other true. Simple examples are

P
1
0

~	P
0	1
1	0

P	⊃	Q
1	1	1
1	0	0
0	1	1
0	1	0

P	·	~	Q
1	0	0	1
1	1	1	0
0	0	0	1
0	0	1	0

P	v	Q
1	1	1
1	1	0
0	1	1
0	0	0

~	P	·	~	Q
0	1	0	0	1
0	1	0	1	0
1	0	0	0	1
1	0	1	1	0

In each pair we say that the propositions are *contradictories*, or that each is the *denial* of the other, or the *negation* of the other, or the *contradiction* of the other.

It is sometimes important to know just what constitutes the denial of a proposition. A careless eye may view the following pair and think they are contradictory, hence concluding that if one is true the other must be false:

Organized labor is dangerous or useless.
Organized labor is safe or useful.

Yet these are not contradictories, as truth tables will show.

P: Organized labor is dangerous.
$\sim P$: Organized labor is safe.
Q: Organized labor is useful.
$\sim Q$: Organized labor is not useful.

P	v	Q		~P	v	~Q
1	1	1		0	0	0
1	1	0		0	1	1
0	1	1		1	1	0
0	0	0		1	1	1

We see that both propositions can be true when one and only one of the constituent atoms is true.

The terms *consistent* and *inconsistent*, formerly used primarily in regard to a single proposition, may also be used to signify relations between a pair of propositions. If, given two propositions, they cannot both be true we say that the *pair* is inconsistent. Examples of inconsistent *pairs* are

$P \cdot Q$ and $\sim P \text{ v} \sim Q;$
$P \cdot Q$ and $\sim P \cdot Q.$

The first pair illustrates one possible *kind* of inconsistency. For the propositions in the first pair cannot both be true, nor can they both be false. In fact, they are not only inconsistent, but they are *also* contradictory. On the other hand the propositions in the second pair, although they cannot both be true, *can* both be false. Two such propositions are said to be *contraries*. Clearly these terms can be extended in a natural way to sets of three or more propositions.

To complete the survey, we call two propositions which *may* both be true but can*not* both be false, *subcontraries*. Examples are

$P \supset Q$ and $P \supset \sim Q;$
$P \text{ v } Q$ and $\sim P \text{ v } Q.$

Finally, we note an evident qualification: Our truth-functional method for showing that a molecule could be true (or false) is to point out an assignment of truth-values for the molecule's parts under which it *would* be true (or false). This involves a presumption that the relevant combination of truth-values is possible—a presumption which might be overthrown by a closer scrutiny of the parts. (For example, the assumption that a certain P and a certain Q could both have truth-value 1 would be wrong if P meant "All men are mortal," and Q meant "Not all men are mortal.") A similar qualification holds when we show by truth-functional means that two different molecules can both be true (or false). Although seldom a practical obstacle, this difficulty cannot be ignored. It is part of the price we pay for abandoning the symbolic uniqueness rule, and is in fact another form of the second "danger" noted in Section 1 of this chapter.

Exercises

1. Show that if P and Q are inconsistent, $P \cdot Q$ is a logical falsehood, and conversely.

2. Show that if P and Q are contradictory, $P \cdot Q$ is a logical falsehood, and $P \vee Q$ is a logical truth.

3. Show that if $P \cdot Q$ is inconsistent, $\sim(P \cdot Q)$ is a logical truth. Next show that if $P \cdot Q$ is inconsistent, $P \supset \sim Q$ is a logical truth.

4. Show that if P and Q are contradictory, the denial of either is equivalent to the other.

*5. Suppose we have a set of propositions, $P_1, P_2, P_3, \ldots, P_n$. If the set is inconsistent show that the conditional

$$(P_1 \cdot P_2 \cdot P_3 \cdot \ldots \cdot P_{n-1}) \supset \sim P_n$$

is a logical truth.

*6. Suppose we have a set of propositions, $P_1, P_2, \ldots, P_n, Q_1, Q_2, \ldots, Q_m$. The set is known to be inconsistent. Show that an argument whose premises consist of $P_1, P_2, \ldots, P_n$, and whose conclusion is

$$\sim Q_1 \vee \sim Q_2 \vee \ldots \vee \sim Q_m$$

is valid.

7. Which of the following pairs of propositions are equivalent, which are contradictory, and which are neither? Among the latter, which are contraries, which are subcontraries, and which are neither?

   a. Either Harry goes or John stays home.
      It is not the case that Harry does not go and John does not stay home.

   b. Harry goes and John stays home.
      It is not the case that either Harry goes or John stays home.

   c. Management is basically honest and well intentioned.
      Management is not basically honest and not well intentioned.

   d. If John and Harry go, then Myrtle stays home.
      If John goes Myrtle stays home, and if Harry goes Myrtle stays home.

   e. If John goes, then Harry and Myrtle stay home.
      If John goes Harry stays home, and if John goes Myrtle stays home.

   f. Either Aristotle is right and Plato too, or Aristotle is right and Zeno wrong.
      Aristotle is right, and Plato is right or Zeno wrong.

   g. Liszt was great or Bach was, and Liszt was either great or he was an innovator.
      Either Liszt was great, or Bach was great and Liszt was an innovator.

   h. Existence is prior to essence, or the existentialist tradition is mistaken.
      Existence is not prior to essence, and the existentialist tradition is not mistaken.

   i. The plane is late or down.
      The plane is not late, nor is it down.

   j. If the plane is down, then if Percy jumped he may be safe.
      If the plane is down, then Percy jumped and he may be safe.

   k. If the plane is down, then if Percy jumped he may be safe.
      If the plane is down and Percy jumped, he may be safe.

   l. If the plane was hit, Percy jumped.
      If Percy jumped, the plane was hit.

   m. If the plane was hit, Percy jumped.
      If Percy did not jump, the plane was not hit.

n. If the plane was hit, Percy jumped.
The plane was not hit, and Percy jumped.

o. If the plane was hit, Percy jumped.
The plane was hit, and Percy did not jump.

p. The bus is hot.
The bus is hot and either there will be cold drinks at the end of the trip or there will not.

q. The bus is hot.
The bus is not hot or there will and will not be cold drinks at the end of the trip.

*r. If, on the one hand, John will be pleased if Mary goes with him and Jean comes with Harry or George, then, on the other hand, John will be satisfied with those other arrangements.
Either, in the first place, John will not be satisfied with those other arrangements, and either Mary will not go with him or Jean will not go with Harry and likewise not go with George, or, in the second place, John will not be satisfied with those other arrangements and John will be pleased.

8. If two propositions are each equivalent to a third, what can be inferred about the relation between the two?

9. If two propositions are each negations of a third, what can be inferred about the relation between the two?

*10. If two propositions are each inconsistent with a third, what can be inferred about the relation between the two?

11. A valid argument has premises P, Q, R, and conclusion C. It is discovered that P is equivalent to Q. Is the argument still valid if one of those premises is dropped? If both are dropped?

12. Which of the following are correct?

a. Any two logical truths are equivalent.

b. Any two logical falsehoods are equivalent.

c. Any logical truth is contradictory to any logical falsehood.

13. How can two propositions be equivalent if they contain totally different atoms? How can two propositions be contradictory if they contain totally different atoms?

14. Given two propositions, such that one has an atom that the other lacks, and both are contingent. Can they be equivalent? Contradictory? Give examples.

13 • INDIRECT TRUTH-TABLE TECHNIQUE

We have so far considered arguments and propositions containing no more than five different atoms. But any arguments contain many more atoms than that. Were we faced with an inference involving eight atoms, the prospect of checking it with truth-table methods would be terrifying, for it would require 2^8, or 256 rows. However, there is a way to approach the analysis of propositional arguments by means of truth tables that will, in the vast majority of cases, yield a decision in a far shorter time than the method we have heretofore employed. It is called the *indirect truth-table technique*; unlike the method used until now, it requires some ingenuity and cannot be relied upon to produce a decision with the same automatic regularity.

Take first an argument of the following form:

P v Q.
Q v R.
Therefore, P v R.

To analyze it we need to form its corresponding conditional:

$[(P \text{ v } Q) \cdot (Q \text{ v } R)] \supset (P \text{ v } R)$.

Imagine that a full truth table for this proposition has been constructed. Our interest in the table is summed up in a single question: "Is there a row in which the conditional is false?" Or, equivalently: "Is there a row in which all the conjuncts of the antecedent (that is, the premises) are true and the consequent (that is, the conclusion) false?" If *one* such row exists the argument is invalid; if none exists it is valid.

But instead of constructing an entire truth table, we will instead try to construct just a single row in which the corresponding conditional is false. That is, we shall try our luck at building, by itself, a truth-table row in which the conjuncts in the antecedent are true and the consequent false. We begin by assuming that such a row exists; then the initial assignment of truth values in the row will be

$$[(P \text{ v } Q) \cdot (Q \text{ v } R)] \supset (P \text{ v } R).$$
$$1 \qquad\quad 1 \qquad 0 \quad 0$$

This initial step *commits us* to further truth-value assignments. For because the consequent is a false disjunction, both of its disjuncts must be false. Hence, we have[16]

$$[(P \text{ v } Q) \cdot (Q \text{ v } R)] \supset (P \text{ v } R).$$
$$1 \qquad\quad 1 \qquad 0 \quad \underline{0}\,0\,\underline{0}$$

But now, because P and R are false in one of their occurrences, they must be false in their other occurrences as well (for we are constructing a *single* truth-table row). Thus we get

$$[(P \text{ v } Q) \cdot (Q \text{ v } R)] \supset (P \text{ v } R).$$
$$\underline{0}\,1 \qquad\quad 1\,\underline{0} \quad 0 \quad 0\,0\,0$$

Lastly, we note that both conjuncts of the antecedent are true disjunctions, one of whose disjuncts is false. This condition can only be satisfied if the other disjunct is true; hence, Q must be true, and the finished row is

$$[(P \text{ v } Q) \cdot (Q \text{ v } R)] \supset (P \text{ v } R).$$
$$0\,1\,\underline{1} \quad \underline{1}\,1\,0 \quad 0 \quad 0\,0\,0$$

But this shows, without further fuss, that the argument is not valid. For we have shown that there is at least one row in the truth table of the corresponding conditional in which that conditional is false; hence, the conditional is not a logical truth, and the corresponding argument is not valid. Or, equivalently, we have shown that there is a possible assignment of truth-values to the atoms of the argument under which the premises are true and the conclusion false.

---

[16]For ease of reading, the next numerals filled in are underlined; this practice will be continued throughout this section.

However, it is not always the case that the attempt to build such a row will work out. In particular, it will *not* work out if the argument is valid and the corresponding conditional is a logical truth. The *fact* that the attempt to build such a row comes to grief (if it does) can then be taken as proof that the corresponding argument is valid. For example consider an argument of the form

P v Q.
$\sim P$.
Therefore, Q.

As before, we form the corresponding conditonal and set out to build a truth-table row in which it will be false. In such a row the conjuncts of the antecedent must be true and the consequent false, so initially we have

$$[(P \text{ v } Q) \cdot \sim P] \supset Q.$$
$$1 \quad\quad 1 \quad\; 0 \; 0$$

This initial step commits us to some further assignments. Because $\sim P$ is true, P must be false, and it must be false wherever it occurs; hence;

$$[(P \text{ v } Q) \cdot \sim P] \supset Q.$$
$$0 \; 1 \quad\; 1\underline{0} \; 0 \; 0$$

Furthermore, because Q is false in the consequent, it must also be false where it appears in the antecedent:

$$[(P \text{ v } Q) \cdot \sim P] \supset Q.$$
$$0 \; 1\underline{0} \quad 10 \; 0 \; 0$$

But now we have arrived at an absurd result, for we have said in effect that the molecule P v Q is true although both its disjuncts are false. We note this contradictory outcome by slashing the truth-value assigned to P v Q:

$$[(P \text{ v } Q) \cdot \sim P] \supset Q.$$
$$0 \; \cancel{1} \; 0 \quad 10 \; 0 \; 0$$

This result is sufficient to establish the validity of the corresponding argument. For we have shown that the attempt to construct a truth-table row in which the conditional turns out false necessarily fails. Because no such row *can* be constructed, we can infer without further labor that no such row exists; the conditional is logically true, and the argument is valid.

In brief, then, if the attempt to construct a row in which the conditional is false succeeds, the argument is invalid. If it necessarily fails, the argument is valid. Evidently this method is simply a systematic application of Tech 2 and Tech 4 of Chapter 1.

To make this method work properly, however, it is essential that each step in the assignment of truth-values be *forced.* Suppose for instance that we return to the first example, and set out the corresponding conditional with initial truth-value assignments:

$$[(P \vee Q) \cdot (Q \vee R)] \supset (P \vee R).$$
$$1 \qquad\quad 1 \qquad\quad 0 \qquad 0$$

Now it is possible that P and Q are false. If we plunge ahead and assign these values we obtain

$$[(P \vee Q) \cdot (Q \vee R)] \supset (P \vee R),$$
$$0\,\underline{\cancel{1}}\,0 \quad 0\,1 \qquad\quad 0\ \underline{0}\ 0$$

where the slash indicates a contradiction arising in the first premise. This proves that in the truth-table row where P and Q are false the entire conditional must indeed be true. But since we are not logically *obliged* by the original assumptions to assign 0 to Q, the possibility is still open that we might have filled in the row without contradiction if Q had been given some other value.

Although the occurrence of a choice in a sequence of moves leading to a contradiction *prevents* us from deciding at once about the validity of the argument, the same does not hold if a choice occurs in a sequence of moves leading to the *successful* construction of the desired row. The reason is obvious: So long as *one* such row exists, the conditional is shown not to be a logical truth, and the argument is shown to be invalid.

It is possible in the course of analyzing an argument by the indirect truth-table method that one may reach a point where choices are unavoidable. The general plan to adopt in such cases is clear: Choose some atom arbitrarily and assume first that it is true and then that it is false. Examine the consequences of each assumption separately. If, under *either* assumption, it is possible to fill out the row without contradiction, the argument is invalid. If, under *both* assumptions, contradictions arise in the subsequent attempt to complete the row, the argument is valid. This applies similarly if there are more than two choices or choices within alternatives.

There are some tactical principles useful in the actual utilization of this method: (i) Avoid choices; that is, develop alternative sets of truth-value assignments to analyze only when forced assignments are not available. (ii) When a choice must be made, look for some atom whose truth-value, once assigned arbitrarily, will lead quickly to further forced moves. (iii) Develop alternatives by the arbitrary assignment of truth-values to *atoms*, not molecules; for this is simpler and usually has simpler consequences. (iv) Just before making an arbitrary assignment of truth-value to some atom, repeat all of the truth-values so far assigned in a second row directly under the first; then, if further analysis of the first row leads to a contradiction, the second row shows at once how far "back" in the sequence one must go to explore the second alternative.

Exercises

1. Using the indirect truth-table technique for determining validity, recheck the following arguments from the exercises at the end of Section 9: 1a, 1d, 1h, 1k, 1u, 1v.

2. Check the following arguments for validity by the indirect truth-table technique.

   a. If death is a pleasant dream we have nothing to fear. If death is a long sleep we have nothing to fear. Death is a pleasant dream or a long sleep. Therefore, we have nothing to fear.

   b. Either death is a pleasant dream and if it is we have nothing to fear, or death is a long sleep and if it is we have nothing to fear. Therefore, we have nothing to fear.

   c. Either we have nothing to fear if death is a pleasant dream or we have nothing to fear if death is a long sleep. Therefore, we have nothing to fear.

d. If Descartes is right the mind does not occupy space. If the mind does not occupy space it is immaterial. If it is immaterial it is not subject to decay. If it is not subject to decay it is immortal. Descartes is right. Therefore, the mind is immortal.

e. If Aquinas was right, reason is dependable. If reason is dependable, then Aquinas' proofs for the existence of God are sound. If Aquinas' proofs for the existence of God are sound, then Kant is wrong. If Kant is wrong then so is Newton. Newton is right. Therefore, Aquinas was wrong.

f. If it is true that if prices generally rise then all salaries rise, then if steel prices go up so will steel wages. Prices will generally rise, and not all salaries will rise. If steel prices go up new car sales will decline. If steel wages do not go up appliance purchases will decline. And if appliance purchases and new car sales decline, we are in for a recession. Therefore, steel prices will go up, and we are in for a recession.

g. If the solution is dilute and the mice do not overeat, then if they got the supplement they will survive. Either the colorimeter is badly calibrated or the solution is dilute. Yet, if the colorimeter is badly calibrated then, still, the solution is dilute. If the mice overeat, then it is not the case that they will either be hungry or frustrated. It is certainly not true that either they will survive or they will not be hungry. Therefore, they did not get the supplement.

*h. If the Patagonians have heavy artillery within range, then, in the first place, it is not the case that they will either miss the chance to use it or avoid the consequent test of strength, and in the second place, if they do not miss the chance to use it they will come over Sinbad's Ridge and deploy in the heights beyond. Hence, if they have heavy artillery within range, then they will not avoid the consequent test of strength and they will deploy in the heights beyond Sinbad's Ridge.

i. If it is not true that if most prices rise steel prices rise, then if steel prices rise wages will be stable. Most prices will rise, and steel prices will not rise. If steel prices do not rise, appliance purchases will fall off. If appliance purchases fall off and wages remain stable, we are in for a recession. Therefore, we are in for a recession and most prices will rise.

j. Repeat Exercise i, but change the *and* in the last premise to *or*.

k. It is false that Mary will go and John will not. If the car will be on time, then either John will go or Mary will. The driver will be sober and the car will be on time. If Harry goes then John will not go. It is not the case that Myrtle and John will go. If the driver is sober and the car on time, then either Myrtle or Harry will go. So, if Mary will go and the car will be on time, then Myrtle will go.

l. If the pea is under the first shell, then if I have been watching I have been fooled. If I have been fooled, my eyes have lost their sharpness. If my eyes have lost their sharpness, I have not been taking proper care of them. If I have been taking proper care of them, then I have been using the right glasses. If my oculist made a mistake, then I have not been using the right glasses. The pea is under the first shell. Therefore, if I have been watching, then my oculist made a mistake.

3. Is the indirect truth-table technique a decision procedure?

4. How can you adapt the indirect truth-table technique to test sets of propositions for consistency? Test the premises in Exercises 2f and 2k, above.

5. Suppose the indirect truth-table technique is used to test an argument containing n premises for validity. There is a sense in which, at the same time, a set in $n + 1$ propositions is being tested for consistency. Explain. (Compare Exercise 6 at the end of Section 11.)

*6. The prosecutor argues thus: "On the night of the murder the defendant was either in Hickville or Henryville. If he was in Hickville he was surely with the deceased's wife. And if that, he had a motive for the crime. On the other hand, if he was in Henryville, he was either at the Star Drive-In or the Victory Roadhouse. If he was at the Star Drive-In he must have seen the deceased leaving work. If he was at the Victory Roadhouse he must have seen the deceased come in to talk to his brother. And if he either saw the deceased leaving work or coming in to talk to his brother, he had the opportunity to follow him. And if that, then he had opportunity to commit the crime. Therefore, the defendant had a motive for the crime or the opportunity."

The defending attorney replies as follows: "On the night of the murder the defendant was either not in Hickville or not in Henryville. If he was not in Hickville he was not with the deceased's wife. And if he was not with the deceased's wife he had no motive for the crime. On the other hand, if he was not in Henryville, then he was not at the Star Drive-In *and* he was not at the Victory Roadhouse. Clearly, if he was not at the Star Drive-In he could not have seen the deceased leaving work. And if he was not at the Victory Roadhouse he could not have seen the deceased come in to talk to his brother. Furthermore, if he did not see the deceased leaving work and did not see him come in to the Victory to talk to his brother, then he had no opportunity to follow him. And if he had no opportunity to follow him, he had no opportunity to commit the crime. Therefore, either the defendant had no motive for the crime or no opportunity."

Which lawyer is arguing validly? Or are both? Or neither? Is it possible that both lawyers are arguing soundly?

*7. What premises can be dropped from the argument of Exercise 2j while preserving its validity?

*8. What premises can be dropped from the argument of Exercise 2k while preserving its validity?

14 • SYNONYMS FOR "AND," "NOT," AND "IF . . . THEN"

Thus far we have developed a considerable logical apparatus in conjunction with just four truth-functional connectives: *and, not, If . . . then,* and *or.* But English discourse is not confined to just these words to indicate truth-functional connections. Here and in the following sections we shall consider some alternative and supplementary expressions that have truth-functional significance, and some obscurities associated with them. In the present section we shall discuss three of the four connectives that have been used heretofore.

I. Consider first the word, *and.* Terms or phrases obviously having the same significance are *furthermore, also, in addition.* In some contexts *meanwhile* and *at the same time* may have a purely truth-functional significance. For example, "Ziblanski is small; *at the same time* he is very fast," means only that "Ziblanski is small *and* he is very fast." On the other hand, "The murder was in Chicago; *at the same time* the accused was in New York," means not only that the two conjoined propositions are both true, but that the events described in them occurred simultaneously. Here the assertion of simultaneity is an essential part of the meaning, and is something more than the mere assertion of the joint truth of the atomic propositions that make up the molecule. We shall see in later chapters how this additional part of the meaning can be captured and symbolized in convenient ways; for the moment, we note that *meanwhile* and *at the same time* may or may not be synonymous with *and*. Other words or phrases sometimes or always synonymous will occur to the reader. Exhaustive lists are not possible, because demands of style may at any time press a word or phrase into service in an unusual or unaccustomed way.

Somewhat surprising, perhaps, is the fact that *but* is fundamentally a synonym for *and*. The proposition, "She is quite old *but* very beautiful," means, at least in part, "She is quite old *and* very beautiful." In this context and in many others, besides having the logical force of *and*, the term *but* also conveys a note of surprise: Either the writer's surprise (or the speaker's), or an anticipated surprise for the reader (or the listener). Yet it is hard to imagine a context in which the note of unexpectedness is essential to the meaning, particularly if our attention is confined to the uses of propositions in arguments. Hence, it is generally safe to translate *but* as *and*, ignoring the connotations of surprise. The same holds good when *but* is used to mark out a contrast, as in "John is going to Harvard, *but* Thomas to Yale," and this will serve adequately if the proposition is intended for literal employment as part of an argument or statement of fact. The words *yet, however,* and *although* may function in exactly the same way as *but*.

II. Next, consider *not*. Denials of molecules, and occasionally of atoms, can be indicated by phrases such as *it is not the case that*,or *it is false that*. Denials of atoms are more commonly expressed by inserting the word *not* somewhere inside an atomic proposition, or by converting a verb or adjective to its negative form. Thus, "Cathy is pretty" can be denied as "Cathy is not pretty," or "Cathy is ugly," or even "Cathy is unpretty."

Difficulty frequently arises concerning the scope of a denial that precedes some molecular expression. Suitable punctuation marks, as we have seen, can provide the clues to structure that we require for logical clarity. Such clues are also furnished on occasion by the presence or absence of verb repetitions. "It is not the case that Malo is sick and Bono is sick," may be intended to have the structure $\sim(P \cdot Q)$, or $\sim P \cdot Q$. The absence of all punctuation suggests that the former structure is meant; still, there is a residue of doubt. But if the proposition were written as, "It is not the case that Malo is sick and so is Bono," we could be confident that the denial extends in scope over the whole of what follows it. Similarly, the contraction of two propositions into what is grammatically a single sentence with a compound subject achieves the same effect. "It is not true that Mary is going and Bob is going," is somewhat ambiguous in the absence of punctuation marks after the "that" or the first "going." Contracted to "It is not true that Mary and Bob are going," all ambiguity vanishes.

It is a commonplace of English grammar to observe that "two negatives make a positive." Hence, the statement, "It is not the case that P is false," simply means P. This is a consequence of the simple fact, which will be very prominent in the next chapter, that $\sim\sim P$ is equivalent to P:

P		$\sim$	$\sim$	P
1		1	0	1
0		0	1	0

As a consequence of this equivalence, certain choices are sometimes available in the translation of negative atoms into logical symbols. Take, "Faith is not wearing a white sweater." We can let P stand for "Faith *is* wearing a white sweater," in which case $\sim P$ will stand for the former expression. Alternatively we could let P stand for the original (negative) expression, and then $\sim P$ would mean that "Faith *is* wearing a white sweater."

III. The connective *If . . . then* can be replaced by a wide variety of expressions. We have already noted that the *then* can be omitted or the order of the clauses inverted. Other words and phrases having the same significance are *when, whenever, in the event that, in case, provided that,* and so on. We have also noted that *implies* can be used as a synonym for *If . . . then,* but this word more often carries one of a number of other meanings.

Exercises

1. Check these arguments for validity.

   a. It is not the case that the pants fit, but the coat fits. Therefore, it is not the case that the pants and coat fit.

   b. It is not the case that the pants and coat fit. Therefore, it is not the case that the pants fit, but the coat fits.

2. Given a valid argument with a premise of the form $\sim(P \cdot Q)$, would it necessarily remain valid if the premise were changed to $\sim P \cdot Q$? If yes, show why. If no, give an appropriate example.

3. Given a valid argument with a premise of the form $\sim P \cdot Q$, would it necessarily remain valid if the premise were changed to $\sim(P \cdot Q)$? If yes, show why. If no, give an appropriate example.

4. Check the following arguments for validity twice each, once symbolizing negative atoms with the aid of the negation sign, and once symbolizing affirmative atoms with the aid of the negation sign. Verify that the results are the same.

   a. When the train comes in the band will strike up, but if the leader is not here the band cannot strike up. Hence, if the leader is not here the train will not come in.

   b. When the train comes in the band will strike up provided the leader is here; however, when the leader is not here the band cannot strike up. Hence, if the leader is not here the train will not come in.

5. Check the following arguments for validity.

   a. In the event that the hypothesis is right the animals would not survive, yet they are surviving. Hence, the hypothesis is wrong.

   b. Were the hypothesis right the acid would get stronger while the animals survived; furthermore, the acid is getting stronger and the animals surviving. Hence, the hypothesis is right.

   c. The hypothesis says that the animals will not survive if the acid gets stronger; however, the acid is getting stronger while the animals are not dying. So the hypothesis must be wrong.

   d. The animals will not survive if the acid gets stronger, provided the hypothesis is true. But the hypothesis is false. Consequently, if the acid gets stronger the animals will not die.

15 • SYNONYMS FOR "OR"; AND EXCLUSIVE DISJUNCTION

Or, as one can hardly help notice, appears often in company with *either,* whose logical function is to indicate the scope of a disjunctive connection. Sometimes English employs long phrases in place of *or* along with the term *or*, particularly if the disjuncts are lengthy and potentially confusing. The phrases *On the one hand . . . on the other hand* are very common in this respect and others are easily thought of:

> "*On the one hand,* the French will be angry and the Germans delighted; *on the other hand,* the French will remain ignorant of the whole thing and the Germans will either be angry or indifferent."

In symbols this has the structure $(P \cdot Q) \text{ v } [R \cdot (S \text{ v } T)]$. Note, however, that in a slightly altered context the same words may lose the significance of *or* and acquire instead the significance of *and:*

> "*On the one hand,* if the French are angry the Germans will be delighted; *on the other hand,* if the French remain ignorant of the whole thing the Germans will either be angry or indifferent."

This has the structure $(P \supset Q) \cdot [R \supset (S \text{ v } T)]$. As always, context must be our guide; inflexible principles are not available.

Of greater importance in the study of *or* is the fact that this term, by itself, is frequently ambiguous. A comparison of two typical cases of its employment will reveal the ambiguity, which is quite commonly noticed:

> (i) If their rifle patrol has seen us *or* their reconnaissance plane has, then we can expect an attack by evening.
>
> (ii) If they begin an artillery bombardment, then we shall retreat beyond range *or* advance to knock out their observation post.

In both cases the disjunction we wish to fix our attention on constitutes part of a conditional: This helps to set a clear context but is irrelevant to the distinction that is illustrated. In (i), the term *or* indicates that *at least one* of the two disjuncts is true, *perhaps both.* In (ii) the term *or* signifies that *one and only one* of the disjuncts is true. In (i) the possibility of both disjuncts being true is not excluded, for if "we" were spotted by both the rifle patrol and the plane, it would be understood that the entire disjunction, "Either their rifle patrol has seen us or their reconnaissance plane has," is true. But in (ii) the possibility that both disjuncts are true is excluded; for "we" could hardly "retreat beyond range" *and* "advance to knock out their observation post."

To repeat, in (i) the possibility that both conjuncts may be true is included; in (ii) it is excluded. Hence, the term *or* as used in the first sense is referred to as the *inclusive or*; as it is used in the second sense it is referred to as the *exclusive or*. The distinction is sometimes marked in ordinary English by the use of the term *and/or* to indicate explicitly the inclusive sense.

To handle arguments in which the exclusive sense appears, we may introduce a new symbol to stand for exclusive or; ∇. Its truth-functional significance is then exhibited as follows:

TT5:	A	B		A ∇ B
	1	1		0
	1	0		1
	0	1		1
	0	0		0

This table should be compared with TT2; the only difference lies in the first row.

As an alternative to the use of a new symbol, we can capture the meaning of exclusive or with symbols already familiar. Because $A \nabla B$ means that either A or (in the inclusive sense) B is true, *and* not both, we can symbolize as

$$(A \text{ v } B) \cdot \sim(A \cdot B).$$

This is exactly equivalent to the sense of $A \nabla B$ shown in TT5.

It will be found that the inclusive *or* is more commonly used by far. Oddly enough, in the one case where exclusive *or* is most clearly intended, it is perfectly adequate to treat it as inclusive instead. For the most evident use of exclusive *or* occurs in logical truths of the form P *or* $\sim P$. But as truth tables will show, $P \nabla \sim P$ and $P \text{ v } \sim P$ are equivalent. In doubtful cases it is generally the best tactic to interpret a given *or* as inclusive, partly because this is more usual and partly because the inclusive meaning is itself *part of* the exclusive meaning (cf. the previous paragraph) and so represents a minimum significance that an expression of the form A *or* B must have.[13]

---

[13]As one might expect there are cases in which this policy, although generally reliable, leads to trouble. This is particularly true if the disjunction in question occurs within the scope of a negation. Compare Exercises 2 and 3 for this section.

Lastly, we note a generally unexpected result: The word *unless* is a synonym for *or*. Dictionaries usually approximate the term *unless* by the phrase *if not*. Hence, the proposition "I will go unless Mary stays home," means "I will go, if it is not the case that Mary stays home." Rearranging clauses, this becomes, "If Mary does not stay home, then I will go." But now this conditional is exactly equivalent to the proposition, "Mary stays home or I will go," as a truth table will show. Thus, we could have captured the meaning of the original statement ("I will go unless Mary stays home") at once by inserting *or* for *unless*. This result holds good quite generally; even the ambiguity of *or* can be found in uses of *unless*.

Exercises

1. Check the following arguments for validity.

   a. The train is on track 7 unless it is on track 9; and it is also the case that it is on track 9 or track 11. Therefore, it is on track 9.

   b. Unless the train is on track 7, then it is on track 9; and it is also the case that unless it is on track 9 it is on track 11. Therefore, it is on track 7 unless it is on track 11.

   c. The train is on track 7 or track 9; and it is also the case that it is on track 9 unless it is on track 11. Again, it cannot be on track 7 unless it is not on track 11 either. Therefore, it is on track 9.

   d. It is not the case that the train will be on track 5 or on track 7. If it is not on track 5 it must be late, furthermore, it is on track 7 unless it has been rerouted. Hence, the train has been rerouted and it is late.

   e. Either their plane will spot us or their radar will. But, either our fighters will escort us or we will hide in the clouds. Hence, either their planes will spot us and our fighters will escort us, or their radar will spot us and our fighters will escort us, or we will hide in the clouds and their radar will spot us, or their planes will spot us and we will hide in the clouds.

   f. It may be that the apples are rotten and the bananas delayed in transit, or the bananas rotten and the apples delayed in transit, or the apples both rotten and delayed, or the bananas both rotten and delayed. Hence, either the apples or the bananas were delayed in transit; furthermore, either the apples or the bananas are rotten.

g. He has to play to win or play clean, he cannot do both. His conscience will be easy if he plays clean. If he plays to win and his conscience is uneasy, he will be a miserable man to get along with tomorrow. He will play to win. Hence, he will be a miserable man to get along with tomorrow.

h. Either the Russians or the French will get there first. If the Russians do not, some of the SS troops may escape. But it will be hard to maintain the supply lines if the French do not get there first. Too, should there be difficulty with the supply lines we may be bogged down here the rest of the winter. So, on the one hand some of the SS troops may escape, or, on the other hand, we may be bogged down here all winter.

i. If we had some ham we could have some ham and eggs, and if we could have some ham and eggs we could last till supper. We could skip lunch if we could last till supper, unless, if we skipped lunch we would be risking our health. If it is not true that we could skip lunch if we could last till supper, then if we did skip lunch we would indeed be risking our health. Hence, if we had some ham, we would be risking our health.

j. If the Bugle is a yellow paper and undependable, then the story is exaggerated or downright false. The Bugle is a yellow paper; too, if it is yellow it is also undependable. Even if the story is exaggerated the Administration is in trouble. If the story is false, the Bugle is in trouble. If either the Administration is in trouble or the Bugle is in trouble, there will be some interesting court actions. Hence, the Bugle is a yellow paper, and it is undependable, and there are going to be some interesting court actions.

2. Show that $P \triangledown Q$ implies $P \vee Q$, but not conversely. Next, show that $\sim(P \vee Q)$ implies $\sim(P \triangledown Q)$, but not conversely.

*3. Each of the following questions is to be answered "Yes" or "No."

If yes, show why. If no, give an appropriate example.

a. Given a valid argument with a premise of the form $P \vee Q$ will it necessarily remain valid if the premise is changed to $P \triangledown Q$?

b. Given a valid argument with a premise of the form $P \triangledown Q$ will it necessarily remain valid if the premise is changed to $P \vee Q$?

c. Given a valid argument with a premise of the form $\sim(P \vee Q)$ will it necessarily remain valid if the premise is changed to $\sim(P \triangledown Q)$?

  d. Given a valid argument with a premise of the form $\sim(P \nabla Q)$ will it necessarily remain valid if the premise is changed to $\sim(P \vee Q)$?

  e.–h. Repeat questions a.–d. with the word *conclusion* in place of the word *premise*.

  i.–p. Repeat questions a.–h. with the word *invalid* in place of the word *valid*.

4. Is the exclusive *or* commutative? Is it associative? (For the meaning of these terms see Chapter 2, Section 5.)

5. Express the logical structure of the following proposition symbolically, without the use of the symbol ∇. "The train is on track 1, or on track 2, or on track 3."

6. Someone proposes to translate the proposition in Exercise 5 as $P \nabla Q \nabla R$. What is wrong with this proposal?

16 • "ONLY IF" AND "IF AND ONLY IF"

A connective of frequent occurrence is the phrase, *only if*. An example is

  (1) This is a robin's egg *only if* it is blue.

From this proposition, if true, we could infer that,

  (2) If this is a robin's egg, then it is blue.

Here we have replaced the phrase *only if* with the word *then* and added an initial *if* to serve correlatively with the *then*. Let us see if the same trick works in reverse. Take

  (3) If shells are falling on our flank, then they have brought in bigger guns.

From this, if true, we could evidently infer the following:

  (4) Shells are falling on our flank *only if* they have brought in bigger guns.

Here we have dropped the initial *if* and replaced the *then* with *only if*. Assuming that similar derivations can be made for any propositions having the same form as the examples, we see that *P, only if Q* implies *If P, then Q*, and conversely. Hence, the two are equivalent, and the general rule for translating *only if* is to substitute *then* in its place.

It is important not to confuse the *if* that precedes the antecedent of a conditional with the *if* that appears in the phrase *only if*, for the latter precedes a consequent, not an antecedent. Thus,

P, if Q means $Q \supset P$;
P, only if Q means $P \supset Q$;
If P, Q means $P \supset Q$; and
Only if P, Q means $Q \supset P$.

It is sometimes thought that propositions of the form P, *only if* Q really mean $P \supset Q$ *and* $Q \supset P$. For example,

(5) Army will win only if they take to the air.

This means, as we have seen, that if Army will win then they will have to take to the air. Does it also mean that if they take to the air then they will win? We might be tempted to say that it *does* mean that, but such a temptation should be resisted. For it is possible to say, "Army will win only if they take to the air, and even then they may lose," which shows that the proposition "If they take to the air, then they will win," is *not* part of the meaning of (5).

Thus, *only if* is a truth-functional connective analogous in function to *then*. The usual awkwardnesses arise when we confront conditionals freighted with more than the minimal truth-functional meaning. For example,

(6) If Navy wins, then they will celebrate.

In our view, this is equivalent to

(7) Navy will win only if they will celebrate.

This seems repugnant, unless we note that (6) implies that Navy's winning is a *cause* of the celebration, whereas the causal connotations in (7), if any, run in the opposite sense. Such connotations aside, the propositions are quite equivalent, a fact that can be underscored by rephrasing them to suppress the causal implications. For (6) we can write

(6') If it is true that Navy wins, then it is true that they will celebrate.

And for (7) we have

(7') It is true that Navy wins only if it is true that they will celebrate.

Such phrasings, however awkward, show that the fundamental logical meaning of (6') and (7'), and hence of (6) and (7), are identical.

The next connective we will discuss is in a sense not a new connective at all, but a combination of two that have already appeared; it is the phrase, *if and only if*. This occurs so frequently that we will assign to it a new symbol, the triple bar, $\equiv$.

As the words suggest, we must interpret molecules of the form, P, *if and only if* Q, as conjunctions of two subsidiary molecules: P, *if* Q, and P, *only if* Q. The first of these goes into symbols as $Q \supset P$, and the second as $P \supset Q$. Thus we have it that $P \equiv Q$ means $(P \supset Q) \cdot (Q \supset P)$.

These results point the way to construction of a sixth fundamental truth table to exhibit the meaning of $P \equiv Q$. The truth-table analysis of $(P \supset Q) \cdot (Q \supset P)$ shows that it is true when and only when both constituent atoms have the same truth-value:

(P	⊃	Q)	·	(Q	⊃	P)
1	1	1	1	1	1	1
1	0	0	0	0	1	1
0	1	1	0	1	0	0
0	1	0	1	0	1	0

Hence, we can set forth the significance of $P \equiv Q$ as follows:

TT6:	A	B	A ≡ B
	1	1	1
	1	0	0
	0	1	0
	0	0	1

This is all in accord with our ordinary understanding of the phrase *if and only if*. For if someone asserts a proposition of the form, P, *if and only if* Q, he is understood to be saying that either P and Q are both true or neither is; this is exactly the condition shown in TT6.

Because the connective *if and only if* is in effect a conjunction of two conditionals, it is sometimes referred to as the *biconditional*.

We now face a terminological difficulty of some seriousness. Because an assertion of the form $P \equiv Q$ means that P and Q have the same truth-value, it is natural to render it as "P is equivalent to Q." This temptation becomes even stronger when we deal with certain symbolic forms of general importance, such as $P \equiv (Q \equiv R)$. How, after all, is such a form read off in words? It is possible but awkward to say "P, if and only if, Q if and only if R." It is much clearer to say "P is equivalent to: Q is equivalent to R."

The trouble in all this is that we have already used the term *equivalent* to refer to molecular propositions that *must logically* have the same truth-value, for example S v T and T v S. But a statement of the form $P \equiv Q$ only asserts that the two components (atoms or molecules) *happen* to have the same truth-value. In other words, "P if and only if Q" asserts a truth-functional relation, $P \equiv Q$, defined in TT6. But "P is equivalent to Q," as we have used it heretofore, says that $P \equiv Q$ is a logical truth (because of the internal molecular structures of P and Q). Hence, ambiguity arises if we also use the term *equivalent* to designate the biconditional.

Nevertheless, we will permit the ambiguity and so use the term. It will usually be clear from the context which meaning of *equivalent* is intended. Where it is important to mark the difference, we can say "P is materially equivalent to Q" when we mean that P and Q are related biconditionally, as in TT6: In this sense P and Q are said to have the relation of *material equivalence*. On the other hand, we may say, "P is logically equivalent to Q," or "P is formally equivalent to Q," when we mean that $P \equiv Q$ is logically true: In this sense P and Q are said to have the relation of *formal equivalence* or *logical equivalence*. These terminological distinctions are analogous to similar definitions that have been discussed in connection with conditional propositions and the term *implies*.

Exercises

1. Is the connective *if and only if* commutative? Is it associative?

2. Which of the following are logical truths?

   a. $(P \equiv Q) \equiv (Q \equiv P)$

   b. $[(P \equiv Q) \equiv R] \equiv [P \equiv (R \equiv Q)]$

   c. $(P \equiv Q) \equiv [(P \cdot Q) \ v \ (\sim P \cdot \sim Q)]$

   d. $(P \equiv Q) \equiv [(P \ v \ Q) \cdot (\sim P \ v \sim Q)]$

   e. $(P \equiv Q) \equiv [(\sim P \ v \ Q) \cdot (P \ v \sim Q)]$

   f. $(P \equiv Q) \equiv \sim (P \triangledown Q)$

3. Consider the proposition, "*P, Q,* and *R* are all (materially) equivalent." Which of the following formulations succeeds in capturing the meaning of this?

   a. $P \equiv Q \equiv R$

   b. $(P \equiv Q) \cdot (Q \equiv R)$

   c. $(P \cdot Q \cdot R) \vee (\sim P \cdot \sim Q \cdot \sim R)$

   d. $[P \supset (Q \cdot R)] \cdot [\sim P \supset (\sim Q \cdot \sim R)]$

4. Check the following arguments for validity.

   a. Frisbee will join a fraternity if they are democratic. They are democratic. Hence, Frisbee will join.

   b. Frisbee will join a fraternity only if they are democratic. They are democratic. Hence, Frisbee will join.

   c. Frisbee will join a fraternity if and only if they are democratic. They are democratic. Hence, Frisbee will join.

   d. Only if fraternities are democratic will Frisbee join. They are democratic. Hence, Frisbee will join.

   e. If and only if fraternities are democratic Frisbee will join. As they are democratic, it follows that he will join.

   f. The enemy will come through the pass if and only if we abandon the forward line. We will abandon the forward line if and only if our supplies fail. Hence, the enemy will come through the pass if and only if our supplies fail.

   g. The enemy will come through the pass only if we abandon the forward line. We will abandon for forward line if our supplies fail. Hence, the enemy will come through the pass only if our supplies fail.

   h. The enemy will come through the pass only if we abandon the forward line. We will abandon the forward line only if our supplies fail. Hence, the enemy will come through the pass only if our supplies fail.

   i. Chicago is west of Detroit if and only if Evanston is west of Denver. It is not the case that: Either Evanston is west of Denver or east of Joliet (but not both). Therefore, Chicago is west of Detroit only if Evanston is east of Joliet.

   j. The solution to the equation is an answer to the problem only if the equation has been properly set up. But the equation has indeed been properly set up. Therefore, the solution to the equation is an answer to the problem.

17 • SUFFICIENT AND NECESSARY CONDITIONS

Propositions containing the phrase *sufficient condition* or *necessary condition* have a fundamentally truth-functional significance. However, that significance is not at all obvious and will require considerable discussion to expose. We shall concentrate first on sufficient conditions, and begin by considering an ordinary conditional proposition:

(1) If Quincy is sixteen, then he can get a license.

In a more verbose way, we can express this as,

(2) If it is true that Quincy is sixteen, then it is true that he can get a license.

The purpose of this awkward phrasing is to expose an important aspect of the meaning. For (2) asserts in effect that the truth (or fact) that Quincy is sixteen is by itself *sufficient* to guarantee the truth of the proposition that he can get a license. Hence we have

(3) The truth (or fact) that Quincy is sixteen is a *sufficient condition* for the truth (or fact) that he can get a license.

We can now compress (3) into a shorter and more natural form by allowing the constituent atomic propositions to be expressed implicitly:

(4) Quincy's being sixteen is a *sufficient condition* for his being able to get a license.

What we have done here could be done equally well with any other similar proposition. It thus appears that from a conditional we can derive a proposition expressing a sufficient-condition relation in which the truth of the antecedent (or the occurrence of the circumstance described by it) is a sufficient condition for the truth of the consequent (or for the occurrence of the circumstance described by it).

Let us now turn to another example and begin from the opposite end, that is, from an expression that explicitly contains the notion of sufficient condition:

(5) The stone's being denser than the water is a *sufficient condition* for its sinking.

We can say this in lengthier form as follows, in order to render the constituent atomic propositions explicit:

(6) The truth (or fact) that the stone is denser than water is a *sufficient condition* for the truth (or fact) that it will sink.

From this we can surely say,

(7) If it is true that the stone is denser than water, then it is true that it will sink.

And lastly, this can be contracted to

(8) If the stone is denser than water, then it will sink.

Because this series of transformations can likewise be worked on any proposition similarly phrased, we see that from a statement expressing a sufficient-condition relation we can derive a conditional in which the antecedent expresses the truth or circumstance that is the sufficient condition, and the consequent states the truth or circumstance that it (the sufficient condition) is a condition *for*. Hence, the two formulations—that is, the conditional and the sufficient-condition statement—are equivalent, because each implies the other.

We are thus equipped to convert many propositions embodying the phrase *sufficient condition* or variations of it into our logical notation. For example, "The presence of acid is a sufficient condition for the litmus paper to turn red," becomes $P \supset Q$, where P means *acid is present*, and Q means *litmus paper turns red*. Similarly, "For this animal to be warm-blooded, it is sufficient to establish that it is a mammal," becomes $P \supset Q$, where P means *this animal is a mammal*, and Q means *it is warm-blooded*.

It is reasonable to raise a certain objection to this result. Consider the proposition,

(9) If the boys are attracted to Baby Jane, then she must be awfully pretty.

On the basis of principles established so far, (9) is equivalent to:

(10) The boys' being attracted to Baby Jane is a sufficient condition for her being awfully pretty.

The objection to be raised is this: The fact that the boys are flocking around Jane can hardly be thought of as a *condition* for Jane's beauty. Rather, it is the other way around; Jane's beauty is the condition that leads to the motions of the boys.

This objection is perfectly natural, and is based on the familiar fact that propositions in natural languages are often loaded with meanings and connotations in one context that are absent in another. When we say that A is a sufficient condition for B, we sometimes, but not always, mean that A is a sufficient *cause* of B. If (10) is understood as asserting that a causal connection runs from the boys' attraction to Jane's beauty, then (10) is clearly false and is not equivalent to (9), which may very well be true. But the minimal meaning that can be attached to (10) or to any proposition phrased like it is the simple truth-functional assertion that *if* the boys are attracted, *then* that alone suffices to show that she must be extraordinarily pretty. Thus, if (10) is explicity stripped of causal connotations, we see that it *is* equivalent to (9).

One qualification must be entered before we pass to other connectives. Our way of dealing with sufficient condition expressions is adequate only when the conditions in question are specific, particular facts or circumstances that can be described in a proposition. We often see statements such as, "Money is a sufficient condition for happiness." This is a complex general proposition asserting that all persons or groups having money are happy; we are not yet equipped to deal with the internal structure of propositions of that sort.

The concept of necessary condition can be analyzed in a similar way; we state the result at once, and abstractly: "If P, then Q," means that P cannot be true without Q being true; hence, Q is a necessary condition for P. Conversely, if Q is a necessary condition for P, P can be true *only if* Q is; that is, "If P, then Q." Thus, the logical force of many necessary-condition statements can be captured by conditionals in which the necessary condition appears as *consequent*, and that which it is a condition *for* as antecedent.

To aid in the translation of statements embodying necessary and sufficient conditions, a simple mnemonic device is available. The word SUN by an obvious twist suggests the form $S \supset N$. This records the fact that sufficient conditions appear as the antecedents of conditionals, and necessary conditions as the consequents.

Exercises

1. How do you symbolize "P is a necessary and sufficient condition for Q"?

2. Which of the following are correct?

   a. In a valid argument, the truth of the premises is a necessary condition for the truth of the conclusion.

   b. In a valid argument, the truth of the conclusion is a necessary condition for the truth of the premises.

   c. In a valid argument, the truth of the premises is a sufficient condition for the truth of the conclusion.

   d. In a valid argument, the truth of the conclusion is a sufficient condition for the truth of the premises.

3. Check the following arguments for validity.

   a. Schooling for Johnny is a necessary condition for his maturing. Only if he matures will it be possible to tolerate him. Consequently, schooling for Johnny is a necessary condition for its becoming possible to tolerate him.

   b. Schooling for Johnny is a sufficient condition for his maturing. Only if he matures will it be possible to tolerate him. Consequently, schooling for Johnny is a sufficient condition for its becoming possible to tolerate him.

   c. Johnny will mature only if he goes to school. It is false that his going to school is a sufficient condition for his becoming easy to live with. Therefore, Johnny will not mature.

   d. Johnny will mature only if he goes to school. It is false that his going to school is a necessary condition for his becoming easy to live with. Therefore, Johnny will not mature.

   e. It is false that the sun's rising is a necessary and sufficient condition for the warmth of the day. Hence, either the sun rises or the day is warm, but not both.

   f. It is false that the sun's rising is a necessary and sufficient condition for the warmth of the day. Hence, the sun rises and/or the day is warm.

   g. That this animal is a bird is a sufficient condition for its having at least rudimentary wings. It is indeed a bird unless it is a bat. Its being a mammal is a necessary condition for its being a bat. In fact it is not a mammal and it has no rudimentary wings. Hence, it is a bird, although it is also a bat.

h. A love of old movies is a necessary condition for Lulubelle's watching late television. A weak mind is a necessary condition for Lulubelle's having a love of old movies. Hence, a sufficient condition for Lulubelle's not watching late television is that she does not have a weak mind.

18 • TRANSLATION TECHNIQUE

Our survey of truth-functional connectives is essentially complete; by far the majority of English truth-functional molecules are expressed in one or another of the ways we have discussed. Of course one may at any time confront other words or phrases bearing truth-functional significance or old words used in novel ways. For such eventualities there can be no general rules: One must simply *understand* the expression and seek for some appropriate symbolic representation. Often more than one translation will be reasonable, and if the alternatives are equivalent, as many times they are, no ambiguity results.

The translation of long molecules into symbols is peculiarly difficult when the order of several parts has to be shifted; for example, "P, if Q is a necessary condition for R," becomes $(R \supset Q) \supset P$. When such cases are severely complex, a tedious but systematic approach will reduce the possibility of error to a minimum: First locate the connective of greatest scope and rewrite the entire proposition, in words, with just that connective put into symbolic form. This leaves two (at most) shorter verbal expressions, joined by (or preceded by) a symbolic connective. Repeat the procedure on these, and so on. Eventually one reaches the atomic level, and on putting letters for atoms the translation is complete.

Exercises

1. Propose appropriate symbolic representations for the structure of the following propositions.

a. Not only will the south side abandon the party, the northwest will go as well. (two atoms)

b. Of the following only one holds: The product of any two odd numbers is even, or the product of any two odd numbers is odd, or the product of any two odd numbers is irrational. (three atoms)

c. Even if Caesar had stayed north of the Rubicon the Republic would have fallen away. (two atoms)

d. To prove that the war would have ended differently had the Germans won the Battle of the Bulge, it is necessary to show that neither Roosevelt nor Churchill was irrevocably committed to the doctrine of unconditional surrender. (four atoms)

e. I must pay the bill on time else I lose the discount. (two atoms)

f. Taking the premises as true and the argument as valid, the conclusion is true as well, in which case the argument is useful. (four atoms)

2. Check the following arguments for validity:

a. If the drive succeeds, then if the collectors are honest the school will be built provided the architect agrees to work free. The Smythes or the Marquands will lead the drive. The Smythe's leading the drive is sufficient guarantee of its success. It cannot be that the Marquands could lead the drive without its succeeding. The collectors will be honest if and only if they are closely supervised or they have some idealism combined with relatively little temptation. It is clearly not the case that if they have some idealism they will also have a great deal of temptation. The school will not be built. Therefore, the architect would not agree to work free.

b. On the one hand, it may be that the product is faulty if and only if the materials are substandard, and the materials are substandard and the deliveries late unless the materials are not substandard and the deliveries on time; or, on the other hand, it may be that the product is faulty, and if so the deliveries are late only when there is quality control and not late only when there is no quality control. The deliveries are not late. Therefore, the product is faulty although there is quality control.

c. Either the Platonists are right and the Aristotelians wrong while the Neoplatonists miss the point entirely, or the Cartesians are right and Newton and Maxwell wrong, or the Platonists' being right is a sufficient condition for the Sceptics to have been on the right path. Neither the Aristotelians nor the Platonists nor the Neoplatonists are right. The Cartesians are wrong unless both Newton and Maxwell are wrong. Hence, the Sceptics were on the right path unless the Platonists are wrong.

d. A sufficient condition for the pea's being under the first shell unless it is under the second is that it not be under the third. Actually it is neither under the first nor the second, unless there is no pea at all. But there is a pea somewhere all right. And it cannot be under both the third and the fourth. Hence, it is not under the fourth.

e. Where *is* the pea in the previous problem?

f. The named insured is covered for theft only if there is evidence of forcible entry. Evidence of a fraudulent application is sufficient to warrant suspension of all coverages. If he is not really covered for theft and yet holds the policy, one can conclude that there is evidence of fraudulent application. There is no evidence of forcible entry, yet he continues to hold the policy. Hence, a suspension of all coverages must be warranted.

*3. If the butler is guilty so is the maid, and the gardener is not guilty only if the shot was fired after two o'clock. The gardener is guilty unless the butler is. It is not the case that either the door or window was closed. If the door was open, then the shot would have been heard if the window was open. But either the maid is not guilty or the shot was not fired after two o'clock, if the window was open. Who is certainly guilty? Who is possibly guilty?

CHAPTER 3

Natural Deduction
for
Propositional
Arguments

ABSTRACT: A reliable and intuitively natural system for the construction of exclusively valid arguments is developed. In Sections 1–6 the use of elementary valid argument forms in the production of formal proofs is discussed. In Section 7 the idea of substitution is treated, and Sections 7–13 add a series of logical equivalences that are also employed in proof-construction. The method is expanded in Sections 14–16, in which the techniques of conditional and indirect proof are introduced. In Section 17 the construction of proofs for logical truths is discussed, and in the final section the methods in this and in the previous chapter are compared. It is shown throughout that the techniques of the two chapters are consistent with each other.

1 • FORMAL PROOF; MODUS PONENS AND MODUS TOLLENS

Although we have developed a complete apparatus for the analysis and evaluation of propositional arguments, we have worked out almost no principles whatever to guide us in the construction of original arguments. Confronted with a set of premises (or facts, or hypotheses), we often wish to know what propositions if any will follow from them. Again, we frequently wish to prove a certain conclusion and therefore have to know what propositions will logically imply the conclusion at hand. Hence, it is desirable to acquire such a sense of logical form that one may be able to discover at will some of the interesting conclusions that flow from certain premises, and to strike quickly on feasible propositions that will permit the deduction of a desired conclusion.

To some extent everyone has such a sense of logical form, and the spontaneous construction of arguments is a natural and ubiquitous activity. The classic example of careful and systematic deductive argument is Euclid's geometry; the previous chapters of this book contain several fairly complex arguments (in the text, not merely as examples for analysis); and the reader who has worked out a number of the problems in Chapter 2 with the indirect truth-table method has already, in effect, constructed some quite long and thoroughly valid deductions.

The outstanding characteristic of natural deduction is its chain-like structure, a feature that is somewhat obscured by truth-table methods of analysis. That is, rather than pass directly from a premise-set to a conclusion, most naturally constructed arguments proceed by a series of relatively simple steps. Intermediate conclusions are derived each of which becomes part of the material that can be appealed to in establishing further conclusions, and so on until the final desired result is reached. It is this process that we will now study in detail.

We begin as usual with discussion of an example:

(1) If the boat is coming the bridge will open.
(2) If the bridge will open the traffic will stop.
(3) The boat is coming.
    Therefore, the traffic will stop.

We have numbered the premises of this argument for ease of reference, a practice that we will continue in the sequel. Faced with the somewhat trivial task of checking this argument for validity, we could of course subject it to some truth-table analysis. However reliable in the long run that method may be, most people would maintain with considerable justice that they can "see" the validity of the argument without resorting to cumbersome symbolic matrices. How should we proceed were we asked to substantiate that claim?

In the first place, we recall that

$P \supset Q$.
P.
Therefore, Q.

is a valid argument form; the fact that it is clearly and intuitively valid was noted in Chapter 1 as a fundamental principle underlying further developments. This argument form appears with such frequency that it has been given a name, which we will hereafter use when referring to it: *modus ponens*.[17] It is evident that the first and third premises of the preceding argument correspond in form to the premises of *modus ponens*. Consequently, from them we can infer a result in accordance with the form of the conclusion of *modus ponens* (compare Tech 1 of Chapter 1). Thus, from (1) and (3) we can say

(4) The bridge will open.

Now we repeat the trick. Because (2) and (4) again correspond in form to the premises of modus ponens, we get from them:

(5) The traffic will stop.

But this last part is just the desired conclusion. Thus we have "seen" that the original argument is valid by means of two intermediate steps of unquestioned validity and one intermediate conclusion (4).

Let us cast this entire process, simple as it is, into symbolic form. As premises of our argument we have, where the letters are constants:

(1) $P \supset Q$.
(2) $Q \supset R$.
(3) P.

---

[17]The name derives from the Latin *ponere*, meaning to affirm. In this case, one affirms the parts of a conditional.

Next we wish to fix our attention on premises (1) and (3), getting from them the proposition Q by *modus ponens*. Hence, we can add,

(4) Q [From (1) and (3) by *modus ponens*]

Again from (2) and (4) we get R in the same way, so we add:

(5) R [From (2) and (4) by *modus ponens*]

The whole process can be briefly recorded in a way that presents it to the eye (and the mind) with a minimum of difficulty and a maximum of conciseness:

1. $P \supset Q$		Pr
2. $Q \supset R$		Pr
3. P		Pr
4. Q		1, 3, MP
5. R		2, 4, MP

In the left-hand column are the various propositions that figure in the argument. In the right-hand column opposite each proposition is a notation indicating the justification for the appearance of the corresponding proposition: *Pr* means premise, and *MP* means *modus ponens*. All of the marks in the right-hand column are collectively referred to as *annotations*. The line under the premises is an optional refinement indicating graphically the separation between premises and conclusions. The whole array is called variously a *formal proof*, or a *formal deduction*, or a *natural deduction*.

Another example is

(1) If the peaches or apples succeed, we will break even provided the truck does not break down.
(2) The truck will not break down.
(3) If the apples succeed, the worms will not invade.
(4) A sufficient condition for the success of either the peaches or the apples is that the worms do not invade.
(5) Really, the apples will succeed no matter what.
   Therefore, we will break even.

The validity or invalidity of this argument is hardly apparent at a glance. Let us first reduce it to symbolic notation:

P: The peaches will succeed.
Q: The apples will succeed.

R: We will break even.
S: The truck will break down.
T: The worms will invade.

Next we will write out the premises in symbolic form. It is sometimes helpful at the beginning of a formal proof to make a notation of the desired conclusion (if there is one); it is convenient to do this by setting out the conclusion at the right, behind a slash, as in the following:

1. $(P \lor Q) \supset (\sim S \supset R)$ *Pr*
2. $\sim S$ *Pr*
3. $Q \supset \sim T$ *Pr*
4. $\sim T \supset (P \lor Q)$ *Pr*
5. Q *Pr* /*R*

Again we can argue as follows: (3) and (5) imply $\sim T$, which in conjunction with (4) clearly implies $(P \lor Q)$, and this in conjunction with (1) yields $(\sim S \supset R)$, and combining that with (2) we obtain the desired result. The formal proof is

1. $(P \lor Q) \supset (\sim S \supset R)$ *Pr*
2. $\sim S$ *Pr*
3. $Q \supset \sim T$ *Pr*
4. $\sim T \supset (P \lor Q)$ *Pr*
5. Q *Pr* /*R*
---
6. $\sim T$ 3, 5, *MP*
7. $P \lor Q$ 4, 6, *MP*
8. $\sim S \supset R$ 1, 7, *MP*
9. R 2, 8, *MP*

The chief difference between this example and the previous one, aside from greater length, lies in the fact that the appeal to *modus ponens* in the present case takes place in a more subtle way. For example, at line (8) we argued that

$(P \lor Q) \supset (\sim S \supset R)$.
$P \lor Q$.
Therefore, $(\sim S \supset R)$.

because this has the form of *modus ponens*.

If the method of proof by stepwise deduction is to be powerful enough to permit construction of a rich variety of arguments, we shall require a stock of simple valid argument-forms to which we can appeal. In particular, we shall need more than *modus ponens* alone. The following argument, although valid, could never be proved with *modus ponens* solely:

(1) If the constable had come to call, the maid was downstairs.
(2) If the maid was downstairs, the water would have been shut off.
(3) If the constable did not come to call, the gate was closed.
(4) The water was not shut off.
    Therefore, the gate was closed.

Symbolically, we have

1. $P \supset Q$ *Pr*
2. $Q \supset R$ *Pr*
3. $\sim P \supset S$ *Pr*
4. $\sim R$ *Pr /S*

We shall now introduce a second valid form and show how it can be used in this argument. It may be recalled that *modus ponens* was employed implicitly in the previous chapter during the course of indirect truth-table analysis; for whenever we appealed to the principle that a true conditional with a true antecedent has to have a true consequent, we implicitly used *modus ponens*. From the same context we now recall the principle that a true conditional with a false consequent has to have a false antecedent; this corresponds to the following argument form:

$$\frac{\begin{array}{c} P \supset Q \\ \sim Q \end{array}}{\sim P}$$

This form, like *modus ponens*, is fairly obvious and extraordinarily frequent; the name given to it is *modus tollens*, abbreviated MT.[18]

Thus, freshly armed we return to the argument. We note that lines (2) and (4) correspond to the premises of MT, so we get

1. $P \supset Q$ *Pr*
2. $Q \supset R$ *Pr*
3. $\sim P \supset S$ *Pr*
4. $\sim R$ *Pr /S*
5. $\sim Q$ 2, 4, MT

---

[18]From the Latin *tollere*, to deny. In this case we deny the parts of a conditional.

Again (1) and (5) have the required form for MT; and the conclusion derived from them, $\sim P$, can be combined with (3) to yield the desired final conclusion by MP. The whole proof is

1. $P \supset Q$		Pr
2. $Q \supset R$		Pr
3. $\sim P \supset S$		Pr
4. $\sim R$		Pr /S
5. $\sim Q$		2, 4, MT
6. $\sim P$		1, 5, MT
7. S		3, 6, MP

In subsequent sections of this chapter further devices for the construction of formal proofs will be added, until we are able to build a proof for any valid deductive argument.

The two forms so far at our disposal are easily confused with two other forms that are *not* valid. The confusions are so notorious that attempts to argue in accordance with the related but fallacious forms are given special names. First, the argument form

$$P \supset Q$$
$$Q$$
$$\overline{P}$$

is called the *fallacy of affirming the consequent.* A common type of example is

> If Armstrong is a member of the high-tariff party, he will oppose the bill. He is opposing the bill. Therefore, he is a member of the high-tariff party.

The other fallacious form is

$$P \supset Q$$
$$\sim P$$
$$\overline{\sim Q}$$

and is called the *fallacy of denying the antecedent.*

> If Armstrong is a member of the high-tariff party, he will oppose the bill. He is not a member of the high-tariff party. Therefore, he will not oppose the bill.

Both of these fallacies have been illustrated by numerous examples and exercises in earlier pages.

The danger of mistaking these invalid forms for *modus ponens* or *modus tollens* is enhanced when conditionals are stated in reversed order:

> Armstrong will oppose the bill if he is a member of the high-tariff party. He will oppose the bill. Therefore, he is a member of the high-tariff party.

Although it "sounds" very good, this is still a case of the fallacy of affirming the consequent. It would be a valid argument if the term *if* in it were replaced by *only if* or by *if and only if*, a fact that further enhances the likelihood of confusion. These two fallacies will at some time or other catch the most trained eye or ear; they are probably the most common logical fallacies appearing in ordinary discourse.

Exercises

1. From Chapter 2, Section 9, review the arguments in Exercises 1a, 1b, 1c, and 1d. If they are valid, construct formal proofs; if not, identify the fallacies involved.

2. Construct formal proofs for the following arguments where possible.

   a. The train will be on time. If it is, Mr. Smith will catch the plane to Washington. The passage of the Smith Bill will guarantee that the dam will be built. His bill will be passed if he catches the plane to Washington. So the dam will be built after all.

   b. If only the relay works, then the temperature will stay up if the generator does not fail. If the generator does not fail, the relay will work. The maintenance staff is not lazy. And the generator will fail only if the maintenance staff is lazy. Hence, the temperature will stay up.

   c. Good rain this month is a necessary condition for a decent corn harvest. If there is a decent corn harvest and a reasonable market, we will make enough for a new tractor or a down payment on the house we want. If there is not a decent corn harvest, we will not make enough for a new tractor or a down payment on the new house. There will not be any rain this month. So, there will not be both a decent corn harvest and a reasonable market.

*d. When the shaft breaks or the power fails, then, if the watchman is not on duty, the police will get a signal if the batteries are fresh. If the watchman is on duty, the power will fail for sure. If the batteries are fresh, the power will not fail. The batteries are fresh. Whenever the batteries are fresh, either the shaft breaks or the power fails. Hence, the police will get a signal.

*3. Are all the premises in 2c needed to justify the conclusion? Which ones are redundant?

4. Which of the following arguments are fallacious? Identify the fallacies where they appear.

    a. Her watching television is a necessary condition for her being up-to-date on the news. She does watch television. Hence, she is up-to-date on the news.

    b. Her watching television is a sufficient condition for her being up-to-date on the news. She is up-to-date on the news. Hence, she watches television.

    c. Fraternities are democratic if they have no discrimination clauses. But they do have discrimination clauses. Hence, they are not democratic.

    d. The number 3 has to be a solution to this equation if it is the answer to that problem. It is a solution to this equation. Therefore, it is the answer to that problem.

5. An *enthymeme* is an argument with an unexpressed premise. What reasonable premises are required in order that the following enthymemes be valid? Construct appropriate formal proofs.

    a. If the clock is right I will be late. And if I miss the appointment I will lose the sale. The clock is right. Hence, I will lose the sale.

    b. If it is a mammal it will learn fast. A necessary condition for its being intelligent is that it become friendly if it is a mammal. It is indeed a mammal. Therefore, it will become friendly.

    c. If this is red then it is ripe, only if it is what we think it is. It is not what we think it is. Therefore, it is not an apple.

    d. If he is so smart, why is he not rich?

6. What interesting conclusions can be inferred from the following premise-sets? Construct appropriate formal proofs.

a. The butler is guilty only if the maid helped. The footman is guilty if the maid helped. The maid did not help.

b. The butler is guilty only if the maid helped. The footman is guilty if the maid helped. If the maid helped she was guilty too. The maid was not guilty. If the maid did not help, then the butler was guilty provided that the footman was innocent. And if the maid did not help, then the footman was guilty provided that the butler was innocent.

2 • SIMPLIFICATION, CONJUNCTION, HYPOTHETICAL SYLLOGISM

In this section we add some other simple valid forms to serve as bases of appeal in formal proofs.

Consider this argument:

(1) If John comes, Harold will be content.
(2) John and Albert are coming.
Therefore, Harold will be content.

Clearly valid, it has the form,

1. $P \supset Q$ Pr
2. $P \cdot R$ Pr /Q

The natural way to prove this by a stepwise deduction is to appeal first to the fact that $P \cdot R$ logically implies P alone. We shall call this the principle of *simplification*, abbreviated as *Simp*. We then complete the desired proof as follows:

1. $P \supset Q$ Pr
2. $P \cdot R$ Pr /Q
3. P 2, *Simp*
4. Q 1, 3, *MP*

Thus, we have added a third valid from to our list. In symbols the simplification argument has the general form

$$\frac{P \cdot Q}{P}$$

This is the first form in our developing list that has only one premise. Note that it has already been used implicitly in the indirect truth-table technique whenever we appealed to the principle that the conjuncts in a true conjunction must be likewise true.

Next consider a somewhat longer argument:

(1) If there are apples and oranges in the package, then it is worth something.
(2) There are apples and bananas in the package.
(3) There are oranges and grapefruits in the package.
   Therefore, it is worth something.

In symbols it is

1. $[(P \cdot Q) \supset R$ *Pr*
2. $P \cdot S$ *Pr*
3. $Q \cdot T$ *Pr* /R

In constructing a formal proof for this it is clear at once that our initial concern must be with the atoms P and Q. With the help of *Simp* we can separate them from the lines in which they appear, as follows:

1. $[(P \cdot Q) \supset R$ *Pr*
2. $P \cdot S$ *Pr*
3. $Q \cdot T$ *Pr* /R
4. P 2, *Simp*
5. Q 3, *Simp*

Next, it is hard to avoid noticing that P and Q expressed together as a joint molecule would correspond to the antecedent of (1), leading to the desired conclusion by *MP*. Because P and Q are expressed on separate lines, they are both true if the premises are, so they can clearly be joined by an *and*, and they can be stated as a single molecule. We call this the process of *conjuction*, abbreviated *Conj*. In general form the argument *Conj* is:

P
Q
$\overline{P \cdot Q}$

Returning to our proof, we can finish it as follows:

1. $[(P \cdot Q) \supset R$ *Pr*
2. $P \cdot S$ *Pr*
3. $Q \cdot T$ *Pr* /R
4. P 2, *Simp*
5. Q 3, *Simp*
6. $P \cdot Q$ 4, 5, *Conj*
7. R 1, 6, *MP*

Next, we turn to another argument of familiar type:

(1) If they promise a tax cut, business will improve.
(2) If business improves, prices will increase.
(3) If prices increase, we will be better off.
    Therefore, if they promise a tax cut, we will be better off.

In symbols it is

1. $P \supset Q$ Pr
2. $Q \supset R$ Pr
3. $R \supset S$ Pr $/P \supset S$

None of the four forms we have listed so far holds out any promise whatever for proceeding with this proof. Yet the argument is clearly valid and we are obliged to select some other valid form to add to the list. The following is intuitively appealing:

$$P \supset Q$$
$$\frac{Q \supset R}{P \supset R}$$

and the argument in question is clearly a repeated application of this form. The form is called *hypothetical syllogism*, abbreviated *Hyp*. We then have the following formal proof for our argument:

1. $P \supset Q$ Pr
2. $Q \supset R$ Pr
3. $R \supset S$ Pr $/P \supset S$
4. $P \supset R$ 1, 2, Hyp
5. $P \supset S$ 4, 3, Hyp

Note that the annotation for the last step is 4, 3, *Hyp* and not 3, 4, *Hyp*. This is to indicate that the fourth and third lines of the proof must be taken in just *that* order to exhibit their correspondence with the form of the premises in the form *Hyp*. This practice is in principle desirable for the sake of perfect clarity. In fact the practice will sometimes become burdensome, and it may be abandoned unless the context is so complicated that confusion is likely to result otherwise.

We now have five simple valid forms specifically listed to justify step-by-step inferences. The validity of each of these forms could be confirmed by truth-table analysis applied directly to the forms themselves. However, it would be a mistake to suppose that a truth table analysis *proves* the validity of these forms in any significant sense. For the technique of truth-table examination was itself constructed in the light of our prior intuitive grasp of the validity of such simple forms as *modus ponens* and simplification. On the other hand no simple argument form that is proposed for use in constructing formal proofs would be reliable if it showed up as invalid under truth-table examination. In succeeding sections we shall enumerate a rather long list of argument forms and supplementary principles to be used in making formal deductions. Most of them will be chosen for their intuitive naturalness, some for more subtle reasons; but all must be such as to produce inferences that appear valid when subjected to the more cumbersome machinery of the truth table.

It is obvious that the steps of a formal proof can sometimes be arranged in different ways, and that different principles can sometimes be employed to reach the same conclusion from the same premises.

Exercises

1. From Chapter 2, Section 9, review the arguments in Exercises 1h, 1i, 1j, and 1t. Construct proofs if they are valid; if not, prove invalidity by some appropriate means.

2. From Chapter 2, Section 13, review the arguments in Exercises 2d and 2e. These are valid. For each argument construct two proofs, one employing *Hyp* and one not.

3. Construct proofs for the following arguments:

   a. If the merchants are generous the drive will succeed. If the merchants are generous the solicitors will be well treated. The merchants are generous. Therefore, the drive will succeed and the solicitors will be well treated.

   b. The merchants are generous and the reporters not. The lawyers are generous and the doctors not. If the merchants are generous the drive will succeed, and if the lawyers are the legal obstacles can be overcome. If the legal obstacles can be overcome and the drive succeeds, the hospital will be built. So it will be built.

c. There is a necessary being and a contingent being. If there is a necessary being then God exists and we should worship him. If we should worship God, then we should join a church. Hence, there is a necessary being and we should join a church.

d. There is no self-sufficient creature. If the devil does not exist and there is no radical evil in creation, then moral virtue is attainable. If the devil exists, then there is a self-sufficient creature. If there is no self-sufficient creature there is no radical evil in creation. Therefore, moral virtue is attainable.

4. For the following arguments construct formal proofs where possible; where not, prove invalidity.

a. If the plane is safe, the train is safer and the car is dangerous. If the train is safer, we will take it. We would arrive on Tuesday in the center of the town were we to take the train. The plane is safe. Hence, we will arrive on Tuesday.

b. If the plane is safe, then we should take it provided there is transportation to the airport. If we take the plane we can get there today. If the plane is safe, then the sale is assured if we can get there today. The sale is by no means assured. The plane is safe, even though the sale is not assured. Hence, there must not be transportion available to the airport.

c. If Plato's theory is at all correct, *a priori* knowledge is possible. But *a priori* knowledge is possible only if Plato's theory is essentially correct. Maserowski's reading of the history of philosophy is right, on the condition that Plato's theory is largely correct if and only if *a priori* knowledge is possible. Maserowski's reading is right. Therefore, Plato's theory is correct.

d. If Maserowski's theory is largely right, then if Plotinus had read Plato he must have understood his thesis, provided the manuscripts were available. Were the manuscripts available, Maserowski's view is right. Again, were the manuscripts available Plotinus had read Plato. If the Romans were in the vicinity at the time and were not totally ignorant of what they had, then the manuscripts were available. The Romans were in the vicinity at the time. If they were ignorant of what they had, they must have been utter barbarians. But the Romans were not utter barbarians. Hence, Plotinus understood Plato's thesis.

e. If they come through the pass, then if the support is here we will meet them directly. They will come through the pass and we will meet them directly. The general will be watching if his plane has been repaired, only if our meeting them directly is a sufficient reason for engaging all the forces. If the general's plane has been repaired, then the telescopes will have been fixed. And if the telescopes have been fixed the general will be watching. Hence, if the support is here all the forces will be engaged.

f. If the Hungarians signed the treaty the Austrians did too; furthermore the English did not sign. If the French did sign, so did the English. If the French did not sign, then if the Austrians signed there will be trouble all over Europe. Hence, if the Hungarians signed there will be trouble all over Europe.

5. What premise is needed to make the following enthymeme valid? "*A* equals *B*. *B* equals *C*. *C* equals *D*. If *A* equals *B* and *B* equals *C*, then *A* equals *C*. Therefore, *C* equals *D*."

6. What curious conclusion can be inferred from the following premise-set? "If the extreme Right favors labor, so do the Liberals. If the Liberals favor labor, so does the extreme Left. If it is true that the Liberals favor labor if the extreme Right does, then it is likewise the case that the Christian Democrats favor labor if the extreme Left does. And if the Christian Democrats favor labor, so does the extreme Right."

3 • THE CHAIN THEOREM

Before expanding the devices needed in constructing formal proofs, we pause to examine one of the presuppositions upon which the entire proof process depends. Suppose we begin with a premise-set *A* and obtain from it a result *B* so that *B* is validly inferred from *A*. Next *B* becomes in effect part of the premises, and in a second step we get, from *A* and *B* together, another result, *C*. We then take it for granted that *C* has been shown to follow from *A* alone, a type of claim inherent in all construction of chain-like proofs (that is, proofs employing intermediate steps to reach a final conclusion). It is desirable to show that this claim can be justified by reference to the understanding of validity developed in Chapters 1 and 2.

We make the following assertion, called the *chain theorem*:

> **Theorem:** If there is a valid argument with premises *A* and conclusion *B*, and another with premises $(A \cdot B)$ and conclusion *C*, then *A* implies *C*.

In virtue of the fundamental theorem (Chapter 2, Section 11), the hypotheses of the chain theorem state in effect that

$$A \supset B \quad \text{and} \quad (A \cdot B) \supset C$$

are logical truths. We then have to show, in effect, that $A \supset C$ is likewise a logical truth. In order for $A \supset C$ to be false, there must be an assignment of truth-values to its constitutent parts such that A is true and C false. Under such conditions B must be true, because by hypothesis $A \supset B$ is logically true. But then, under those conditions, $(A \cdot B) \supset C$ would be false, which is impossible by hypothesis. Hence, $A \supset C$ is logically true, and A implies C.

This result can clearly be extended to cover any number of further steps. The chain theorem says in effect that propositions inferred from premises with the help of intermediate conclusions are validly inferred from the premises. In a certain sense our demonstration of the chain theorem is circular, because we have *used* chain-like arguments from the very outset while developing and justifying the methods of Chapter 2. We have again used a chain-like argument in demonstrating the chain theorem. It is possible that the entire study of deductive logic is only the transformation into explicit and precise terms of principles that are already understood implicitly and employed vaguely.

Despite the circularity our demonstration of the chain theorem by reference to the ideas and methods of Chapter 2 does establish an important fact: It shows that the stepwise procedure employed in formal proofs is *consistent* or *harmonious* with truth-table methods, in the sense that any propositional argument established through intermediate steps that are all demonstrably valid under truth-table analysis will itself be valid under truth-table analysis. In subsequent sections of this chapter we will show that *every* technique adopted in formal proof-construction is similarly consistent with truth-table methods.

Exercises

1. Suppose an argument with premise-set A and conclusion C is valid. Another proposition, B, which may or may not be logically related to A or C, is added to the premise-set. Show that the argument with this new premise-set (A and B) and conclusion C is likewise valid.

2. "If A logically implies B, and B logically implies C, then A logically implies C." Show that this follows from the chain theorem and Exercise 1. Also, prove it independently of the chain theorem.

3. Prove the chain theorem for the case where there are two intermediate arguments. That is, assuming that a premise-set A implies B; and A and B together imply C; and A, B, and C together imply D; show that A implies D.

4. Given an invalid argument with premises A and conclusion B, and another invalid argument with premise B and conclusion C, does it follow that the argument with premises A and conclusion C is likewise invalid?

5. Given an invalid argument with premises A and conclusion B, and another invalid argument with premises A and B and conclusion C, does it follow that the argument with premises A and conclusion C is likewise invalid?

6. Given an invalid argument with premises A and B and conclusion C, does it follow that the argument with premises B and conclusion C is likewise invalid?

7. Exercise 1 asks in effect for a proof of this theorem: If any premises are added to a valid argument, the argument remains valid. State and prove a corresponding theorem for invalid arguments.

8. Show that a premise can be used more than once in a valid proof.

4 • DISJUNCTIVE SYLLOGISM, CONSTRUCTIVE DILEMMA, ADDITION

We have until now stated no argument forms involving disjunctions. In this section we introduce three, following our usual method of discussion by means of sample arguments.

I. Take first:

(1) I have missed him unless the train is late.
(2) The train is not late and has already gone.
Therefore, I have missed him.

Clearly valid, it is rendered symbolically as:

1. $P \lor Q$ Pr
2. $\sim P \cdot R$ $Pr \ /Q$

We see at first that R is not relevant to the proof, and we clear it away:

    3. $\sim P$ 2, *Simp*

We now have an assertion that a certain disjunction, $P \lor Q$, is true, and one of its disjuncts, namely P, is false. In other contexts we have already employed the principle that in such cases the other disjunct must be true. This principle can now be formalized as an argument form called the *disjunctive syllogism*, abbreviated *Dis*; in symbols:

$$P \lor Q$$
$$\frac{\sim P}{Q}$$

Applied to our present problem it permits us to finish as follows:

    1. $P \lor Q$ *Pr*
    2. $\sim P \cdot R$ *Pr* /Q
    3. $\sim P$ 2, *Simp*
    4. Q 1, 3, *Dis*

II. Next consider this argument, of quite familiar form:

    (1) If I lie, I will please men.
    (2) If I tell the truth, I will please God.
    (3) I must lie or tell the truth.
        Therefore, I will either please men or please God.

It is not possible to construct a formal proof for this argument with the aid of any of our current argument forms. Yet is *is* a valid argument, as a truth table will show; so common are arguments of this type that we shall take the form itself as one of our simple valid forms. It is called the *constructive dilemma*, abbreviated *Dil*. In symbols it has the form

$$P \supset Q$$
$$R \supset S$$
$$\frac{P \lor R}{Q \lor S}$$

This is the only simple form that we have, or will have, involving three premises and four different constituent propositions.

III. Consider now this argument:

  (1) If the apples or the peaches are rotten, we cannot sell the crop.
  (2) The apples are rotten.
       Therefore, we cannot sell the crop.

In symbols the argument is

  1. $(P \vee Q) \supset R$ *Pr*
  2. P *Pr* /R

Intuitively we see that this is valid. For if a disjunction has one true disjunct, the disjunction itself must be true. As the second line asserts that P is true, the disjunction $P \vee Q$ is true, and hence the consequent R follows. What we must do here is formalize the principle that allows us to infer the truth of a disjunction from the truth of one of its disjuncts. In symbols, the required form is

$$\frac{P}{P \vee Q}$$

We shall call this the principle of *addition*, abbreviated *Add*. The proof is then completed as follows:

  1. $(P \vee Q) \supset R$ *Pr*
  2. P *Pr* /R
  3. $P \vee Q$ 2, *Add*
  4. R 1, 3, *MP*

The addition principle is sometimes repugnant when carelessly considered. For it looks as if we can, with its aid, introduce any proposition whatever into a proof at any time. For instance, if we have it as a premise or in some subsequent line of a proof that "The moon is made of rock," we can infer by addition that "Either the moon is made of rock or Genghis Khan is the mayor of Toledo." Although it is hard to see why anyone would want to make such an inference, it is perfectly valid. It must be noted that the added proposition has not been introduced in such a way as to allow it to be stated in a line by itself; it is and presumably would remain part of a disjunction of no particular use or interest.

We now have a total of eight valid argument forms which permit the construction of some lengthy proofs (see the subsequent exercises); it is thus reasonable to look for ways to shorten the written presentation of formal proofs without a loss of clarity. This may be done by combining two or more very simple steps in a single line, omitting the explicit statement of the intermediate conclusion(s) appealed to. Thus, one may go in a single step from $(P \cdot Q)$ and $(P \supset R)$ to R, retaining in the annotation an indication of the two (or more) principles appealed to. *Conj* and *Simp* are obvious candidates for such combination.

Exercises

1. Review the following arguments from Chapter 2. Construct formal proofs where valid, prove invalidity where not.

   Section 8, Exercises 1d, 1g, 1h.
   Section 9, Exercises 1v, 1w.
   Section 15, Exercises 1a, 1b.

2. Construct proofs for the following arguments where possible.

   a. If mercy or charity is a virtue, Eloise is virtuous. Mercy is a virtue. Hence, Eloise is virtuous.

   b. Mercy is not a virtue unless charity is not a virtue. It is not the case that mercy is not a virtue. Therefore, charity is not a virtue.

   c. Mercy is a virtue unless vindictiveness is. Mercy is not a virtue and cruelty is a vice. Were vindictiveness a virtue, so would selfishness be. Therefore, selfishness is a virtue.

   d. Harry will go or Manuel will not, but Gene will definitely go. If Harry goes his wife will accompany him. But his wife will not go. If Joseph goes so will Manuel. Hence, Joseph will not go.

   e. If the rose wins Mrs. Miniver will be pleased. If the aster wins she will be put out. If the judge is not competent either the rose or aster will win. If the judge is competent the prize will not even be awarded. It is not the case that the prize will not be awarded. Hence, Mrs. Miniver will be pleased or put out.

   f. If Mrs. Miniver is pleased provided the rose wins, and she is in a normally good humor, then the gardener will get a week off. If her husband is not here or her brother is, she will be in a normally good humor. If her husband is here, the judges will be intimidated. The judges will not be intimidated, and Mrs. Miniver will be pleased. The judges will be intimidated, unless Mrs. Miniver is pleased provided the rose wins. Thus, the gardener will get a week off.

g. If the car is sound, then if the driver lasts it out they will come in first. If the fees are paid, then if the shares are fair they will receive a tidy sum. The car is sound. And the fees are paid. Provided the car is sound and the fees are paid, nothing can go wrong. If nothing goes wrong, then either the driver will last it out or the shares will be fair, perhaps both. Hence, they will come in first or receive a tidy sum, perhaps both.

h. If all three animals survive, the serum is effective. If there is movement in the first cage, the first animal has survived. If there is a sign of escape in the second cage, the second animal has survived. And if there are noises in the third cage, the third animal has survived. There is movement in the first cage, a sign of escape in the second, noise in the third, and a healthy animal in the fourth. Hence, the serum is effective.

i. A sufficient condition for the serum's not being effective is that if the animal was not treated, he survived. If the serum is effective, all animals are dead or dying. But not all treated animals are dead or dying. If it is not the case that this animal survived if he was not treated, then further inquiry is useless. Hence, further inquiry is useless.

j. There will be a sea fight tomorrow. There will not be a sea fight tomorrow. Therefore, the serum is effective.

3. Viewing the following as a propositional enthymeme, what premise is needed to make it valid? "If Socrates is mortal he will die. He will die, for all men are mortal."

4. What significant conclusion can be inferred from the following premise-set? "If the spray is no good the insects will thrive. A necessary condition for the plants' health is that the insects do not thrive and the rainfall continues. The plants are healthy."

5 • THE REPLACEMENT THEOREMS

We pause again in the development of devices for proof-construction to discuss a presupposition that underlies the process and that, in fact, underlies any method of argument that depends on appeal to admittedly valid *forms*. The principle in question is simply our supposed right to appeal to standard forms even when they appear in very complex contexts. For example, we regard the following as cases of disjunctive syllogism:

$$(P \vee Q) \vee (R \cdot S)$$
$$\underline{\sim(P \vee Q)}$$
$$R \cdot S$$

$$\sim[R \cdot (S \supset Q)] \vee \sim(P \cdot Q)$$
$$\underline{\sim\sim[R \cdot (S \supset Q)]}$$
$$\sim(P \cdot Q)$$

Consider the form *Dis* as originally expressed:

$$P \vee Q$$
$$\underline{\sim P}$$
$$Q$$

Here we usually think of P and Q as variables. We may, however, regard them for the moment as atomic constants and then construct the corresponding conditional with a truth table:

[(P	v	Q)	·	~P]	⊃	Q
1	1	1	0	0	1	1
1	1	0	0	0	1	0
0	1	1	1	1	1	1
0	0	0	0	1	1	0

This is a logical truth.[19] We infer that an argument of this type where P and Q stand for specific atoms is valid. One might reasonably maintain, of course, that the validity of *Dis* does not really depend upon this demonstration, but is guaranteed by an independent intuition or by some other method. That is of no matter; the demonstration still shows that the decision to take two-atom arguments of the form of *Dis* as valid *will not conflict with our earlier methods of evaluation* (that is, no such use of *Dis* will lead us to put forward as valid an argument that appears *in*valid by truth-table methods).

But can we similarly justify the use of *Dis* (or show its harmony with earlier methods) when it is applied to complex cases, with P or Q or both replaced by complex molecules? To state the problem precisely we first define the idea of *uniform replacement*. If, in any

---

[19]It is easily verified that the same result may be obtained for every standard argument form which we have mentioned, or will mention.

argument or proposition, some atom is replaced by another atom or molecule, the same replacing-atom or replacing-molecule being used throughout, the process is called *uniform replacement*; it is essential to this idea that the repla*ced* atom be replaced in the same way at every instance of its occurrence. Thus, for the proposition

$(S \text{ v } T) \cdot \sim S$

the following are uniform replacements for S,

$[(P \text{ v } Q) \text{ v } T] \cdot \sim (P \text{ v } Q)$
$[(P \cdot S) \text{ v } T] \cdot \sim (P \cdot S)$
$(\sim T \text{ v } T) \cdot \sim \sim T$

and the following are not,

$[(P \cdot S) \text{ v } T] \cdot \sim S$
$[(P \cdot S) \text{ v } T] \cdot \sim (P \text{ v } Q)$
$(S \text{ v } T) \cdot \sim T$.

This applies similarly for entire arguments. Note that the process of uniform replacement does *not* include the replacement of molecules by atoms or other molecules.

Now that which justifies *Dis* (or shows its harmony with earlier methods) is the fact that its corresponding conditional is seen to be a logical truth when the letter symbols are understood as constants. When we appeal to complex forms of *Dis*, we are in effect asserting the validity of arguments in which the P or Q (or both) are uniformly replaced by molecular structures.[20] Equivalently, we are asserting that propositions generated by uniform replacement from

$[(P \text{ v } Q) \cdot \sim P] \supset Q$

(P and Q atomic constants) are also logical truths.

But these assertions are easily seen to be correct, because a truth table constructed under the preceding proposition shows that the proposition is true for all possible true-false combinations of its constituent atoms. When the constituent atoms are replaced by molecules or other atoms, no new true-false combinations of the parts (that is,

---

[20]Trivially, *Dis* arguments with just two atoms symbolized by letters other than P and Q might also be regarded as results of uniform replacement on the original symbolic statement of *Dis*.

segments of the structure corresponding to the original atoms) can arise, for the replacing structures have no possible truth-values other than the ones (truth and falsity) already exhibited by the original atoms. Hence, the new proposition is also a logical truth, and the corresponding argument is also valid.

Parenthetically, we note that some possible combinations exhibited in the truth table for the original proposition may vanish after replacement because of internal structural details. For instance, if P in the proposition is replaced by $(S \cdot \sim S)$, no line can arise in which the first part of the proposition (that is, the left-most disjunct) is true. This does not affect the conclusions of the previous paragraph.

Evidently the conclusions we have reached in regard to *Dis* and its corresponding conditional hold good for any valid propositional argument and any logically true proposition. Without further discussion we therefore state the following, called the *replacement theorems*.

> **Theorem:** Any argument obtained by uniform replacement from a valid argument is itself valid.

> **Theorem:** Any proposition obtained by uniform replacement from a logically true proposition is itself logically true.

These theorems provide a precise meaning and justification for the practice of speaking about valid argument *forms* rather than particular valid arguments. If we have some particular argument symbolized with atomic constants P, Q, and so forth, the theorems guarantee that any argument obtained by uniform replacement of one or more letters is likewise valid. It is then natural to think of the letters as representing indifferently any of the infinite number of possible replacement-atoms or replacement-molecules that can be inserted for them: Thus, the letters take on the significance of variables, and the result is a *form* whose *substitution instances* are all valid arguments. This clarifies the informal method of Tech 1 as applied to propositional arguments.

One naturally wonders whether Tech 3 can be similarly clarified. Tech 3 states that an argument is proved invalid if it is shown to have the same form as an argument already known to be invalid, or if it is shown to be a substitution instance of an invalid form (provided the requirements of symbolic uniqueness are satisfied). However, no results corresponding exactly to the replacement theorems hold good for invalidity, or for propositions not logically true. It is easy to see why. We know, for instance, that "*P*, *Q*, therefore, *R*" is trivially invalid if *P*, *Q*, and *R* stand for distinct atoms, for it is possible to assign 1 to both premises and 0 to the conclusion. Now if we replace *Q* by the molecule $(P \supset R)$, the result is valid (MP). What has happened in terms of truth tables is that the second premise can no longer be assigned the value 1 when the first premise is also 1 and the conclusion 0. Thus, a valid argument has been generated by uniform replacement from an invalid one; or, if we consider the corresponding conditionals, we may say that a logical truth has been generated by uniform replacement from a proposition not logically true.

However, suppose we replace atoms in "*P*, *Q*, therefore, *R*" with structures that are entirely unique (that is, contain no atoms in common with the original argument or with each other) and that are themselves contingent (neither logically true nor logically false). In that event the possibility of assigning 1 to both premises and 0 to the conclusion could not be overturned, and the result would likewise be an invalid argument. Or, if we again think of the corresponding conditionals, the result of such restricted uniform replacement in a proposition not logically true would be another proposition that is likewise not logically true.

Evidently these conclusions hold in general for any invalid arguments and any propositions not logically true. Hence, we state the following *restricted replacement theorems*:

> **Theorem:** Any argument obtained by uniform replacement from an invalid argument is itself invalid, provided the structures used in replacement are unique and contingent.

> **Theorem:** Any proposition obtained by uniform replacement from a proposition not logically true is itself not logically true, provided the structures used in replacement are unique and contingent.

These theorems clarify Tech 3 as applied to propositional arguments in the same way that the unrestricted replacement theorems clarify Tech 1. The restrictions—uniqueness and contingency—can be compared with the requirement of symbolic uniqueness employed in Chapter 1.

Exercises

1. Show that any proposition obtained by uniform replacement from an inconsistent proposition is itself inconsistent.

2. Construct a truth table for $(P \cdot Q) \supset P$. Then replace the *molecule* $(P \cdot Q)$ with R, and construct another table (this is not uniform replacement). Considering $(P \cdot Q)$ as a part of the first proposition, show that there is a combination of truth-values for the parts of the second proposition that does not exist for the first.

3. Construct a truth table for $[\sim P \cdot (Q \supset P)] \supset \sim Q$ and replace the first Q with R, but not the second. Show that there is a combination of truth-values for the parts of the second proposition that does not exist for the first (consider each atom a separate part).

4. State why the replacement theorems would not hold if the meaning of uniform replacement were extended to include the replacement of molecules by atoms.

5. State why the replacement theorems would not hold if one were permitted to replace an atom in one of its occurrences and not in the other(s).

6. Construct a truth table for $P \supset Q$. Replace P by Q and construct another table. Which rows in the first table have no counterparts in the second?

7. Repeat Exercise 6, but replace P by $R \cdot \sim R$.

8. Repeat Exercise 6, but start with $P \cdot Q$, then replace P by $\sim Q$.

9. Repeat Exercise 6, but start with $P \cdot Q$, then replace P by $R \cdot \sim R$.

10. Is it the case that any proposition obtained by uniform replacement from a contingent proposition is itself contingent? Under what circumstances or restrictions would this hold?

6 • COMMUTATIVITY AND ASSOCIATIVITY

We have seen in a prior chapter that conjunction and disjunction are commutative; that is, $P \cdot Q$ is logically equivalent to $Q \cdot P$, and $P \vee Q$ to $Q \vee P$. Because the members of these pairs are equivalent each logically implies the other. It follows that any proposition of the form $P \cdot Q$ implies another of the form $Q \cdot P$, and similarly for disjunction. Hence, we can add the following simple valid argument forms to our list:

$$\frac{P \cdot Q}{Q \cdot P} \quad \text{and} \quad \frac{P \vee Q}{Q \vee P}$$

We call them both by the same name, *commutativity*, abbreviated *Com*. An example of its use:

> (1) If the apples are ripe and the peaches almost ready, I will go to the market today.
> (2) The peaches are almost ready and the apples ripe.
>   Therefore, I will go to the market today.

1. $(P \cdot Q) \supset R$	Pr
2. $Q \cdot P$	$Pr \; / R$
3. $P \cdot Q$	2, *Com*
4. R	1, 3, *MP*

In this example the appeal to commutativity is so evident that there is good reason to combine the two steps into a single line:

1. $(P \cdot Q) \supset R$	Pr
2. $Q \cdot P$	Pr
3. R	1, 2, *Com, MP*

There are many cases in which one may wish to omit entirely the explicit reference to commutativity. For example, consider the fact that we have stated the simplification principle as

$$\frac{P \cdot Q}{P} \quad \text{and not as} \quad \frac{P \cdot Q}{Q}$$

That is, we have given it in such a form that one can isolate the left-hand conjunct but not the right-hand one. Suppose we have premises $(P \vee Q) \cdot R$ and wish to infer R. If we are to keep strictly to our forms, we should write

1. $(P \vee Q) \cdot R$	$Pr \; / R$
2. $R \cdot (P \vee Q)$	1, *Com*
3. R	2, *Simp*

Yet the appeal to the commutativity principle is so evident and natural that there can be no objection to combining it with the other step and even omitting all reference to it entirely. Thus, we could write

1. $(P \lor Q) \cdot R$ Pr
2. R 1, $Simp$

Along with commutativity goes the principle of *associativity*, abbreviated *Ass*. We state it formally in two ways, both referred to by the same name:

$$\frac{(P \cdot Q) \cdot R}{P \cdot (Q \cdot R)} \quad \text{and} \quad \frac{(P \lor Q) \lor R}{P \lor (Q \lor R)}.$$

As in the case of commutativity, these argument forms are just as valid in reverse, taking the conclusions as premises and the premises as conclusions. An example of its use is

(1) Either the first or second is true, or the third.
(2) The first is false.
     Therefore, the second or third is true.

1. $(P \lor Q) \lor R$ Pr
2. $\sim P$ $Pr / Q \lor R$
3. $P \lor (Q \lor R)$ 1, Ass
4. $Q \lor R$ 3, 2, Dis

Of course chain disjunctions and conjunctions, such as $P \lor Q \lor R$, or $P \cdot Q \cdot R$, are not usually grouped by pairs as in the first line of the proof here, precisely because commutativity and associativity principles render such groupings unnecessary for most purposes. In short, both commutativity and associativity principles are often applied implicitly or even unconsciously in verbal argument, and there is no need to demand in all cases of formal proof that explicit reference to every use of those principles be provided.

Exercises

1. Construct completely detailed proofs for the following arguments.

    a. Either the apples or pears are ripe. The pears are not ripe. Hence, the melons or apples are ripe.

    b. The melons, pears, apples, and cucumbers are ready. If the cucumbers and pears are ready, we can make a market trip today. Hence, we can make a market trip today.

c. If the trees are tall, the wind will not blow through. If the trees are strong, the ground will not erode. The trees are tall or strong. Therefore, the trees will need further care or the ground will not erode or the wind will not blow through.

d. The trees are tall or strong or resistant to cold or heavily leafed. They are not resistant to cold, nor tall, nor heavily leafed. Hence, they are strong.

2. What reasonable premise makes the following valid? "If he is kindly to children, he will help us. If he is inordinately cruel he will actively hinder us and prevent our helping. If he prevents our helping and actively hinders us, or he helps us, then we shall have to punish him or reward him. Hence, we shall indeed have to reward or punish him."

3. What significant conclusion can be inferred from the following? "If the president fails to act, then if the banks fail there will be a lack of currency. If the courts take a hand, then if appeals are made money will be released. Either the president will fail to act or the courts will take a hand. If there is a lack of currency there will be a serious depression. It is not the case that money will be released when appeals are made."

7 • SUBSTITUTION

Thus far we have shown how commutativity and associativity can be used to rearrange the order or grouping of propositions that themselves occupy an entire line of proof. But now consider the following premises:

1. $[P \text{ v } (Q \cdot R)] \supset T$.
2. $P \text{ v } (R \cdot Q)$.

From these, could we infer T? Intuition claims we can, because $Q \cdot R$ and $R \cdot Q$, being logically equivalent, can be substituted one for the other, so that T follows by MP. What we are trying to do here differs from any case in which we infer $R \cdot Q$ from $Q \cdot R$ where both occupy separate lines of proof. Rather, we now desire to *substitute* one for the other *within* a larger context. Using the letter S as an annotation for this operation, we might indicate the inference as follows.

1. $[P \text{ v } (Q \cdot R)] \supset T$ Pr
2. $P \text{ v } (R \cdot Q)$ $Pr \ /T$
3. $P \text{ v } (Q \cdot R)$ 2, S, Com
4. T 1, 3, MP

Here the annotation S, Com tells that one proposition has been substituted within a context for another. Another proof of the same sort is

1. $[\sim P \cdot (Q \cdot R)] \supset S$ Pr
2. $T \supset [(\sim P \cdot Q) \cdot R]$ $Pr \ /T \supset S$
3. $T \supset [\sim P \cdot (Q \cdot R)]$ 2, S, Ass
4. $T \supset S$ 3, 1, Hyp

It must be emphasized that the legitimacy of substitution (discussed subsequently) requires that one part of an expression be replaced by another that is logically *equivalent* to it, not merely *implied* by it. For instance, if we start with $(P \cdot Q) \supset R$ and substitute P for $(P \cdot Q)$, on the ground that the latter implies the former, the result will not be a valid inference, and the process will not be what is meant by substitution. Note also how substitution differs from uniform replacement: The structure for which substitution is made may be (and usually is) a molecule; and even if it occurs in the original proposition more than once, *one* act of substitution means that just *one* of its occurrences is replaced by some equivalent.

The following expresses our claims in respect to substitution:

Theorem: If a proposition A contains some part B, and a new proposition A' is generated by substituting for B a proposition B' which is logically equivalent to B, then A and A' are logically equivalent.

The soundness of this theorem is fairly evident. Visualize truth tables constructed for A and A'. Because A and A' are exactly alike except that the former has B where the latter has B', A and A' can have different truth values only in some case where B and B' have different values. But as B and B' are by hypothesis equivalent, no such case can arise, and A and A' are also equivalent. Hence, either can be inferred from the other.

In due course we shall develop a list of standard *forms* of equivalence, which may be appealed to for making substitutions in formal proofs. So far, we are familiar with the fact that the following are logically true:

$$(P \cdot Q) \equiv (Q \cdot P)$$
$$(P \text{ v } Q) \equiv (Q \text{ v } P)$$
$$[P \cdot (Q \cdot R)] \equiv [(P \cdot Q) \cdot R]$$
$$[P \text{ v } (Q \text{ v } R)] \equiv [(P \text{ v } Q) \text{ v } R]$$

We take these as our first standard equivalence forms, annotated by *Com* and *Ass* as before. In Section 6 we employed these principles to deduce one expression from another where both occupied entire lines of proof by themselves. We can now view such usage as a subcase of substitution, in which the wider context has degenerated to the vanishing point. Hence, the argument forms given in Section 6 may now be abandoned, for the logical equivalences listed here *include* them as part of their significance. However, in making annotations we shall continue to write *Com* or *Ass* without an *S* when the relevant expressions do not occur within a wider context.

Exercises

1. Show by truth tables that the following pairs are equivalent and identify in each the equivalent subparts that are substituted for each other.

   a. $P \supset (R \text{ v } S)$ and $P \supset [(R \text{ v } S) \text{ v } (T \cdot \sim T)]$.

   b. $P \supset (R \cdot T)$ and $P \supset \{[R \text{ v } (R \cdot S)] \cdot T\}$.

   c. $\sim[P \cdot \sim(R \text{ v } \sim R)]$ and $\sim[P \cdot \sim\sim(S \cdot \sim S)]$.

   d. $\sim\sim[\sim(P \text{ v } Q) \cdot R]$ and $\sim(Q \text{ v } \sim R \text{ v } P)$.

2. We claim that the equivalence of $P \cdot Q$ and $Q \cdot P$ can be regarded as a *form* that can be invoked to justify the interchange of conjuncts in any context, even if the conjuncts are themselves molecules. Justify that claim.

8 • DOUBLE NEGATION, CONTRAPOSITION, TAUTOLOGY

In this section we shall introduce and discuss three logical equivalences of general usefulness.

I. Consider first this argument:

    (1) If this is not a whale, it is a fish.
    (2) It is not a fish.
        Hence, it is a whale.

The natural way to throw this into symbols is with the following dictionary:

    P: This is a whale.
    Q: This is a fish.

Then we have

1. $\sim P \supset Q$		Pr
2. $\sim Q$		$Pr\ /P$

The only available principle for moving forward with the deduction is *modus ponens*:

    3. $\sim(\sim P)$ 1, 2, MT

In this line the use of the parentheses is redundant, because $\sim(\sim P)$ means $\sim\sim P$. But now how shall we arrive at the desired conclusion, which is simply P?

One way is to go back to the original dictionary and redefine the symbols. If we take P for "This is *not* a whale" and $\sim P$ for "This *is* a whale," all will go smoothly:

1. $P \supset Q$		Pr
2. $\sim Q$		$Pr\ /P$
3. $\sim P$		1, 2, MT

Although this would suffice for a way out of the present difficulty we can hardly view it as a happy solution, for it is cumbersome and logically intolerable to make the feasibility of a deduction depend upon the accidents of symbolic translation. Instead of altering the original dictionary, we can introduce instead the obvious logical equivalence

$$P \equiv\ \sim\sim P$$

called *double negation*, abbreviated *DN*. Using the original dictionary, our sample argument is then proved as follows.

1. $\sim P \supset Q$	Pr
2. $\sim Q$	Pr /P
3. $\sim\sim P$	1, 2, MT
4. P	3, DN

The principle can be employed similarly to overcome other purely symbolic obstacles; of course, it can also be used for substitutions.

II. Next consider the following argument:

If it is a whale, it is a mammal.
Hence, if it is not a mammal, it is not a whale.

In symbols, and evidently valid, we have

$$\frac{P \supset Q}{\sim Q \supset \sim P}$$

Clearly the same argument works in reverse, so the following is a logical equivalence:

$$(P \supset Q) \equiv (\sim Q \supset \sim P).$$

It is called the principle of *contraposition,* abbreviated *Cont.* An example of its use is

1. $P \supset Q$	Pr
2. $\sim R \supset \sim Q$	$Pr /P \supset R$
3. $Q \supset R$	2, $Cont$
4. $P \supset R$	1, 3, Hyp

III. Lastly we consider this familiar argument:

(1) If death is a sleep, we need not fear it,
(2) If death is a dream, we need not fear it.
(3) Death is a sleep or a dream.
    Therefore, we need not fear it.

It is clearly a dilemma, and we can get very close to the desired conclusion with our constructive dilemma form:

1. $P \supset Q$	Pr
2. $R \supset Q$	Pr
3. P v R	Pr /Q
4. Q v Q	1, 2, 3, Dil

It is evident that Q v Q is equivalent to simply Q. We formalize this as a principle and add it to our list:

$P \equiv (P \text{ v } P)$

We call this *tautology*, abbreviated *Taut*. The proof is then completed by writing,

5. Q 　　　　　　　　　　　　　　　4, *Taut*

The tautology principle is not often needed apart from dilemma arguments, having just the form of this one. But such arguments are fairly frequent, and the equivalence here is surely evident, so we will add it to our list of official logical equivalences.

Parenthetically, we note that it is somewhat inaccurate to state our fundamental logical equivalences, such as $P \equiv \sim\sim P$, with the aid of the $\equiv$. For this sign does not mean *logical* equivalence any more than the $\supset$ means logical implication. As we have seen, P logically implies Q if and only if $P \supset Q$ is logically true; and P is logically equivalent to Q if and only if $P \equiv Q$ is logically true. However, we shall not burden ourselves with additional symbols; it will be understood from the context that in stating logical equivalences, the biconditionals such as $P \equiv \sim\sim P$ are thought of as logical truths.

Exercises

1. Review the following arguments from Chapter 2, and construct formal proofs or show invalidity as appropriate.

　　Section 8, Exercises 1b, 1j, 1k.
　　Section 9, Exercises 1e, 1f, 1g, 1p, 1q, 1t, 1y, 1z.
　　Section 13, Exercise 2a.
　　Section 14, Exercises 4a, 5b.
　　Section 15, Exercise 1j.

2. Construct proofs or show invalidity for the following:

　a. If the rain stops, the wind will die down and the temperature will rise. If the temperature rises and the wind dies down, we will be comfortable here. Hence, if the rain stops we will be comfortable here.

　b. If the rain stops, then the wind will die down or the temperature will rise. If the temperature rises or the wind dies down, we will be comfortable here. Hence, if the rain stops we will be comfortable here.

c. If the rain stops, then if the wind dies down the temperature will rise. Provided that if the temperature rises the wind will die down, we will be comfortable here. Hence, if the rain stops we will be comfortable here.

d. If the rain stops, then if the wind dies down the temperature rises. Provided that if the temperature does not rise the wind will not die down, we will be comfortable here. Hence, if the rain stops we will be comfortable here.

e. If the rain stops, then if the wind dies down the temperature will not rise. Provided that if the temperature rises the wind will not die down, we will be comfortable here. Hence, if the rain stops we will be comfortable here.

3. Supply the unquestionably true premise that the following argument omits to express, then determine its validity. "If he has a dog, and his animal is even-tempered, then he has a good pet. If his animal is even-tempered, it must be a collie. In fact he has a collie. Hence, he must have a good pet."

4. What significant conclusion can be drawn from the following? "If it is teased it will not snap, only if it is a good dog. If it is not teased it will snap, only if it is a bad dog. If it has been fed, then if it will not snap it is being teased. It has been fed."

9 • DE MORGAN'S RULES

In this section we develop two more equivalences frequently needed. First consider this valid argument:

(1) If the merchants are justified or the police correct, then we need more patrolmen.

(2) But we do not need more patrolmen.
Therefore, the merchants are not justified.

1. $(P \lor Q) \supset R$ *Pr*
2. $\sim R$ *Pr* / $\sim P$

Evidently, only *modus tollens* will get us started:

3. $\sim(P \lor Q)$ 1, 2, *MT*

The assertion in (3) can be read as "neither P nor Q," and this certainly implies "$\sim P$," which is the conclusion we want. In fact, "neither P nor Q" is equivalent to "$\sim P$ and $\sim Q$," and we now introduce this as a new principle:

$$\sim(P \lor Q) \equiv (\sim P \cdot \sim Q)$$

For historical reasons this is known as *De Morgan's rule,* abbreviated DM. Our proof then continues:

4. $\sim P \cdot \sim Q$ 3, *DM*
5. $\sim P$ 4, *Simp*

Similar to this argument is the following one, also valid:

(1) If the merchants are justified and the police correct, then we need more patrolmen.
(2) But we do not need more patrolmen.
 Therefore, either the merchants are not justified or the police not correct.

In symbols, with the first step completed, we have

1. $(P \cdot Q) \supset R$ *Pr*
2. $\sim R$ *Pr* $/\sim P$ v $\sim Q$
3. $\sim(P \cdot Q)$ 1, 2, *MT*

In words, line (3) says it is not the case that P and Q are both true, and this is evidently the same as saying that one or the other is false. We are thus moved to introduce a second equivalence also known as one of De Morgan's rules:

$$\sim(P \cdot Q) \equiv (\sim P \text{ v } \sim Q)$$

The proof is then completed with:

4. $\sim P$ v $\sim Q$ 3, *DM*

Here is another example of the use of these principles, slightly more complex:

(1) If the glass is down or the sea rolling, they will be covering the hatches and lowering sail.
(2) If the glass is not down and the wind not blowing, they will be fishing.
 Hence, if they are not covering the hatches or not lowering sail, they will be fishing.

P: The glass is down.
Q: The sea is rolling.
R: They are covering the hatches.
S: They are lowering sail.
T: They are fishing.

1. $(P \text{ v } Q) \supset (R \cdot S)$ *Pr*
2. $(\sim P \cdot \sim Q) \supset T$ *Pr* $/(\sim R \text{ v } \sim S) \supset T$
3. $\sim(R \cdot S) \supset \sim(P \text{ v } Q)$ 1, *Cont*
4. $\sim(R \cdot S) \supset (\sim P \cdot \sim Q)$ 3, *S, DM*
5. $\sim(R \cdot S) \supset T$ 4, 2, *Hyp*
6. $(\sim R \text{ v } \sim S) \supset T$ 5, *S, DM*

In effect the De Morgan rules state the way to rewrite denials of conjunctions and disjunctions so that the negation signs appear on the disjuncts or conjuncts themselves.

The careless use of symbols (or words) sometimes leads to the substitution of $\sim P \text{ v } \sim Q$ for $\sim(P \text{ v } Q)$, or the substitution of $\sim P \cdot \sim Q$ for $\sim(P \cdot Q)$. Such manipulations are quite fallacious, for these pairs are not logically equivalent.

Exercises

1. Construct proofs or show invalidity for the following.

   a. It is not the case that men and boys are cruel. But boys are cruel. Therefore, men are not.

   b. It is not the case that either men or boys are cruel. If boys are not cruel, neither are girls. Hence, girls are not cruel.

   c. It is not the case that men are cruel, or it is not the case that boys are cruel. If men are not cruel, neither are women. If boys are not cruel, neither are girls. Hence, girls are not cruel.

   d. The corn is not high. Therefore, it is false that the corn is high and the cattle thriving.

   e. If the corn is high we cannot put a tractor through that field. If it rains today, we must pick up the grass. It is not the case that we must pick up the grass while the corn is not high. Hence, it is not the case that we can put a tractor through that field while it is raining today.

   f. If murder is always evil, then war is criminal and so is self-defense. If war is criminal we must submit to any attack. It is not true that we must either submit to any attack or go underground. Therefore, murder is not always evil.

   g. Either murder is not pardonable or the law is unjust. It is not the case that either murder is pardonable or juries too lenient. Hence, the law is unjust.

h. The defendant was in town at the time or he was on the highway. He was neither in town nor in the suburbs. If it is not the case that if he is innocent he was in the suburbs, then he was not on the highway. Therefore, he is guilty.

i. If the defendant was in the vicinity, then he was in town or in the suburbs. If he was not guilty, then he was not in town and not in the suburbs. Therefore, the defendant is guilty if he was in the vicinity.

j. If God exists, then there is some rationality to things. If Aquinas is wrong, then if scripture is reliable it is purely historical in significance. If Spinoza is right, then neither Aquinas nor Augustine is. Spinoza is right. It is not the case that scripture is unreliable and God nonexistent. Therefore, either there is some rationality to things or scripture is purely historical in significance.

2. Which of the following are inconsistent with the proposition, "High wages are either dangerous or useless."?

a. High wages are not dangerous or not useless.

b. It is not true that high wages are dangerous or useless.

c. It is not true that high wages are dangerous and useless.

d. High wages are not dangerous and not useless.

3. Socrates argues as follows. "If I tell the truth, I will be loved by the gods. If I tell lies, I will be loved by men. As I must either tell the truth or tell lies, I will be loved by gods or men." Callicles insists that without denying those premises he can show that Socrates must be hated by gods or men. How?

4. If the butler did it, neither the window nor the door could have been open. If the cook did not do it, then either the window or the door was open. If the cook did it, the maid did not. If the gardener did it, the cook did not. It is false that neither the maid nor the gardener did it. If the gardener did not do it, the butler did. Who did it for sure? Who might have done it? Who could not have done it?

5. Refer to Section 1, Exercise 2c, in this chapter. Show that the conclusion of the argument there can be established with only two of the premises.

10 • CHANGE OF CONNECTIVES

The conditional proposition $P \supset Q$ is logically equivalent to a denial of a certain conjunction: $\sim(P \cdot \sim Q)$. This fact, familiar from the second chapter, can be used in constructing a proof for the following argument:

(1) If the light is green and the track not blocked, then the train will start.
(2) The train is not starting.
   Hence, if the light is green the track must be blocked.

1. $(P \cdot \sim Q) \supset R$	Pr
2. $\sim R$	$Pr / P \supset Q$
3. $\sim(P \cdot \sim Q)$	1, 2, MT
4. $P \supset Q$	3, CC

Here the annotation CC is used as an abbreviation for a principle of *change of connectives*. The appeal in this case arises from the fact that

(i) $(P \supset Q) \equiv \sim(P \cdot \sim Q)$

is logically true.

The equivalence in (i) shows how a conditional can be re-expressed in terms of negation and conjunction. We have also seen in the second chapter that a conditional can be expressed in terms of disjunction and negation:

(ii) $(P \supset Q) \equiv (\sim P \vee Q)$.

We shall employ both (i) and (ii) in the construction of formal proofs, using the same name (change of connectives) and the same abbreviation, CC, for both. In fact, however, both are not needed. For, as we shall show directly, any substitution that could be made by an appeal to (ii) could also be made by an appeal to (i) and some other principles already established. Thus, once we have (i), (ii) is strictly speaking *redundant*; but we shall retain it as a separate form for convenience.

To show that (ii) is redundant, we shall suppose that we have some proposition of the form $P \supset Q$ and wish to obrain $\sim P \vee Q$ without the use of (ii). The proof proceeds as follows.

1. $P \supset Q$ *Pr*
2. $\sim(P \cdot \sim Q)$ 1, *CC* [i.e. (i)]
3. $\sim P$ v $\sim\sim Q$ 2, *DM*
4. $\sim P$ v Q 3, *S*, *DN*

Because each step is justified by an appeal to an equivalence, the steps will work just as well in reverse, or by substitution inside a larger context. This is not the first case of redundancy in the list of argument forms and equivalences that we are accumulating, nor will it be the last. For example, *Dil* is now redundant in the light of the *CC* principles and other rules established previously (proof is left as an exercise); yet we retain it because of its convenience and naturalness, we shall do likewise in many other cases of redundancy.

The connectives ·, v , and $\supset$ are sometimes called *binary connectives* because they express truth-functional relations between *two* atoms or molecules. In this they are distinguished from $\sim$, which in an ideal vocabulary would not be called a connective at all. The two change-of-connective rules that we have set out allow us to transform any conditional into an expression involving negation and conjunction (i), or into an expression involving negation and disjunction (ii). One naturally wonders whether similar equivalences hold with respect to the other binary connectives.

The answer is of course in the affirmative. In the first place a disjunction can be transformed into an expression involving negation and the conditional sign,

    (iii) $(P$ v $Q) \equiv (\sim P \supset Q)$

or into an expression involving negation and conjunction,

    (iv) $(P$ v $Q) \equiv \sim(\sim P \cdot \sim Q)$.

Secondly, a conjunction can be transformed into an expression using negation and the conditional sigh,

    (v) $(P \cdot Q) \equiv \sim(P \supset \sim Q)$

or into an expression using negation and disjunction:

    (vi) $(P \cdot Q) \equiv \sim(\sim P$ v $\sim Q)$.

All of these are genuine logical equivalences, and they are one and all redundant if we have (i) and (ii), or even if we have (.) alone or (ii) alone. Inspection shows that (iv) and (vi) are very close relatives of the De Morgan rules. For the sake of symmetry and completeness, we will retain all six change-of-connective equivalences as forms available in proof-construction. In fact only the first three are likely to be in much demand, and no very great inconvenience will result if the remaining three are largely ignored. In particular, (v) is usually used only with a considerable sense of awkwardness.

To this list we must add the two equivalences that are needed on those occasions when the signs ∇ and $\equiv$ are introduced into proofs. They are

(vii) $(P \nabla Q) \equiv [(P \text{ v } Q) \cdot \sim(P \cdot Q)]$

(viii) $(P \equiv Q) \equiv [(P \supset Q) \cdot (Q \supset P)]$

The last statement is symbolically peculiar, for it is understood that its first $\equiv$ does not connote *logical* equivalence, whereas its second one does. The entire list of eight principles will all be called by the same name and abbreviated by *CC*.

Exercises

1. Show that the *CC* equivalences (iii), (iv), (v), and (vi), are redundant in the light of (i) and (ii). That is, show how each of the former equivalences can be established by reference to (i) and (ii) alone.

2. Show that the *DM* rule, $\sim(P \cdot Q) \equiv (\sim P \text{ v } \sim Q)$, is redundant in the light of the first two *CC* rules. Hint: Express $\sim(P \cdot Q)$ as $\sim[P \cdot \sim(\sim Q)]$.

3. Show that the *DM* rule, $\sim(P \text{ v } Q) \equiv (\sim P \cdot \sim Q)$, is redundant in the light of the first two *CC* rules and *DN*.

4. Review the following arguments from Chapter 2, and construct proofs or show invalidity as appropriate:

   Section 2; Exercises 3, 4.
   Section 8; Exercises 1a, 1c, 1e, 1i, 1l.
   Section 9; Exercises 1l, 1m, 1n, 1o.
   Section 10; Exercises 5a, 5b, 5c.
   Section 14; Exercises 1a, 1b, 5c, 5d.
   Section 15; Exercises 1c, 1h.
   Section 16; Exercises 4c, 4e, 4f, 4i.
   Section 17; Exercises 3c, 3d, 3e, 3f.
   Section 18; Exercises 2a, 2d, 2f.

5. Show that *Dis* and *Dil* are redundant in the light of *CC* and other principles established previously.

11 • EXPORTATION AND DISTRIBUTION

We now add three more equivalences to our list; there will be no more.

The following argument can be shown to be valid by truth tables, or by the construction of a formal proof:

> If nothing is clogged, then if the machine is operated continuously we will finish by evening. Hence, if nothing is clogged and the machine is operated continuously we will finish by evening.

1. $P \supset (Q \supset R)$	Pr
2. $\sim P$ v $(Q \supset R)$	1, CC
3. $\sim P$ v $(\sim Q$ v $R)$	2, S, CC
4. $(\sim P$ v $\sim Q)$ v R	3, Ass
5. $\sim(P \cdot Q)$ v R	4, S, DM
6. $(P \cdot Q) \supset R$	5, CC

Because each step in the proof is justified by appeal to an equivalence, it is clear that each step is reversible, and the conclusion implies the premise. Thus, the follow ng is logically true:

$$[P \supset (Q \supset R)] \equiv [(P \cdot Q) \supset R].$$

This is called the principle of *exportation*, abbreviated *Exp*. Although clearly redundant, it is extraordinarily convenient and frequently desired.

We now turn to the last pair of equivalences that we shall formulate for use in proof-construction. They have some usefulness in the usual business of proving arguments; but they will play an extremely prominent role in the next chapter, when we seek to prove some general theorems *about* the logical system we have been developing. Consider this argument:

> The mayor is in; furthermore, either the alderman is with him or he is having lunch. Hence, either the mayor is in and the alderman is with him, or the mayor is in and having lunch.

Although rather unlikely, it is clearly valid; its form is

$$\frac{P \cdot (Q \text{ v } R)}{(P \cdot Q) \text{ v } (P \cdot R)}$$

and it is also valid in reverse. It is convenient to add this equivalence at once to our list:

$$[P \cdot (Q \text{ v } R)] \equiv [(P \cdot Q) \text{ v } (P \cdot R)].$$

It is called *distribution*, abbreviated *Dist*. The name derives from an analogous rule in algebra, which states that for any numbers x, y, and z:

$$x(y + z) = xy + xz.$$

We illustrate the importance of *Dist* by showing its use in a more natural argument:

> Either the mayor is here conferring with the alderman, or the mayor is here having lunch. But hence, in any case, the mayor is here.

1. $(P \cdot Q) \text{ v } (P \cdot R)$	Pr /P
2. $P \cdot (Q \text{ v } R)$	1, *Dist*
3. P	2, *Simp*

It is an instructive but frustrating exercise to try to prove this simple argument by any of the principles already at our disposal.

There is another equivalence analogous in structure to the one we have just listed. It is

$$[P \text{ v } (Q \cdot R)] \equiv [(P \text{ v } Q) \cdot (P \text{ v } R)].$$

We shall also add this one and call it by the same name. This principle allows a disjunction, "P v —", to be distributed through a conjunction and attached as it were to each of the terms in the conjunction. The first distribution principle similarly allows a conjunction, "$P \cdot$ —", to be distributed through a disjuncton and attached to each of the terms in the disjunction. It should be noted that there is *no* analogous law of algebra corresponding to the second distribution principle.

We illustrate the use of the second *Dist* rule in the following argument.

If the peaches come in, we will make a fortune and go to Europe. Hence, if the peaches come in, we will go to Europe.

1. $P \supset (Q \cdot R)$	$Pr\ /P \supset R$
2. $\sim P$ v $(Q \cdot R)$	1, CC
3. $(\sim P$ v $Q) \cdot (\sim P$ v $R)$	2, $Dist$
4. $\sim P$ v R	3, $Com, Simp$
5. $P \supset R$	4, CC

This completes a list of twenty fundamental equivalence forms to be used in proof-construction. Some are quite trivial, and a few are rarely needed or rarely helpful. But with the possible exception of some of the CC rules, all are fairly natural and should become part of our arsenal of elementary logical manipulat ons. We list them all here:

Commutativity, *Com*	$(P \cdot Q) \equiv (Q \cdot P)$
	$(P$ v $Q) \equiv (Q$ v $P)$
Associativity, *Ass*	$[(P \cdot Q) \cdot R] \equiv [P \cdot (Q \cdot R)]$
	$[(P$ v $Q)$ v $R] \equiv [P$ v $(Q$ v $R)]$
Contraposition, *Cont*	$(P \supset Q) \equiv (\sim Q \supset \sim P)$
Double Negation, *DN*	$P \equiv \sim\sim P$
Tautology, *Taut*	$P \equiv (P$ v $P)$
De Morgan Rules, *DM*	$\sim(P \cdot Q) \equiv (\sim P$ v $\sim Q)$
	$\sim(P$ v $Q) \equiv (\sim P \cdot \sim Q)$
Change of Connectives, *CC*	$(P \supset Q) \equiv \sim(P \cdot \sim Q)$
	$(P \supset Q) \equiv (\sim P$ v $Q)$
	$(P$ v $Q) \equiv (\sim P \supset Q)$
	$(P$ v $Q) \equiv \sim(\sim P \cdot \sim Q)$
	$(P \cdot Q) \equiv \sim(P \supset \sim Q)$
	$(P \cdot Q) \equiv \sim(\sim P$ v $\sim Q)$
	$(P \triangledown Q) \equiv [(P$ v $Q) \cdot \sim(P \cdot Q)]$
	$(P \equiv Q) \equiv [(P \supset Q) \cdot (Q \supset P)]$
Exportation, *Exp*	$[P \supset (Q \supset R)] \equiv [(P \cdot Q) \supset R]$
Distribution, *Dist*	$[P \cdot (Q$ v $R)] \equiv [(P \cdot Q)$ v $(P \cdot R)]$
	$[P$ v $(Q \cdot R)] \equiv [(P$ v $Q) \cdot (P$ v $R)]$

Exercises

1. Show that the second *Dist* rule is redundant in the light of the first *Dist* rule and other equivalences established previously.

2. Review these arguments from Chapter 2 and construct proofs or show invalidity as appropriate:

> Section 9; Exercises 1r, 1s.
> Section 15; Exercises 1e, 1f.

3. Construct proofs or show invalidity for the following.

> a. If the tree is green; then if my glasses are on, my sight is failing if the light is normal. Hence, if the light is normal; then if my glasses are on, my sight is failing if the tree is green.

> b. If the tree is green; then if my glasses are on, my sight is failing if the light is normal. Hence, if my glasses are on; then if the light is normal, my sight is failing if the tree is green.

> c. If the light is right assuming the tree appears green, then his vision is normal. Hence, if the tree appears green, the light is right and his vision is normal.

> d. If the light is right assuming the tree appears green, then his vision is normal. Hence, if his vision is normal assuming the tree appears green, then the light is right.

> e. Serum A works or serums B and C work. Hence, either serums A and B work, or serums A and C work.

> f. Serum A works, and serum B or C works. Hence, serum A or B works, and serum A or C works.

> g. Serums A and B work, or serums A and C work. Hence, serum A works.

> h. If I get a ticket I must go to court and pay a fine. Thus, if I get a ticket I must pay a fine.

> i. If I get a ticket I must go to court. And if I get a ticket I must pay a fine. Thus, if I get a ticket I must go to court and pay a fine.

> j. If I speed or drive in the center I will get a ticket. Hence, if I speed I will get a ticket.

> k. If I speed I will get a ticket. Therefore, if I speed and drive in the center I will get a ticket.

> l. Mary or George will go; but furthermore, Mary or Henry will go. Either George or Henry will not go. Therefore, Mary will.

> m. If Mary or George goes and Mary or Henry goes, then Sally will go. But Sally will not go. Therefore, neither will Mary.

n. Having adequate rain is a necessary condition for the following:—
If the corn ripens assuming there is adequate fertilizer, then there
will be a satisfactory harvest this year. The corn has not ripened this
year. Hence, if there was adequate fertilizer there was inadequate rain.

12 • TACTICS

The system of principles now developed is rich enough to allow the
construction of most valid propositional arguments.[21] The actual construction of proofs is a task requiring some wit and ingenuity. There
are, however, some tactical principles that may be helpful when used
flexibly; the reader will find that he has already been using some of
them implicitly or otherwise. In the subsequent discussions, we assume
that a valid argument with a known conclusion is given.

I. One may simply begin the attempt at proof-construction by
making any likely looking deductions from the premises, keeping a
record of the (intermediate) conclusions inferred and the means by
which they are inferred. After one or two false starts, it often happens
that the route to the conclusion will become apparent, and one or
more of the inferences made in the beginning may then be discarded.

II. After one acquires some experience with the deductive process,
one also attains a sense of the likely ways in which a given result can
be obtained. It is then possible to begin with the conclusion, determine likely (intermediate) conclusions that would al'ow the final
conclus'on to be established, then look for routes from the premises to
the intermediate conclusions, and so on. This is merely the reverse of
the first procedure; both methods are usually combined consciously or
otherwise in any process of proof-construction.

III. It happens that in most valid arguments it will be necessary to
appeal to each premise once and only once. Of course it sometimes is
necessary to use a premise two or more times, and there may be
premises not needed at all; but *usually* each is needed once. Hence,
it may be helpful to check off each premise as it is used, and look to
the remaining premises for clues to the construction of subsequent

---

[21]However, it does not allow the construction of all such arguments: see Appendix B. This section may be omitted with no loss of continuity.

steps. For example, suppose we have the following argument, in symbols, proposed for proof:

1. $U \supset P$ *Pr*
2. $(U \cdot T) \text{ v } (W \cdot T)$ *Pr*
3. $T \supset (W \supset P)$ *Pr*
4. $(P \text{ v } Q) \supset (R \supset S)$ *Pr*
5. $\sim R \supset \sim T$ *Pr /S*

We see that the conclusion, S, appears in only one premise. It could be obtained if we could first get $R \supset S$ and R on separate lines. We record this observation in the following auxiliary diagram:

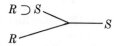

But $R \supset S$ could be obtained from line (4) if we could first prove P v Q. This tentative plan can be incorporated into the auxiliary diagram as follows:

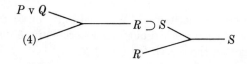

We note next that Q never occurs in the other premises. This suggests that we must work to prove P, and let P v Q come by addition:

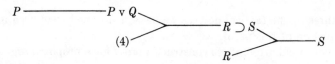

If this approach is to succeed, we have two tasks: (i) prove P, and (ii) prove R.

(i) How shall we prove P? It appears in the first and third premises as a consequent of conditionals. Shall we try to prove U and get P from (1)? Or shall we try to prove T and W, and thus get P from (3)? At this point let us make some simple inferences from the premises first: Perhaps these will then suggest a path to P. We note first that T is common to both disjuncts in (2). So we can write

6. $T \cdot (U \text{ v } W)$	2, *Dist, Com*
7. T	6, *Simp*
8. $U \text{ v } W$	6, *Com, Simp*

Next (7) combines readily with (3):

9. $W \supset P$	3, 7, *MP*

Now we note that we have yet to refer to the first and last premises. Referring to the first, we see that (1), (8), and (9) share the three terms U, W, and P. In fact, they form the premises for a dilemma:

10. $P \text{ v } P$	1, 9, 8, *Dil*
11. P	10, *Taut*

This completes the first part of the preliminaries: We have arrived at P.

(ii) Next we must find a way to deduce R. But this is easy if we return to the remaining neglected premise:

12. $T \supset R$	5, *Cont*
13. R	12, 7, *MP*

The rest is mechanical: We need only follow the sequence that has already been worked out—backward—in the diagram that originally suggested the search for P and R.

14. $P \text{ v } Q$	11, *Add*
15. $R \supset S$	14, 4, *MP*
16. S	15, 13, *MP*

All three of the tactical devices we have mentioned were used in the completion of this proof.

If continual attempts to construct a proof for a proposed argument fail to yield results, one must *suspect* that the argument is invalid.

IV. In using equivalence forms (or argument forms), it is sometimes difficult to grasp the similarities of formal structure involved. For example, suppose we wish to alter $[\sim\sim P \cdot \sim(\sim Q \cdot R)]$ to some equivalent expression by application of one of the *DM* rules. It may not be easy to see at a glance that this is equivalent to $\sim[\sim P \text{ v } (\sim Q \cdot R)]$. In such cases it may help to write out the *form* one is appealing to and then tabulate explicitly the correspondences between the elements of the form and the parts of the propositions under manipulation. In the present example we first will write the relevant *DM* rule:

$$\sim(P \text{ v } Q) \equiv (\sim P \cdot \sim Q)$$

Referring to the *right* side of this form, and the original proposition that we want to alter, we see that P in the form corresponds to $\sim P$ in the proposition, and Q in the former to $(\sim Q \cdot R)$ in the latter. Thus

$$P - \sim P$$
$$Q - (\sim Q \cdot R)$$

The application of these correspondences to the *left* side of the form then yields the desired result.

Exercises

1. Determine without truth tables which of the following are logically equivalent to each other.

   a. $\sim\sim(Q \cdot \sim R) \supset \sim[\sim P \cdot \sim(\sim S \cdot T)]$

   b. $\sim\{\sim(\sim P \cdot Q) \supset [(\sim S \cdot R) \text{ v } T]\} \text{ v } (P \supset T)$

   c. $(P \cdot \sim T) \supset \sim\{[(\sim R \text{ v } S) \cdot \sim T] \supset \sim\sim[\sim(Q \supset P)]\}$

   d. $P \text{ v } (T \cdot \sim S) \text{ v } \sim Q \text{ v } R$

2. Supply one reasonable needed premise for each of the following.

   a. The litmus turned blue. If the acid was too strong or just right, the litmus would not turn blue. If Mr. Quincy checked the apparatus, then it is impossible that the acid is right and the burette improperly calibrated. The acid is not too weak and the indicator is too old, unless the indicator bottle is wrongly labeled and the acid is not too weak. Therefore, Mr. Quincy did not check the apparatus.

   b. If there is no necessary being, then nothing exists necessarily. If it is possible that nothing exists at all, then utter nonexistence is conceivable. But utter nonexistence is not conceivable. Therefore, there is a necessary being.

13 • MATERIAL SUBSTITUTION

It has already been established that logically equivalent propositions can be substituted for each other within larger contexts. But these are not the only cases in which substitution of one proposition for another within a context is desirable. Consider the following argument:

(1) Either the director was incompetent, or the actors were nervous and insufficiently rehearsed.
(2) If the actors were nervous, they were inexperienced.
(3) And they could not have been inexperienced unless they really were nervous.
Hence, unless the director was incompetent, the actors were inexperienced and insufficiently rehearsed.

P: The director was incompetent.
Q: The actors were nervous.
R: The actors were insufficiently rehearsed.
S: The actors were inexperienced.

The premises, along with some natural steps, are

1. P v $(Q \cdot R)$	Pr
2. $Q \supset S$	Pr
3. $\sim S$ v Q	Pr / P v $(S \cdot R)$
4. $S \supset Q$	3, CC
5. $(Q \supset S) \cdot (S \supset Q)$	2, 4, $Conj$
6. $Q \equiv S$	5, CC

We have now derived the assertion that Q and S are equiva'ent, and it would be natural to finish the proof by substituting S for Q in the first premise, thus arriving at the result:

7. P v $(S \cdot R)$	1, 6, S

The annotation indicates the two prior propositions concerned in the substitution step, one in which the requisite equivalence is set out, and one in which the substitution is carried through.

The obstacle to this procedure lies in the fact that our substitution theorem (Section 7) justifies only the interchange of *logically* equivalent propositions. What we have in line (6) of the proof is only an assertion that Q and S have the same truth-value if the premises are true; that is, line (6) states that Q and S are *materially* equivalent, assuming the premises are true. The claim that substitution is legitimate in this case may be expressed precisely in the following:

> **Theorem:** Let there be an argument with premises P such that P implies A, A contains a part B, and P implies $(B \equiv B')$. If A' is obtained from A by substituting B' for B, then P implies A'.

To demonstrate this theorem, set out the propositions

$$P \supset A \quad \text{and} \quad P \supset A'$$

and imagine truth tables ranged beneath them. We show first that they are equivalent. For they can have different truth-values only when P is true and A and A' have different values. Because of the way they are formed, A and A' can have different values only when B and B' do; but because P implies $(B \equiv B')$, this cannot occur when P is true. Hence, the propositions set out are equivalent. Because the one on the left is by hypothesis a logical truth, so is the one on the right, and P implies A'.

To distinguish this type of substitution from the kind discussed earlier (Section 7) we shall call this *material substitution*. To annotate it we continue to use the letter S along with *two* numerals to indicate the *two* prior lines of proof involved. It happens that all propositions proved with the aid of material substitution could also be proved without it,[22] but as it is a natural and convenient procedure we here adopt it as a separate principle of proof-construction.

Exercises

The following arguments are all valid. Construct two proofs for each, one using the principle of material substitution and one without it.

1. The jury will acquit if and only if the judge uses our proposed instructions. The judge will use our proposed instructions if and only if he remembers that I went to Yale, too. Hence, the jury will acquit if and only if the judge remembers that I went to Yale, too.

2. The jury will acquit or recommend leniency. The jury will recommend

---

[22]See Appendix A.

leniency if and only if the judge encourages them. Hence, the jury will acquit or the judge will encourage them to recommend leniency.

3. Either you install a gold tooth or you install a plastic one and use inferior cement. You run the risk of losing the tooth if and only if you use inferior cement. Hence, you install a gold tooth unless you install a plastic one and run the risk of losing the tooth.

4. Either gold fillings are dependable or silver fillings may be used. If special cements are employed or gold fillings are dependable; and if furthermore he works carefully and silver fillings may be used, or he is very experienced; then it would be right to let him do the work. He is very experienced, or he works carefully and special cements are employed. If special cements are employed the objections to silver can be met. Silver fillings may be used if the objections to silver can be met. If silver fillings can be used special cements are also employed. Therefore, it would be right to let him do the work.

14 • CONDITIONAL PROOF

The system of formal deduction we have developed will permit the construction of proofs for most but not all valid propositional arguments. In this section we introduce a further procedure. With its aid it can be shown that formal proofs exist for all valid propositional arguments.[23] The significance of the new method, called *conditional proof*, is not restricted to the fact that it permits deduction of a small residue of hitherto unprovable arguments. The method, as we shall see, is intuitively quite natural; and its use facilitates to an extraordinary degree many deductions that are otherwise difficult and clumsy.

The subsequent argument, although trivial, is clearly valid. It can be shown that with the principles so far at our disposal no formal proof for it could possibly be constructed:[24]

If the clock is right, then Cora is late.
Therefore, if the clock is right, then the clock is right and Cora is late.

$$\frac{P \supset Q}{P \supset (P \cdot Q)}$$

---

[23]See Chapter 4, Section 6.
[24]See Appendix B.

It is instructive to approach this at the verbal level. Quite reasonably, it may be urged that it is valid as follows:

> Suppose the premise is true. Next, suppose the antecedent of the conclusion is also true, that is, the clock *is* right. From this and the premise it would follow that Cora is late (by *MP*). Hence, assuming that the antecedent of the conclusion is true, it would follow that (i) the clock is right and (ii) Cora is late. In other words, assuming the clock is right, it follows that the conjunction "The clock is right and Cora is late," is true. That is, we have shown that *if* the clock is right, *then* the clock is right and Cora is late. But this last is just the desired conclusion of the argument.

This verbal justification, perhaps dizzying, is entirely valid and proper; but it corresponds to no method of proof-construction that we have yet seen. For the moment we ignore the problem of *proving* that it is logically correct to argue in this way. Let us first concentrate on developing a clear way to portray in symbols the essence of the verbal justification.

We begin by assuming the premise to be true. This is no different from our ordinary procedure; we simply assert, or write down, the premise as follows:

$$1.\ P \supset Q \qquad\qquad Pr\ /P \supset (P \cdot Q)$$

Next we assumed that the antecedent of the desired conclusion, P, was true. This in itself is not a premise, nor does it follow from the given premise. It is rather an assumption or hypothesis made for the sake of continuing the argument, and it is understood that the final conclusion will not depend upon it. We shall indicate this subsidiary assumption in a second line of proof, indented to the right:

$$1.\ P \supset Q \qquad\qquad Pr\ /P \supset (P \cdot Q)$$
$$2.\ \ \ \ P \qquad\qquad\qquad CP$$

We call line (2) an *assumption for conditional proof*, abbreviated *CP*. No numerals are included in the annotation, for the assertion of that line is not warranted by reference to any previous lines.

Next, we note that from (1) and (2) together certain inferences can be drawn. The first inference is Q, from (1) and (2) by *MP*. It is clear that this intermediate conclusion, Q, depends upon the assumption in (2) as well as on the premise, and it does not follow from the premise alone. Hence, to show its (partial) dependence on the assumption in (2), we write it in the same indented column:

1. $P \supset Q$ $Pr /P \supset (P \cdot Q)$
    2. P CP
    3. Q 1, 2, MP

Continuing, we see that the conjunction $P \cdot Q$ follows from lines (2) and (3). Because it is indirectly dependent upon the assumption in (2)—for it does not follow from the premise alone—we continue to write in the indented column:

1. $P \supset Q$ $Pr /P \supset (P \cdot Q)$
    2. P CP
    3. Q 1, 2, MP
    4. $P \cdot Q$ 2, 3, $Conj$

At this stage, we note that (2) is the antecedent of the desired final conclusion and (4) the consequent. In the *verbal* argument here, the final move was made by pointing out that, in effect, we have shown (4) to follow *if* (2) is true. That is, under the initial premise, we have shown that if (2) is assumed, (4) follows. Which is to say, the proposition $P \supset (P \cdot Q)$ has been demonstrated. The validity of that conclusion, $P \supset (P \cdot Q)$, does not depend upon the assumption made in line (2); rather it incorporates it. Hence, we can write the conclusion back at the left-hand margin, to indicate that it follows from the premise alone:

1. $P \supset Q$ $Pr /P \supset (P \cdot Q)$
    2. P CP
    3. Q 1, 2, MP
    4. $P \cdot Q$ 2, 3, $Conj$
5. $P \supset (P \cdot Q)$ 2–4, CP

The annotation 2–4 indicates that the justification for line (5) is based on the auxiliary argument set out in lines (2) *through* (4); that argument, based as it is on the assumption of P as a condition, is reasonably called a *conditional argument*, or a *hypothetical argument*. In the fifth line we assert in effect that if the condition (or hypothesis) of the conditional argument does indeed hold, so does its conclusion. To indicate that (5) is justified specifically by a sequence of lines forming a conditional argument, its full annotation is then 2–4, CP.

To see the power and convenience of this method, let us examine an argument that can be proved both with and without it:

$$\frac{(P \vee Q) \supset R}{(P \cdot Q) \supset R}$$

Without conditional proof methods we have

1.	$(P \vee Q) \supset R$	$Pr \, / (P \cdot Q) \supset R$
2.	$\sim(P \vee Q) \vee R$	1, *CC*
3.	$(\sim P \cdot \sim Q) \vee R$	2, *S, DM*
4.	$(\sim P \vee R) \cdot (\sim Q \vee R)$	3, *Com, Dist*
5.	$\sim P \vee R$	4, *Simp*
6.	$(\sim P \vee R) \vee \sim Q$	5, *Add*
7.	$(\sim P \vee \sim Q) \vee R$	6, *Ass, Com*
8.	$\sim(\sim P \vee \sim Q) \supset R$	7, *CC*
9.	$(P \cdot Q) \supset R$	8, *S, CC*

With conditional proof we write

1.	$(P \vee Q) \supset R$	$Pr \, / (P \cdot Q) \supset R$
2.	$P \cdot Q$	*CP*
3.	P	2, *Simp*
4.	$P \vee Q$	3, *Add*
5.	R	1, 4, *MP*
6.	$(P \cdot Q) \supset R$	2–5, *CP*

The second proof is far simpler, easier to follow or construct, and shorter.

Before discussing the use of this method in further detail, we shall show that it is consistent with our earlier procedures and can be justified by reference to them. The demonstration is almost trivial. For purposes of illustrat on we refer to the last formal proof here, and formulate in general terms the various steps in the use of conditional proof:

1.	$(P \vee Q) \supset R$ } —————— A
2.	$P \cdot Q$ } —————— B
3.	P
4.	$P \vee Q$
5.	R } —————— C
6.	$(P \cdot Q) \supset R$ } —————— $B \supset C$

We begin with premise(s) A, then add an assumption or hypothesis B. Taking A and B together we infer an intermediate conclusion C. That is, we show that $(A \cdot B) \supset C$ is a logical truth. But by the principle of exportation this is equivalent to $A \supset (B \supset C)$; hence, this last is also a logical truth. But that shows that A alone implies $B \supset C$. The technique of conditional proof can be employed, then, whenever we wish to establish a conclusion having the form of a conditional.

There is no reason why a sequence of conditional argument has to begin immediately after the premises. It can begin anywhere:

1. $P \supset [Q \supset (R \cdot S)]$	Pr
2. P	Pr /$Q \supset S$
3. $Q \supset (R \cdot S)$	1, 2, MP
4. Q	CP
5. $R \cdot S$	3, 4, MP
6. S	5, Com, $Simp$
7. $Q \supset S$	4–6, CP

Here the first *three* lines may be regarded as a set of premises and (4) as an additional hypothesis for the sake of the conditional argument in (4) to (6). The last line follows from the first three lines alone, and because the third follows from the premises alone, so does the last line (chain theorem). Obviously, conditional proof can also be used to establish some intermediate conclusion in a proof rather than only the last line.

It is important to avoid confusion regarding which propositions are available as premises for a given line. Throughout the sequence of indented steps in a conditional argument, any prior proposition in or out of that sequence can be appealed to. For the propositions within the sequence are said to be true assuming that the conditional assumption *and* the premises are true. Hence, the premises and anything that follows directly from them, appearing at the left-hand margin, are all available while constructing steps within the conditional sequence.

But the reverse is not the case. Once the conditional-proof sequence has been terminated and the deduction returns to the left-hand margin, none of the propositions within the scope of the assumption (that is, none of the indented propositions) is available as a source of appeal for further steps. The following, for instance, is wrong.

1. $P \supset Q$ *Pr*
2. $Q \supset R$ *Pr*
3. $R \supset S$ *Pr*
     4. P *CP*
     5. Q 1, 4, *MP*
     6. R 2, 5, *MP*
7. $P \supset R$ 4–6, *CP*
8. S 3, 6, *MP* (wrong)

The mistake here is in the last step, where an appeal is made to a proposition, R, that appeared only within the conditional sequence. For R is true only under the assumption that P is true, whereas propositions written at the left-hand margin are supposed to be free of that restriction; hence, to appeal to R (or to P or Q) as justification for propositions written at the margin is forbidden.

In sum, when a conditional assumption such as P is made, it is indented to the right and all deductions that depend upon it, likewise indented, are said to lie within its *scope*. Once the conditional sequence is terminated and the proof returns to the left-hand margin, all of the propositions that lie within the scope of the conditional assumption must so to speak be forgotten or sealed off.

Exercises

1. Review the following arguments from *this* chapter, and construct conditional proofs for each.

    Section 8; Exercises 2a, 2b, 2d, 2e.
    Section 11; Exercises 3h, 3i, 3j, 3k.

2. Write conditional proofs for the following.

    a. If John goes Harry goes. If Harry goes Jim goes. If Jim goes there may be trouble. Hence, if John goes there may be trouble.

    b. If John goes, then if Jim goes Harry will go. John will go, but if Harry goes there will be trouble. Hence, if Jim goes there will be trouble.

    c. If John goes Harry goes. If Harry goes Jim goes. Hence, either John does not go or Jim does.

d. If John goes, then if Harry goes Jim will go. If John does not go Martin will. Martin will not go, but if Jim goes there will be trouble. Hence, there will be trouble unless Harry does not go.

e. If death is a sleep it is restful. If death is a dream it is pleasant. Death is a sleep or a dream. Therefore, it is restful or pleasant.

f. If death is a sleep it is not terrible. If death is a dream it is not terrible. Death is a sleep or a dream. Therefore, it is not terrible. (Hint: Take "death is terrible" as a conditional assumption and work to prove something of the form $P \supset \sim P$.)

g. The train is late and on track 3, or the train is late and not in the station. Hence, the train is late.

h. The train is late or my watch is fast. And the train is late or the schedule is wrong. Hence, either the train is late or my watch is fast and the schedule wrong.

i. The train is late and on track 3, or the train is late and not in the station. Hence, the train is on track 3 or not in the station.

j. If the train is late, I will sue the railroad. If the train is late, I will miss my appointment. And if the train is late, I will lose the sale. Therefore, if the train is late I will sue the railroad, miss my appointment, and lose the sale.

3. Construct a proof for the argument in Exercise 2j here, without using conditional-proof methods.

4. Review the following arguments from *this* chapter, and construct conditional proofs for each.

> Section 2; Exercises 4e, 4f.
> Section 9; Exercises 1i, *1j.

5. From Section 13 of Chapter 2, review the following arguments and construct conditional proofs for each: 2h, 2k (are all the premises needed?), and 6 (both parts).

15 • MULTIPLE CONDITIONAL PROOFS

It is possible and often convenient to employ two or more sequences of conditional proof within a larger deduction. As an example we can study the following:

1.	$P \supset U$	Pr
2.	$(U \vee W) \supset Q$	Pr
3.	$R \supset (S \cdot T)$	Pr
4.	$P \vee R$	Pr /$Q \vee S$
5.	P	CP
6.	U	1, 5, MP
7.	$U \vee W$	6, Add
8.	Q	2, 7, MP
9.	$P \supset Q$	5–8, CP
10.	R	CP
11.	$S \cdot T$	3, 10, MP
12.	S	11, $Simp$
13.	$R \supset S$	10–12, CP
14.	$Q \vee S$	9, 13, 4, Dil

Note that at step (11) we reach back to a line—(3)—that appears prior to the first conditional sequence. This is of course permissible, because (3) is part of the premises that govern the entire argument. It would also be permissible if (3) were not part of the premises but followed directly from them.

However, within the scope of the assumption R—lines (10) to (12) —it would not be permissible to appeal to lines that lie within the scope of the previous conditional sequence in lines (5) to (8). For the latter are true if the premises and P are true; whereas propositions under R are true if the premises and R are true, and they are not supposed to depend logically upon P. No confusion can arise if one clings to the principle that a conditional sequence, once terminated, is permanently sealed off from the balance of the proof: None of its constituent propositions can be referred to for justification of subsequent lines of any kind, under any circumstances. (Of course it might happen, through inadvertence, that a line appearing inside a conditional sequence *could* appear outside it and would be *needed* outside it, at the left-hand margin. In such cases, the line could simply be reproved at the appropriate place.)

Finally, we note that there can be conditional sequences lying within conditional sequences, as in the following.

1. $P \supset [R \text{ v } (S \cdot {\sim}Q)]$	Pr
2. $S \supset T$	Pr
3. $T \supset U$	$Pr \ /P \supset (R \text{ v } U)$
4. $S \supset U$	2, 3, Hyp
5. P	CP
6. $R \text{ v } (S \cdot {\sim}Q)$	1, 5, MP
7. ${\sim}R$	CP
8. $S \cdot {\sim}Q$	6, 7, Dis
9. S	8, $Simp$
10. U	4, 9, MP
11. ${\sim}R \supset U$	7–10, CP
12. $R \text{ v } U$	11, CC
13. $P \supset (R \text{ v } U)$	5–12, CP

Here it should be noted that throughout the inner conditional sequence—lines (7) through (10)—it is permissible to appeal to the outer
conditional sequence as so far developed; this happens for instance
at line (8). It is also permissible in the inner conditional sequence to
appeal all the way over to the left-hand margin—that is, to the original premises or things that follow directly from them—such as
occurs at line (10). However, no appeal to the inner conditional sequence can be made during subsequent stages of the outer sequence
—lines (11) and (12). And, of course, no appeals to a line in either of
the conditional sequences can be make in justifying a line at the
left-hand margin.

Exercises

1. From Section 11 of this chapter, review the arguments in Exercises
   3a and 3b. Construct formal proofs for them using conditional sequences
   inside conditional sequences.

2. Construct conditional proofs for the following arguments. Refrain from
   using distribution principles.

   a. If raising the temperature is a sufficient condition for speeding the
      reaction and increasing the voltage is a sufficient condition for in-
      creasing the output of the heater, then we will be finished by noon

tomorrow. If the temperature is raised the bath will boil and the reaction will speed up. If the voltage is increased the amperage will likewise increase. If the amperage increases and the voltage increases, the output of the heater will be increased. Hence, we will be finished by noon tomorrow.

b. If raising the temperature is a sufficient condition for making the bath boil, and it is a sufficient condition for increasing the reaction speed, and it is a sufficient condition for successful synthesis, then we will be finished by noon tomorrow. The bath will boil, the reaction speed increase, and the synthesis succeed, if we raise the temperature. Hence, we will be finished by noon tomorrow.

c. John goes unless Mary and Martha go. Hence, John goes unless Mary goes, and John goes unless Martha goes.

d. John and Jim go, or Mary and Martha go. If John and Jim go, then Harry and Hal will stay home. If Mary and Martha go, then Nancy and Irene will stay home. Therefore, Harry or Nancy will stay home.

e. Fluid A is light enough, or fluids B and C are. If fluid A is light enough, we have succeeded. If B and C are light enough, then we know how to proceed, and we have again succeeded. Hence, we have succeeded.

f. Either A is light enough, and if it is we have succeeded, or B is light enough, and if it is we have succeeded. Hence, we have succeeded.

g. If the line is clogged or the ignition disconnected, then the motor will not catch and the generator will not be switched in. Either the line is clogged or the ignition disconnected or the plugs worn out. If the plugs are worn out the motor will not catch. Hence, the motor will not catch.

h. The line is clogged or the ignition disconnected or the plugs worn out. If the line is clogged the motor will not catch. Likewise, if the ignition is disconnected. And again likewise if the plugs are worn out. Hence, the motor will not catch.

i. Either Mary, Martha, Hal, or Quincy found the right stuff. If Mary found it, it is substance A. If Martha, it is substance B. If Hal, it is C. And if Quincy, D. Hence, the right stuff is substance A or B or C or D.

*j. Speed is important, and either skill or experience essential. Hence, either speed is important and skill essential, or speed important and experience essential.

*3. Show that the *Dist* principles are redundant in the light of conditional proof, material substitution, and other principles at our disposal.

16 • INDIRECT PROOF

There remains one further useful technique for constructing formal deductions. In the first chapter, we showed that an argument could be proved valid if, combining the premises with a denial of the conclusion, some absurdity resulted (Tech 4). This same technique was applied to propositional arguments in Chapter 2, through the method of indirect truth-table analysis; for in that procedure one assumes in effect that the premises and a denial of the conclusion are all true and then seeks a contradiction.

These earlier techniques suggest the following conjecture: Suppose we have a set of premises with a proposed conclusion and add the denial of the conclusion as an extra premise or assumption, as we do for conditional proof. Suppose, with this addition, we can derive a contradiction. Will this suffice to show that the original argument is valid? The answer to this question is in the affirmative, as we shall prove shortly. In using this procedure, we indent to the right when adding the denial of the conclusion as an extra assumption or hypothesis just as we do for a conditional argument; and we use the abbreviation *IP* to annotate the procedure, which is called *indirect proof*.

As an example, consider this argument, which, it happens, is easily provable by other means:

1. $P \supset Q$
2. $Q \supset R$
✓3. P /R
     4. $\sim R$ IP
     5. $\sim Q$ 2, 4, MT
  ✓6. $\sim P$ 1, 5, MT

Here we have a contradiction between the checked lines. A more complicated example is the following.

1. $P \supset U$	
2. $(U \text{ v } W) \supset Q$	
3. $R \supset (S \cdot T)$	
4. $P \text{ v } R$	/$Q \text{ v } S$
5. $\sim(Q \text{ v } S)$	*IP*
6. $\sim Q \cdot \sim S$	5, *DM*
7. $\sim Q$	6, *Simp*
✓8. $\sim S$	6, *Com, Simp*
9. $\sim(U \text{ v } W)$	2, 7, *MT*
10. $\sim U \cdot \sim W$	9, *DM*
11. $\sim U$	10, *Simp*
12. $\sim P$	1, 11, *MT*
13. R	4, 12, *Dis*
14. $S \cdot T$	3, 13, *MP*
✓15. S	14, *Simp*

Here the contradiction appears between two lines lying within the scope of the extra assumption.

We now need to show that the appearance of the contradict'ons in these circumstances is sufficient to guarantee that the argument is valid. Suppose we return to the first example here and assume there is some doubt as to whether the proposed conclusion, R, really follows from the premises. We shall show that it must so follow, by the following device: Change the annotation *IP* to *CP*; this done, we have in effect a formal proof with an unterminated sequence of conditional argument within it. We can terminate the sequence and finish the argument in the following way:

1. $P \supset Q$		
2. $Q \supset R$		
3. P	/R	
4. $\sim R$	*CP* ——— (Changed)	
5. $\sim Q$	2, 4, *MT*	
6. $\sim P$	1, 5, *MT*	
7. $\sim P \text{ v } R$	6, *Add*	⎫
8. R	7, 3, *Dis*	⎪
9. $\sim R \supset R$	4–8, *CP*	⎬ ——— (Continuation)
10. $R \text{ v } R$	9, *CC*	⎪
11. R	10, *Taut*	⎭

The same trick can be worked on the second example:

1. $P \supset U$
2. $(U \lor W) \supset Q$
3. $R \supset (S \cdot T)$
4. $P \lor R$ /$Q \lor S$

   5. $\sim(Q \lor S)$ CP ———————— (Changed)
   6. $\sim Q \cdot \sim S$ 5, DM
   7. $\sim Q$ 6, $Simp$
   8. $\sim S$ 6, Com, $Simp$
   9. $\sim(U \lor W)$ 2, 7, MT
  10. $\sim U \cdot \sim W$ 9, DM
  11. $\sim U$ 10, $Simp$
  12. $\sim P$ 1, 11, MT
  13. R 4, 12, Dis
  14. $S \cdot T$ 3, 13, MP
  15. S 14, $Simp$
  16. $S \lor (Q \lor S)$ 15, Add
  17. $Q \lor S$ 16, 8, Dis
18. $\sim(Q \lor S) \supset (Q \lor S)$ 5–17, CP ——(Continuation)
19. $(Q \lor S) \lor (Q \lor S)$ 18, CC
20. $Q \lor S$ 19, $Taut$

The continuations of these two proofs may be compared; it should be evident without further discussion that the same moves in the same order can be made whenever a contradiction appears subsequent to initiating a conditional sequence with a denial of the proposed conclusion. Hence, we conclude that the appearance of the contradiction is itself sufficient to warrant the claim that the argument is valid. Also, we see that indirect proof can be regarded as a subcase of conditional proof. Accordingly, whenever the sought-for contradiction does in fact appear, we will adopt the practice of writing the conclusion immediately at the left-hand margin, annotating with the letters IP and numerals indicating the sequence formed under the extra assumption. Hence, our first example can be regarded as a finished deduction when written in the following form:

1. $P \supset Q$
2. $Q \supset R$
✓3. P /R

   4. $\sim R$ IP
   5. $\sim Q$ 2, 4, MT
 ✓6. $\sim P$ 1, 5, MT
7. R 4–6, IP

It is helpful to include the checks or other marks to show where the contradiction is exhibited. Similarly, the other example, which we do not repeat in full, can be finished by writing as follows:

$$5. \sim(Q \text{ v } S) \qquad IP$$
....
$$\checkmark \; 8. \sim S \qquad 6, \textit{Com, Simp}$$
....
$$\checkmark 15. \; S \qquad 14, \textit{Simp}$$
$$16. \; Q \text{ v } S \qquad 5\text{--}15, \textit{IP}$$

As the examples show, it makes no difference whether the contradiction breaks out between two lines both lying within the scope of the extra assumption, or one within and one without. If *both* lie without, then the argument is valid because the premises are themselves inconsistent.

Indirect proof can be used to establish any conclusion, any time. It is also possible to combine sequences of indirect proof with sequences of conditional proof in the same deduction, or to place one within the other.

Exercises

1. Construct indirect proofs for arguments having the form of *MP, MT Dis, Hyp, Simp, Add, Dil*, and *Conj*.

2. From this chapter, review the arguments in Section 14, Exercise 2. Construct indirect proofs for each.

3. From this chapter, review the arguments in Section 15, Exercises 2e, 2g, 2h, and 2i. Construct indirect proofs for each.

4. From Chapter 2, review the arguments in Section 10, Exercises 6a, 6b, 6c, and 6d. Construct *ordinary* proofs for each.

5. Contrive a proof for the following argument with an indirect proof sequence inside a conditional proof sequence. "If the marble is hard, then the building will last unless there is an earthquake. If there is an earthquake we would have to be on a fault. We are not on a fault. If the building lasts it will be a fitting memorial. Hence, if the marble is hard the building will be a fitting memorial."

6. Contrive a proof for the following argument with a conditional proof sequence inside an indirect proof sequence. "If it is true that if the marble

is hard the building will last, then we are not on a fault. We are on a fault.
If the marble is hard the building will be a fitting memorial. Therefore, the
building will be a fitting memorial even though it will not last."

7. Write two proofs for the following argument, one using a single sequence
of conditional proof, and one using a single sequence of indirect proof.
"If chemicals A or B are adequate, then if A is applied the whole treatment will succeed. If the laboratory does not guarantee the chemicals,
then it is not the case that the whole treatment will succeed unless the
patient is run down to start with. If the patient is not run down to
start with, then A will be applied. So if the laboratory does not guarantee
the chemicals, chemical A is not adequate."

*8. Write a proof for the argument in Exercise 7 without using conditional
or indirect proof sequences.

17 • PROVING LOGICAL TRUTHS

Our system of proof construction is now complete in the sense
that a formal proof can be constructed for any valid propositional
argument.[25] It will be recalled that any argument whose conclusion
is logically true is valid, no matter what the structural relations between premises and conclusion. It is instructive to see how formal
proofs for such arguments are constructed.

Consider the following:

1. P	Pr
2. $Q \cdot R$	CP
3. Q	2, $Simp$
4. $(Q \cdot R) \supset Q$	2–3, CP

The annotations for lines subsequent to the premise make no mention
of the premise. The same lines could therefore appear after any other
premise, or even *after no premises whatever*. In the latter sense we
could write

1. $Q \cdot R$	CP
2. Q	1, $Simp$
3. $(Q \cdot R) \supset Q$	1–2, CP[26]

---

[25]See Chapter 4, Section 6.

[26]The close relation between the conclusion of this proof and the argument form
Simp does not affect the technical adequacy of the proof itself. Strictly, the letters
in the last line should be thought of as constants; on seeing that the last line is

Any logical truth can be proved similarly, that is, after any premises or after no premises at all. Such proofs will always begin with some conditional or hypothetical premise taken as a starting point for a sequence of conditional or indirect proof. Here are three further examples:

1. $P \equiv Q$		CP
2. $P \supset Q$		1, CC, Simp
3. $Q \supset P$		1, CC, Simp
4. $\sim Q \supset \sim P$		2, Cont
5. $\sim P \supset \sim Q$		3, Cont
6. $\sim P \equiv \sim Q$		4, 5, Conj, CC
7. $(P \equiv Q) \supset (\sim P \equiv \sim Q)$		1–6, CP

1. P	CP
2. $P \vee P$	1, Taut
3. P	2, Taut
4. $P \supset P$	1–3, CP
5. $\sim P \vee P$	4, CC

1. $\sim(P \vee \sim P)$	IP
2. $\sim P \cdot \sim\sim P$	1, DM
3. $\sim P$	2, Simp
4. P	2, Simp, DN
5. $P \vee \sim P$	1–4, IP

This method of establishing logical truths is an alternative to truth-table analysis, and in subsequent chapters it will emerge as more than a theoretical curiosity. For the moment, its practical importance rests on the fact that it is sometimes convenient or natural to introduce logical truths into formal deductions. For example, take a set of premises that suggests repeated use of *Hyp*.

---

deducible from no premises whatever, we then interpret it as a logical truth, and because of the fundamental and replacement theorems we associate that truth with the form *Simp*. The proof could not be a *justification* for *Simp*, because the latter is already *used* for one step of the proof. But the proof does indicate a general method for *mentioning*, *within* a formal deduction, any logical truth that is a substitution instance of an argument form that is *used* in proof-construction.

1. $P \supset Q$	Pr
2. $Q \supset (R \cdot S)$	Pr
3. $S \supset T$	Pr /$P \supset T$
4. $R \cdot S$	CP
5. S	4, Com, $Simp$
6. $(R \cdot S) \supset S$	4–5, CP
7. $P \supset T$	1, 2, 6, 3, Hyp (4 times)

Again, consider an argument whose form suggests completion through *Dil*:

1. $P \supset Q$	Pr
2. $\sim P \supset R$	Pr /Q v R
3. $\sim\sim(P \cdot \sim P)$	IP
✓4. P	3, DN, $Simp$
✓5. $\sim P$	3, DN, $Simp$
6. $\sim(P \cdot \sim P)$	3–5, IP
7. $\sim P$ v P	6, DM, DN
8. Q v R	1, 2, 7, Dil

Both of these examples could also be proved by other means.

It is possible to develop a standard list of logically true forms and permit the introduction into proofs, at any place, of any substitution instances thereof. Because this procedure would clearly be redundant, we shall not adopt it as an "official" device. It can be shown that if one permits the introduction at any time of logical truths having the P v $\sim P$, the techniques of conditional and indirect proof become redundant.[27]

Exercises

1. Show by formal proofs that the following are logical truths.
   a. $P \equiv (P \cdot P)$
   b. $P \equiv [P \cdot (Q$ v $\sim Q)]$
   c. $P \equiv [P$ v $(Q \cdot \sim Q)]$
   d. $\sim(P \cdot Q \cdot R) \equiv (\sim P$ v $\sim Q$ v $\sim R)$
   e. $\sim(P$ v Q v $R) \equiv (\sim P \cdot \sim Q \cdot \sim R)$
   f. $(P$ v $\sim P) \equiv (Q$ v $\sim Q)$
   g. $(P \cdot \sim P) \equiv (Q \cdot \sim Q)$

---

[27]See Appendix B.

h. $[P \cdot (Q \vee R \vee S)] \equiv [(P \cdot Q) \vee (P \cdot R) \vee (P \cdot S)]$
i. $[P \vee (Q \cdot R \cdot S)] \equiv [(P \vee Q) \cdot (P \vee R) \cdot (P \vee S)]$
j. $\sim\{P \supset [Q \supset (R \supset S)]\} \equiv (P \cdot Q \cdot R \cdot \sim S)$

2. Prove the following theorems:

   a. A valid argument with a logical truth among its premises remains valid if the logical truth is dropped from the premises.

   b. An invalid argument remains invalid if any logical truth is added to its premises.

   c. A valid argument remains valid when any further premises are supplied.

   d. An invalid argument remains invalid when any premises are dropped.

   e. The validity or invalidity of any argument is unaffected by the addition or subtraction of logical truths to or from the premises.

18 • COMPARISON OF METHODS

We have now completed our development of methods for coping with propositional arguments; they fall into two main types, truth-table analyses and formal proof techniques.

The cardinal advantage of truth tables lies in the fact that they furnish a decision procedure, because the construction of a truth table for the conditional corresponding to any argument *must* provide a decision about its validity after a finite number of steps is carried out. In contrast to this, the attempt to build a formal proof *may* issue in a decision if a proof is discovered, but the failure to find a proof is no demonstration of invalidity. To show that an argument is invalid, one must generally resort, again, to truth tables or some modification thereof.

On the other hand, truth tables are notoriously cumbersome, and one can generally establish validity more rapidly with a formal proof. Even when an argument given for analysis turns out to be invalid, it frequently happens that the attempt to construct a proof provides rapid insight into the relevant structural details and suggests a road to the demonstration of invalidity. Furthermore, formal proof methods furnish principles and *habits* for the construction of original valid arguments. Almost all of our intuitive argument-making (of the deductive kind) involves some more or less vague employment of the methods formalized in this chapter. Of course the specific system developed here is not the only one possible, and it contains many more principles than are absolutely required; but all of the listed principles are fairly simple, and they constitute an arsenal of proof devices that is at once adequate and complete.

The two types of method merge completely in the technique of indirect truth-table analysis, which is clearly a type of indirect (formal) proof.

Exercises

1. An argument is given for analysis. One of the premises is denied, and the remainder accepted. It is shown that from this new premise-set one can prove the original conclusion. Does this show that the original argument is invalid? That it is unsound?

2. An argument is given as in Exercise 1. All of the premises are denied. It is shown that from this new premise-set one can prove the original conclusion. Does this show that the original argument is invalid? That it is unsound?

3. An argument is given as in Exercise 1. It is shown that from the premises one can prove the denial of the original conclusion. Does this show that the original argument is invalid? That it is unsound?

4. An argument is given as in Exercise 1. The conclusion is added to the premises. From this new premise-set it is shown that one can prove the denial of one of the original premises. Does this show that the original argument is invalid? That it is unsound?

5. Determine what significant conclusions, if any, can be inferred from the following premise-sets. Determine also whether there are any critical ambiguities of expression. Construct formal proofs or show invalidity where appropriate.

   a. A necessary condition for the diet being too rich in fats is that the animal show one of the following symptoms at least: high cholesterol, empty gall bladder, unusual lethargy. A coronary is likely unless the cholesterol level is not high. If a coronary is not likely, then there will not be any unusual lethargy. If the gall bladder is empty, then a coronary is likely.

b. The set is closed only if any arbitrarily selected pair generates another member of the set. Any arbitrarily selected pair will generate another member of the set if and only if any arbitrarily selected pair has the property of rho-convertibility. Any arbitrarily selected pair has the property of rho-convertibility if and only if this pair does. But this pair is rho-convertible.

c. If the glass is broken, then if the insured has coverage A, the company will pay *unless* he also has coverage C. The insured has coverage A and C.

d. The driver or the inspector did it, but not both. The inspector or the constable did it, but not both. If it is the case that if it was raining at the time then the driver did it, then it is not the case that either the driver or the postman did it. If the constable did it, then if the driver did not the postman did.

6. Determine what reasonable premises if any are needed in order that the following arguments be valid. Construct proofs or show invalidity where appropriate.

a. If he has coverage C or some coverage that includes the provisions of coverage C, then the company will pay for the glass. If he has coverage A, then he has in effect a coverage that includes the provisions of C unless he has coverage B. If he has coverage B then he has C. Hence, it must be the case that the company will pay for the glass.

b. If Williams knows his business and says the play is no good, it is no good. If he went to Yale, then either he knows his business or he is well trained. He did go to Yale, but he says the play is no good. So it is no good.

c. Unless counsel has forgotten the precedent he must know that this can be regarded as grand larceny. If he knows this can be regarded as grand larceny and hopes we will ignore the precedent, we must conclude that his handling of the case is questionable. If he hopes we will not notice the relevance of the precedent, he must think the jury's competence is questionable. Hence, either his handling of the case is questionable or he thinks the jury's competence is.

d. If the general understanding of the Egyptologists is reliable, then an oppressive central autocracy or an unusually rich supply of slaves is a necessary condition for their having a slave society. They had a slave society if the evidence of the pyramids is accepted. If there were some unusually rich supply of slaves, the general understanding of the Egyptologists is unreliable. If the general understanding is unreliable the documents are suspect and the evidence of the pyramids unacceptable. Therefore they had an oppressive central autocracy. [Supply at most a single premise of one atom.]

*7. Formalize the following argument, supplying premises and/or interpretations as needed.

"The rational numbers are not sufficient to represent *every* point on the real number axis. Even the Greek mathematicians recognized that when a given line segment of unit length is chosen there are intervals whose lengths cannot be represented by rational numbers; these are the so-called segments incommensurable with the unit. Thus, for example, the hypotenuse of a right-angled isosceles triangle with sides of unit length is not commensurable with the unit of length. For, by the theorem of Pythagoras, the square of this length must be equal to 2. Therefore, if $\sqrt{2}$ were a rational number and consequently equal to p/q, where p and q are integers different from 0, we should have $p^2 = 2q^2$. We can assume that p and q have no common factors, for such common factors could be cancelled out to begin with. Since, according to the above equation, p^2 is an even number, p itself must be even, say $p = 2p'$. Substituting this expression for p gives us $4p'^2 = 2q^2$, or $q^2 = 2p'^2$; consequently q^2 is even, and so q is also even. Hence, p and q both have the factor 2. But this contradicts our hypothesis that p and q have no common factor. Thus, the assumption that the hypotenuse can be represented by a fraction p/q leads to contradiction and is therefore false."[28]

---

[28]R. Courant, *Differential and Integral Calculus*, 2nd. ed. rev. (New York: Interscience Publishers, Inc., 1937), vol. I, p. 7.

CHAPTER 4

Generalizations
and
Normal Forms

ABSTRACT: Some of the concepts and methods presented in Chapter 3 are generalized and supplemented, partly to establish certain facts *about* the symbol system
used in Chapters 2 and 3, and partly to prepare for Chapter 5. In Section 1 generalizations of frequently used logical truths are discussed. In Sections 2–4 certain
normal (that is, standard) forms into which any truth-functional molecule may be
equivalently transformed are defined; some theoretical applications of those forms
are exhibited in Sections 5 and 6. From these studies a question arises concerning the
minimum number of truth-functional connectives theoretically required; this question
is answered in Section 7, which may be omitted with no loss of continuity.

195

1 • GENERALIZED LOGICAL TRUTHS

Many of the forms of logical truths we discussed in Chapter 3 may be extended to similar forms having more atoms or having any finite number of atoms whatever. Because some of these generalized forms are valuable for later purposes, we shall discuss some here and list some others in the exercises following this section.

I. Consider the following De Morgan rule:

$$\sim(P \cdot Q) \equiv (\sim P \text{ v } \sim Q).$$

It is easy to see that a similar statement with three atoms is likewise logically true:

$$\sim(P \cdot Q \cdot R) \equiv (\sim P \text{ v } \sim Q \text{ v } \sim R).$$

This can be verified with truth tables or established by transforming the left side into the right side with two applications of the original De Morgan rule. Similarly, for any n, the following is logically true:

$$\sim(P_1 \cdot P_2 \cdot \ldots \cdot P_n) \equiv (\sim P_1 \text{ v } \sim P_2 \text{ v } \ldots \text{ v } \sim P_n).$$

For we may set out the left side and by the suitable grouping of its terms, transform it into the right side by $n - 1$ applications of the the original De Morgan rule:

1. $\sim[P_1 \cdot (P_2 \cdot P_3 \cdot P_4 \cdot \ldots \cdot P_n)]$	*Pr*
2. $\sim P_1$ v $\sim[P_2 \cdot (P_3 \cdot P_4 \cdot \ldots \cdot P_n)]$	1, *DM, Ass*
3. $\sim P_1$ v $\sim P_2$ v $\sim[P_3 \cdot (P_4 \cdot \ldots \cdot P_n)]$	2, *S, DM, Ass*
. . . .	. . . .
n. $\sim P_1$ v $\sim P_2$ v $\sim P_3$ v $\sim P_4$ v $\ldots$ v $\sim P_n$	n–1, *S, DM, Ass*

Because each step proceeds by appeal to equivalences, the steps are reversible and the last line is equivalent to the first.

II. With a somewhat different argument we can also establish the generalized forms of certain logically true conditionals, such as

$$[(P_1 \supset P_2) \cdot (P_2 \supset P_3) \cdot \ldots \cdot (P_{n-1} \supset P_n)] \supset (P_1 \supset P_n).$$

Taking the conjuncts in the antecedent as premises of an argument,

$$P_1 \supset P_2$$
$$P_2 \supset P_3$$
$$\ldots \ldots$$
$$\underline{P_{n-1} \supset P_n \quad /P_1 \supset P_n}$$

we see that the desired conclusion can be reached with $n - 2$ uses of *Hyp*. We therefore conclude that the original conditional is logically true for any n.

III. Lastly, we illustrate how further cases of generalized logical truths can be established through an appeal to some already in our possession. Take the following generalized *CC* rule:

$$(P_1 \cdot P_2 \cdot \ldots \cdot P_n) \equiv \sim(\sim P_1 \text{ v } \sim P_2 \text{ v } \ldots \text{ v } \sim P_n).$$

We begin with the left-hand side and transform it to the right side as follows:

1. $P_1 \cdot P_2 \cdot \ldots \cdot P_n$	*Pr*
2. $\sim[\sim(P_1 \cdot P_2 \cdot \ldots \cdot P_n)]$	1, *DN*
3. $\sim[\sim P_1 \text{ v } \sim P_2 \text{ v } \ldots \text{ v } \sim P_n]$	2, *S*, and generalized *DM* rule established here

Exercises

1. Show that the following are logically true, if they are, for all values of n.

   a. $\sim(P_1 \text{ v } P_2 \text{ v } \ldots \text{ v } P_n) \equiv (\sim P_1 \cdot \sim P_2 \cdot \ldots \cdot \sim P_n)$

   b. $[P \cdot (Q_1 \text{ v } Q_2 \text{ v } \ldots \text{ v } Q_n)] \equiv [(P \cdot Q_1) \text{ v } (P \cdot Q_2) \text{ v } \ldots \text{ v } (P \cdot Q_n)]$

   c. $[P \text{ v } (Q_1 \cdot Q_2 \cdot \ldots \cdot Q_n)] \equiv [(P \text{ v } Q_1) \cdot (P \text{ v } Q_2) \cdot \ldots \cdot (P \text{ v } Q_n)]$

   d. $[(P \text{ v } Q_1 \text{ v } Q_2 \text{ v } \ldots \text{ v } Q_n) \cdot \sim Q_1 \cdot \sim Q_2 \cdot \ldots \cdot \sim Q_n] \supset P$

   e. $[(P_1 \text{ v } P_2 \text{ v } \ldots \text{ v } P_n) \cdot (P_1 \supset Q_1) \cdot (P_2 \supset Q_2) \cdot \ldots \cdot (P_n \supset Q_n)] \supset$
     $(Q_1 \text{ v } Q_2 \text{ v } \ldots \text{ v } Q_n)$

   *f. $[(P_1 \cdot P_2 \cdot \ldots \cdot P_n) \supset Q] \equiv [P_1 \supset (P_2 \supset (\ldots \supset (P_n \supset Q) \ldots))]$

2. Show that the generalized form of $(P \text{ v } Q) \equiv \sim(\sim P \cdot \sim Q)$ is logically true, without any direct appeal to this rule itself.

*3. Show that $(P_1 \text{ v } P_2 \text{ v } \ldots \text{ v } P_m) \cdot (Q_1 \text{ v } Q_2 \text{ v } \ldots \text{ v } Q_n)$ is logically equivalent to
   $[(P_1 \cdot Q_1) \text{ v } (P_2 \cdot Q_1) \text{ v } \ldots \text{ v } (P_m \cdot Q_1)] \text{ v } [(P_1 \cdot Q_2) \text{ v } (P_2 \cdot Q_2) \text{ v } \ldots \text{ v }$
     $(P_m \cdot Q_2)] \text{ v } \ldots \text{ v } [(P_1 \cdot Q_n) \text{ v } (P_2 \cdot Q_n) \text{ v } \ldots \text{ v } (P_m \cdot Q_n)]$

*4. Show that $(P_1 \cdot P_2 \cdot \ldots \cdot P_m) \text{ v } (Q_1 \cdot Q_2 \cdot \ldots \cdot Q_n)$ is logically equivalent to
   $[(P_1 \text{ v } Q_1) \cdot (P_2 \text{ v } Q_1) \cdot \ldots \cdot (P_m \text{ v } Q_1)] \cdot [(P_1 \text{ v } Q_2) \cdot (P_2 \text{ v } Q_2) \cdot \ldots$
     $\cdot (P_m \text{ v } Q_2)] \cdot \ldots \cdot [(P_1 \text{ v } Q_n) \cdot (P_2 \text{ v } Q_n) \cdot \ldots \cdot (P_m \text{ v } Q_n)]$

2 • ELEMENTARY NORMAL FORM

In this and the following two sections we shall develop some technical conceptions of largely theoretical interest; their practical significance will be apparent in connection with certain problems arising in Chapter 5.

The symbolic system of Chapters 2 and 3 employs six different connective signs. The signs $\equiv$ and $\triangledown$ are used less frequently than the others, and it is obvious that any expression containing those signs can be transformed into an equivalent expression *not* containing them through appeal to *CC* rules. Clearly we could carry this simplification a step further by eliminating all conditional signs, leaving an expression with negations, conjunctions, and disjunctions only. It happens that such expressions can be further transformed so that negation signs extend *only over atoms*; they are then said to be in *elementary normal form*. The following exhibit elementary normal form; for each one, if it employs any connectives at all, employs only negation, conjunction, or disjunction, and no negation signs extend over molecules:

$P \vee Q,$
$P \cdot R,$
$\sim P \vee Q,$
$P \cdot \sim R,$
$\sim P \cdot \sim R,$
$P \cdot (\sim Q \vee R),$
$[P \vee (\sim Q \cdot R)] \cdot [(\sim P \cdot \sim S) \vee T],$
$\sim P,$
$P.$

On the other hand, the following are not in elementary normal form:

$P \supset Q,$
$P \supset \sim Q,$
$\sim (P \vee Q),$
$[\sim P \vee (Q \cdot R)] \cdot \sim (T \cdot S),$
$\sim \sim P.$

The first two fail because they contain an "If . . . then" connective; the last three fail because they have a negation sign that extends over a molecule.

It is easy to prove that any expression *can* be put into elementary normal form. After eliminating all connectives other than negation, conjunction, and disjunction, one then locates the negation sign of largest scope; that is, the one extending over the largest number of symbols, not counting parantheses, brackets, and so on. (It does not matter if two or more negation signs extend over the same number of symbols; because they cannot extend over each other, the molecules that they extend over can be treated separately according to the procedure outlined shortly.) If this sign extends over a conjunction or disjunction, we apply a *DM* equivalence to it, thus replacing the original negation with two others of *smaller* scope (this will not affect the scope of negations lying within the expression so altered). If this sign extends over a proposition that is itself a negation (that is, if the negation sign in question appears to the left of another negation sign), an application of *DN* will cause it to vanish. Repeating the procedure systematically on negation signs of successively smaller scope, we eventually reach elementary normal form.

As an example, let us suppose that we begin with

$$\sim[(P \supset Q) \cdot (R \lor \sim S)].$$

We first replace the conditional:

$$\sim[(\sim P \lor Q) \cdot (R \lor \sim S)].$$

We have here three negations, but only the first extends over a molecule. By *DM* we get,

$$\sim(\sim P \lor Q) \lor \sim(R \lor \sim S).$$

Now there are two new negation signs extending over four symbols. We treat the left-hand one first:

$$(\sim\sim P \cdot \sim Q) \lor \sim(R \lor \sim S).$$

Then we treat the right-hand one:

$$(\sim\sim P \cdot \sim Q) \lor (\sim R \cdot \sim\sim S).$$

There are now two negations extending over molecules, and both vanish under application of *DN*:

$$(P \cdot \sim Q) \lor (\sim R \cdot S).$$

This is in elementary normal form.

Exercises

1. Examine the list of five propositions not in elementary normal form given in the text of this section. Put them into elementary normal form.

2. Cast the following into elementary normal form:

   a. $P \triangledown Q$

   b. $P \equiv Q$

   c. $[P \cdot (P \supset Q)] \supset Q$

   d. $[Q \cdot (P \supset Q)] \supset P$

   e. $[(P \supset Q) \cdot (Q \supset R)] \supset (P \supset R)$

   f. $\sim\{[P \cdot (Q \vee R)] \cdot \sim[(P \cdot Q) \vee (P \cdot R)]\}$

3 • DISJUNCTIVE NORMAL FORM

In the following, we shall use the term *element* to speak of a single atom with or without an antecedent negation sign; if the atom does have such a sign before it, the sign is itself part of the element. Hence, P is an element, $\sim P$ is an element, $(\sim P \cdot Q)$ contains two elements, and $(\sim\sim P)$ contains one element but is not itself an element.

All truth-functional molecules can be expressed in a peculiarly simple formal structure known as *disjunctive normal form*, or simply *disform*. Roughly speaking, a disform consists of a series of *dis*juncts, each one of which contains a series of *con*joined *elements*. Thus, taking the letters as atoms, the following are disforms:

$(P \cdot Q \cdot \sim R) \vee (S \cdot \sim T \cdot P) \vee (P \cdot W),$
$(P \cdot Q \cdot \sim R) \vee (S \cdot \sim T \cdot \sim P \cdot T).$

It is possible for a disform to contain only one disjunct; in this sense the following are also disforms:

$P \cdot Q \cdot \sim R,$
$S \cdot \sim T \cdot \sim P \cdot T,$
$P \cdot W.$

Also, one or more of the disjuncts could contain only a single conjunct; in this sense the following are also disforms.

$(P \cdot Q \cdot {\sim} R)$ v $(S \cdot {\sim} T \cdot P)$ v Q,
$(P \cdot Q \cdot {\sim} R)$ v S v Q,
P v S v ${\sim} Q$.

Clearly, a single element also counts as a disform; it may be thought of as a disform with only one disjunct, itself containing only one conjunct.

The following are not disforms:

$P \supset Q$,
$P \cdot (Q$ v $R)$,
$(P \cdot Q \cdot {\sim} R)$ v ${\sim}(P \cdot W)$,
${\sim}{\sim} P$.

and the reader should satisfy himself as to the reasons why.

We see that a disform contains only conjunction and disjunction signs, and negation signs that extend only over atoms; hence, it meets all the requirements of elementary normal form. In addition, conjunction signs are never inserted between expressions that are themselves disjunctions. These considerations suggest a precise definition: *A proposition exhibits disjunctive normal form if and only if (i) it exhibits elementary normal form, and (ii) no conjunction sign extends over a disjunction sign.* With this formulation we may prove that any expression can be converted into an equivalent disform.

By the methods of the previous section, any expression can be converted into elementary normal form. The remainder of the conversion into disform depends upon the following generalized distribution principle:

$$[P \cdot (Q_1 \text{ v } Q_2 \text{ v } \ldots \text{ v } Q_n)] \equiv [(P \cdot Q_1) \text{ v } (P \cdot Q_2) \text{ v } \ldots \text{ v } (P \cdot Q_n)].$$

We first state two lemmas (preliminary theorems):

Lemma I.   A disjunction of two disforms is itself a disform.

This is evident from the definition of disform.

Lemma II.   A conjunction of two disforms may be transformed into an equivalent disform.

To prove Lemma II we imagine ourselves to be given any conjunction of two disforms; it will have the form

$(C_1 \text{ v } C_2 \text{ v } \ldots \text{ v } C_m) \cdot (D_1 \text{ v } D_2 \text{ v } \ldots \text{ v } D_n)$

where the C's and D's stand for strings of conjoined elements. We can apply the distribution principle to this expression, first taking the left-hand side as a unit. This gives

$$[(C_1 \text{ v } C_2 \text{ v } \ldots \text{ v } C_m) \cdot D_1] \text{ v}$$
$$[(C_1 \text{ v } C_2 \text{ v } \ldots \text{ v } C_m) \cdot D_2] \text{ v}$$
$$\ldots\ldots\ldots\ldots\ldots\ldots\ldots\ldots \text{ v}$$
$$[(C_1 \text{ v } C_2 \text{ v } \ldots \text{ v } C_m) \cdot D_n].$$

Within each set of brackets we again apply the same rule, getting:

$$[(C_1 \cdot D_1) \text{ v } (C_2 \cdot D_1) \text{ v } \ldots \text{ v } (C_m \cdot D_1)] \text{ v}$$
$$[(C_1 \cdot D_2) \text{ v } (C_2 \cdot D_2) \text{ v } \ldots \text{ v } (C_m \cdot D_2)] \text{ v}$$
$$\ldots\ldots\ldots\ldots\ldots\ldots\ldots\ldots\ldots\ldots\ldots \text{ v}$$
$$[(C_1 \cdot D_n) \text{ v } (C_2 \cdot D_n) \text{ v } \ldots \text{ v } (C_m \cdot D_n)].$$

Because the C's and D's are strings of conjoined elements, this last expression is a disform; this proves Lemma II. Combining Lemmas I and II, it is apparent that if two disforms are joined by a conjunction *or* disjunction sign, the result is or can be made into a disform.

Suppose now we are given an arbitrary proposition P in elementary normal form. If it is not already a disform we can locate its connective of greatest scope; because this will be a conjunction or disjunction it will effectively divide the expression into two smaller parts. If those parts are disforms, then by the Lemmas P can be made into a disform. If the parts are not disforms, they can be similarly broken into subparts. If the subparts are disforms, then the parts can be made into disforms (by the Lemmas); if not, we seek still smaller (subsub-)parts, and so forth. In this way the problem of transforming P into a disform is reduced to the problem of transforming successively smaller groups of symbols into disforms. But single elements and strings of conjoined or disjoined elements are already disforms, so the process of looking for parts which are already disforms must reach a successful end. Then it is only necessary to work back "up" through larger and larger sub-parts, transforming into disforms at each stage; eventually P must emerge as a disform. This completes the proof.

We apply the systematic procedure outlined in the proof to a specific example. Suppose we start with

$$[(P \text{ v } Q) \cdot (R \text{ v } S)] \text{ v } [P \cdot (T \text{ v } U \text{ v } W)].$$

Assuming the letters are elements, this is already in elementary normal form. The major connective divides it into two bracketed parts, neither of which is a disform. The left-hand part is a conjunction, and both conjuncts are disforms. Hence, we can make the left-hand part into a disform at once:

$$[(P \cdot R) \text{ v } (Q \cdot R) \text{ v } (P \cdot S) \text{ v } (Q \cdot S)] \text{ v } [P \cdot (T \text{ v } U \text{ v } W)].$$

Similarly with the right-hand part:

$$[(P \cdot R) \text{ v } (Q \cdot R) \text{ v } (P \cdot S) \text{ v } (Q \cdot S)] \text{ v } [(P \cdot T) \text{ v } (P \cdot U) \text{ v } (P \cdot W)].$$

But now this is a disjunction of two disforms and is itself a disform.

The systematic but tedious procedure outlined above may be shortened in many cases by ingenuity, or by contraction of structures having the form

$$P \text{ v } P,$$
$$P \cdot P, \text{ or}$$
$$P \text{ v } (Q \cdot \sim Q \cdot R),$$

to P.

Exercises

1. For each of the following, find an equivalent proposition in disjunctive normal form that contains the same atoms.

   a. $P \triangledown Q$

   b. $P \equiv Q$

   c. $(P \text{ v } \sim P) \cdot (Q \text{ v } \sim Q)$

   d. $\sim [(P \cdot Q) \supset P]$

   e. $[(P \supset Q) \cdot P] \supset Q$

   f. $\sim \{[(P \supset Q) \cdot P] \supset Q\}$

   g. $[(P \supset Q) \cdot Q] \supset P$

   h. $\sim \{[(P \supset Q) \cdot Q] \supset P\}$

   i. $[(P \text{ v } Q \text{ v } R) \cdot \sim P \cdot \sim Q] \supset R$

   j. $\sim \{[(P \text{ v } Q \text{ v } R) \cdot \sim P \cdot \sim Q] \supset R\}$

2. Can a string of two or more conjoined elements be logically true? Can it be logically false?

4 • CONJUNCTIVE NORMAL FORM

There exists another standard form of some interest, very much like disjunctive normal form but with the roles of disjunction and conjunction interchanged. It is called *conjunctive normal form*, or *conform*. A conform is a series of *con*juncts, each one of which consists of a string of *dis*joined *elements*. Thus, the following are conforms:

$(P$ v Q v $\sim R) \cdot (S$ v $\sim T$ v $P) \cdot (P$ v $W)$,
$(P$ v Q v $\sim R) \cdot (S$ v $\sim T$ v $\sim P$ v $T)$.

A conform could contain only one conjunct; in this sense the following are also conforms:

P v Q v $\sim R$,
S v $\sim T$ v $\sim P$ v T,
P v W.

Also, one or more of the conjuncts could contain only a single disjunct; in this sense the following are also conforms:

$(P$ v Q v $\sim R) \cdot (S$ v $\sim T$ v $P) \cdot Q$,
$(P$ v Q v $\sim R) \cdot S \cdot Q$,
$P \cdot S \cdot \sim Q$.

Clearly, a single element can be regarded as a conform with only one conjunct, itself containing only one disjunct.

More precisely defined, *a proposition is said to exhibit conjunctive normal form if and only if* (*i*) *it exhibits elementary normal form and* (*ii*) *no disjunction sign extends over a conjunction sign.* Any truth-functional molecule can be converted into a conform by first putting it into elementary normal form, and then applying the generalized distribution rule,

$$[P \text{ v } (Q_1 \cdot Q_2 \cdot \ldots \cdot Q_n)] \equiv [(P \text{ v } Q_1) \cdot (P \text{ v } Q_2) \cdot \ldots \cdot (P \text{ v } Q_n)].$$

Proof is left as an exercise. The process of converting expressions into conforms can sometimes shortened by contracting molecules of the form

$P \text{ v } P,$
$P \cdot P, \quad$ or
$P \cdot (Q \text{ v } \sim Q \text{ v } R),$

to P.

Exercises

1. Show that two conforms joined by a disjunction sign can be converted into a conform.

2. Show that any proposition in elementary normal form can be converted into an equivalent conform.

3. Convert the expressions in Exercise 1, Section 3 (of this chapter) into conforms.

4. Can a string of two or more disjoined elements be logically false? Can it be logically true?

5 • USE OF DISFORMS AND CONFORMS

The application of disforms and conforms to the analysis of arguments rests on the following facts: It is remarkably easy to tell by inspection whether or not a disform is inconsistent and whether or not a conform is logically true. To develop the required criteria, we first define a special term: We shall say that a pair of elements of the form P and $\sim P$ constitutes a *conjugate pair*.

Now consider a string of *con*joined elements. Clearly, if such a string contains a conjugate pair, it is inconsistent. And if not, it is consistent, for then one can without conflict assign 1 to all the un-negated atoms in the string and 0 to all the negated ones, making the whole string true. Thus, *a string of conjoined elements is inconsistent if and only if it contains a conjugate pair*. Next consider a conform. It consists of a series of conjuncts, each one of which is a series of disjoined elements. Clearly, the whole disform is consistent if it has at least one consistent disjunct, otherwise it is inconsistent. It follows that a *dis-*

form is inconsistent if and only if every disjunct contains a conjugate pair. With this result, we can tell at a glance that the following are inconsistent:

$(P \cdot \sim P \cdot Q \cdot \sim S \cdot R)$ v $(P \cdot R \cdot \sim W \cdot T \cdot W)$ v $(\sim S \cdot T \cdot S)$,
$(P \cdot \sim Q \cdot R \cdot \sim R)$ v $(\sim S \cdot S)$ v $(P \cdot \sim P \cdot S \cdot \sim T \cdot W \cdot T)$.

And these are consistent:

$(P \cdot \sim P \cdot Q \cdot \sim S \cdot R)$ v $(P \cdot R \cdot \sim W \cdot S \cdot T)$ v $(\sim S \cdot T \cdot S)$,
$(P \cdot \sim P)$ v $(P \cdot Q \cdot \sim R \cdot R \cdot \sim Q)$ v P.

Conversely, consider a string of *dis*joined elements. Clearly, if such a string contains a conjugate pair it is logically true. And if not, it is not logically true, for then one can without conflict assign 0 to all the un-negated atoms and 1 to all the negated ones, making the whole string false. Thus, *a string of disjoined elements is logically true if and only if it contains a conjugate pair*. Next consider a conform. It consists of a series of conjuncts, each one of which is a series of disjoined elements. Clearly, the whole conform is *not* logically true if it has at least one conjunct that is *not* logically true, otherwise it *is* logically true. It follows that *a conform is logically true if and only if every conjunct contains a conjugate pair*.

With this result we can tell at a glance that the following are logically true:

$(P$ v $\sim P$ v Q v $\sim S$ v $R) \cdot (P$ v R v $\sim W$ v T v $W) \cdot (\sim S$ v T v $S)$,
$(P$ v $\sim Q$ v R v $\sim R) \cdot (\sim S$ v $S) \cdot (P$ v $\sim P$ v S v $\sim T$ v W v $T)$.

And these are not:

$(P$ v $\sim P$ v P v $\sim S$ v $R) \cdot (P$ v R v $\sim W$ v S v $T) \cdot (\sim S$ v T v $S)$,
$(P$ v $\sim P) \cdot (P$ v Q v $\sim R$ v R v $\sim Q) \cdot P$.

It is now possible to state two new methods for the evaluation of given arguments. By the fundamental theorem, an argument is valid if and only if its corresponding conditional is logically true. Hence, we can test an argument by forming the corresponding conditional, by converting into conjunctive normal form, and by inspecting each of the conjuncts. The argument will be valid if and only if every conjunct contains a conjugate pair.

Alternatively, consider the denial of an argument's corresponding conditional. This converts to a conjunction of all the premises along with a denial of the conclusion: The latter is called the *corresponding conjunction.* Evidently an argument is valid if and only if its corresponding conjunction is inconsistent. Hence, to test an argument we can form its corresponding conjunction, convert to disjunctive normal form, and inspect each of the disjuncts. The argument will be valid if and only if every disjunct contains a conjugate pair.

It is obvious that these methods are too cumbersome for routine employment, unless they are incorporated into mechanical or electronic devices that carry out the requisite manipulations automatically.

Exercises

1. Test the following propositions for inconsistency by inspection of equivalent disforms.

   a. $[(P \supset Q) \cdot {\sim}Q] \supset {\sim}P$

   b. ${\sim}\{[(P \supset Q) \cdot {\sim}Q] \supset {\sim}P\}$

   c. $(P \supset Q) \cdot {\sim}Q \cdot {\sim}{\sim}P$

   d. $[(P \supset Q) \cdot Q] \supset P$

   e. $(P \supset Q) \cdot Q \cdot {\sim}P$

2. Test the propositions in Exercise 1 for logical truth by inspection of equivalent conforms.

3. Test the following arguments for validity by one or the other of the two methods developed in this section.

   a. $\dfrac{P \supset {\sim}P}{{\sim}P}$

   b. $\dfrac{P \supset {\sim}P}{P}$

   c. $\dfrac{P \equiv Q}{P \supset Q}$

   d. $\dfrac{{\sim}(P \equiv Q)}{{\sim}(P \supset Q)}$

   e. $P \vee Q$
      P
      $\overline{{\sim}Q}$

   f. ${\sim}(P \vee Q)$
      P
      $\overline{R}$

   g. $P \supset Q$
      $R \supset S$
      $\dfrac{{\sim}Q \vee {\sim}S}{{\sim}P \vee {\sim}R}$

   h. ${\sim}(P \cdot {\sim}Q)$
      P
      $\dfrac{(Q \vee R) \supset S}{S}$

6 • A COMPLETENESS PROOF

It is now possible to show with very little difficulty that the system of formal deduction worked out in Chapter 3 is *complete*, in the sense that a formal proof can be constructed for any valid propositional argument. To show this, we indicate in a general way how a proof *could* be constructed for any valid argument; no claim is made that the general procedure outlined here is likely to be brief, convenient, or natural: In most cases it is quite the opposite.

Assume we have a valid argument with premises P and conclusion C. The general plan is to build an indirect proof: We begin by taking $\sim C$ as an assumption on an indented line. On subsequent (indented) lines we may conjoin P and $\sim C$, arriving at an expression that is in fact logically false. By repeated appeals to CC, DM, DN, and $Dist$, this can be rearranged into disjunctive normal form (as in Section 3). We will then have, on an indented line, something of the following structure:

$$D_1 \text{ v } D_2 \text{ v } D_3 \text{ v} \ldots \text{v } D_n.$$

Each disjunct will contain a string of conjoined elements. Furthermore each disjunct will in fact be inconsistent, so it will have somewhere within itself a conjugate pair. Hence, the first disjunct, for example, has the form

$$Q \cdot \sim Q \cdot R$$

where Q is an atom and R is an element or a string of conjoined elements.

Next, within the original indirect proof sequence we indent again and set out another short indirect proof, as follows (using i, j, and so on for the line numbers):

$i.$	$\sim\sim(Q \cdot \sim Q \cdot R)$	IP
$j.$	$Q \cdot \sim Q \cdot R$	i, DN
$k.$	Q	$j, Simp$
$l.$	$\sim Q$	$j, Simp$
$m.$	$\sim(Q \cdot \sim Q \cdot R)$	$i\text{--}l, IP$

Having now established the denial of the first disjunct D_1, we may infer by disjunctive syllogism,

$$D_2 \text{ v } D_3 \text{ v} \ldots \text{v } D_n.$$

But then by a similar procedure we can introduce denials of each successive disjunct, and by repeated appeals to *Dis* we can eventually obtain, simply

D_n.

Then by simplification we set out separately the conjugate pair in this last disjunct, arriving at a contradiction. This completes the proof.

As an example, consider the following argument:

$$(P \cdot Q) \supset R$$
$$\sim R$$
$$\overline{P \supset \sim Q}$$

The proof as constructed by the general method is

1.	$(P \cdot Q) \supset R$	*Pr*
2.	$\sim R$	*Pr*
3.	$\sim(P \supset \sim Q)$	*IP*
4.	$P \cdot Q$	3, *CC, DN*
5.	$[(P \cdot Q) \supset R] \cdot \sim R \cdot P \cdot Q$	1, 2, 4, *Conj*
6.	$[\sim(P \cdot Q) \lor R] \cdot \sim R \cdot P \cdot Q$	5, *S, CC*
7.	$(\sim P \lor \sim Q \lor R) \cdot \sim R \cdot P \cdot Q$	6, *S, DM*
8.	$(\sim P \cdot \sim R \cdot P \cdot Q) \lor (\sim Q \cdot \sim R \cdot P \cdot Q)$ $\lor (R \cdot \sim R \cdot P \cdot Q)$	7, Dist
9.	$(P \cdot \sim P \cdot \sim R \cdot Q) \lor (Q \cdot \sim Q \cdot \sim R \cdot P)$ $\lor (R \cdot \sim R \cdot P \cdot Q)$	8, *S, Com*
10.	$\sim\sim(P \cdot \sim P \cdot \sim R \cdot Q)$	*IP*
11.	$P \cdot \sim P \cdot \sim R \cdot Q$	10, *DN*
✓12.	P	11, *Simp*
✓13.	$\sim P$	11, *Simp*
14.	$\sim(P \cdot \sim P \cdot \sim R \cdot Q)$	10–13, *IP*
15.	$(Q \cdot \sim Q \cdot \sim R \cdot P) \lor (R \cdot \sim R \cdot P \cdot Q)$	9, 14, *Dis*
16.	$\sim\sim(Q \cdot \sim Q \cdot \sim R \cdot P)$	*IP*
17.	$Q \cdot \sim Q \cdot \sim R \cdot P$	16, *DN*
✓18.	Q	17, *Simp*
✓19.	$\sim Q$	17, *Simp*
20.	$\sim(Q \cdot \sim Q \cdot \sim R \cdot P)$	16–19, *IP*
21.	$R \cdot \sim R \cdot P \cdot Q$	15, 20, *Dis*
✓22.	R	21, *Simp*
✓23.	$\sim R$	21, *Simp*
24.	$P \supset \sim Q$	3–23, *IP*

Obviously the same argument can be established in a shorter and simpler way; but this proof illustrates the general method that must succeed for every valid argument.

Exercises

1. Construct formal proofs for the following arguments, using the general method outlined in the text of this section.

   a. $P \supset Q$
   $$\overline{P \supset (P \cdot Q)}$$

   b. $P \vee Q$
   $\sim P$
   $\sim Q$
   $$\overline{R}$$

2. State a general method of constructing proofs for valid propositional arguments using conjunctive normal forms instead of disjunctive normal forms. Then carry out the method on the two arguments in Exercise 1.

7 • FUNCTIONALLY COMPLETE SETS OF CONNECTIVES[29]

It has been seen that every truth-functional molecule can be expressed equivalently with the use of negation, conjunction, and disjunction signs purely. Hence, we say that negation, conjunction, and disjunction constitute a *functionally complete* set of connectives. Obviously one can further remove all disjunction signs in favor of additional conjunctions and negations (by appeal to appropriate CC rules). Hence, negation and conjunction alone also constitute a functionally complete set. By appeal to various CC rules it is easy to see that negation and disjunction, and negation and "If . . . then", also constitute functionally complete sets.

It happens that there is a *single* binary connective that is functionally complete by itself. It is symbolized with a slash and defined by the following truth table.

---

[29]This section is of purely theoretical interest and can be omitted with no loss of continuity.

A	B	A/B
1	1	0
1	0	1
0	1	1
0	0	1

We see that A/B is false when A and B are both true, otherwise true. Hence, we may render it in words as "Not both A and B," or "A and B are incompatible". The truth-functional relations symbolized by the other frequently used connectives can all be expressed with the slash alone, as the subsequent tables demonstrate.

∼	P		P	/	P
0	1		1	0	1
1	0		0	1	0

P	v	Q	(P	/	P)	/	(Q	/	Q)
1	1	1	1	0	1	1	1	0	1
1	1	0	1	0	1	1	0	1	0
0	1	1	0	1	0	1	1	0	1
0	0	0	0	1	0	0	0	1	0

P	·	Q	(P	/	Q)	/	(P	/	Q)
1	1	1	1	0	1	1	0		
1	0	0	1	1	0	0	1		
0	0	1	0	1	1	0	1		
0	0	0	0	1	0	0	1		

P	⊃	Q	P	/	(P	/	Q)
1	1	1	1	1	0	1	
1	0	0	1	0	1	0	
0	1	1	0	1	1	1	
0	1	0	0	1	1	0	

The equivalences indicated in these tables facilitate the transformation of any given proposition into an equivalent expression employing just the slash. For example, we start with

$(P \text{ v } Q) \cdot \sim R$

and eliminate the disjunction by referring to the appropriate table:

$[(P/P)/(Q/Q)] \cdot \sim R.$

Next we eliminate the conjunction in accordance with the tables:

$$\{[(P/P)/(Q/Q)]/\sim R\}/\{[(P/P)/(Q/Q)]/\sim R\}.$$

And lastly we eliminate the negation:

$$\{[(P/P)/(Q/Q)]/(R/R)\}/\{[(P/P)/(Q/Q)]/(R/R)\}.$$

Exercises

1. Express the following with negation and conjunction alone; also negation and disjunction; and negation and "If . . . then":

   a. $P \triangledown Q$

   b. $P \equiv Q$

   c. $\sim[P \supset (Q \cdot R)] \vee S$

2. Express the propositions in Exercise 1 with the slash alone.

3. Is it possible to express $\sim P$ with some combination of conjunction, disjunction, and "If . . . then" signs? Why?

*4. Aside from the slash, there is another binary connective that is functionally complete by itself. Find it, and show how to express the other connectives in terms of it.

CHAPTER 5

Simple
Quantificational
Arguments

ABSTRACT: Methods are developed for arguments containing propositions that must be analyzed in greater detail than hitherto. In Sections 1–3 a method of interpreting and symbolizing certain kinds of propositions (*universal*, *particular*, and *singular*) that appear most frequently in such arguments is developed. The results are employed in a preliminary way to examine some logical relations between propositions (Sections 4, 5, 6, and 8). Section 7 contains a lengthy digression on the puzzling matter of vacuous truths. In Sections 9–13 a complete decision procedure is stated for the evaluation of arguments with constituent propositions of the types under discussion. In Section 14 two commonly used methods of symbolic compression and their implications are reviewed. The entire chapter is governed by an assumption (later dropped) that the universe contains a finite number of objects.

1 • SINGULAR AND GENERAL PROPOSITIONS

The last three chapters have been concerned exclusively with propositional arguments. We must now extend our treatment beyond that somewhat limited scope, although the principles and techniques worked out in connection with propositional arguments will remain with us to be used and expanded as the occasion requires.

We shall begin by listing three simple arguments of the kind we wish eventually to discuss; both the arguments and their constituent propositions are typical examples of frequently occurring types:

All men are mortal.
Socrates is a man.
Therefore, Socrates is mortal.

All cigarettes are irritants.
All irritants are harmful.
Therefore, all cigarettes are harmful.

All whales are mammals.
Some marine animals are whales.
Therefore, some marine animals are mammals.

Under the methods of previous chapters each of these arguments has the invalid form *P, Q, therefore R*; yet each is valid, and we must now find some more detailed mode of analysis that will expose the structural relations upon which that validity depends. That is, our first task is to devise some method for representing symbolically the inner structure of the propositions concerned.

We note first that there are three *types* of propositions in the arguments displayed:

I. Propositions in which an assertion is made about one designated entity, such as "Socrates is a man," or "Socrates is mortal." We shall call these *singular propositions*.

II. Propositions in which an assertion is made about all the members of a class or type of entity, such as "All men are mortal," or "All whales are mammals." We shall call these *general* or *universal* propositions.

III. Propositions in which an assertion is made about some members of a class or type of entity, such as "Some marine animals are whales," or "Some marine animals are mammals." We shall call these *particular* propositions.

We look first at what is apparently the simplest type: the singular proposition. It is a commonplace of grammatical analysis that most sentences in English (or any other Indo-European language) are thought of as exhibiting a fundamental subject-predicate form. That is, they express a judgment in which some property or attribute is ascribed to one or more individuals constituting the subject. Thus, the sentence "Socrates is mortal" is understood as ascribing the property of mortality to the individual subject Socrates. If we adopt this approach, a symbolism then suggests itself: We can use, for example, upper case letters to stand for properties and lower case letters for individuals. Then, using M for mortality and s for Socrates, we form the expression Ms. If we let H stand for the property of being a man (or a human), then Hs means "Socrates is a man." Similarly, using obvious symbols, "Abigail is lovely" may be rendered La. The decision to use upper case letters for properties and lower case letters for individuals is purely arbitrary; it is likewise a matter of pure convention that the upper case letter comes first.

Next we turn to general propositions. It is tempting to continue in the same way and represent "All men are mortal" as Mm, where M means mortal and m means all men. The objection to this procedure is that we have already agreed to use lower case letters for (single) individuals; if we now allow the same symbols to stand for *groups* of individuals we may obscure essential logical relations. For example, take the argument

> All men are mortal.
> Socrates is a man.
> Therefore, Socrates is mortal.

Using this dictionary:

> M: mortal
> H: human
> m: all men
> s: Socrates

the argument would go into symbols as

$$\frac{\begin{array}{l} Mm \\ Hs \end{array}}{Ms}$$

Here all three constituent propositions have symbolically the same structure. But it is clear that the validity of the argument depends upon the fact that the first premise enjoys a structure quite different from that of the second premise or the conclusion, and it is just such differences of logical structure that we wish to expose. Hence, we must find a more satisfactory presentation.

To develop the needed alternative, we first lay down an assumption that will simplify our current task. We assume, somewhat arbitrarily, that *in any context of discussion the objects under consideration are finite in number*. This assumption will remain in force throughout the present chapter, and we shall have frequent occasion to refer to it; accordingly, it is given a name: the *finitude postulate*.

There is an evident objection to the finitude postulate; namely, there are many general propositions that encompass an infinite number of individuals (for example, "All whole numbers are odd or even," or "All possible propositions are true or false"). It will be shown at a later stage that the finitude postulate can be dropped without invalidating any of the techniques that at first seem to depend upon it. The postulate is therefore to be regarded as a temporary device, employed to facilitate the erection of an analytical structure; like a scaffold, it can be discarded after the structure is built. Temporarily (that is, throughout this chapter) we shall take the view that our analysis does not include propositions or arguments that involve reference to infinite classes.

Now we again attack the proposition "All men are mortal". Under the finitude postulate we take it for granted that there is only a finite number of men.[30] Hence, we can imagine that a list of men is drawn up, and lower case letters are assigned to each one. The symbolic list of men is then "$a, b, c, d, \ldots$", where a is the letter associated with the first man in the list, b is the letter associated with the second man, and so on. Thus, the letters are to be thought of as proper names. Of course there are more men than letters in the alphabet, so it will make matters clearer if we use one letter with numerical subscripts, say x_1, x_2, and so on. Then we can represent all men as follows:

$$x_1, x_2, x_3, \ldots, x_n.$$

---

[30]It happens that in fact there is only a finite number of men. But this *fact* is irrelevant to the discussion, which employs the class of men only to illustrate an analysis equally applicable in other cases.

Here each symbol refers to some man in the group, and the letter n signifies the number of men (and hence the number of symbols) altogether. It does not matter that the list would be terribly long, and it does not matter that we do not know just how long it would be. What does matter is that the number of entities is assumed to be finite, so that the list therefore *can* be made (theoretically), and will sometime come to an end.

Next, we can form a series of *singular* propositions stating that each man (one by one) is mortal:

$$Mx_1, Mx_2, Mx_3, \ldots, Mx_n.$$

Here Mx_1 means that the first listed man is mortal, Mx_2 means that the second listed man is mortal, and so on. Evidently the proposition "All men are mortal" amounts to the *conjunction* of all the singular propositions displayed here. Hence, we can render "All men are mortal" symbolically as

$$Mx_1 \cdot Mx_2 \cdot Mx_3 \cdot \ldots \cdot Mx_n.$$

Similarly, "All whales are mammals" could be symbolized in the same way, with the understanding that M means mammal and the x's stand for whales. And "All cigarettes are irritants" could be symbolized as

$$Ix_1 \cdot Ix_2 \cdot Ix_3 \cdot \ldots \cdot Ix_n,$$

using I for irritant and the X's for cigarettes. Although we are now close to a satisfactory symbolism for general propositions, there are still two difficulties.

In the first place, the symbolism is cumbersome, for it involves ellipses and numerical subscripts to symbolize a single proposition. To meet this difficulty, we note first that the subscript n is clearly an inessential part of the symbol, because it merely records the fact that the series, however long, terminates. Also, each conjunct has the same form, say Mx, followed by a subscript. So it is natural to abbreviate the whole series of conjuncts with the single symbol Mx. Then we have to add some auxiliary symbol to denote the fact that Mx does not stand for a singular proposition, but for a series of conjoined singular propositions. For this purpose we introduce the symbol (x) to precede the expression Mx. Thus,

$$(x)Mx \quad \text{means} \quad Mx_1 \cdot Mx_2 \cdot \ldots \cdot Mx_n.$$

Similarly

$(x)Ix$ means $Ix_1 \cdot Ix_2 \cdot \ldots \cdot Ix_n$.

In general, for any predicate letter F,

$(x)Fx$ means $Fx_1 \cdot Fx_2 \cdot \ldots \cdot Fx_n$.

The expressions on the left are to be regarded as abbreviations for the longer expressions on the right. In any discussion we can legitimately pass back and forth from one representation to the other.

It happens that we shall have far more use for the abbreviated form than for the unabbreviated, so it is essential to have some sort of verbal equivalent for its parts. To indicate in words the logical significance of the symbol (x) we can use the phrase "for any x," or "for every x." Hence, when x's stand for men and M for mortal, $(x)Mx$ can be read as, "For any man, that man is mortal," or "For every man, that man has the property of mortality"; clearly, these have the same meaning as "All men are mortal". In general, the expression $(x)Fx$ can be suggested in words as "For any x, x is an F," or "For any x, x has the property F"; these expressions are obviously equivalent in meaning to "All x's are F."

Secondly, there remains a further and more profound objection to the symbolism. Consider this argument:

> All cigarettes are irritants.
> All irritants are harmful.
> Therefore, all cigarettes are harmful.

This would go naturally into symbols as follows:

$$\frac{(x)Ix}{(x)\,Hx}$$
$$(x)\,Hx$$

At once we see the difficulty: The second premise and the conclusion are symbolized identically, because the letter x means one thing (irritants) in the second premise and something else (cigarettes) in the conclusion. An obvious way around this difficulty is to use different lower case letters. If we write out a full dictionary

$I:$ irritant
$H:$ harmful
$x:$ cigarettes
$y:$ irritants

we can symbolize the argument without ambiguity as

$(x)Ix$
$(y)\,Hy$
$\overline{(x)\,Hx}$

But we still have some troubles: The cogency of the argument evidently depends upon the fact that the same term—irritant—appears in both premises. Our symbolization fails to reflect this. We might then try using a lower case i for irritants in the second premise, in order to mark a connection with the upper case I used in the first premise for the property of irritability. But this device would not be more than a palliative; our eventual purpose is to develop ways of checking the validity of arguments in which these propositions occur. It is not likely that practical techniques can be molded around such subtle symbolic features as the connection between upper and lower case versions of the same letter. And where the arguments are longer, there may be several terms *each* occurring more than once as subject and more than once as predicate, thus presenting a bewildering network of symbolically subtle connections whose logical significance must somehow be traced—a discouraging prospect.

The solution to this difficulty lies along the line of a further modification of the devices already suggested. Instead of allowing the x's to represent men, or cigarettes, or irritants, we can let x stand for any physical object whatever. By the finitude postulate there is only a finite number of objects whatever the context. Then we can (theoretically) draw up a list of them: $x_1, x_2, \ldots, x_n$.

Now suppose it *is* the case that all cigarettes are irritants. Evidently this means that any object, *if* it is a cigarette, is *also* an irritant. Or, it will be true of any object that, *if* it is a cigarette, *then* it is an irritant. Specifically it will be true of x_1; hence, we can write

$Cx_1 \supset Ix_1.$

In words this is, "If x_1 is a cigarette, then x_1 is an irritant." And so on:

$Cx_2 \supset Ix_2,$
$Cx_3 \supset Ix_3,$
$\ldots\ldots\ldots,$
$Cx_n \supset Ix_n.$

Clearly the statement "All cigarettes are irritants" is then a *conjunction* of all the preceding propositions:

$$(Cx_1 \supset Ix_1) \cdot (Cx_2 \supset Ix_2) \cdot \ldots \cdot (Cx_n \supset Ix_n).$$

Using the same abbreviation device as before, we can write this as

$$(x)(Cx \supset Ix).$$

In words this is, "For any object, if it is a cigarette then it is an irritant." Or, more simply, "For any x, if x is a cigarette then x is an irritant." And it should be evident that this has the same meaning as "All cigarettes are irritants.[31] Generally, any proposition of the form "All F's are G" goes into symbols as $(x)(Fx \supset Gx)$.

Now let us write again the argument about cigarettes:

All cigarettes are irritants.
All irritants are harmful.
Therefore, all cigarettes are harmful.

Using our modified symbolism, the argument is exhibited as

$$\frac{\begin{array}{l}(x)(Cx \supset Ix) \\ (x)(Ix \supset Hx)\end{array}}{(x)(Cx \supset Hx)}$$

The argument is now unambiguously symbolized, and the important fact that the term *irritant* appears in both premises is prominently displayed. The x's have the same meaning throughout, a meaning (*physical object*) that is clear from the context and does not require specification in the dictionary.[32]

---

[31] There may perhaps be some *difference* in the meaning, because the term cigarette appears originally as a grammatical *subject* and in the final symbolization as a *predicate*. But if this shift involves a distortion of the meaning, it is too subtle to concern us here.

[32] It is technically possible to let the x's refer to any objects whatsoever rather than physical objects: The symbolism would be unchanged and would be equally effective. But this would bring into view a series of philosophical problems surrounding the term *object*. For instance, what constitutes an *individual* object? Can one object be part of another? What sorts of objects can there be? And so on. In the case of the argument discussed in the text, we side-step these difficulties by giving to x the fairly well-understood meaning, "any physical object." Although narrower than the concept of any object whatsoever, this is still broad enough to provide a single framework of reference within which all of the argument's constituent propositions can be suitably understood and symbolized.

In other contexts, other kinds of objects may be involved, such as numbers,

To sum up, we now adopt the following procedure for symbolizing general propositions of the form "All F are G." We first re-express the proposition (mentally) as "For any x, if x is an F then x is a G." Then we write this in symbols as $(x)(Fx \supset Gx)$. It is understood that the number of objects to which x can refer is finite. It is also understood that the expression $(x)(Fx \supset Gx)$ is a convenient abbreviation for the longer symbol

$$(Fx_1 \supset Gx_1) \cdot (Fx_2 \supset Gx_2) \cdot \ldots \cdot (Fx_n \supset Gx_n).$$

Exercises

1. Using the dictionary supplied, symbolize the following propositions. If there are both abbreviated and unabbreviated possibilities, give both.

      H: man
      A: animal
     M: mortal
      I: Italian
      G: generous soul
      F: forgiving
      T: talking
      C: child in the room
      a: Abigail
      b: Benjamin
      c: the child in the corner

  a. All men are animals.

  b. All animals are mortal.

  c. All animals die.

---

ideas, or gods; and in some contexts the notion of any object whatsoever may indeed be the only one appropriate, whatever the difficulties. But in almost all contexts of argument there will be some clear (although implicit) understanding as to a class or type of object to which the appropriate predicates can be meaningfully applied. If not, any attempt at symbolic analysis must be accompanied by an explicit statement of the significance attached to the x's.

It can be shown rigorously that this approach (that is, through some limitation on the meaning of the x's) will not qualify the reliability of the methods for evaluating arguments that develop in the sequel. At a later place the reader is invited to formulate an appropriate demonstration (Section 14, Exercises 3–5).

   d. All men die.

   e. All Italians are generous souls.

   f. All generous souls are forgiving.

   g. All Italians are forgiving.

   h. Abigail is Italian.

   i. Abigail is forgiving.

   j. Abigail and Benjamin are Italians.

   k. The child in the corner has a generous soul.

   l. If the child in the corner is talking, then Benjamin is talking.

   m. If the child in the corner is talking, then Abigail and Benjamin are too.

   n. If the child in the corner is talking, then all the children in the room are talking.

2. Using the dictionary of Exercise 1, translate the following into ordinary English.

   a. Ac

   b. $(x)(Cx \supset Gx)$

   c. $(Mx_1 \supset Fx_1) \cdot (Mx_2 \supset Fx_2) \cdot \ldots \cdot (Mx_n \supset Fx_n)$

   d. $(x)(Ix \supset Mx)$

   e. $Ab \cdot Aa$

   f. $(Tx_1 \supset Hx_1) \cdot (Tx_2 \supset Hx_2) \cdot (Tx_3 \supset Hx_3) \cdot \ldots \cdot (Tx_n \supset Hx_n)$

   g. $\sim Ac$

   h. $\sim[(x)(Hx \supset Mx)]$

 *i. $(x)[(Fx \cdot Ix) \supset Gx]$

 *j. $Hx_1 \lor Hx_2 \lor Hx_3 \lor \ldots \lor Hx_n$

3. Using the dictionary supplied and unabbreviated symbols, construct formal proofs for the following arguments:

   H: man
   M: mortal
   T: tragic figure
   x_1: Socrates

   a. All men are mortal. Socrates is a man. Therefore, Socrates is mortal.

b. All men are mortal. All mortals are tragic figures. Socrates is a man. Therefore, Socrates is a tragic figure.

2 • PARTICULAR PROPOSITIONS; TECHNICAL TERMS

We turn now to particular propositions; the examples we have are "Some marine animals are whales," and "Some marine animals are mammals." If we proceed exactly as in our discussion of general propositions, we will first imagine that a list of marine animals is drawn up: $x_1, x_2, x_3, \ldots, x_n$. The finitude postulate guarantees that the list can theoretically be made; and we are here using x's to refer only to marine animals. Next we form a series of singular propositions stating that *each* marine animal is a whale:

$$Wx_1, Wx_2, Wx_3, \ldots, Wx_n.$$

If we take it as true that "Some marine animals are whales," then *some* of the singular propositions in this list must be true. How many? The word *some* is vague in this regard. Usually it connotes more than one, but minimally it must mean *at least one*. Hence, we can approximate to the meaning of "Some marine animals are whales" by forming a *disjunction* of all the singular propositions listed:

$$Wx_1 \text{ v } Wx_2 \text{ v } \ldots \text{ v } Wx_n.$$

This means that at least one marine animal is a whale: It does not exclude the possibility that more than one is a whale, and it does not exclude the possibility that *all* are whales. We will take this as a standard interpretation of the meaning of some—that is, at least one, perhaps more, maybe even all. The awkward symbol

$$Wx_1 \text{ v } Wx_2 \text{ v } \ldots Wx_n$$

for "Some marine animals are whales" can be abbreviated as

$$(\exists x)Wx,$$

using the new symbol $(\exists x)$ to indicate a series of disjoined Wx's. Similarly, taking M for mammal, "Some marine animals are mammals" can be rendered as

$$Mx_1 \text{ v } Mx_2 \text{ v } \ldots \text{ v } Mx_n$$

and abbreviated as

$$(\exists x)Mx.$$

As a verbal equivalent for the new symbol $(\exists x)$ we can use the phrase, "There is at least one x such that," or in brief, "There is an x such that." Hence $(\exists x)$ Mx can be read, "There is an x (at least one) such that x is an M." Or, in the present context, it can be read, "There is at least one marine animal such that it is a mammal." Clearly these phrasings are identical or extremely close in meaning to "Some x's are M," or "Some marine animals are mammals."

As in the case of general propositions, we shall eventually run into difficulty if we allow the letter x to take on specific meanings. It is better to let x refer to any individual objects at all (of whatever sort happens to be appropriate to the context—usually physical objects). Then we can modify our approach along lines parallel with the treatment of general propositions.

We first list (in theory) all the objects, $x_1, x_2, \ldots, x_n$. The proposition "Some marine animals are whales" asserts that at least one of the listed objects is a marine animal *and* a whale. Taking A for marine animal and W for whale, it is therefore symbolized as

$$(Ax_1 \cdot Wx_1) \text{ v } (Ax_2 \cdot Wx_2) \text{ v } \ldots \text{ v } (Ax_n \cdot Wx_n)$$

and abbreviated as

$$(\exists x)(Ax \cdot Wx).$$

With M for mammals, "Some marine animals are mammals" is given by $(\exists x)(Ax \cdot Mx)$. Again, using obvious symbols, "Some swans are black" is symbolized $(\exists x)(Sx \cdot Bx)$. In general, any proposition of the form "Some F's are G" can be represented symbolically as $(\exists x)$ $(Fx \cdot Gx)$.

To see how well this method is suited to the analysis of arguments, consider,

> All whales are mammals.
> Some marine animals are whales.
> Therefore, some marine animals are mammals.

This is symbolized as follows:

$$(x)(Wx \supset Mx)$$
$$\underline{(\exists x)(Ax \cdot Wx)}$$
$$(\exists x)(Ax \cdot Mx)$$

It will be noted that the symbolic version is entirely unambiguous, and exhibits clearly the crucial fact that *whales* appears in both premises. The development of criteria for the evaluation of this argument (and others) belongs to a later stage of discussion.

There is a critical point of contrast between the symbolic representations of general and particular propositions: The symbol for a general proposition employs a *conditional* form, whereas the symbol for a particular proposition employs a *conjunctive* form. It is easy to confuse these, and it is instructive to see what happens if the roles are reversed. Given the statement "Some apples are red," we should symbolize with $(\exists x)(Ax \cdot Rx)$; that is, there is an x (at least one) that is an apple and is red. Suppose one symbolized the same statement as $(\exists x)(Ax \supset Rx)$? Would this do equal justice to the meaning?

The answer to this query is emphatically in the negative. For $(\exists x)$ $(Ax \supset Rx)$ is an abbreviation of

$$(Ax_1 \supset Rx_1) \text{ v } (Ax_2 \supset Rx_2) \text{ v } \ldots \text{ v } (Ax_n \supset Rx_n)$$

and this proposition would be true if there were *one* object that was not an apple.[33] Yet the statement "Some apples are red" can hardly follow from the fact that there are other things in the world besides apples. This shows that $(\exists x)(Ax \supset Rx)$ is an incorrect translation.

On the other hand, take the statement "All apples are red." Our way of translating this is to write (x) $(Ax \supset Rx)$. Suppose one tried to effect the same result by writing $(x)(Ax \cdot Rx)$. In unabbreviated form, this is

$$(Ax_1 \cdot Rx_1) \cdot (Ax_2 \cdot Rx_2) \cdot \ldots \cdot (Ax_n \cdot Rx_n),$$

which implies that every object is an apple (also that every object is red). But "All apples are red" does not imply that everything is an apple. This shows that $(x)(Ax \cdot Rx)$ is an improper translation.

To summarize, singular propositions of the form "*a is an F*" may be symbolized Fa; general propositions of the form "All F's are G" may be symbolized $(x)(Fx \supset Gx)$; particular propositions of the form "Some F's are G" may be symbolized $(\exists x)(Fx \cdot Gx)$. There are to be sure other forms of singular, general, and particular propositions; in

---

[33]Suppose x_1 is not an apple; then Ax_1 is false, and $(Ax_1 \supset Rx_1)$ is true; this suffices to make the entire chain disjunction true.

the following section we will show how some of them yield to similar methods of symbolization.

To facilitate further discussion of these symbols we require a technical vocabulary for referring to their parts. The lower case letters a, b, x_1, x_2, and x are *individual letters*; all but the last are *individual constants*, and the last is an *individual variable*. Upper case letters are called *predicate letters*, and are usually used as constants rather than variables.[34] In the symbol for a universal proposition, $(x)(Fx \supset Gx)$, the part (x) is called a *universal quantifier* because it signifies that what follows is meant to hold for all x's. The expression following the quantifier, $(Fx \supset Gx)$, is not exactly a proposition: It may be rendered in words as "if x is an F then x is a G," which lacks precise meaning because the x has a deliberately unspecified significance; hence, we call the part $(Fx \supset Gx)$ an *open proposition*. In the symbol for a particular proposition, $(\exists x)(Fx \cdot Gx)$, the part $(\exists x)$ is called an *existential quantifier* because its verbal equivalent "there is an x such that" asserts the existence of something. The expression following the quantifier, $(Fx \cdot Gx)$, is again an open proposition. Because particular propositions are characteristically symbolized with existential quantifiers, they are also called *existential propositions*.

We shall find that it is often desirable to consider expressions such as Fx, $Fx \supset Gx$, $Fx \cdot Gx$ and $\sim Fx \vee Gx$ alone, without preceding quantifiers, and with the understanding that the x's are variables, not constants. These may all be understood as open propositions; they are roughly equivalent to English expressions employing indefinite pronouns, such as "it is friendly," or "if it is friendly then it is good," and so on. Like their symbolic counterparts these verbal statements have no definite significance and are not strictly speaking propositions. Because we will often need to use the cumbersome phrase "open proposition," we shall also use the artificial term *prop* as a synonym. This device emphasizes the fact that a prop (that is, an open proposition) is an incomplete proposition.[35]

---

[34]The terms *predicate* and *property* are frequently used interchangeably without causing confusion, although strictly speaking a predicate is a symbolic entity denoting a property.

[35]What are here termed *open propositions*, or *props*, are often called *propositional functions* or *sentential functions*, because the significance and truth-value of the relevant expressions are functions of whatever constants are put for the vari-

Exercises

1. Using the given dictionary, write symbolic translations for the following propositions. Where there are both abbreviated and unabbreviated possibilities, give both.

H: man
M: mortal
A: animal
E: Englishman
S: serious
G: grave
h: Herbert

a. Some men are mortal.

b. Some men are animals.

c. Some animals are mortal.

d. All Englishmen are serious.

e. Some Englishmen are serious.

f. Herbert is serious.

g. Herbert is an Englishman.

h. Herbert is a serious Englishman.

i. It is serious.

j. It is serious and it is grave.

k. There is something that is both serious and grave.

l. If it is serious, then it is grave.

m. It is true of anything that if it is serious then it is grave.

n. All serious things are grave.

---

ables; this terminology is also attractive because of its evident analogy with mathematics. We have not employed the function terminology in the sequel on the ground that the mathematical analogy may be more confusing than illuminating, whereas the term *open proposition* practically compels attention to the logical significance of the expressions in question.

2. Using the dictionary of Exercise 1, translate the following into ordinary English:

   a. $(\exists x)(Ex \cdot Mx)$

   b. $(\exists x)(Mx \cdot Sx)$

   c. $(\exists x)(Ex \cdot Ax)$

   d. $(\exists x)(Ax \cdot Ex)$

   e. Mh

   f. $Mh \cdot Hh$

   g. Ax

 *h. $(\exists x)(Ax \supset Mx)$

   i. $(x)(Ax \cdot Mx)$

 *j. $\sim[(\exists x)(Hx \cdot Mx)]$

3. Using the dictionary supplied and unabbreviated symbols, construct formal proofs for the following arguments:

   H: man
   M: mortal
   x_1: Socrates

   a. Socrates is a man and Socrates is mortal. Therefore, some men are mortal.

   b. All men are mortal. Socrates is a man. Therefore, some men are mortal.

3 • EXTENSIONS OF THE METHOD

In this section we shall show through illustrations how the symbolizing techniques of the first two sections can be extended to cover a variety of similar but distinct forms. The quantifiers are always to be understood as abbreviations for serial conjunctions (universal) or disjunctions (existential), as in the earlier examples. It is desirable to cultivate the habit of passing (in the mind) directly from English expressions to *abbreviated* symbolic representations. In some of the examples offered here, more than one symbolic translation is given;

the appropriate response to such alternatives at this stage is to inspect the symbols in detail and persuade oneself that the alternatives given are equally correct; techniques for *demonstrating* the equivalences will be studied later.

I. We have dealt heretofore only with affirmative propositions. Evidently we can employ our usual sign for negation wherever it will help to exhibit logical structures. In the simplest instance, we can write $\sim Fa$ for "Abraham is not foolish." In a more complex vein, "No apples are red" can be translated $(x)(Ax \supset \sim Rx)$. "Some apples are not red" becomes $(\exists x)(Ax \cdot \sim Rx)$. Other examples are

No men are mortal.	$(x)(Hx \supset \sim Mx)$
Some men are not mortal.	$(\exists x)(Hx \cdot \sim Mx)$
All men are immortal.	$(x)(Hx \supset \sim Mx)$
Not all men are mortal.	$\sim[(x)(Hx \supset Mx)]$ or
	$(\exists x)(Hx \cdot \sim Mx)$
Everything not an animal is unconscious.	$(x)(\sim Ax \supset \sim Cx)$
No animals are unconscious.	$(x)(Ax \supset \sim\sim Cx)$ or
	$(x)(Ax \supset Cx)$
Some things that are not animals are not mortal.	$(\exists x)(\sim Ax \cdot \sim Mx)$
Some animals are not immortal.	$(\exists x)(Ax \cdot \sim\sim Mx)$ or
	$(\exists x)(Ax \cdot Mx)$

II. Occasionally we find general and particular propositions containing only one term suitable for translation into a predicate letter, such as "Everything is good," or "Something is good." These may be translated as $(x)Gx$ and $(\exists x)(Gx)$, respectively. It is understood that, in accordance with what is now our general practice, the x's stand for any objects whatsoever.[36] Other examples are

Everything is material.	$(x)Mx$
Something is material.	$(\exists x)Mx$
Nothing is good.	$(x)(\sim Gx)$ or
	$\sim[(\exists x)Gx]$
Something is not good.	$(\exists x)(\sim Gx)$
Not everything is good.	$\sim[(x)Gx]$ or
	$(\exists x)(\sim Gx)$

---

[36]Or perhaps any physical objects, depending on the relevant context.

III. Some propositions are appropriately symbolized with the aid of connectives, or combinations of connectives, not heretofore employed for this purpose. Examples are

Everything is good or bad.	$(x)(Gx \text{ v } Bx)$
Something is good or bad.	$(\exists x)(Gx \text{ v } Bx)$
Nothing is good or bad.	$\sim[(\exists x)(Gx \text{ v } Bx)]$ or
	$(x)[\sim(Gx \text{ v } Bx)]$
Everything is desirable and precious.	$(x)(Dx \cdot Px)$
Anything is perfect if and only if it is not earthly.	$(x)(Px \equiv \sim Ex)$

IV. Many propositions contain three or more terms that can be singled out for symbolic treatment. For example, we earlier translated "Some marine animals are whales" as $(\exists x)(Ax \cdot Wx)$, taking W for whale and A for marine animal. We could, however, refine this by taking W for whale as before, M for marine, and A for animal (simply). Then we would have, for the same English expression, $(\exists x)$ $(Mx \cdot Ax \cdot Wx)$. Other examples are

All rich men are virtuous.	$(x)[(Rx \cdot Mx) \supset Vx]$
Some rich men are virtuous.	$(\exists x)(Rx \cdot Mx \cdot Vx)$
Some men are neither rich nor virtuous.	$(\exists x)(Mx \cdot \sim Rx \cdot \sim Vx)$
All men are virtuous and rich.	$(x)[Mx \supset (Vx \cdot Rx)]$
Not all men are virtuous and rich.	$\sim\{(x)[Mx \supset (Vx \cdot Rx)]\}$ or
	$(\exists x)[Mx \cdot (\sim Vx \text{ v } \sim Rx)]$
No rich men are virtuous.	$(x)[(Rx \cdot Mx) \supset \sim Vx]$ or
	$\sim[(\exists x)(Rx \cdot Mx \cdot Vx)]$
Some men who are not rich are not virtuous.	$(\exists x)(Mx \cdot \sim Rx \cdot \sim Vx)$
All wealthy Turks are honest if they are self-educated.	$(x)[(Wx \cdot Tx) \supset (Sx \supset Hx)]$
Oranges and grapefruits are fruits.	$(x)[(Ox \text{ v } Gx) \supset Fx]$
Oranges and grapefruits are citrus fruits.	$(x)[(Ox \text{ v } Gx) \supset (Fx \cdot Cx)]$

V. Certain expressions presenting themselves at first glance as singular propositions can be profitably reinterpreted as general or particular types. For instance, "John is faster than everyone" is naturally translated Fj, where F denotes the property of being faster than everyone. However, it is possible to absorb the proper noun John into a predicate and render the sentence as a general proposition in the following way: Let J stand for the property of being slower than John; that is, Jx means John is faster than x. Then "John is faster than everyone" can be symbolized $(x)Jx$. The advantage of this method is that it exhibits more of the logical detail of the proposition's structure. In some contexts such detail may be critical, in some not. Other examples are

John can outrun everyone on the team. (Tx: x is on the team, Jx: John can outrun x)	$(x)(Tx \supset Jx)$
Someone loves Mary. (Lx: x loves Mary)	$(\exists x)Lx$
Harry hates some Republicans from California. (Hx: Harry hates x; R: Republican, C: California)	$(\exists x)(Rx \cdot Cx \cdot Hx)$
Socrates is not smarter than any Greek. (Sx: Socrates is smarter than x)	$(x)(Gx \supset {\sim}Sx)$

In these examples the dictionaries are specified, because the predicates formed are somewhat awkward. Note also the device of indicating the meaning of a cumbersome predicate by writing it along with a variable; for instance,

Jx: John can outrun x

is easier to grasp than

J: outrunnable by John

or some similar circumlocution.

VI. Finally, we add a few words concerning notational practice. It has been our habit to enclose the open proposition that follows a quantifier with parentheses. For example, we write $(x)(Fx \supset Gx)$ and not $(x)Fx \supset Gx$. We shall continue this practice, partly because of the clarity it furnishes, but mainly because it will be needed to avoid confusion at a later stage (where it becomes necessary to employ a multiplicity of quantifiers to symbolize certain propositions). There are two convenient exceptions to this rule:

When the open proposition following a quantifier consists of a single atom, such as Fx, we do not enclose it.[37] For instance, we have been writing $(x)Fx$ rather than $(x)(Fx)$. We will continue this practice. Also, when an open proposition following a quantifier begins with a negation sign we do not enclose it. Thus, instead of writing (x) $[\sim(Fx \vee Gx)]$, we write $(x)\sim(Fx \vee Gx)$; and instead of $(\exists x)(\sim Fx)$ we can write $(\exists x)\sim Fx$. This represents a departure from earlier practice: It greatly facilitates the handling of complicated forms.

One further change in previous practice will be instituted at this point. When negating a proposition that begins with a quantifier (that is, a *quantified* proposition), we have heretofore enclosed the entire expression in brackets, $\sim[(x)(Fx \supset Gx)]$ for the denial of (x) $(Fx \supset Gx)$. Hereafter we shall take it as conventionally understood that a negation sign preceding a quantifier extends over the whole of the quantified proposition. Hence, instead of $\sim[(x)(Fx \supset Gx)]$ we write simply $\sim(x)(Fx \supset Gx)$; and instead of $\sim[(\exists x)(Fx \cdot Gx)]$, simply $\sim(\exists x)(Fx \cdot Gx)$.

Exercises

1. Put the following propositions into symbolic form, using in each case the number of predicate letters indicated.

   a. God exists. (1)

   b. Some horses are not animals. (2)

   c. All Republican senators are conservative. (3)

   d. Republican senators are conservative. (3)

---

[37]The term *atom* is here used in a somewhat different way than earlier, for Fx is strictly not a proposition and hence not an atomic proposition. Yet it is clear enough that Fx is atomic in a sense in which $(Fx \supset Gx)$ is not. To be fussy, we could at this stage define an atom as any proposition *or* open proposition that does not contain truth-functional connectives.

e. Republicans and senators are conservative. (3)

f. All men are good. (2)

g. All men are good unless ignorant. (3)

h. All good men are ignorant. (3)

i. It is not the case that some apples are not red. (2)

j. There are red apples. (2)

k. There are no red apples. (2)

l. Not all bees buzz. (2)

m. No buzzing bees are bothersome. (3)

n. All of the jurors who have read the newspapers are prejudiced. (3)

o. The prejudiced jurors have either read the newspapers or failed to listen to the judge. (4)

p. John can out-think any student in the class. (2)

q. John can out-think every student in the class. (2)

r. John cannot out-think any student in the class. (2)

s. John cannot out-think every student in the class. (2)

t. Molly is adored by some men who find red hair attractive. (2)

u. Molly is adored by some men who find red hair attractive. (3)

v. Molly is adored by all men who find red or blonde hair attractive. (4)

w. Hockey players are small but strong. (3)

x. There are hockey players who are neither small nor strong. (3)

y. Some hockey players are not both small and strong. (3)

z. Not all who are strong but small are hockey players. (3)

2. Which of the following is the correct translation for "Boys and girls are children"?

a. $(x)[(Bx \cdot Gx) \supset Cx]$

b. $(x)[(Bx \text{ v } Gx) \supset Cx]$

*3. Which of the following is the correct translation for "All those who are smart, if they are brave, are desirable"?

    a. $(x)[Sx \supset (Bx \supset Dx)]$

    b. $(x)[(Sx \supset Bx) \supset Dx]$

4. Using the dictionary supplied, state the following in ordinary English.

    C: carnivore
    A: animal
    L: large
    Sx: Sambo can escape x

    a. $(x)[(Cx \cdot Ax) \supset Lx]$

    b. $(x)[Cx \supset (Lx \cdot Ax)]$

    c. $(x)[Ax \supset (Cx \vee \sim Lx)]$

    d. $(x)[(Cx \cdot Ax) \supset \sim Lx]$

    e. $(\exists x)(Lx \cdot Cx \cdot Ax)$

    f. $(\exists x)(Lx \cdot Ax \cdot \sim Cx)$

    g. $(\exists x)(Cx \cdot Ax \cdot \sim Lx)$

    h. $(\exists x)(\sim Cx \cdot Ax \cdot \sim Lx)$

    i. $\sim(x)(Ax \supset Cx)$

    j. $\sim(x)[(Lx \cdot Ax) \supset Cx]$

    k. $\sim(\exists x)(Cx \cdot Ax)$

    l. $\sim(\exists x)(Lx \cdot Ax \cdot Cx)$

*m. $(x) \sim (Ax \cdot \sim Lx)$

*n. $(\exists x) \sim (Lx \vee Ax)$

    o. $(x) \sim Ax$

    p. $(\exists x) \sim Ax$

*q. $\sim(x) \sim Ax$

*r. $\sim(\exists x) \sim Ax$

    s. $(x)(Ax \supset Sx)$

t. $(x)[(Ax \cdot \sim Lx) \supset Sx]$

u. $(\exists x)(Ax \cdot Sx)$

v. $(\exists x)(Ax \cdot \sim Cx \cdot Sx)$

w. $(x)(Ax \supset \sim Sx)$

x. $(x)(\sim Cx \supset Sx)$

y. $(\exists x)(Ax \cdot Lx \cdot \sim Sx)$

z. $(\exists x)(\sim Lx \cdot Ax \cdot Sx)$

*5. Using unabbreviated symbols, determine which of the following pairs are logically equivalent:

a. $\sim(x)Fx$ and $(\exists x) \sim Fx$

b. $(x)(Fx \supset Gx)$ and $(x)(\sim Fx \lor Gx)$

c. $(x)(Fx \cdot Gx)$ and $(\exists x)(Fx \cdot Gx)$

d. $(x)(Fx \supset Gx)$ and $\sim(\exists x)(Fx \cdot \sim Gx)$

4 • Q EQUIVALENCE RULE

Before working out methods for evaluating arguments in which general, particular, and singular propositions appear, it is necessary to study some of the logical relations (equivalence, contradiction, and so on) that obtain between propositions symbolized with quantifiers. In so doing we will develop elementary rules for the transformation of symbols involving quantifiers into *other* symbols (also involving quantifiers) that are logically equivalent.

Consider first the following pair of statements:

All whales are mammals.
Anything not a mammal is not a whale.

It is natural to translate these as follows:

$(x)(Wx \supset Mx)$
$(x)(\sim Mx \supset \sim Wx)$.

It is *intuitively* evident that the original propositions are logically equivalent. Furthermore, the symbolic translations are suspiciously alike, for the two open propositions

$$(Wx \supset Mx) \quad \text{and} \quad (\sim Mx \supset \sim Wx)$$

have the appearance of a pair of truth-functional molecules that are (logically) equivalent by the principle of contraposition. We are thus moved to raise the following conjecture: *Is it possible to manipulate open propositions as if they were genuine propositions, applying all the truth-functional principles developed in Chapter 2?* For if it *is* possible we can conclude at once that $(x)(Wx \supset Mx)$ is equivalent to $(x)(\sim Mx \supset \sim Wx)$, and similarly that $(\exists x)\sim(Fx \cdot Gx)$ is equivalent to $(\exists x)(\sim Fx \vee \sim Gx)$, and so on for countless other pairs. We shall show that the conjecture is justified.

Observe first that a prop can be regarded as a kind of *form* that generates (genuine) propositions when constants are substituted for the variable x. The propositions so generated are naturally called *substitution instances* of the corresponding prop.[38] Examples are

Prop	*Substitution instances*
$(Fx \supset Gx)$	$(Fa \supset Ga)$, $(Fb \supset Gb)$, $(Fx_1 \supset Gx_1)$, $(Fx_2 \supset Gx_2)$, $(Fx_n \supset Gx_n)$, etc.
$(Fx \cdot Gx)$	$(Fa \cdot Ga)$, $(Fb \cdot Gb)$, $(Fs \cdot Gs)$, $(Fx_1 \cdot Gx_1)$, $(Fx_7 \cdot Gx_7)$, $(Fx_n \cdot Gx_n)$, etc.
Fx	Fa, Fb, Ff, Fx_1, Fx_2, Fx_n, etc.
$[(Fx \cdot Gx) \supset Hx]$	$[(Fa \cdot Ga) \supset Ha]$, $[(Fb \cdot Gb) \supset Hb]$, $[(Fx_1 \cdot Gx_1) \supset Hx]$, $[(Fx_5 \cdot Gx_5) \supset Hx_5]$, $[(Fx_n \cdot Gx_n) \supset Hx_n]$, etc.
$\sim(Fx \vee \sim Gx)$	$\sim(Fd \vee \sim Gd)$, $\sim(Fe \vee \sim Ge)$, $\sim(Fx_{12} \vee \sim Gx_{12})$, $\sim(Fx_{23} \vee \sim Gx_{23})$, $\sim(Fx_n \vee \sim Gx_n)$, etc.

It should be noted that a substitution instance is generated by putting the same constant for the x throughout; $(Fa \supset Gb)$ is not a substitution instance of $(Fx \supset Gx)$. Note also that the atoms appearing in one substitution instance of a given prop are entirely distinct from those appearing in every other substitution instance of the same prop. It follows that if one such substitution instance is logically true, so are all the others—likewise if one is contingent or inconsistent.[39]

---

[38]The expression *substitution instance* was also employed in Chapter 1 in a somewhat different (broader) context.

[39]Compare the replacement and restricted replacement theorems of Chapter 3, Section 5.

Now consider a pair of props, Ax and Bx, and assume they are truth-functionally equivalent; that is, assume that when the x's are momentarily treated as constants, Ax and Bx can be seen as logically equivalent by the methods of Chapter 2 or Chapter 3.[40] Then

$$Ax \equiv Bx$$

is logically true, and likewise so are

$$Ax_1 \equiv Bx_1, Ax_2 \equiv Bx_2, \text{ etc.}$$

When we compare the unabbreviated versions of $(x)Ax$ and $(x)Bx$,

$$Ax_1 \cdot Ax_2 \cdot \ldots \cdot Ax_n = (x)Ax,$$
$$Bx_1 \cdot Bx_2 \cdot \ldots \cdot Bx_n = (x)Bx,$$

we see that each A term must always have the same truth-value as its corresponding B term. Therefore $(x)Ax$ and $(x)Bx$ are equivalent.

Conversely, suppose Ax and Bx are *not* equivalent. This means it is possible to assign truth-values to constituent atoms to make Ax true and Bx false, or the reverse (x taken momentarily as a constant). Suppose Ax can be true while Bx is false. Then the same thing holds for Ax_1 and Bx_1, for Ax_2 and Bx_2, and so forth. Turning again to the unabbreviated versions of $(x)Ax$ and $(x)Bx$, we see that truth-values can be so assigned to make every A term true (each one contains different atoms, so no conflicts can emerge between them) and every B term false. This makes $(x)Ax$ true and $(x)Bx$ false and shows that they are also *not* equivalent.

To sum up, propositions of the form $(x)Ax$ and $(x)Bx$ are equivalent *if and only if* Ax and Bx are equivalent. The same holds for $(\exists x)Ax$ and $(\exists x)Bx$; proofs are left as exercises. These results taken together may be called the *equivalence rule for quantified propositions*, or simply the *Q equivalence rule*.

---

[40]Here A and B are predicate variables. Moreover, it is understood that they may stand for *molecular predicates*, that is predicates requiring truth-functional connectives in their complete symbolization. Thus, the complex symbol Ac (A, a variable) is a stand-in for such things as $Fc \supset Gc$, and $Fc \cdot Gc$ (F and G constants). Likewise, the symbol Ax (A, a variable) is a stand-in for such things as $Fx \supset Gx$, and $Fx \cdot Gx$ (F and G constants).

Exercises

1. Show that if any two props Ax and Bx are equivalent (x taken momentarily as a constant), so are $(\exists x)Ax$ and $(\exists x)Bx$.

2. Show that if any two props Ax and Bx are not equivalent (x taken momentarily as a constant), neither are $(\exists x)Ax$ and $(\exists x)Bx$.

3. Determine which of the following pairs are equivalent:

   a. All whales are mammals. All mammals are whales.

   b. No whales are mammals. No mammals are whales.

   c. Some whales are mammals. Some mammals are whales.

   d. Some whales are not mammals. Some mammals are not whales.

   e. All bald men are virile. All virile men are bald.

   f. All apples are red. Everything is either red or not an apple.

   g. All the French are clever and witty. Everything is both clever or not French, and witty or not French.

   h. Some fools are strong but not brave. There is something such that (i) it is not the case that if it is strong then it is brave, and (ii) it is not a fool.

   i. There are some things (that is, at least one) that are plump and juicy, or not ripe. There are some things that are plump or not ripe, and if ripe then juicy.

   j. Everything is either material or not material. All whales are whales.

   k. Some men are not men. Not all whales are whales.

   l. Some men are not men. There is something such that it is not the case that if it is a whale then it is a whale.

   m. Everything is good. Everything is either good or it is black and not black.

   n. Something is corrupt. There is something such that, if it is corrupt then it is large and not large.

4. Suppose two props Ax and Bx are inconsistent but not contradictory, that is, contrary. Are $(x)Ax$ and $(x)Bx$ necessarily contrary? What about $(\exists x)Ax$ and $(\exists x)Bx$?

5. Suppose two props Ax and Bx are contradictory. Are $(x)Ax$ and $(x)Bx$ necessarily contradictory? What about $(\exists x)Ax$ and $(\exists x)Bx$?

5 • CHANGE-OF-QUANTIFIER RULES

We employ two kinds of quantifiers, universal and existential, corresponding to general and particular propositions. It happens that any proposition involving a quantifier of one sort is logically equivalent to some proposition involving the *other* sort of quantifier. The rules embodying this fact are easy to establish. First let us write $(x)Fx$ unabbreviated:

$$(Fx_1 \cdot Fx_2 \cdot \ldots \cdot Fx_n).$$

In virtue of the generalized form of one of our *CC* rules (Chapter 2), this is equivalent to:

$$\sim(\sim Fx_1 \text{ v } \sim Fx_2 \text{ v } \ldots \text{ v } \sim Fx_n).$$

But the part within the parentheses may be abbreviated $(\exists x)\sim Fx$. Hence, we have established that $(x)Fx$ and $\sim(\exists x)\sim Fx$ are equivalent.

Next we show similarly that $\sim(x)Fx$ is equivalent to $(\exists x)\sim Fx$. For the former may be written as

$$\sim(Fx_1 \cdot Fx_2 \cdot \ldots \cdot Fx_n)$$

which, by a generalized *DM* rule, is equivalent to

$$\sim Fx_1 \text{ v } \sim Fx_2 \text{ v } \ldots \text{ v } \sim Fx_n.$$

But this is just $(\exists x)\sim Fx$, which shows what we set out to prove. By similar methods it can be shown that $(\exists x)Fx$ is equivalent to $\sim(x)\sim Fx$, and that $\sim(\exists x)Fx$ is equivalent to $(x)\sim Fx$. Proofs are left as exercises.

In sum, the following four biconditionals are logically true for any prop Fx:

$$(x)Fx \equiv \sim(\exists x)\sim Fx,$$
$$\sim(x)Fx \equiv (\exists x)\sim Fx,$$
$$(\exists x)Fx \equiv \sim(x)\sim Fx,$$
$$\sim(\exists x)Fx \equiv (x)\sim Fx.$$

These are called, collectively, the *change-of-quantifier rules*, or *Q rules*. They are used so often that it is desirable to have a mnemonic device to facilitate their employment. The following may be helpful.

> To change a quantified proposition into a logically equivalent expression employing a different quantifier, carry out these steps: (i) If there is a negation sign directly to the left of the quantifier, drop it; if not, put one in. (ii) Change the quantifier, from universal to existential or conversely, as required. (iii) If there is a negation sign directly to the right of the quantifier extending over the whole of the prop, drop it; if not, put one in.

Inspection of the Q rules will show that these three steps will always effect the desired change, with a logically equivalent result.

The Q rules and Q equivalence rule together permit us to test any pair of quantified propositions (of the types so far discussed) to see if the propositions are equivalent. We have seen that pairs of the form

$$(x)Fx \quad \text{and} \quad (x)Gx, \quad \text{or}$$
$$(\exists x)Fx \quad \text{and} \quad (\exists x)Gx,$$

are equivalent if and only if their props are equivalent. With the Q rules we can treat pairs such as

$$(x)Fx \quad \text{and} \quad \sim(\exists x)Gx, \quad \text{or}$$
$$\sim(x)Fx \quad \text{and} \quad (\exists x)Gx,$$

by applying a Q rule to the negated member of the pair and then proceeding as before. For instance, $(x)(Fx \supset Gx)$ and $\sim(\exists x)(Fx \cdot Gx)$ can be shown *not* to be equivalent by transforming the second into $(x)\sim(Fx \cdot Gx)$ and then observing that $(Fx \supset Gx)$ and $\sim(Fx \cdot Gx)$ are not equivalent.

Obviously, pairs such as

$$\sim(x)Fx \quad \text{and} \quad \sim(x)Gx, \quad \text{or}$$
$$\sim(\exists x)Fx \quad \text{and} \quad \sim(\exists x)Gx,$$

are equivalent if and only if they are also equivalent when the initial negation signs are erased, and the analysis can then be treated as in the preceding example. The remaining possibilities are pairs of the form

$$(x)Fx \quad \text{and} \ (\exists x)Gx, \qquad \text{or, equivalently,}$$
$$\sim(x)Fx \quad \text{and} \quad \sim(\exists x)Gx.$$

Such pairs are very rarely equivalent; in fact, it can be shown by scrutiny of the unabbreviated forms that they are equivalent if and only if both members of the pair are logically true or logically false.[41] We leave this proof as an exercise.

Finally, two propositions are contradictory if and only if the denial of either is equivalent to the other; hence, we can also test any pair for contradictoriness.

Exercises

1. Show by an appeal to unabbreviated forms that $(\exists x)Fx$ and $\sim(x) \sim Fx$ are logically equivalent. In the same way show that $\sim(\exists x)Fx$ and $(x) \sim Fx$ are equivalent.

2. Show that $\sim(x)(Sx \supset \sim Px)$ and $(\exists x)(Sx \cdot Px)$ are logical equivalents.

3. Translate into symbols, "Not all apples are not red."

4. Determine which of the following pairs are equivalent, which contradictory, and which neither.

   a. All senators are idiots. There is no senator who is not an idiot.

   b. Any violet is blue. No violets are not blue.

   c. All animals are warm-blooded if they are vertebrates. It is not true that there is a vertebrate animal that is not warm-blooded.

   d. Some Democrats are Communists. Everything is either a non-Communist or a non-Democrat.

   e. No roses are red. Not all roses are red.

   f. Not all swans are not white. Some swans are white.

   g. Not all swans are not white. Everything white is other-than-a-swan.

   h. There is something that does not have the property that, if it is not physical, then it is either illusory or mental. Everything is mental unless it is illusory or physical.

---

[41]Also, a particular and a general proposition with equivalent props are equivalent if there is only one object in the world, for then the quantifiers make no difference. As this is a logically conceivable circumstance, it must be noted that we generally assume that the number of objects x_1, x_2, and so on, although finite, is very large.

   i.   All bald men are virile. Some virile men are bald.

   j.   All honest politicians are wealthy. Some poor politicians are honest.

   k.   All red or pink apples are ripe. There are no apples that are either not ripe and red or not ripe and pink.

   l.   Some brave and strong men are noble. All brave men are strong or not noble.

   m.   Some strong and noble men are brave. Every brave man is either strong or noble.

   n.   Some brave and noble men are strong. It is not the case that all noble men are neither brave nor strong.

   o.   John can out-talk anyone on the block. There is someone on the block whom John can out-talk.

   p.   John can out-talk anyone on the block. There is someone on the block whom John cannot out-talk.

   q.   John cannot out-talk anyone on the block. Anyone whom John can out-talk is not on the block.

   r.   John can out-talk any girl in his class. Any girl whom John cannot out-talk is not in his class.

5. Show that a proposition of the form $(x)Fx$, where Fx is any prop, is logically true or false if and only if Fx is logically true or false. Show the same for a proposition of the form $(\exists x)Fx$.

6. Assuming there are at least two objects x_1, x_2, and so on, in the world, show that a pair of propositions of the form $(x)Fx$ and $(\exists x)Gx$ is equivalent if and only if both propositions are logically true or logically false.

6 • SQUARE OF OPPOSITION

To illustrate the employment of the analytical methods we have so far worked out, we shall scrutinize in detail the logical relations between four simple types of propositions, types that occur so frequently that they have at times been taken as the fundamental forms of expression requiring logical treatment. They are

All S are P.	(e.g., All apples are red.)
Some S are P.	(e.g., Some apples are red.)
No S are P.	(e.g., No apples are red.)
Some S are not P.	(e.g., Some apples are not red.)

As the first two forms are affirmative, they have been labeled A and I propositions, respectively (from the first two vowels in the Latin word *affirmo—I* affirm).[42] The next two, being negative in style, are labeled E and O propositions, respectively (from the vowels in the Latin word *nego—I* deny). It is convenient to arrange the four expressions in a square, called the *traditional square of opposition*, with universals at the top, particulars at the bottom, affirmatives to the left, and negatives to the right. In the square shown here we add the appropriate symbolic translations:

A	*E*
All S are P.	No S are P.
$(x)(Sx \supset Px)$	$(x)(Sx \supset \sim Px)$
I	*O*
Some S are P.	Some S are not P.
$(\exists x)(Sx \cdot Px)$	$(\exists x)(Sx \cdot \sim Px)$

Suppose we wish to contradict an A proposition. Under the Q rules we see that $\sim(x)(Sx \supset Px)$ is equivalent to $(\exists x)\sim(Sx \supset Px)$. In virtue of the fundamental equivalence rule for quantifiers, this in turn is equivalent to $(\exists x)(Sx \cdot \sim Px)$. Thus, it turns out that an O proposition is the contradictory of a corresponding A proposition. (*Corresponding* here means having the same predicate letters in the same order; or in terms of the grammatical structure of the English expressions, it means having the same subject and predicate.) Hence to deny that all apples are red, one must assert—or show—that some apples are not red. This is in harmony with our intuitive sense of the logic of general propositions. For in order to refute a general proposition of the form "All S are P" we ordinarily search for a counterexample: An S that is not a P. But to produce such an S is, in effect, to establish the proposition "Some S are not P."

Also, we can now see that the expression "Not all apples are red," which is naturally and properly translated as the denial of an A proposition, is equivalent to the O proposition "Some apples are not red." In general, we may now say that "Not all S are P" is an alternative rendering of "Some S are not P."

---

[42] These labels, and the ones that follow, derive from a medieval tradition. Also, it should be clear that the A and I propositions are called affirmative in virtue of their mode of expression in ordinary language; for symbolically any affirmative proposition P is equivalent to some negative proposition $\sim\sim P$.

Just as the A and O propositions, which occupy diagonally opposite corners, are contradictory, so also are the diagonally opposite E and I propositions. Proof of this is left as an exercise. Aside from the contradictions that hold along the two diagonals of the square, other logical relations obtain between adjacent corners. We enumerate them one by one:

I. Under ordinary circumstances corresponding A and E propositions are contraries, for they cannot both be true but might both be false. It is obvious that they can both be false, for if some S's are P and some are not, then "All S are P" and "No S are P" are both false. To see that one of them *must* be false we write them symbolically in full:

A: $(Sx_1 \supset Px_1) \cdot (Sx_2 \supset Px_2) \cdot \ldots \cdot (Sx_n \supset Px_n)$.
E: $(Sx_1 \supset \sim Px_1) \cdot (Sx_2 \supset \sim Px_2) \cdot \ldots \cdot (Sx_n \supset \sim Px_n)$.

Under ordinary circumstances there will be some object (at least one) that has the property S: Indeed this is what we *mean* by ordinary circumstances. Suppose it is x_1 that has the property S. In this case the atom Sx_1 is true, and one of the two conditionals, $(Sx_1 \supset Px_1)$ or $(Sx_1 \supset \sim Px_1)$, must be false. Whichever one it is, it suffices to make the entire proposition in which it appears false. Hence, A or E must be false, provided there is at least one object that has the property S.

But suppose nothing has the property S; suppose, that is, that the *class* of things that are S's is *empty*. Then every atom $Sx_1, Sx_2, \ldots$ Sx_n will be false, and every conjunct in A and E will be true (because every conjunct will be a conditional with a false antecedent). Then A and E are both true. Thus, the relation of contrariety that ordinarily holds between A and E fails if the grammatical subject of the propositions does not exist.

This result can be extended to other cases, for it now appears that any general proposition ascribing properties to a class of objects having no members is true. For an assertion about all objects having the property F will take the form $(x)(Fx \supset \ldots)$, or

$(Fx_1 \supset \ldots) \cdot (Fx_2 \supset \ldots) \cdot \ldots \cdot (Fx_n \supset \ldots)$.

And if there are no F's, every antecedent will be false, every conditional true, and the whole proposition true. Thus, it is true that all the twentieth-century kings of France are handsome, and it is equally true that none of them is. (This discovery may be at first bewildering. It is discussed at length in the following section.)

II. It may be shown that under ordinary circumstances (that is, when there are some S's) the I and O propositions are subcontraries: They cannot both be false, and they might both be true. Under the unusual circmstance that there is nothing that is an S, then both would be false. Proofs are left as exercises.

III. If all apples are red, would it follow that some apples are? The answer is yes, assuming that there are apples at all. That is, under ordinary circumstances the A proposition logically implies the corresponding I proposition. For the A proposition we have

$$(Sx_1 \supset Px_1) \cdot (Sx_2 \supset Px_2) \cdot \ldots \cdot (Sx_n \supset Px_n).$$

Assuming at least one thing is an S, suppose it is x_1. Then we have the ingredients for a *modus ponens* argument:

$$\frac{\begin{array}{l} Sx_1 \supset Px_1 \\ Sx_1 \end{array}}{Px_1}$$

Then x_1 is an S and also a P; by *Conj* we can assert $(Sx_1 \cdot Px_1)$. And thence by addition it follows that

$$(Sx_1 \cdot Px_1) \lor (Sx_2 \cdot Px_2) \lor \cdots \lor (Sx_n \cdot Px_n).$$

But this is the corresponding I proposition.

In case there are no S's this argument fails to hold. Also, in that case, the A proposition is true and the corresponding I clearly false, so no relation of implication obtains.

IV. As with the relation between A and I, the E proposition implies the corresponding O, provided there are S's. If not, the implication does not hold. Proofs are left as exercises.

It is desirable to emphasize that the relation of contradiction that holds between the diagonally opposite corners of the square is independent of the existence or nonexistence of classes of objects; and it is this relation that is the single most important logical fact exhibited in the square.

Exercises

1. Show that corresponding I and O propositions are ordinarily subcontraries. Also show why the relation fails if the subject of the propositions is an empty class.

2. Show that an E proposition ordinarily implies the corresponding O proposition. Also show why the relation fails if the subject of the propositions is an empty class.

3. Show that corresponding A and O propositions are contradictory, whether or not their subject is an empty class. Show the same for corresponding E and I propositions.

4. Definition: A proposition is *converted* when its grammatical subject and predicate are interchanged. Which propositions in the square of opposition can be converted without change of meaning (that is, with a logically equivalent result)?

7 • VACUOUS TRUTHS

We have seen in Section 6 that statements ascribing some property to all members of a nonexistent class are true; such statements are conveniently termed *vacuous truths*. The word *vacuous* has a double significance in this context: A vacuous truth is about a vacuous or empty class of objects; also, it is of no importance for most purposes, because if one says truly that every member of an empty class has property F, it is just as true to say that none of them has property F. Because this last feature is a frequent cause of perplexity, the present section is devoted to a more detailed examination of statements about empty classes.

We do not often (knowingly) say things about empty classes, other than to say that they are empty. And *that* kind of statement, along with its denial, can be made and analyzed without any perplexity. For instance, suppose we wish to say (truly, as it happens), "There are no twentieth-century French kings." This goes naturally into symbols as $\sim(\exists x)Kx$ where K is for twentieth-century French kings; it is equivalent to $(x)\sim Kx$, and in unabbreviated form we have:

$$\sim Kx_1 \cdot \sim Kx_2 \cdot \ldots \cdot \sim Kx_n.$$

Given our factual knowledge that no object is a twentieth-century French king, every conjunct in the series is true, and the entire proposition is true. Next, we may wish to say (wrongly), "There *are* twentieth-century French kings." In symbols we get $(\exists x)Kx$, or

$$Kx_1 \text{ v } Kx_2 \text{ v } \ldots \text{ v } Kx_n.$$

Every disjunct is false, and the entire proposition is false. These results accord with our intuitive expectations.

The significance of the examples lies in the fact that the first, "There are no twentieth-century French kings," may in a way be regarded as a general assertion about an empty class. This would emerge more clearly if we phrased it as, "No twentieth-century French kings exist." Yet we do not think of this as a vacuous truth, but as a significant and important (true) statement. In fact we are not obliged to regard it as vacuous, and ought not to do so, for when its logical structure is exhibited in symbols it lacks the form of a string of conditionals, which is precisely the feature that makes most other assertions about empty classes vacuously true. Hence, we are moved to say: *All general assertions about empty classes are true, including the the bare assertion that the class is empty.* (As we have seen, the assertion that an empty class is *not* empty is a particular proposition.) Furthermore, *those general propositions that ascribe to an empty class some property other than the bare fact of nonexistence are vacuously true.* Clearly, vacuous truth is not a purely logical property, for we cannot tell merely by inspection of the form of a proposition whether or not it is vacuously true; that determination depends on factual knowledge about the existence or nonexistence of certain sorts of objects.

There remains a residue of difficulty.[43] Consider the following propositions:

(i) All twentieth-century French kings hunt.
(ii) No twentieth-century French kings hunt.
(iii) No twentieth-century French kings exist.

---

[43]The discussion that begins here and runs to the end of this section may be omitted without loss of continuity. But the problems it treats are likely to arise sooner or later for anyone who tries to use the symbolism in a wide variety of contexts. Hence, a cursory reading at least is recommended.

In symbols, the first two are

    (i) $(x)(Kx \supset Hx)$.
    (ii) $(x)(Kx \supset {\sim}Hx)$.

Evidently these are vacuously true, because every atom of the form Kx_1, Kx_2, and so on, is false. Indeed (i) and (ii) illustrate the most prominent and significant feature of vacuous truths, which is that corresponding A and E propositions, ordinarily contrary, are in this case both true. It may now be tempting to translate (iii) in the same way, as $(x)(Kx \supset {\sim}Ex)$, where Ex means x exists. But then we seem to be saying that (iii) is also vacuously true, because its constituent conditionals,

$$(Kx_1 \supset {\sim}Ex_1) \cdot (Kx_2 \supset {\sim}Ex_2) \cdot \ldots \cdot (Kx_n \supset {\sim}Ex_n)$$

all contain false antecedents:—a peculiar situation to say the least, because the circumstance that all those antecedents are false is just what (iii) itself says, reflecting the fact that (iii) is *not* a vacuous truth but a very significant one.

To make matters worse, if we take (iii) as a kind of E proposition, we are then moved to form a corresponding A statement:

    (iv) All twentieth-century French kings exist.

It is hard to imagine precisely what this means. And if, in analogy with (iii), we put it into symbols as $(x)(Kx \supset Ex)$, we must conclude at once that it is (vacuously) true, a conclusion that is logically impeccable but surely awkward.

These and many other difficulties along the same lines are avoided if we adopt the practice of capturing the notion of existence through quantifiers rather than through predicate letters. Then (iii) is translated ${\sim}(\exists x)Kx$, or $(x){\sim}Kx$; it is then *not* an E proposition, does not belong in the square of opposition at all, is not *vacuously* true, and no difficulties arise in regard to it.

There remains a puzzle about (iv), a puzzle that can be solved or side-stepped only by reference to philosophical considerations. The expression (iv) has the form "All F's exist." If the concept of existence is a simple and unambiguous notion, there could be no occasion for saying such a thing. For given some phrase describing a class of objects, such as "having the property F," there are only two possibilities: Either there *are* objects having the property F, or not. The first possibility is expressed as "There are F's" or "Some F's exist"; the second possibility is expressed as "There are no F's or "No F's exist." In neither case is there any point in saying "All F's exist," nor is there any clear meaning that could be attached to that expression not already contained in the statement "There are F's" (that is, "Some F's exist").

On the other hand, there *are* cases in which one may want to make statements of the form "All F's exist"; for instance, "Everything I clearly conceive exists." But such cases arise only in contexts where there are two or more senses of existence; thus, in the example, "things I clearly conceive" might be regarded as having an existence in the mind, and the statement that "things I clearly conceive also *exist*" would probably mean that they exist outside the mind as well, giving a double sense to the word. Whether or not there *are* two permissible senses of existence is not relevant here: The fact is that only under such conditions is it reasonable to utter a proposition of the form "All F's exist," intending thereby to signify something different from what is meant by "Some F's exist."

The analysis and evaluation of philosophical arguments concerning existence—the meaning of the concept or the proper uses of the term—lie quite beyond the scope of this text. The concept has entered into our symbolism as an auxiliary notion, via the existential quantifier, introduced in order to facilitate the analysis of particular propositions. Hence, the symbolism is suited primarily for situations where philosophical issues about the nature of existence are not relevant, that is, situations where existence can be thought of in a simple and unambiguous way without loss of precision or meaning. Most contexts of argument are of course of this sort. Our symbolic techniques may or may not be helpful in the analysis of arguments of the other sort, arguments that are about, or play on the ambiguities in, the notion of existence; certainly they can be used in such contexts only with the greatest care.

Meanwhile, we shall assume that the arguments and propositions that fall under our scrutiny do not entail such complexities; and to avoid the needless introduction of irrelevant puzzles we will avoid forming props of the type Ex (x exists). Instead, we shall symbolize the notion of existence, wherever possible, with the aid of quantifiers. And expressions of the form "All twentieth-century French kings exist," and others of its ilk, we shall set aside as meaningless— not really propositions at all.

Observe that if "All K's exist" were accepted as a proposition, its contradictory would be "Some K's do not exist," or "There *is* at least one K that does *not* exist." On the face of it this seems as meaningless as the other. We adopt the view that in ordinary contexts (that is, where existence has a simple meaning) *neither* is a proposition.[44] In this respect they are to be treated like the expression, "Duplicity runs twelve," which is grammatically impeccable but does not appear to be a meaningful expression.[45]

To summarize this digression, we have adopted the following principles: (1) Any general proposition about an empty class is true. (2) Any general proposition about an empty class other than the proposition that expresses the fact that it is empty is vacuously true. (3) Any expression of the form "All F's exist" or "Some F's do not exist" is rejected as meaningless, unless it appears in a context that admits of more than one sense of existence. (4) Wherever possible the notion of existence will be symbolized through quantifiers rather than predicate letters.

Exercises

1. Suppose the entire universe contains just three objects, a, b, and c. Starting with the premise "There are no unicorns," construct a formal proof getting

---

[44] Compare G. E. Moore, "Is Existence a Predicate?" in his *Philosophical Papers* (London: George Allen & Unwin, Ltd., 1959), pp. 115–126. This essay first appeared in *Aristotelian Society, Supplementary Vol. XV*, 1936.

[45] The idea of rejecting an expression as meaningless cannot be extended to other general statements about empty classes. In the first place we reject "All F's exist" by inspection of its form, independently of the question of whether or not there are F's. In contrast, the expressions "All F's are G" and "No F's are G" do not even become puzzling until *after* the discovery that there are no F's (if indeed there are none). It is quite foreign to our conception of logical form to suppose that a statement that is apparently meaningful and that has to be true or false can be made meaningless by *factual* discoveries. Furthermore, the contradictories of "All F's are G" and "No F's are G" are, respectively, "There is an F that is not G" and "There is an F that is G." Whether of not there are F's, these (particular) propositions are quite meaningful and no perplexity arises in their interpretation. If we rejected the corresponding general statements we should have to say that the denials of certain particular propositions with clear significance are meaningless—which is evidently intolerable.

to the conclusion "All unicorns are black." Next, starting with the same premise, construct a formal proof getting to the conclusion "No unicorns are black."

2. Suppose the entire universe contains just three objects, a, b, and c. Starting with the premises "All unicorns are black" and "No unicorns are black," construct a formal proof getting to the conclusion "There are no unicorns."

3. A philosopher argues:

Everything I clearly conceive exists.
I clearly conceive x_1.
Therefore, there *exists* something I clearly conceive.

A logician objects that the argument is silly, because it would be valid without the first premise. The philosopher disagrees. What is the difficulty?

8 • FURTHER EXTENSIONS; Q DISTRIBUTION RULES

In this section we shall refine and extend the use of our symbolism in exhibiting the structure of various propositions. We shall then be ready for (indeed we shall hardly be able to avoid) the rapid development of a decision procedure for the evaluation of arguments whose constituent propositions are among the types so far discussed.

As a general principle it must be observed that no mechanical rules will suffice for the symbolic analysis of English expressions. Often different words and phrases are obviously translated the same way, and sometimes the same words or phrases, appearing in different contexts, require a different interpretation.

Notorious in this regard are the words *any* and *every*. The following propositions, for example, are all identical in meaning:

All men are animals.
Any man is an animal.
Every man is an animal.

Here *any* and *every* are precisely alike in significance, both being synonymous with *all*. Yet, if we change things slightly,

Not all men are animals.
Not any man is an animal.
Not every man is an animal.

the situation with regard to *any* and *every* also changes; for the first and third of these propositions are still equivalent and can be translated $(\exists x)(Mx \cdot \sim Ax)$, but the second is $(x)(Mx \supset \sim Ax)$.

The same shift can occur in other ways. The sentences

> Mary can recite any poem in the book.
> Mary can recite every poem in the book.

mean the same, and can be given as $(x)(Px \supset Mx)$ with obvious symbols. But

> Mary cannot recite any poem in the book.
> Mary cannot recite every poem in the book.

differ; the first is $(x)(Px \supset \sim Mx)$, and the other is $(\exists x)(Px \cdot \sim Mx)$. Again, we see that where *any* and *every* are alike in an affirmative context, their meanings diverge when used negatively.

With this general principle (that is, that context rules) in mind, we can employ the symbolism for some forms of expression that have not been discussed. For instance,

> (i) Only the brave deserve the fair.

This does not mean "All the brave deserve the fair"; for it might be the case that "Only the brave deserve the fair—and not even all of them." Rather, (i) seems to mean

> (ii) There are no persons deserving of the fair who are not brave.

In symbols, this is $\sim(\exists x)(Dx \cdot \sim Bx)$, or $(x)(Dx \supset Bx)$. Thus, "Only the brave deserve the fair" turns out to be equivalent to "All who deserve the fair are brave." We can diagram the relation between the phrase "only the brave" and the symbolic version of the sentence:

Only the brave deserve the fair.

$(x)(Dx \supset Bx).$

We see that the part of the sentence that follows the *only* appears in the symbolized version as the consequent of a conditional: This is exactly in accord with the behavior of the truth-functional phrase *only if*. Other propositions of the form "Only *F*'s are *G*" (so-called *exclusive* propositions) can be similarly rendered as $(x)(Gx \supset Fx)$.

Somewhat more complicated are expressions that hinge on the word *except* or some equivalent (sometimes called *exceptive* propositions). For example:

All except the brave are suspect.
All Scotsmen are clever except the lowlanders.

In the first case, the statement evidently means that any person not brave is suspect, and also any person who *is* brave is *not* suspect. That is, anyone is suspect if and only if he is not brave. This leads to the following translation:

$(x)(Sx \equiv {\sim}Bx)$.

The other example is treated similarly, for it seems to mean that any Scotsman is clever if and only if he is not a lowlander, hence:

$(x)[Sx \supset (Cx \equiv {\sim}Lx)]$.

In general we may approximate to the meaning of *except* with the awkward phrase *if and only if not*. In view of the fact that $(P \equiv {\sim}Q)$ is equivalent to $(P \triangledown Q)$, the translations can be given in somewhat shorter form with the aid of the exclusive disjunction sign; but then it is hard to formulate a verbal equivalent for *except* that would lead directly to the appropriate translation.

The word *but*, which we have already seen as a connective meaning *and*, often serves as a synonym for *except*, as in "All but the brave are suspect." The phrase *none but* evidently means *only*, as in "None but the brave deserve the fair."

We can now also form or analyze expressions in which quantified statements are joined with truth-functional connectives. For example:

Everything is physical or nothing is colored.
If all men are mortal then no man is safe.

These are clearly symbolized as

$(x)Px \vee {\sim}(\exists x)Cx$.
$(x)(Hx \supset Mx) \supset (x)(Hx \supset {\sim}Sx)$.

Other cases can be handled similarly.

In this connection, there are two principles of great usefulness in the evaluation of arguments. First, the propositions

Everything is material and palpable.
Everything is material and everything is palpable.

appear to be equivalent, and appearances in this case do not deceive. In fact, any two propositions of the form $(x)(Fx \cdot Gx)$ and $(x)Fx \cdot (x)Gx$ are equivalent; this may be proved by writing out the unabbreviated version of the former and rearranging terms to obtain the unabbreviated version of the latter. Similarly, propositions of the form $(\exists x)(Fx \lor Gx)$ and $(\exists x)Fx \lor (\exists x)Gx$ are equivalent; proof is left as an exercise.

In sum, then, the following biconditionals are logically true for any props Fx and Gx:

$$(x)(Fx \cdot Gx) \equiv [(x)Fx \cdot (x)Gx],$$
$$(\exists x)(Fx \lor Gx) \equiv [(\exists x)Fx \lor (\exists x)Gx].$$

These may be called *distribution rules for quantifiers*, or simply *Q distribution rules*. Note that the following pairs are *not* equivalent:

$(x)(Fx \lor Gx)$	and	$[(x)Fx \lor (x)Gx];$
$(\exists x)(Fx \cdot Gx)$	and	$[(\exists x)Fx \cdot (\exists x)Gx].$

These are easy to confuse with the Q distribution rules; proof that they are not equivalent is left as an exercise.

Exercises

1. Show that for any props Fx and Gx,

$$(\exists x)(Fx \lor Gx) \equiv [(\exists x)Fx \lor (\exists x)Gx]$$

is logically true.

2. Translate into symbols:

   a. None but the brave deserve the fair.

   b. No athletes have time for study.

   c. No athletes have time for study unless they take a part-time program.

   d. No athletes have time for study except those who take a part-time program.

   e. Only athletes who take a part-time program have time for study.

   f. Men only. (A sign on a door.)

g. The barber will shave only those men who do not shave themselves.

h. The barber will shave any man who does not shave himself.

i. The barber will not shave any man who does not shave himself.

j. The barber will not shave every man who does not shave himself.

3. Determine which of the following pairs are equivalent. For those that are not, describe some set of circumstances under which one will be true and the other false.

a. If everything is physical, then everything is real.
Everything that is physical is real.

b. Everything is physical or everything is spiritual.
Everything is physical or spiritual.

c. Everything is physical and everything is real.
Everything is physical and real.

d. If something is physical, then something is real.
There is something such that, if it is physical, then it is real.

e. Something is physical or something is spiritual.
Something is either physical or spiritual.

f. Something is physical and something is spiritual.
Something is physical and spiritual.

g. Apples are fruits and oranges are fruits.
Apples and oranges are fruits. (Translate as one universal proposition.)

h. Apples are fruits and oranges are fruits.
All nonfruits are either not apples or not oranges.

*i. None but the lonely are wise.
None are wise but the lonely.

*j. Priests alone can speak to God.
Anyone who speaks to God is a priest.

4. Show that the following pairs are not equivalent:

$$(x)(Fx \lor Gx) \quad \text{and} \quad (x)Fx \lor (x)Gx;$$
$$(\exists x)(Fx \cdot Gx) \quad \text{and} \quad (\exists x)Fx \cdot (\exists x)Gx.$$

5. One use of a logical symbolism is to exhibit, and hence resolve, ambiguities that plague ordinary discourse. Consider:

(i) Everything intellectual is not pleasant —
although it might seem so at first.

(ii) Everything intellectual is not pleasant —
although at first it might seem that there *are*
intellectual things that *are* pleasant.

In (i) the part that comes before the dash means $(\exists x)(Ix \cdot \sim Px)$. In (ii) the same words mean $(x)(Ix \supset \sim Px)$. The following expressions are all ambiguous. State in symbols the two meanings to which each is susceptible, and invent contexts that illustrate each meaning.

a. Everything progressive is not wise.

b. Not any woman can be a truly good mother.

c. It is not true that any man can be a god.

d. Any wrestler is not an athlete.

9 • TEST FORMS

It is now possible to state a systematic procedure for the evaluation of any argument whose constituent propositions are of the types discussed in the foregoing sections. We shall begin by examining only arguments whose premises and conclusion contain a single quantified proposition; this will exclude from consideration all arguments containing quantified propositions joined by (binary) truth-functional connectives; it will also exclude arguments containing singular propositions (except insofar as singular propositions are implicitly contained in quantified expressions). Extension of our results to include these cases will be relatively easy at a later stage.

Any argument with premises $P_1, P_2, \ldots, P_n$, and conclusion C is valid if and only if its corresponding conjunction

$$P_1 \cdot P_2 \cdot \ldots \cdot P_n \cdot \sim C$$

is inconsistent. Our method for evaluating arguments will consist of forming the corresponding conjunction and examining it for consistency. However, it will be convenient to put the corresponding conjunction, once formed, into a standard *test form*, which is implicitly defined in the following instructions:

Step 1: To evaluate an argument, first form the corresponding conjunction (conjunction of all premises and denial of conclusion). The conjuncts will consist of four possible types: Propositions symbolized with universal quantifiers, propositions symbolized with existential quantifiers, and among each of these classes propositions with quantifiers preceded by negation signs and propositions not preceded by negation signs.

Step 2: Apply a Q rule to each proposition in which the quantifier is preceded by a negation sign. This will leave only conjuncts with universal or existential quantifiers, none preceded by negations.

Step 3: Collect all universal propositions into a single universal proposition by appeal to the appropriate Q distribution rule. The result will be an expression of the form

$$(x)Fx \cdot (\exists x)G_1x \cdot (\exists x)G_2x \cdot \ldots \cdot (\exists x)G_mx.$$

This is the standard test form. It is a string of conjoined quantified expressions, none preceded by negation signs; it contains at most one universal proposition and any number of existential propositions (including zero).

As an example, we construct the test form for the following familiar type of argument:

$$(x)(Wx \supset Mx)$$
$$\underline{(x)(Mx \supset Ax)}$$
$$(x)(Wx \supset Ax)$$

The corresponding conjunction:

$$(x)(Wx \supset Mx) \cdot (x)(Mx \supset Ax) \cdot \sim(x)(Wx \supset Ax).$$

As the second step, we convert the negative to an affirmative:

$$(x)(Wx \supset Mx) \cdot (x)(Mx \supset Ax) \cdot (\exists x) \sim (Wx \supset Ax).$$

And lastly we collect the general propositions:

$$(x)[(Wx \supset Mx) \cdot (Mx \supset Ax)] \cdot (\exists x) \sim (Wx \supset Ax).$$

This is the test form.

Exercises

1. Construct test forms for the following arguments:

   a. All boys are men. All men are mortal. Therefore, all boys are mortal.

   b. All whales are warm-blooded. Some animals are whales. Therefore, some animals are warm-blooded.

   c. Some clever men are witty. All witty men are popular. Only the deserving are popular. Therefore, some deserving men are clever.

   d. Everything is material. Everything material is palpable. Therefore, something is palpable.

   e. Nothing green is red. Some apples are red. Some apples are green. Therefore, some apples are not red.

   f. Everything is green. Therefore, something is not red.

   g. Everything silver is precious. Everything precious is expensive. I cannot afford anything expensive. Therefore, I cannot afford anything silver. (Take Ax for "I can afford x.")

   h. All kangaroos are marsupials. There are no marsupials that live anywhere but in Australia. There are kangaroos. Any Australian kangaroo is a potential pest. Therefore, any Australian marsupial is a potential pest.

2. Assume that any proposition of the form $(x)Fx$ is consistent if and only if Fx, taken as a proposition, is consistent. Under this assumption determine whether arguments 1d and 1f here are valid.

*3. Can there be an argument whose test form consists of *one* particular proposition?

10 • SHORT TEST FORMS

The simplest test form that can arise consists of a single universal proposition. That is, where Fx represents any prop, it will have the form $(x)Fx$, or

(i) $\quad Fx_1 \cdot Fx_2 \cdot Fx_3 \cdot \ldots \cdot Fx_n.$

This proposition is consistent if and only if Fx, viewed as if it were a proposition, is itself consistent. The proof is easy, for if Fx is inconsistent, then every substitution instance is likewise inconsistent, and therefore so is (i). Conversely, if Fx is consistent, each conjunct in (i) is consistent. Then, because each conjunct is distinct from every other (for each is a statement about a different individual object), it is possible for all of them to be true simultaneously, This would make (i) true, showing that (i) is consistent.

As an example, take the argument

> All men are mortal.
> Therefore, some men are mortal.

In symbols it is

$$\frac{(x)(Hx \supset Mx)}{(\exists x)(Hx \cdot Mx)}$$

The corresponding conjunction is

$$(x)(Hx \supset Mx) \cdot \sim(\exists x)(Hx \cdot Mx).$$

By using a Q rule and then combining universals through one of the Q distribution rules we get

$$(x)[(Hx \supset Mx) \cdot \sim(Hx \cdot Mx)].$$

This is the test form. To see if it is consistent we examine the prop alone for consistency:

$$(Hx \supset Mx) \cdot \sim(Hx \cdot Mx).$$

If Hx is false both conjuncts in this expression are true. Therefore, this is consistent, the test form is consistent, and the argument is invalid.

This result, abstractly arrived at, is no more than an application of Tech 2 (Chapter 1), which requires that one demonstrate invalidity by describing possible circumstances under which the premises of an argument are true and its conclusion is false. But an argument's corresponding conjunction is a complex statement *asserting* that the premises are true and the conclusion false, whereas the test form is just a convenient version of that statement. In showing that the test form is consistent we have shown that that assertion may be true. *Furthermore,* we have implicitly provided a concrete description of a conceivable state of affairs that makes the premises true and the conclusion false. For we saw that

$$(Hx \supset Mx) \cdot \sim(Hx \cdot Mx)$$

is true when Hx is taken as false. Clearly, then, the test form

$$(x)[(Hx \supset Mx) \cdot \sim(Hx \cdot Mx)]$$

is true in a universe of one entity that is not a man, or many entities not any of which are men. This outcome is important because it points the way to a sympathetic reinterpretation of the argument (if such is desired) that may make it valid. In this case, we are moved to try adding the (probably understood) premise, "There are men." The test form for that expanded version of the argument will be studied shortly. Although the suggested addition is obvious in the present instance merely from consideration of the verbal argument, this is not generally the case.

Usually no test form will arise consisting of a single *particular* proposition. For every argument contains at least two propositions, and the corresponding conjunction will also contain at least two propositions. These may be two universals, two particulars, or one of each. In the first case they combine into a single *universal*. In the other cases, there simply are not principles for the combination of two particulars, or one particular and one universal, into one equivalent particular.[46] Nevertheless, it is important to note that a proposition of the form $(\exists x)Fx$ is consistent if and only if Fx itself is consistent. The proof exactly parallels the preceding proof for a universal proposition and will not be repeated.

The most common type of test form contains one universal proposition and one particular. That is, it has the form $(x)Fx \cdot (\exists x)Gx$. Written in full, it is

(ii) $(Fx_1 \cdot Fx_2 \cdot \ldots \cdot Fx_n) \cdot (Gx_1 \text{ v } Gx_2 \text{ v } \ldots \text{ v } Gx_n)$.

We show that this is consistent if and only if $(Fx \cdot Gx)$, taken as a proposition, is itself consistent. First suppose $(Fx \cdot Gx)$, is consistent. Then so is every one of its substitution instances. In particular $(Fx_1 \cdot Gx_1)$ is consistent. This means that Fx_1 and Gx_1 can be simultaneously

---

[46] In fact such combination is possible only under very peculiar circumstances, as, for instance, if two particulars are themselves equivalent.

true whatever their internal structures; let us then assign the truth-value 1 to those two terms. Because $(Fx \cdot Gx)$ is consistent, Fx alone must be likewise; then all the remaining F terms (Fx_2, Fx_3, and so on) can also be assigned the value 1. This would suffice to render the whole of (ii) true and shows that (ii) can be true and is consistent.

Now suppose $(Fx \cdot Gx)$ is inconsistent. Then so are its substitution instances $(Fx_1 \cdot Gx_1)$, $(Fx_2 \cdot Gx_2)$, and so on. Therefore, any time we assign the truth-value 1 to an F term (such as Fx_1 or Fx_2) we should have to assign zero to the corresponding G term. Now in order for (ii) to be true, *every* F term would have to be true. But then every G term would be false, the series of disjoined G terms as a whole would be false, and hence (ii) itself would be false. This shows that (ii) cannot be true and must be inconsistent.[47]

An example is

> All men are mortal.
> There are men.
> Therefore, some men are mortal.

$$(x)(Hx \supset Mx)$$
$$(\exists x)Hx$$
$$\overline{(\exists x)(Hx \cdot Mx)}$$

The corresponding conjunction is

$$(x)(Hx \supset Mx) \cdot (\exists x)Hx \cdot \sim(\exists x)(Hx \cdot Mx).$$

Applying a Q rule we have

$$(x)(Hx \supset Mx) \cdot (\exists x)Hx \cdot (x) \sim (Hx \cdot Mx).$$

Rearranging, and combining universals, the test form is

$$(x)[(Hx \supset Mx) \cdot \sim(Hx \cdot Mx)] \cdot (\exists x)Hx.$$

We then examine the conjoined props and find them inconsistent:

$(Hx$	$\supset$	$Mx) \cdot$	$\sim$	$(Hx$	$\cdot$	$Mx) \cdot$	$Hx.$
Ø	1	0	1	1	0	0	1
(8)	(1)	(7)	(2)	(4)	(5)	(6)	(3)

---

[47]It may happen that Fx alone is inconsistent, thus making it impossible to assign 1 to the F terms. But in that case (ii) would already be shown to be inconsistent.

The numerals in parentheses record the order in which truth-values have been assigned. The argument is valid.

A final example is

> All Communists favor labor.
> There are no Republicans who are Communists.
> Therefore, no Republicans favor labor.

$$(x)(Cx \supset Lx)$$
$$\sim(\exists x)(Rx \cdot Cx)$$
$$\overline{(x)(Rx \supset \sim Lx)}$$

The corresponding conjunction is

$$(x)(Cx \supset Lx) \cdot \sim(\exists x)(Rx \cdot Cx) \cdot \sim(x)(Rx \supset \sim Lx).$$

Applying Q rules to the negative propositions we get

$$(x)(Cx \supset Lx) \cdot (x) \sim (Rx \cdot Cx) \cdot (\exists x) \sim (Rx \supset \sim Lx).$$

Combining the universals, the test form is

$$(x)[(Cx \supset Lx) \cdot \sim(Rx \cdot Cx)] \cdot (\exists x) \sim (Rx \supset \sim Lx).$$

We examine the conjoined props:

$$(Cx \supset Lx) \cdot \sim(Rx \cdot Cx) \cdot \sim(Rx \supset \sim Lx).$$

This is consistent, as we see by taking Rx and Lx as true and Cx as false. Hence, the argument is invalid.

What are the concrete circumstances implicit in this finding? We have found the test form to be possibly true by taking "Rx and Lx as true, and Cx as false,"—that is, by taking x to be a non-Communist Republican who favors labor. Therefore, the test form is satisfied on the hypotheses that the world contains just one entity having those properties, or many entities all having those properties. This result can be further checked by returning to the verbal form of the argument and verifying that under that hypothesis all the premises are true and the conclusion is false.

To facilitate rapid analysis of test forms, various notational conveniences are available. For instance, it may be helpful to use a slash as a sign for *and* between quantified propositions. And when examining props for consistency it is clear that the x's play no functional role and can be dropped. Neither of these devices is adopted in the text.

Exercises

1. Prove that any proposition of the form $(\exists x)Fx$ is consistent if and only if Fx is consistent.

2. Refer to the exercises at the end of Section 9 of this chapter; test the arguments in the following for validity: 1a, 1b, 1c, 1d, 1f, 1g.

3. Test the following arguments for validity:

   a. No wars are just. Therefore, some wars are not just.

   b. No wars are just. There are wars. Therefore, some wars are not just.

   c. All men reason. Therefore, it is not the case that no men reason.

   d. All men reason. There are men. Therefore, it is not the case that no men reason.

   e. All Communists favor labor. All Socialists favor labor. Therefore, all Socialists are Communists.

   f. Only the brave deserve the fair. None but the noble are brave. Therefore, anyone who is brave and deserving of the fair must be noble.

   g. All capable teachers are learned. Only the diligent are capable. There is not anyone who is learned that is not capable. Therefore, all diligent teachers are capable.

   h. Painters and sculptors are artists. Artists are sensitive. Therefore, any sensitive artist is a painter or a sculptor.

   i. Some employers are tyrannical and generous. Anyone who is tyrannical or severe is neurotic. All employers are basically fair. Therefore, some basically fair neurotics are employers.

   j. All liberals and southerners are in favor of the bill. All Democrats are liberals or southerners. Therefore, all Democrats are in favor of the bill.

   k. All liberals are in favor of the bill. All southerners are in favor of the bill. All Democrats are liberals or southerners. Therefore, all Democrats are in favor of the bill.

   l. All liberal southerners are in favor of the bill. All Democrats are liberals or southerners. Therefore, all Democrats are in favor of the bill.

4. The argument in Exercise 3g here is invalid. Describe in words a set of circumstances under which the premises would be true and the conclusion false.

*5. The development of the test-form method for evaluating arguments does not depend in any way upon the Q equivalence rule. Prove that rule by appeal to the test form technique for evaluation.

11 • LONGER TEST FORMS

A test form may contain no universal proposition at all, but two particular ones. Suppose there arises a test form of the type $(\exists x)Fx \cdot (\exists x)Gx$, or:

(i) $(Fx_1 \vee Fx_2 \vee \ldots \vee Fx_n) \cdot (Gx_1 \vee Gx_2 \vee \ldots \vee Gx_n)$.

To state the outcome at once, this form is consistent if and only if Fx and Gx, considered separately, are consistent.

First suppose Fx and Gx are not both consistent. For instance, let Fx be inconsistent. Then obviously every F term in (i) will have to be false under any circumstances (in other words $(\exists x)Fx$ will be inconsistent), and (i) itself will have to be false, hence inconsistent. This is true also if Gx is inconsistent.

Next suppose Fx and Gx are both consistent. Then whatever their internal structures, any F term could be true, and likewise any G term could be true. Let us suppose truth-values are assigned so as to make Fx_1 true. Note that Fx_1, be it an atom or a molecule, is wholly distinct from Gx_2, because they are statements about different individuals. Hence, without running into any conflict with the truth-value assignments in Fx_1, we can make further truth-value assignments that render Gx_2 true. But if Fx_1 and Gx_2 are both true, then (i) itself is true, and is therefore consistent.

Observe that we selected Fx_1 and Gx_2, rather than corresponding terms from each series. The reason is this: Despite the fact that Fx and Gx are (by hypothesis) consistent, their conjunction $(Fx \cdot Gx)$ could be inconsistent.[48] Then the assignment of 1 to Fx_1 would prevent the assignment of 1 to Gx_1; but we could still assign 1 to Gx_2 without conflict. That is, by choosing the first atom in the first series of disjuncts and the second atom in the second series, we are able to show that each series considered as a whole can be simultaneously

---

[48]For instance, if Fx were $(Sx \supset Tx)$ and Gx were $(Sx \cdot \sim Tx)$.

true, even if $(Fx \cdot Gx)$ is inconsistent. Clearly this device would *fail* if there were only one object x_1 in the world. Consequently, we shall assume, here and hereafter, that there are at least as many objects x_1, x_2, and so on, as there are nonuniversal propositions in the test form —a reasonable postulate, although not *logically* necessary.

To recapitulate, then, a proposition of the form $(\exists x)Fx \cdot (\exists x)Gx$ is consistent if and only if Fx and Gx are themselves consistent; it does not matter if the prop formed by the conjunction $(Fx \cdot Gx)$ is consistent or not. This result can be easily generalized for test forms containing three or more particular propositions.

As an example, consider this argument:

> Some whales are mammals.
> Therefore, all whales are mammals.

The corresponding conjunction and test form are

$(\exists x)(Wx \cdot Mx) \cdot \sim(x)(Wx \supset Mx),$
$(\exists x)(Wx \cdot Mx) \cdot (\exists x) \sim (Wx \supset Mx).$

The two props $(Wx \cdot Mx)$ and $\sim(Wx \supset Mx)$ are each consistent, so the argument is invalid (of course). Note that the two props taken together are inconsistent, but this does not affect the outcome.

In what sort of a world is the premise of the argument true and its conclusion false? Clearly, in a world containing *two* types of individuals, one type satisfying $(Wx \cdot Mx)$ and one satisfying $\sim(Wx \supset Mx)$; that is, a world consisting partly of mammalian whales and partly of nonmammalian whales.

At the next level of complexity, we need to examine a form containing *one* general proposition and *two* particulars: $(x)Fx \cdot (\exists x)Gx \cdot (\exists x)Hx$. In unabbreviated form we would have

(ii) $(Fx_1 \cdot Fx_2 \cdot Fx_3 \cdot \ldots \cdot Fx_n) \cdot$
$(Gx_1 \text{ v } Gx_2 \text{ v } Gx_3 \text{ v } \ldots \text{ v } Gx_n) \cdot$
$(Hx_1 \text{ v } Hx_2 \text{ v } Hx_3 \text{ v } \ldots \text{ v } Hx_n).$

We will prove that (ii) is consistent if and only if $(Fx \cdot Gx)$ and $(Fx \cdot Hx)$ are each consistent.

First, if either $(Fx \cdot Gx)$ or $(Fx \cdot Hx)$ is inconsistent, then either $(x)Fx \cdot (\exists x)Gx$ or $(x)Fx \cdot (\exists x)Hx$ would be inconsistent, as we have already seen. In either case, (ii) itself would be inconsistent as well.

Next suppose $(Fx \cdot Gx)$ and $(Fx \cdot Hx)$ are both consistent. Then $(Fx_1 \cdot Gx_1)$ and $(Fx_2 \cdot Hx_2)$ are consistent. Then we can without fear of conflict assign the truth-value 1 to every F term and to Gx_1 and Hx_2. This would suffice to make (ii) true, and hence (ii) would be consistent.

In brief, to check for consistency a form of the type $(x)Fx \cdot (\exists x)Gx \cdot (\exists x)Hx$, conjoin each prop from the particular propositions (one at a time) with the prop from the universal, and test for consistency as before. If either is inconsistent, so is the test form; if both are consistent, so is the test form. This result can also be extended to test forms with one universal and three or more particular propositions.

Finally, consider this example:

All men are mortal.
Some men are not brave.
Some mortals are brave.
Only the brave are noble.
Therefore, some mortals are noble.

The corresponding conjunction and test form are

$(x)(Hx \supset Mx) \cdot (\exists x)(Hx \cdot \sim Bx) \cdot (\exists x)(Mx \cdot Bx) \cdot (x)(Nx \supset Bx)$
$\quad \cdot \sim (\exists x)(Mx \cdot Nx),$
$(x)[(Hx \supset Mx) \cdot (Nx \supset Bx) \cdot \sim(Mx \cdot Nx)] \cdot (\exists x)(Hx \cdot \sim Bx)$
$\quad \cdot (\exists x)(Mx \cdot Bx).$

We first combine the prop from the universal with the prop from the first particular:

$(Hx \supset Mx) \cdot (Nx \supset Bx) \cdot \sim(Mx \cdot Nx) \cdot (Hx \cdot \sim Bx).$

This is consistent, as we may see if we take Hx and Mx as true and Nx and Bx as false. (If this had turned up inconsistent we would be finished: We could have concluded that the argument is valid, without any need for examining the next combination.) Next we combine the prop from the universal with the prop from the second particular:

$(Hx \supset Mx) \cdot (Nx \supset Bx) \cdot \sim(Mx \cdot Nx) \cdot (Mx \cdot Bx).$

This too is consistent, for we could take Hx, Mx, and Bx as true, and Nx as false. Therefore, the argument is invalid. We have implicitly described a world consisting partly of men who are mortal but neither noble nor brave, and partly of men who are mortal and brave but not noble.

Exercises

1. Show that a test form containing three particular propositions is consistent if and only if each proposition is consistent considered separately (but compare Exercise 2).

2. Assume the world contains just two objects, *a* and *b*. Under this assumption, and by direct inspection of unabbreviated forms, show that the following is inconsistent:

$$(\exists x)(Fx \supset Gx) \cdot (\exists x)(Gx \supset Hx) \cdot (\exists x)(Fx \cdot \sim Hx).$$

3. Show that a test form containing one universal and three particular propositions is consistent if and only if the prop from the universal forms a consistent pair when conjoined (one by one) with the props from each of the particulars.

4. Refer to the arguments in Exercises 1e and 1h at the end of Section 9; test these for validity.

5. Test the following arguments for validity:

   a. Some white men are mortal. Some black men are mortal. Some yellow men are mortal. Therefore, all men are mortal.

   b. Some white men are clever. Some men are mean if they are clever. Therefore, all men who are white are mean.

   c. All men who are white are also clever. All clever men are mean. Therefore, every white man is mean.

   d. All white men are clever. Only the mean are clever men. There are men. Therefore, some mean men are white.

   e. There are men. There are animals. There are vegetarians. Therefore, some animals are human vegetarians.

   f. There are men. There are animals. There are vegetarians. All vegetarians are men. All men are animals. Therefore, some animals are human vegetarians.

   g. Harry can eat apples and oranges. There are Cortlands in the basket. All Cortlands are apples. Therefore, there is something in the basket that Harry can eat.

h. Harry can eat apples and oranges. There are some Cortlands in the basket. Some Cortlands are apples. Therefore, there is something in the basket that Harry can eat.

i. Some ships are fast. Nothing fast is a ship. Therefore, all ships are fast.

j. All planes are safe. Only slow things are safe. Not all planes are slow. Therefore, all peasants aspire to royal marriage.

6. The argument in Exercise 5f is valid, and would still be valid if two of its premises were dropped. Which two?

7. The argument in Exercise 5b is invalid. Describe in words a set of circumstances under which the premises would be true and the conclusion false.

*8. Show that any valid argument (of the type we have been discussing) with consistent premises whose test form contains more than two propositions has at least one unnecessary premise.

12 • TEST FORMS WITH SINGULAR PROPOSITIONS

The method of evaluation through test forms has the advantage of being a decision procedure. But it has the disadvantage of being lengthy and awkward in use, even though we have so far examined only arguments whose premises and conclusion contain just one universal or particular proposition. When we expand our view to other types (subsequently), the method becomes still more cumbersome and cannot be regarded as suitable for routine employment. More natural devices are developed in Chapter 6. But meanwhile, the existence of a decision procedure for further types of arguments is of considerable theoretical (and sometimes practical) significance.

Suppose the premises and conclusion of an argument contain one quantified proposition *or* one singular proposition. By *one singular proposition* we mean a statement, atomic or molecular, about *one* individual object. Thus $(Fa \cdot Ga)$ is one singular proposition, and so is $(Fa \text{ v } Ga)$; but $(Fa \text{ v } Gb)$ and $(Fx_1 \supset Gx_3)$ are not, because two different individual constants appear.

As before, we may form the corresponding conjunction for any such argument, apply Q rules to quantified expressions preceded by negation signs, and collect all universals into one. We then have a conjunction of at most one universal, any number of particular, and any number of singular propositions.[49] We extend the meaning of test form to include such types. What are their consistency-criteria?

If a test form contains *only* singular propositions we can test it for consistency immediately by the methods of Chapter 2. Suppose we have a form containing one universal proposition and one singular, $(x)Fx \cdot Gx_1$. Unabbreviated, we have

$$(Fx_1 \cdot Fx_2 \cdot \ldots \cdot Fx_n) \cdot Gx_1.$$

Obviously, if $(Fx_1 \cdot Gx_1)$ is inconsistent, so is the test form. If $(Fx_1 \cdot Gx_1)$ is consistent, Fx_1 alone is consistent and so are the remaining F terms. Then Gx_1 and all the F terms can be simultaneously assigned the truth-value 1, and the the whole test form is consistent. In sum $(x)Fx \cdot Gx_1$ is consistent if and only if $(Fx_1 \cdot Gx_1)$ is consistent.

An example:

All men are mortal.
Socrates is a man.
Therefore, Socrates is mortal.

$(x)(Hx \supset Mx) \cdot Hs \cdot \sim Ms.$

In accordance with our convention we regard this as a conjunct of two propositions, one universal and one singular. It is already in standard test form and may be written more suggestively as:

$(x)(Hx \supset Mx) \cdot (Hs \cdot \sim Ms).$

To test for consistency we take a substitution instance of the prop corresponding to the constant s, conjoin it with the singular proposition, and examine the result:

$(Hs \supset Ms) \cdot (Hs \cdot \sim Ms).$

This is evidently inconsistent, and the argument is valid. (At last.)

---

[49]Obviously no case will arise in which a binary connective other than "·" extends over *different* individual constants. Note, again, that every conjunct that contains the *same* individual constant is regarded as a part of *one* singular proposition, not two. Thus $[Fb \cdot (x)Gx \cdot Hb \cdot Ka]$ contains, in this context, two singular propositions, Ka and $(Fb \cdot Hb)$. This understanding is needed to avoid ambiguity later.

Next, there may be *two* singular propositions conjoined with a universal, as $(x)Fx \cdot Gx_1 \cdot Hx_2$. Unabbreviated, we have

$$(Fx_1 \cdot Fx_2 \cdot Fx_3 \cdot \ldots \cdot Fx_n) \cdot Gx_1 \cdot Hx_2.$$

If $(Fx_1 \cdot Gx_1)$ or $(Fx_2 \cdot Hx_2)$ is inconsistent, so is the whole test form. Suppose $(Fx_1 \cdot Gx_1)$ and $(Fx_2 \cdot Hx_2)$ are both consistent. Then Fx_1, Gx_1, Fx_2, Hx_2, and all the remaining F terms can be simultaneously true, and the whole proposition is consistent. Thus, the form in question is consistent if and only if $(Fx_1 \cdot Gx_1)$ and $(Fx_2 \cdot Gx_2)$ are both consistent.

As a last case for explicit treatment, suppose we have a test form of the type $(x)Fx \cdot (\exists x)Gx \cdot Hx_1$. The unabbreviated form is

$$(Fx_1 \cdot Fx_2 \cdot \ldots \cdot Fx_n) \cdot (Gx_1 \text{ v } Gx_2 \text{ v } \ldots \text{ v } Gx_n) \cdot Hx_1.$$

Clearly, this is inconsistent if $(Fx \cdot Gx)$ or $(Fx_1 \cdot Hx_1)$ is inconsistent. And if both of those are consistent, we may assign 1 to all the F terms to Hx_1, and to Gx_2, making the whole true. Thus, the form in question is consistent if and only if $(Fx \cdot Gx)$ and $(Fx_1 \cdot Hx_1)$ are both consistent.

Evidently there is a parallel between the role played by singular propositions in test forms and the role played by particular propositions. In fact the parallel is complete, and extends to all possible combinations. We state the results at once, omitting further proofs

> A test form with one universal and any number of nonuniversal (particular or singular) propositions is consistent if and only if the props in each particular form consistent expressions when conjoined with the prop in the universal, and each singular forms a consistent expression when conjoined with a corresponding substitution instance of the prop in the universal.

and

> A test form with no universal but any number of nonuniversal (particular or singular) propositions is consistent if and only if each proposition i consistent considered separately.

One does not frequently encounter test forms with a plurality of nonuniversal conjuncts. For consider a *valid* argument (of the type under discussion) whose test form contains three or more propositions. Inconsistency is established because some pair is inconsistent, o because some proposition is inconsistent considered alone. In eithe case there are propositions in the test form that are not needed for the finding of validity. If they are derived from premises, then those premises, are dispensable; and if they are derived from the conclusion, the premises alone are inconsistent. Thus, upon confronting such test forms we may infer at once that the corresponding arguments are invalid, are overweighted with premises, or contain inconsistent premises; further work with the test form will reveal which is the case.

Exercises

1. Test the following arguments for validity.

   a. Abigail is pretty. Therefore, there are pretty things.

   b. Abigail is pretty. Therefore, everything is pretty.

   c. There is something pretty. Therefore, Abigail is pretty.

   d. Everything is pretty. Therefore, Abigail is pretty.

   e. All Frenchmen are witty. Maurice is a Frenchman. Therefore, Maurice is witty.

   f. All Americans are pragmatic. Harold is pragmatic. Therefore, Harold is an American.

   g. All Englishmen are sober. Ewing is not sober. Therefore, Ewing is not English.

   h. All Italians are gay. Angelo is not Italian. Therefore, Angelo is not gay.

   i. Socrates is a mortal man. All men are animals. Therefore, Socrates is a mortal animal.

   j. Arthur is going. Harold is not taking a car. Anyone who is going has to have money. Only those who have no driver's license are not taking a car. Therefore, someone has some money but no driver's license.

   k. Same as Exercise j, but with *or* in place of *but* in the conclusion.

   l. Sample number 1 is a bromide. Sample number 2 is a flouride. Sample number 3 is an iodide. There are halides. Therefore, all bromides are halides.

   m. Moriarty is crafty. Watson is persevering. Holmes is intelligent. Anyone who is crafty or persevering is intelligent. There are intelligent people. Therefore, only the intelligent are persevering.

n. Moriarty is crafty. Watson is persevering. All the crafty are persevering. Only the intelligent are crafty or persevering. Therefore, Moriarty is crafty and intelligent.

2. The argument in Exercise 1n would be valid even if some of the premises were dropped. Which ones?

3. "In my many years of experience," said Holmes, "I have discovered that human beings in the normal course of affairs tend to make mistakes and tell untruths, quite innocently. Hence, in a case of this sort, I would proceed as follows. First, write down the testimony of the suspects, and ask yourself if it is possible that all of them together could be telling the truth. If it is, then they are probably all in it together, but then you will get no further help from that quarter, so you will have to go back to the house to look for more clues. On the other hand, it may be that it is not possible that they could all be telling the truth. In that case, see if there is one suspect's testimony that is harmonious with the testimony of each one of the other suspects. If there is, begin by investigating *him*."

The testimony of the suspects is as follows:

Allison: "Any piece of silver that had not been polished would not be in the drawer."

Burns: "The silver spoon that the master brought back from the Punjab was in the drawer, although it was not polished."

Coates: "There was some piece of silver that was neither in the drawer nor polished."

Would Holmes go back to the house for more clues or would he start investigating someone; and if the latter, which one?

4. It is shown in the text that a valid argument whose test form contains more than one nonuniversal proposition has unnecessary premises, or inconsistent premises. If a valid argument has a test form that does *not* contain more than one nonuniversal proposition, does it follow that the premises are consistent? Does it follow that there are no unnecessary premises?

5. Give proofs for the general consistency-criteria enunciated in the text for all possible types of test forms.

13 • TRUTH-FUNCTIONAL COMBINATIONS

Finally, consider an argument whose premises and conclusion contain universal, particular, or singular propositions, *or any truth-functional combinations thereof*. The decision procedure for such cases is simple in principle, lengthy in execution. We begin as before by forming the corresponding conjunction. Taking each quantified expression and each singular proposition as a single unit, *we recast it into disjunctive normal form,* and then apply a Q rule to any quantified expression that is immediately preceded by a negation sign. The result is a series of disjuncts, each one of which has the shape of a test form. Evidently the whole series is consistent if and only if at least one of the disjuncts is consistent. Example:

> If there are any gods, then all unjust acts are fruitless.
> If there are reliable historians, there are certainly fruitless acts.
> But there are reliable historians.
> And Alexander of Macedon is a god.
> Therefore, there are unjust acts.

> Gx: x is a god.
> Ux: x is an unjust act.
> Fx: x is fruitless.
> Rx: x is a reliable historian.
> a: Alexander of Macedon.

$$(\exists x)Gx \supset (x)(Ux \supset Fx)$$
$$(\exists x)Rx \supset (\exists x)Fx$$
$$(\exists x)Rx$$
$$Ga$$
$$\overline{}$$
$$(\exists x)Ux$$

It is convenient to construct an auxiliary dictionary before writing down the corresponding conjunction.

> P: $(\exists x)Gx$
> Q: $(x)(Ux \supset Fx)$
> R: $(\exists x)Rx$
> S: $(\exists x)Fx$
> G: Ga
> T: $(\exists x)Ux$

Then the argument is

$$P \supset Q$$
$$R \supset S$$
$$R$$
$$G$$
$$\overline{}$$
$$T$$

The corresponding conjunction is

$$(P \supset Q) \cdot (R \supset S) \cdot R \cdot G \cdot {\sim}T.$$

We put this into an equivalent disform by stages:

$$(\sim P \text{ v } Q) \cdot [(\sim R \text{ v } S) \cdot R \cdot G \cdot {\sim}T],$$
$$(\sim P \text{ v } Q) \cdot [(\sim R \cdot R \cdot G \cdot {\sim}T) \text{ v } (S \cdot R \cdot G \cdot {\sim}T)],$$
$$(\sim P \text{ v } Q) \cdot (S \cdot R \cdot G \cdot {\sim}T),$$
$$(\sim P \cdot S \cdot R \cdot G \cdot {\sim}T) \text{ v } (Q \cdot S \cdot R \cdot G \cdot {\sim}T).$$

Referring to the auxiliary dictionary, we examine the left-hand disjunct:

$$\sim(\exists x)Gx \cdot (\exists x)Fx \cdot (\exists x)Rx \cdot Ga \cdot \sim(\exists x)Ux.$$

The corresponding test form is

$$(x)(\sim Gx \cdot \sim Ux) \cdot (\exists x)Fx \cdot (\exists x)Rx \cdot Ga,$$

which is inconsistent because of $(\sim Ga \cdot \sim Ua \cdot Ga)$. Then we turn to the right-hand disjunct, which retranslates into

$$(x)(Ux \supset Fx) \cdot (\exists x)Fx \cdot (\exists x)Rx \cdot Ga \cdot \sim(\exists x)Ux.$$

The test form is

$$(x)[(Ux \supset Fx) \cdot \sim Ux] \cdot (\exists x)Fx \cdot (\exists x)Rx \cdot Ga.$$

The universal is clearly consistent when conjoined with the last two conjuncts. It is also consistent when conjoined with $(\exists x)Fx$:

$$\frac{(Ux \supset Fx) \cdot \sim Ux \cdot Fx.}{0 \quad 1 \quad 1 \quad 1 \quad 0 \quad 1}$$

Therefore, the right-hand disjunct is consistent and the argument is not valid.

It is important to observe that the word *any*, always troublesome, continues to exhibit shifting meanings when it appears in the sorts of contexts that have now come into view. For example, in the following pair of statements *any* and *every* are synonymous:

Any man in the group is a hard worker.
Every man in the group is a hard worker.

But now consider the following pair:

> If any man in the group is a hard worker, we will have an honor platoon.
> If every man in the group is a hard worker, we will have an honor platoon.

Here, *any* has shifted its meaning from *every* to *some*.

Exercises

1. Determine the validity or invalidity of the following:

1. Either everything is material or everything is spiritual. Therefore, everything is either material or spiritual.

b. Everything is either material or spiritual. Therefore, either everything is material or everything is spiritual.

c. Something is material and something is spiritual. Therefore, something is material and spiritual.

d. Something is material and spiritual. Therefore, something is material and something is spiritual.

e. If everything is material then everything is tangible. Therefore, everything material is tangible.

f. Everything material is tangible. Therefore, if everything is material then everything is tangible.

g. If something is material then something is tangible. Therefore, there is something such that, if it is material then it is tangible.

h. There is something such that, if it is material then it is tangible. Therefore, if something is material then something is tangible.

i. If there is a just God, all sins are punished. But malice sometimes goes unpunished, and all malice is sinful. On the other hand, there cannot be any such thing as an unjust God. Therefore, there is no God.

j. If there is food, and there is drink, and there are tameable animals, the planet is habitable. Anything that is not drink is not water. All plants are food. There is no such thing as a cat that is not an animal. It is true of everything that its being tameable is a necessary condition for its being a cat. There is water, and there are plants and cats. Therefore, the planet is habitable.

k. There are rotten apples. The existence of rotten apples is a sufficient condition for the existence of deceptive fruits. Any rotten apple or ripe banana contains sugar. All deceptive fruits tend to create illusions. Therefore, there are some fruits that contain sugar and some that create illusions.

l. Either no compounds contain benzene rings or no compounds are relatively heavy or some compounds are producible in this laboratory. Some aromatics are carcinogens. All carcinogens contain hydrogen. Any aromatic contains benzene rings. Any aromatic that contains hydrogen is relatively heavy. Therefore, some compounds are producible in this laboratory.

m. If all bearded men are Communists, there is someone who is not bearded. Either everyone is bearded or everyone is a Communist. Therefore, if all Communists are bearded, there is at least one non-Communist who is bearded.

n. If Angelo is late, everyone will be angry. If anyone is angry, Maria will be disappointed. If Maria is disappointed, this party is a failure. Therefore, if Angelo is late this party is a failure.

2. Consider the arguments in Exercises 1e, 1h, and 1k. For each, describe circumstances under which the premise(s) would be true and the conclusion false. What additional and quite reasonable premise will suffice to make the argument in 1k valid?

3. Consider the arguments from the following exercises appearing earlier in this chapter. For each one, if invalid, describe circumstances under which the premises are true and the conclusion false.

Section 11:   5e, 5f, 5h.
Section 12:   1f, 1h, 1j.

14 • COMPRESSED SYMBOLIZATIONS

It frequently happens that an argument contains a propositon that *can* be symbolized with the methods of this chapter, but that is repeated unchanged two or three times in the course of the argument. Experience shows that in such cases it is often sufficient to symbolize the entire proposition in question with an isolated upper case letter, as in Chapters 2–4; these symbols can be called *propositional constants.* Propositional constants can be freely mixed in with more detailed symbols, and tests for validity can be applied as before. This procedure involves some loss of complete and automatic decidability. If we come down to test forms such as

$(x)(Sx \supset Tx) \cdot (\exists x)(Sx \cdot \sim Tx) \cdot P$, or
$(x)(Sx \supset Tx) \cdot (\exists x)Sx \cdot P \cdot \sim P \cdot Q$,

we can infer with certainty that they are inconsistent. However, a form such as

$(x)(Sx \supset Tx) \cdot (\exists x)Sx \cdot \sim Ta \cdot P \cdot \sim Q$,

which appears consistent, may turn out otherwise when the internal structures of P and/or Q are exhibited.[50]

However, the use of propositional constants along with other symbols expands the number of arguments that we can evaluate; for many arguments that are not purely propositional, and that contain some propositions amenable to symbolization by the methods of this chapter and some not, will yield to this mixed approach. Examples follow in the exercises.

Another frequently used device for shortening the number of symbols required in a given problem is to impose an explicit restriction on the kind of entity that individual letters (constants or variables) can refer to. A commonplace example is the following argument:

All thoughtful persons are considerate.
Some careful persons are thoughtful.
Therefore, some careful persons are considerate.

Tx: x is thoughtful.
Px: x is a person.
Cx: x is considerate.
Fx: x is careful.

$(x)[Px \supset (Tx \supset Cx)]$
$(\exists x)(Px \cdot Fx \cdot Tx)$
―――――――――――――
$(\exists x)(Px \cdot Fx \cdot Cx)$

―――――――――

[50]This qualified stance in regard to consistency-findings does not arise here for the *first* time. In affirming that, say, $(x)(Sx \cdot Tx)$ is consistent, where S and T are constants, we have always assumed implicitly that the symbols S and T do not conceal vital structural details. Also, compare the principle of symbolic uniqueness (Chapter 1), and the opening paragraphs of Chapter 2.

With the restriction that x's refer exclusively to persons we have the following simpler translation:

$$(x)(Tx \supset Cx)$$
$$\underline{(\exists x)(Fx \cdot Tx)}$$
$$(\exists x)(Fx \cdot Cx)$$

Obviously, this device works only on condition that every proposition in the argument can be understood as being about the type of entity mentioned in the restriction. When this condition is satisfied, it is not difficult to show that the reliability of our methods of testing for validity is unaffected by such symbolic compressions; the demonstration is suggested in Exercises 3 and 4 that follow.

Exercises

1. Check the following arguments for validity:

   a. All persuasive Socialists are dangerous. Jones is a Socialist. All Socialists are persuasive. If Jones is dangerous, then the person who hired him ought to be fired. Therefore, the person who hired Jones ought to be fired.

   b. If the person who hired Jones ought to be fired, then twelve other people will have to be fired as well. If everyone is potentially seditious, then twelve other people will have to be fired. Therefore, if the person who hired Jones ought to be fired, then someone is potentially seditious.

   c. If substance 112 is alkaline, then further research will *have* to be conducted. If there is any Q-type polysaccharide that is nontoxic, then every one is nontoxic. If substance 112 is not alkaline, then it is a nontoxic Q-type polysaccharide. Hence, if no further research *has* to be conducted, no Q-type polysaccharide is toxic.

   d. If there are two members of the Q series that are identical in all inorganic properties, then either there is some organic test that will distinguish between any two members of the Q series, or we have to admit the existence of distinct but indistinguishable chemicals. We do not admit the existence of distinct and indistinguishable chemicals. All organic tests run to completion in a finite time. No test that runs to completion in a finite time will distinguish between any two members of the Q series. Therefore, no two members of the Q series are identical in all inorganic properties.

e. If Watson and the author, and no others, were in the garden, or Holmes was in the house, then anyone who saw Watson or Holmes was in on the plot. Smythe was in the house. If anyone was in the house, certainly Holmes was. Therefore, Smythe was in on the plot.

f. Either someone was in the garden watching the house, or someone was in the house watching the garden, or Holmes has misinterpreted the case and should be replaced. If there was anyone in the garden, then there was just one person in the house. If there was anyone in the house, then there was just one person in the garden. But in fact there was not just one person in the garden, nor just one person in the house. Hence, Holmes has misinterpreted the case and should be replaced.

2. Consider the argument in Exercise 1e. Describe in detail a set of circumstances that would make the premises true and the conclusion false. Also suggest an additional and reasonable premise that would make the argument valid.

3. Let there be a universe U containing some objects that have the property F and some that do not. Imagine another universe formed from U by striking out all the objects that fail to have the property F, and retaining all those that do; the result is called an *F-contraction of U*. Show that: (i) a proposition of the form $(x)(Fx \supset Gx)$ is true in U if and only if $(x)Gx$ is true in the F-contraction of U, (ii) a proposition of the form $(\exists x)(Fx \cdot Gx)$ is true in U if and only if $(\exists x)Gx$ is true in the F-contraction of U, (iii) a proposition of the form Ga, where a is understood to have the property F, is true in U if and only if it is true in the F-contraction of U.

4. Suppose a certain argument can be symbolized and evaluated with the methods of this chapter, every proposition having the form $(x)(Fx \supset \ldots)$, or $(\exists x)(Fx \cdot \ldots)$, or Ga (and a is somewhere asserted to be an F), or some truth-functional combination thereof. Appealing to Exercise 3, show that the argument can be resymbolized and reevaluated with the understanding that individual variables and constants refer only to F's, without affecting the outcome of the evaluation.

5. Suppose a certain argument can be symbolized with the methods of this chapter, with the understanding that individual variables and constants refer only to a specified type of entity, say F's. Appealing to Exercise 3, show that the reliability of the methods developed in this chapter for evaluating the argument is unaffected if there are other sorts of entities beside F's.

CHAPTER 6

Natural Deduction for Simple Quantificational Arguments

ABSTRACT: A system of natural deduction appropriate to the arguments considered in chapter 5 is stated, just as a system appropriate to the arguments considered in Chapter 2 was stated in Chapter 3. However, the assumption that the universe contains only a finite number of objects is dropped at the outset; the discussion is therefore placed in a wider context than that governing Chapter 5. The last section (5) of the present chapter shows that the system is complete (that is, proofs exist for all arguments known to be valid by Chapter 5 criteria), and that the decision procedure of Chapter 5 can be employed reliably even when infinite numbers of objects are in view. It is also claimed, but not proved, that the system is *consistent* in the sense that no proofs exist for arguments known to be invalid by Chapter 5 criteria.

1 • A FRESH START; UNIVERSAL INSTANTIATION

The program we now embark upon is the establishment of a system of formal proof for arguments of the type studied in Chapter 5, analogous to the system we developed for propositional arguments in Chapter 3. The motivation is largely the same: We wish to acquire principles for the easy and rapid constriction of exclusively valid arguments. All of the rules and methods of Chapter 3 will be taken over without qualification here; they form the framework on which the new system is built.

To some extent we shall only work out explicitly and in detail certain principles of argument that have been employed many times in previous discussions, especially in Chapter 5. But in another sense we start afresh, for *we now drop the finitude postulate*. That is, we no longer assume that the individual objects our propositions refer to are necessarily finite in number. Consequently, we can no longer assume that lists of such individuals can theoretically be drawn up. In further consequence, we cannot always regard universal and particular propositions as chains of conjoined or disjoined singular propositions. This means that the techniques developed in Chapter 5 must be suspended until they can be reestablished on some other foundation (they will).[51]

There are, however, three respects in which the procedures of the previous chapter can be carried over unchanged. (i) Because singular propositions involve no reference to indefinite sets or classes of objects, it is clearly appropriate to translate such propositions into logical symbolism with predicate constants and individual constants, as before.

(ii) We shall continue to employ quantifiers and individual variables to translate universal and particular propositions into symbols, in the same way as before. Thus, we still convert "All F's are G's" into $(x)(Fx \supset Gx)$, and "Some F's are G's" into $(\exists x)(Fx \cdot Gx)$. What

---

[51]One may ask, "Why not regard universal and particular propositions as *un*-ending conjunctions or disjunctions? *Everything is an F*, for instance, could be $(Fx_1 \cdot Fx_2 \cdot \ldots \cdot Fx_n \ldots)$." This suggestion appears reasonable if we are dealing with infinite sets whose members can be systematically enumerated, that is, sets for which one can construct a systematic list that predictably includes every member. These are called *denumerable* sets; the primary example is the set of natural numbers, 1, 2, $\ldots$, n, $\ldots$. All finite sets are of course denumerable. But there are also non-denumerable sets, such as the set of points in a finite line segment. It is desirable to have logical techniques that can be applied to both kinds.

is changed is that the symbolic expressions can no longer be understood as abbreviations for certain conjunctions or disjunctions. Instead we shall interpret "All F's are G's" as a claim that "All things, if they are F's, are G's"; and $(x)(Fx \supset Gx)$ is now to be understood as a direct translation of the latter. Similarly, we interpret "Some F's are G's" as a claim that "Some things are both F and G"; and $(\exists x)$ $(Fx \cdot Gx)$ is now to be understood as a direct translation of the latter. This applies similarly for other quantified expressions.

In the balance of this chapter we shall develop some standard forms of argument suitable for use with universal and particular propositions as presently understood. Although some of these are *suggested* by our experiences in Chapter 5, we cannot regard them as *justified* by reference to those experiences, because we are now moving in a wider context (without the finitude postulate). The argument forms will be essentially just rules of reasoning in respect to the concepts *all* and *some*, and we take them as intuitively evident.

(iii) The method for demonstrating *in*validity employed in Chapter 5 can also be employed in this new context. If we suspect that an argument is invalid, we can assume momentarily that the universe of objects that its propositions refer to is finite, and we can apply the procedures of Chapter 5. Suppose we then reach a finding of invalidity; implicitly, we shall have described a finite universe in which the premises are true and the conclusion false. But because it *is* logically *possible* that the relevant universe is finite, this suffices to establish invalidity even though we have dropped the finitude postulate.[52]

Now to begin the development of a system of natural deduction, consider any universal proposition $(x)Fx$; in words, "Everything is an F." It is evident that if this holds, any named individual among the x's will also have the property F. That is, $(x)Fx$ logically implies Fa, Fb, Fx_1, and so on. Schematically, where Fx is any open proposition of the sort studied in Chapter 5 and a is any constant, the following is a valid argument form:

$$\frac{(x)Fx}{Fa}$$

---

[52]Nor would the argument be valid if we stipulated, as an additional premise, that the relevant universe *is infinite*. For it is easily proved that the premises would still be true, and the conclusion false, in an infinite universe containing all those *types* of objects (and no others) which appear in the described finite universe.

We call this the rule of *universal instantiation,* abbreviated *UI.* With its aid we can at once make a formal proof for a familiar argument:

All men are mortal.
Socrates is a man.
Therefore, Socrates is mortal.

1. $(x)(Hx \supset Mx)$		Pr
2. Hs		Pr
3. $Hs \supset Ms$		1, UI
4. Ms		2, 3, MP

Universal instantiation can also be employed in connection with conditional or indirect proofs:

All men are animals.
All animals are mortal.
Therefore, if Socrates is a man then Socrates is mortal.

1. $(x)(Hx \supset Ax)$	Pr
2. $(x)(Ax \supset Mx)$	Pr
3. Hs	CP
4. $Hs \supset As$	1, UI
5. As	3, 4, MP
6. $As \supset Ms$	2, UI
7. Ms	5, 6, MP
8. $Hs \supset Ms$	3–7, CP

This argument could easily have been proved without the conditional sequence, but the example is quite natural and logically correct.

Another example is

If everything was in the house then everything is lost.
The dining room table is not lost.
Therefore, not everything was in the house.

1.	$(x)Hx \supset (x)Lx$	Pr
✓2.	$\sim Lt$	Pr
3.	$\sim\sim(x)Hx$	IP
4.	$(x)Hx$	3, DN
5.	$(x)Lx$	1, 4, MP
✓6.	Lt	5, UI
7.	$\sim(x)Hx$	3–6, IP

Finally, it is obvious that *UI* can be applied repeatedly to the same proposition:

All Greeks are wise.
Therefore, if Socrates and Pericles are Greeks, they are wise.

1.	$(x)(Gx \supset Wx)$	Pr
2.	$Gs \cdot Gp$	CP
3.	Gs	2, *Simp*
4.	$Gs \supset Ws$	1, *UI*
5.	Ws	3, 4, *MP*
6.	Gp	2, *Simp*
7.	$Gp \supset Wp$	1, *UI*
8.	Wp	6, 7, *MP*
9.	$Ws \cdot Wp$	5, 8, *Conj*
10.	$(Gs \cdot Gp) \supset (Ws \cdot Wp)$	2–9, *CP*

There are two types of symbolic manipulations that are easily mistaken for *UI*. The rule of universal instantiation as we have formulated it permits one to pass from *one* universal proposition to one of its substitution instances. The rule cannot be used on an expression containing two or more quantifiers. Thus, for instance, we cannot pass from

$(x)Fx \supset (x)Gx$

to

$Fa \supset Ga.$

Nor can we go from

$(x)Fx \text{ v } (x)Gx$

to

$Fa \text{ v } Ga.$

It happens that the first of these is not a valid deduction and the second is, but neither is to be regarded as a use of *UI*. The second could be proved as follows.

1.	$(x)Fx$ v $(x)Gx$	Pr
2.	$(x)Fx$	CP
3.	Fa	2, UI
4.	$(x)Fx \supset Fa$	2–3, CP
5.	$(x)Gx$	CP
6.	Ga	5, UI
7.	$(x)Gx \supset Ga$	5–6, CP
8.	Fa v Ga	1, 4, 7, Dil

Next, we note that $(x)Fx$ logically implies Fa, but the two are not logically equivalent. Hence, it would be quite illegitimate to use UI within a larger context of symbols appearing on the same line. Thus, we cannot pass by UI from

$$(x)Fx \supset (x)Gx$$

to

$$Fa \supset (x)Gx.$$

Nor can we go from

$$\sim(x)Fx$$

to

$$\sim Fa.$$

Both of these are in fact invalid arguments.

Exercises

1. For each of the following arguments either show invalidity or construct a formal proof of validity. Use universal quantifiers only.

   a. All whales are mammals. Moby Dick is a whale. Therefore, Moby Dick is a mammal.

   · b. All whales are mammals. Moby Dick is not a mammal. Therefore, Moby Dick is not a whale.

   c. All whales are mammals. Hence, if Moby Dick is not a whale he is not a mammal.

   d. No whales are mammals. Moby Dick is a whale. Therefore, Moby Dick is not a mammal.

   e. No whales are mammals. Therefore, if Moby Dick is a mammal he is not a whale.

f. No whales are mammals. Therefore, if Moby Dick is not a whale he is a mammal.

g. If everyone is valuable then everyone is divine. Therefore, if Socrates is valuable everyone is divine.

h. If everyone is valuable then everyone is divine. Therefore, if everyone is valuable Socrates is divine.

i. If everyone is valuable then everyone is divine. Therefore, if Socrates is valuable then Socrates is divine.

j. Everything is valuable or everything is divine. Therefore, Socrates is divine or everything is valuable.

k. If everything is worthless then everything is material. The chalice is not worthless. Therefore, the chalice is not material.

l. If everything is worthless then everything is material. The chalice is not material. Therefore, the chalice is not worthless.

2. Construct formal proofs for the following valid arguments:

a. Socrates is wise but not mortal. Therefore, it is not the case that all wise men are mortal.

b. If all evidence is based on the senses, then any evidence based on the senses is reliable. Either exhibit *A* is evidence, or exhibit *B* is evidence based on the senses but not reliable. Exhibit *A* is not evidence. Therefore, it is not the case that all evidence is based on the senses.

c. All apples and oranges in the basket are rotten. This is not rotten. Therefore, this is not an apple unless it is not in the basket.

d. Anyone is worth a chance if and only if he is educated. Either Sir Newcombe is worth a chance or the Home Secretary is educated. Hence, either Sir Newcombe is educated or the Home Secretary is worth a chance.

2 • UNIVERSAL GENERALIZATION AND (AGAIN) INSTANTIATION

Consider this familiar argument:

All men are animals.
All animals are mortal.
Therefore, all men are mortal.

Challenged to justify this in words, we might with good reason proceed as follows: Take some arbitrarily chosen object in the world, any object at all. Call it x. The first premise says it is true of any object that, if it is a man, then it is an animal. Hence, if our randomly chosen object x is a man, it is an animal. The second premise says it is true of any object that if it is an animal, it is mortal. Hence, if our chosen object x is an animal, then it is mortal. This gives us two statements about the chosen object x. By hypothetical syllogism we conclude that if x is a man, then x is mortal. But because x was arbitrarily chosen, the same argument will obviously hold good for any other x (even if there is an infinite number of them). Hence, it is true of any object that, if it is a man, it is mortal. Or, in other words, all men are mortal.

We must now put this into a suggestive symbolism. The premises are

1. $(x)(Hx \supset Ax)$ Pr
2. $(x)(Ax \supset Mx)$ Pr

As the first step of the proof, we claim that the universal statement in line 1 holds for an arbitrarily chosen individual; it is natural and convenient to use the letter x for that individual. Hence, we write

1. $(x)(Hx \supset Ax)$ Pr
2. $(x)(Ax \supset Mx)$ Pr
3. $Hx \supset Ax$ $1, UI$

In words, line 3 means "An arbitrarily chosen object x is an A if it is an H." Several comments must be made concerning this procedure.

(i) We regard the inference at line 3 as a kind of universal instantiation. Although different in form from the UI rule of the previous section, the logical idea is evidently the same, or at least close enough to warrant the use of the same name for both forms. Hence, we now have, in effect, two UI rules,

$$\frac{(x)Fx}{Fa} \quad \text{and} \quad \frac{(x)Fx}{Fx}$$

(ii) We must be as clear as we can on the interpretation of the expression Fx, or $Hx \supset Ax$. In chapter 5 we called such symbols open propositions but often viewed them as (genuine) propositions for the sake of some manipulation or analysis. In doing so, we temporarily thought of the x as a constant instead of a variable. Clearly, we want to do something very similar here, for we wish to think of Fx, or $Hx \supset Ax$, as a genuine proposition about an arbitrarily chosen individual; the fact that the individual is arbitrarily chosen is recorded in the continued use of the letter x after the quantifier has been removed.

(iii) The x's that appear in the premises have a somewhat different logical significance from the x's in line 3. The latter have so to speak been freed from an antecedent quantifier, and in subsequent lines we can manipulate the expression in line 3, or appeal to it, in accordance with the principles governing truth-functional propositions. No such manipulation or appeal is possible (at this stage of development) with regard to the expressions following the quantifiers in lines 1 and 2. Hence, we shall speak of the x's in line 3 as *free variables* and the x's in lines 1 and 2 as *bound variables*. In general, a bound variable is one that lies within the scope of an antecedent quantifier, and a free variable is one that does not. In the expression $(x)[(Fx \cdot Gx) \supset Hx]$ all the variables are bound; in $(x)(Fx \cdot Gx) \supset Hx$ the first two are bound and the third is free; and in $Fx \lor Gx$ all are free. In this chapter we use x as the only variable, free or bound.

Now we return to our proof. The next step is to make the same inference from premise 2 that we formerly made from premise 1:

1. $(x)(Hx \supset Ax)$	Pr
2. $(x)(Ax \supset Mx)$	Pr
3. $Hx \supset Ax$	1, UI
4. $Ax \supset Mx$	2, UI

We assume without explicit statement in the proof that the same individual selected (in imagination—and randomly) at line 3 is again selected at line 4. The continued use of the letter x suggests this interpretation, which is in any case vital to the cogency of the argument. For lines 3 and 4, given that interpretation, can now be used to infer yet another statement (about the same randomly chosen object):

5. $Hx \supset Mx$	3, 4, Hyp

In words, line 5 says that if x is an H then it is an M. But as x was, to begin with, chosen at random from the universe of available objects, we conclude that what holds for x under the given premises holds for all individuals, because the same argument could be constructed for any of them. This last step is a type of argument form which we have not formalized heretofore. It can be called *universal generalization*, abbreviated *UG*. The proof is then completed by writing

6. $(x)(Hx \supset Mx)$ 5, *UG*

The new argument form *UG* states in effect that if an arbitrarily chosen individual is known to have a certain property, then all individuals have the same property.[53] Symbolically, *UG* permits us to place a universal quantifier before an expression composed of predicate letters and free variables. Schematically it is

$$\frac{Fx}{(x)Fx}$$

Another example of the use of *UI* and *UG* in connection with free variables:

> All bats are winged.
> No mammals are winged.
> Therefore, no mammals are bats.

1. $(x)(Bx \supset Wx)$ *Pr*
2. $(x)(Mx \supset \sim Wx)$ *Pr*
3. $Bx \supset Wx$ 1, *UI*
4. $Mx \supset \sim Wx$ 2, *UI*
5. $\sim Wx \supset \sim Bx$ 3, *Cont*
6. $Mx \supset \sim Bx$ 4, 5, *Hyp*
7. $(x)(Mx \supset \sim Bx)$ 6, *UG*

This formal proof can be given a verbal and intuitively appealing interpretation in the same way as the previous one, provided we retain the understanding that the two uses of *UI* issue in the selection of the *same* object. Hereafter in this chapter we shall take it as understood that *all* uses of *UI* to produce free variables in a given proof issue in

---

[53]This procedure is familiar from plane geometry. We draw a sketch of *one* triangle (*UI*) and say things about it that depend simply upon its being a triangle (that is, things that hold equally well for all other triangles); then we make deductions from those statements, and claim that the conclusions hold for *all* triangles (*UG*).

the selection of the same object. Thus, only the first use of *UI* in a given context must be understood as a process of random selection.

The idea of selecting an individual at random to reason about can can be profitably employed in connection with conditional or indirect sequences, but in a slightly different way. For instead of choosing some individual *x* and concluding that it has a certain property because all *x*'s do (*UI*), we choose an arbitrary *x* and *assume* (with equal arbitrariness) that it has a certain property. For example, we can give an alternative proof of the previous argument by selecting an *x* at random and assuming it is a mammal (line 3):

1.	$(x)(Bx \supset Wx)$	*Pr*
2.	$(x)(Mx \supset \sim Wx)$	*Pr*
3.	Mx	*CP*

Then the argument proceeds

4.	$Mx \supset \sim Wx$	2, *UI*
5.	$\sim Wx$	3, 4, *MP*
6.	$Bx \supset Wx$	1, *UI*
7.	$\sim Bx$	5, 6, *MT*
8.	$Mx \supset \sim Bx$	3–7, *CP*

We have now shown (line 8) that the arbitrarily chosen individual is not a *B* if it is an *M*, and this holds independently of the assumption (in line 3) that it is an *M*. Hence, what has here been shown for *x* could be shown equally well for any other object, and we finish the proof by writing:

9.	$(x)(Mx \supset \sim Bx)$	8, *UG*

However, when we choose *x*'s at random and assume they have given properties in order to generate a conditional sequence, a certain danger appears: We may be seduced into an illegitimate use of *UG*. The fundamental idea behind *UG* is that all objects have property *F* if it can be shown that an arbitrarily chosen *x* has property *F*. But it is one thing to *show* that the chosen *x* has property *F*, and quite another to *assume* that it has property *F*. And when we assume that it does, we cannot, within the scope of that assumption, conclude that everything has property *F*. To state the matter somewhat differently, universal generalization is allowable because anything proved about arbitrary x can be proved equally well and in the same way about any other object. If, however, we make some arbitrary assumption *about* x, then however randomly x is chosen, subsequent conclusions about x could not (necessarily) be drawn with regard to any other object. Hence, so long as we are moving within the scope of a conditional assumption about an arbitrary x, *UG* cannot be used. The following is an invalid argument that could be proved if we made that mistake:

If all the wheels are disconnected, then all the wheels are motionless.
Therefore, all disconnected wheels are motionless.

x's: wheels
 D: disconnected
 M: motionless

1. $(x)Dx \supset (x)Mx$	*Pr*	
2. Dx	*CP*	
3. $(x)Dx$	2, *UG* (wrong)	
4. $(x)Mx$	1, 3, *MP*	
5. Mx	4, *UI*	
6. $Dx \supset Mx$	2–5, *CP*	
7. $(x)(Dx \supset Mx)$	6, *UG*	

To state the situation formally, we impose the following restriction on the use of *UG*: *UG cannot be used within the scope of a conditional assumption in which x appears free.* Note that this restriction does not forbid us to use *UG* within conditional sequences under any circumstances. The following, for instance, is quite proper:

All disconnected wheels are motionless.
Therefore, if all the wheels are disconnected, then all the wheels are motionless.

1. $(x)(Dx \supset Mx)$	*Pr*	
2. $(x)Dx$	*CP*	
3. Dx	2, *UI*	
4. $Dx \supset Mx$	1, *UI*	
5. Mx	3, 4, *MP*	
6. $(x)Mx$	5, *UG* (right)	
7. $(x)Dx \supset (x)Mx$	2–6, *CP*	

In this case the first line of the conditional sequence assumes that all x's have the property D, which is logically quite distinct from the assumption that some one x has property D.

Lastly, we caution against certain misuses of UG. First, the principle allows us to place a universal quantifier before an expression containing free variables; it is assumed that the quantifier extends in scope over the whole of the previous expression. Thus, from $Fx \vee Gx$ we can infer $(x)(Fx \vee Gx)$, but not $(x)Fx \vee Gx$. Such misuse would in fact be an attempt to employ UG within a larger context, something that is never permissible with argument forms given as implications rather than equivalents. Secondly, one may confront an expression containing free variables and constants, such as $Fx \vee Ga$, or an expression containing free and bound variables, such as $Fx \supset (x)Fx$. It is logically possible to apply UG to such expressions, but the results would be propositions of somewhat different form than any we have discussed heretofore. Such propositions, along with others, are treated systematically in a later chapter. Consequently in *this* chapter we will regard UG as applicable only to a line of proof that is composed solely of free variables (always x's) associated with predicate letters, with or without truth-functional connectives.

The rule of universal generalization can be finally stated as follows: Given any expression containing only predicate letters and free variables, perhaps joined by truth-functional connectives, we can place a universal quantifier before the expression and extending over the whole of it, provided the given expression does not lie within the scope of a conditional assumption in which x appears free.

Exercises

1. Construct proofs for the following *valid* arguments:

   a. It is true of everything that if it is human it is animal, and if it is human it is mortal. Therefore, all men are animals and all men are mortals. (Take man and human as synonymous.)

   b. All men are animals. All men are mortals. Therefore, it is true of everything that if it is human it is animal, and if it is human it is mortal.

   c. All Republicans and Conservatives are wealthy. Therefore, all Republicans are wealthy and all Conservatives are wealthy.

d. All Republicans are wealthy. All Conservatives are wealthy. Therefore all Republicans and Conservatives are wealthy.

e. Everything is either not healthy or valuable. Therefore, all healthy things are valuable.

f. All healthy things are valuable. Therefore, everything is either not healthy or valuable.

g. All kangaroos are leapers. All leapers are strong-legged. Therefore, nothing that is not strong-legged is a kangaroo.

h. All kangaroos are leapers. All leaping kangaroos are Australian. Therefore, all kangaroos are Australian.

i. If it is not the case that all merchants are greedy, then everyone is essentially honest. Either the greedy are all cruel, or Ardelot is essentially honest. But Ardelot is not essentially honest. Therefore, all merchants are cruel.

j. If everyone who is neither an organizer nor a member is dependable, then everyone is either dependable or leftist. Everyone who is neither dependable nor an organizer is a member. Cording is not dependable. Therefore, Cording is a leftist.

k. If it is not the case that every double-checked experiment is reliable, then all certainties are suspect. But all certainties are reliable and nothing suspect is reliable. Datum #717 is a certainty, and it is double-checked. Therefore, if all experiments are double-checked, then all experiments are reliable.

l. All fluorides and chlorides are halides, or all fluorides and halides are chlorides, or all chlorides and halides are fluorides. Sample 1 is a fluoride but not a chloride. Sample 2 is a halide but not a fluoride. If Sample 1 is a halide, then all halides are electron-acceptors. Therefore, all fluorides are electron-acceptors.

2. Refer to the arguments in the following exercises at the end of Section 10 of Chapter 5: 3f, 3j, 3k. Construct proofs or show invalidity for each.

3. Construct proofs or show invalidity for the following:

a. Either any sleep is painless and anything painless is desirable, or any dream is desirable. Any death is either a sleep or a dream. Therefore, any death is desirable.

b. Either any sleep is painless and anything painless is desirable, and any death is a sleep, or any dream is desirable and any death is a dream. Therefore, any death is desirable.

3 • EXISTENTIAL INSTANTIATION AND GENERALIZATION

Again, we begin with consideration of an argument:

All who study will pass.
Some study.
Therefore, some will pass.

Intuitively we could argue as follows: Because some study, there is an individual who does in fact study. Call him m. We can thus assert that m studies. Next, because all who study will pass, it is true that if m studies, m will pass. By *modus ponens* we infer that m will pass. Hence, clearly, there is at least one individual who will pass, or, in other words, some will pass.

In this verbal justification we employed the letter m instead of x to signify the individual chosen for discussion. The motive for this choice lies in the necessity for distinguishing such an individual— which satisfies a given *particular* proposition—from a purely arbitrarily chosen individual, which satisfies a given *universal* proposition. For if we start with a universal statement $(x)Fx$ and select one individual for specific treatment, we can select any one at all, and whatever holds true for that one will also hold true for all. But if we start with $(\exists x)Fx$ and select one individual for specific treatment, we must choose an individual that *does* have property F, and what holds for that individual will not (necessarily) hold for all.

Now let us put the verbal argument into symbolic form. The premises are

1. $(x)(Sx \supset Px)$ *Pr*
2. $(\exists x)Sx$ *Pr*

As the first step in the proof, we choose one of the individuals that happens to have the property described in the particular (second) premise, and call it m. We will want to say that m has property S. This is clearly a kind of instantiation, but to mark its difference from the earlier rule of universal instantiation, we call it *existential instantiation*, abbreviated *EI*:

3. Sm 2, *EI*

As the next step, we propose that the universal proposition given in the first premise must hold for m. This is an obviously legitimate extension of the rule of universal instantiation, so we will call it by the same name:

4. $Sm \supset Pm$	1, UI
5. Pm	3, 4, MP

Lastly, because m has now been shown to have the property P it is evident that *something* has property P. Thus, from Pm we infer $(\exists x)Px$. This is analogous to the earlier rule of universal generalization, except that instead of prefixing simply a universal quantifier, we prefix an existential quantifier and change the m to x. We call this process *existential generalization*, abbreviated *EG*. The proof is then finished by writing:

6. $(\exists x)Px$	5, EG

Before exploring other arguments, we shall discuss and state schematically the new argument forms that have been introduced into the deduction system.

I. The first new addition is the rule EI:

$$\frac{(\exists x)Fx}{Fm}$$

Here Fx may be any prop[54] and m is a new type of symbol, not representing an exactly specified individual and not representing an arbitrarily chosen individual either. We shall refer to it as a *particulate variable*; correspondingly, x is called a *general variable*. The argument form EI permits us to drop the existential quantifier preceding a prop and change the prop to a substitution instance using the letter m in place of x.

We quite often come upon arguments containing two or more particular premises, say $(\exists x)Fx$ and $(\exists x)Gx$. If we apply EI to the first we get Fm. Suppose we then wish to apply EI to the second. We cannot in this case write Gm, for then we would be assuming in effect that the same individual, m, that satisfies the first proposition also

---

[54]That is, of the type so far treated—containing only predicate letters each associated with an x and, perhaps, truth-functional connectives.

satisfies the second, an assumption that may be true but need not be. Hence, in using *EI* the second time (in one and the same proof) we have to shift to some other lower case letter, say *n*. Then we could infer *Gn* from $(\exists x)Gx$. It would be understood that *m* and *n* can refer to the same individual, but maybe not. The same holds for further uses of *EI* in the same context; for individuals satisfying further particular propositions in the same proof would have to be designated by letters *o*, *p*, *q*, and so on.

Thus, we are constrained to reformulate the rule of *EI* in the following way: The letters *m*, *n*, *o*, and so on are to be regarded as a stock of particulate variables that can be used successively in any given proof. From a given particular proposition $(\exists x)Fx$ we infer *Fm*, or *Fn*, or *Fo*, *provided the variable chosen does not appear earlier in the proof.* Without this restriction on *EI*, we could prove that some men are both short and tall:

> Some men are short.
> Some men are tall.
> Therefore, some men are short and tall.

1. $(\exists x)(Hx \cdot Sx)$	*Pr*
2. $(\exists x)(Hx \cdot Tx)$	*Pr*
3. $Hm \cdot Sm$	1, *EI*
4. $Hm \cdot Tm$	2, *EI* (wrong)
5. Tm	4, *Simp*
6. $Hm \cdot Sm \cdot Tm$	3, 5, *Conj*
7. $(\exists x)(Hx \cdot Sx \cdot Tx)$	6, *EG*

(In this proof we have again used *EG* in the last line. The rule is discussed subsequently, but its significance here is clear.)

Like *UI*, *EI* permits us to pass from a quantified proposition to a substitution instance. Like *UI*, it can be applied only to propositions involving *one* quantifier and cannot be applied to propositions embedded in a context of other symbols appearing on the same line of proof. Unlike *UI* it does not permit us to pass to any substitution instance, but only to substitution instances employing (new) particulate variables.

II. We have in effect broadened the old rule of *UI*. We now regard *UI* as a principle permitting us to pass from *(x)Fx* to *Fx*, or to *Fa*, *Fb*, *Fc*, and so on, or to *Fm*, *Fn*, *Fo*, and so on. This extension clearly falls within the original intention of UI and requires no further justification.

III. Finally, we have introduced the rule EG, schematically:

$$\frac{Fm}{(\exists x)Fx}$$

Here Fm means any proposition ascribing properties F to an individual designated by the particulate variable m; but in the light of our modification of EI involving the use of *other* particulate variables it is evident that Fm could equally well be Fn, or Fo, and so forth. Furthermore, if we have a statement of the form Fa, or Fx, we are equally entitled to infer $(\exists x)Fx$. For the former means that a named individual has property F, the latter that a randomly chosen individual has property F; both imply that at least one individual *does* have property F. Hence, we regard all of the following as forms of EG:

$$\frac{Fm}{(\exists x)Fx}$$ where m is any particulate variable

$$\frac{Fa}{(\exists x)Fx}$$ where a is any constant

$$\frac{Fx}{(\exists x)Fx}$$

Like the analogous rule UG, EG permits us to place a quantifier in front of an expression occupying an entire line of proof, with the understanding that the quantifier then extends over the whole of that expression. Like UG and other rules, EG cannot be employed within a context of other symbols appearing on the same line. Again like UG, we will not *in this chapter* permit the application of EG to lines containing two or more different lower case letters; hence, EG cannot *here* be used on expressions such as $Fx \lor Gm$, or $Fm \cdot Gn$, or $Fx \supset Gn$, or $Fa \equiv Gb$. Unlike UG, EG can be applied to an expression involving any (one) lower case letter, whether constant, particulate variable, or general variable. And unlike UG, EG can be employed without restraint within conditional sequences.

To sum up, we now have the following rules permitting the addition or subtraction of quantifiers.

Universal Instantiation, *UI*

$$\frac{(x)Fx}{Fx}$$

$$\frac{(x)Fx}{Fm} \quad \text{(or } Fn, \text{ or } Fo, \text{ etc.)}$$

$$\frac{(x)Fx}{Fa} \quad \text{(or } Fb, \text{ or } Fc, \text{ etc.)}$$

Restrictions: None.

Universal Generalization, *UG*

$$\frac{Fx}{(x)Fx}$$

Restriction: The rule may not be employed if Fx lies in a conditional sequence and x appears free in the first line of that sequence.

Existential Instantiation, *EI*

$$\frac{(\exists x)Fx}{Fm} \quad \text{(or } Fn, \text{ or } Fo, \text{ etc.)}$$

Restriction: The particulate variable must not appear earlier in the proof.

Existential Generalization, *EG*

$$\frac{Fx}{(\exists x)Fx}$$

$$\frac{Fm}{(\exists x)Fx} \quad \text{(or } Fn, \text{ or } Fo, \text{ etc.)}$$

$$\frac{Fa}{(\exists x)Fx} \quad \text{(or } Fb, \text{ or } Fc, \text{ etc.}$$

Restrictions: None.

We now exhibit some examples of the use of these rules. It should be clear that each of the proofs set out subsequently corresponds to a natural series of verbal remarks that might be made in support of the argument concerned. The verbal process of choosing unspecified individuals for treatment corresponds symbolically to the dropping of quantifiers and the introduction of free variables (x, m, n, and so on). Such a procedure is always an intermediate device in the course of extended argument; accordingly, we regard no proof as complete unless all variables appearing in the last line are bound.

Everything is physical.
Therefore, something is physical

1. $(x)Px$	Pr
2. Px	1, UI
3. $(\exists x)Px$	2, EG

All whales are mammals.
Some quadrupeds are not mammals.
Therefore, some quadrupeds are not whales.

1. $(x)(Wx \supset Mx)$	Pr
2. $(\exists x)(Qx \cdot \sim Mx)$	Pr
3. $Qm \cdot \sim Mm$	2, EI
4. Qm	3, $Simp$
5. $\sim Mm$	3, $Simp$
6. $Wm \supset Mm$	1, UI
7. $\sim Wm$	5, 6, MT
8. $Qm \cdot \sim Wm$	4, 7, $Conj$
9. $(\exists x)(Qx \cdot \sim Wx)$	8, EG

Pericles is wise.
If anyone is wise, then everyone is cautious.
Therefore, Pericles is cautious.

1. Wp	Pr
2. $(\exists x)Wx \supset (x)Cx$	Pr
3. $(\exists x)Wx$	1, EG
4. $(x)Cx$	2, 3, MP
5. Cp	4, UI

If anyone is in the garden, then anyone in the garden or the house is
   under suspicion.
Holmes is in the garden.
Watson is in the house.
Therefore, Holmes and Watson are under suspicion.

1. $(\exists x)Gx \supset (x)[(Gx \text{ v } Hx) \supset Sx]$	Pr
2. Gh	Pr
3. Hw	Pr
4. $(\exists x)Gx$	2, EG
5. $(x)[(Gx \text{ v } Hx) \supset Sx]$	1, 4, MP
6. $(Gh \text{ v } Hh) \supset Sh$	5, UI
7. $Gh \text{ v } Hh$	2, Add

8. Sh	6, 7, MP
9. $(Gw \lor Hw) \supset Sw$	5, UI
10. $Gw \lor Hw$	3, Add, Com
11. Sw	9, 10, MP
12. $Sh \cdot Sw$	8, 11, $Conj$

If anything is evil, then everything is suspect.
Therefore, everything evil is suspect.

1. $(\exists x)Ex \supset (x)Sx$	Pr
2. Ex	CP
3. $(\exists x)Ex$	2, EG
4. $(x)Sx$	1, 3, MP
5. Sx	4, UI
6. $Ex \supset Sx$	2–5, MP
7. $(x)(Ex \supset Sx)$	6, UG

No Frenchmen are witty.
Some Frenchmen are witty.
Therefore, Anna is the king of Siam.

1. $(x)(Fx \supset \sim Wx)$	Pr
2. $(\exists x)(Fx \cdot Wx)$	Pr
3. $Fm \cdot Wm$	2, EI
4. Fm	3, $Simp$
5. $Fm \supset \sim Wm$	1, UI
6. $\sim Wm$	4, 5, MP
7. Wm	3, $Simp$
8. $Wm \lor Ka$	7, Add
9. Ka	6, 8, Dis

Exercises

1. Why is it that UG and EI are not extended to three different forms, as with UI and EG?

2. Write out verbal equivalents for the proofs constructed in the text of this section.

3. Someone objects that the principle EI cannot be valid, because it permits us to infer that there are at least two entities satisfying a given condition from a premise stating only that at least one entity satisfies the condition.

For example, from $(\exists x)Fx$ we can infer Fm, and then by a second use of EI we can, in the same proof, infer Fn. By conjunction we can write $Fm \cdot Fn$, and this asserts that *two* entities have the property F, whereas $(\exists x)Fx$ can be true where only *one* entity has the property F. Dispose of this objection.

4. The following arguments are all valid; construct proofs for each of them:

   a. Everything is mortal. Therefore, something is mortal.

   b. Abigail is graceful and clever. Therefore, something is graceful, something is clever, and some graceful things are clever.

   c. Jim is tall and John is not. Therefore, something is tall and something is not.

   d. Some mammalian quadrupeds are ungulates. Therefore, there are mammals, there are quadrupeds, and there are ungulates.

   e. Everything is material. Therefore, it is not the case that there is something that is not material. (Hint: Try an indirect proof.)

   f. For any object, it is not the case that if it is a coat then it will not be stolen. Therefore, there is nothing that is not a coat unless it is not going to be stolen.

   g. Something is material. Therefore, it is not the case that everything is not material.

   h. Some Roman senators were inhumane. Therefore, it is not the case that all Roman senators were humane.

   i. All electrons spin. Some particles do not spin. Therefore, some particles are not electrons.

   j. No electrons radiate. Some particles radiate. Therefore, some particles are not electrons.

   k. All electrons spin. Some particles are electrons. Therefore, there is something for which it is not the case that if it is a particle then it does not spin.

   l. Only the smart deserve high pay or good working conditions. There is someone for whom it is not true that: He is smart unless he deserves high pay. Therefore, someone does not deserve good working conditions.

   m. If some men feel inferior and some do not, then all braggarts must be regarded with suspicion. Men brag if and only if they feel inferior.

Some men brag and some do not. Therefore, some men have to be regarded with suspicion.

n. Smith does not have to be regarded with suspicion. If all braggarts have to be regarded with suspicion, and some brag and some do not, then any member of the Liars Club is possibly neurotic. If Smith is possibly neurotic, so is Jones. If Smith is not possibly neurotic, then all braggarts are innately unstable. Anyone innately unstable has to be regarded with suspicion. Therefore, if Jones is not possibly neurotic and Black brags, then neither Smith nor Jones is a member of the Liars Club.

o. All men are mortal. Some men are not mortal. Therefore, some men are mortal, and all angels have wings.

*p. Some men drink and some do not. Men drink if and only if they are disturbed. Either everyone is disturbed or no one is. Therefore, Napoleon was the king of Denmark.

5. Examine the following arguments from the exercises in Chapter 5. For each, construct a proof or show invalidity:

   Section 9, Exercises 1b, 1c, 1d, 1e, 1f, 1g.
   Section 10, Exercises 3b, 3c, 3d, 3i.
   Section 11, Exercises 5f, 5i.

6. Find formal proofs or show invalidity for the following:

   a. Some New York bookies are honest. If there are any bookies, then there are criminals. All criminals are socially maladjusted. If anyone is socially maladjusted, then everyone socially maladjusted needs treatment. Therefore, some need treatment.

   b. The same argument as in 2a, but with the conclusion: "Some bookies need treatment."

   c. The same argument as in 2a, but with the conclusion: "Some New Yorkers need treatment."

   d. It is not true that some chemical tests are unreliable. If some aromatics are poisonous, then either some chemical tests are unreliable, or some animals got the wrong dose, or everything poisonous and pungent is unstable. All aromatics are poisonous and pungent. If any aromatic is pungent, then no animals got the wrong dose. Substance 1 is an aromatic. Consequently, substance 1 is unstable unless it is not aromatic.

7. For the sentence, "No man who is a defendant in this court will be convicted if he is innocent," two translations are offered:

  a. $(x)[Dx \supset (Ix \supset \sim Cx)]$
  b. $(x)[Dx \supset \sim(Ix \supset Cx)]$

Only one of these can be correct. Which one? Show that the wrong one permits a deduction that no one asserting the proposition would allow, and that the same deduction cannot be made from the right one.

8. For the sentence, "Any man who is tried will be acquitted if and only if he is innocent," two translations are offered:

  a. $(x)[(Tx \supset Ax) \equiv Ix]$
  b. $(x)[Tx \supset (Ax \equiv Ix)]$

Proceed as in Exercise 7.

4 • Q EQUIVALENCE, Q RULES, AND Q DISTRIBUTION RULES

In the previous chapter we showed that expressions lying within the scope of a quantifier could be altered in accordance with truth-functional (propositional) equivalences, just as if they were themselves truth-functional molecules. It is easy to see that identical manipulations are justified in the deductive system of this chapter. For instance, to pass from $(x)\sim(Fx \supset Gx)$ to $(x)(Fx \cdot \sim Gx)$ we need only drop the quantifier by UI, make appropriate changes by appeal to CC and DN, and then replace the quantifier by UG.

If the expression we want to alter occurs within some larger context more steps are (theoretically) required. Suppose we want to pass from

  (i) $(x)Hx \text{ v } (\exists x) \sim (Fx \supset Gx)$

to

  (ii) $(x)Hx \text{ v } (\exists x)(Fx \cdot \sim Gx)$.

We could first take $(\exists x)\sim(Fx \supset Gx)$ as an assumption for conditional proof and establish

  $(\exists x) \sim (Fx \supset Gx) \supset (\exists x)(Fx \cdot \sim Gx)$.

The converse can be established in the same way, and the two combined into a biconditional. The principle of material substitution then permits the desired inference from (i) to (ii).

However, all these lengthy maneuvers can clearly be accomplished in the same manner for any pair of truth-functionally equivalent props. Accordingly, we adopt the policy of applying truth-functional equivalences *immediately* to expressions lying within the scope of quantifiers and treating the process annotationally as a case of substitution. Thus, in the example we would simply write

1. $(\exists x) \sim (Fx \supset Gx)$ *Pr*
2. $(\exists x)(Fx \cdot \sim Gx)$ 1, *S, CC, DN*

and similarly within larger contexts.

An analogous approach may be taken to the Q rules of Chapter 5, which are summarized as follows:

$$
\begin{aligned}
(x)Fx &\equiv \sim(\exists x)\sim Fx \\
\sim(x)Fx &\equiv (\exists x)\sim Fx \\
(\exists x)Fx &\equiv \sim(x)\sim Fx \\
\sim(\exists x)Fx &\equiv (x)\sim Fx
\end{aligned}
$$

These expressions implicitly contain *eight* forms of conditional proposition. It happens that any instance of *four* of those forms could be established by conditional sequence in any proof (that is, deduced from no premises whatever) without appeal to principles of inference other than the ones already listed. To establish the other four, however, we require an additional postulate: We assume that any argument of the form

$$
\frac{\sim(x)Fx}{(\exists x)\sim Fx}
$$

is valid. In words it is expressed as follows: If it is not true that everything is an F, then it follows logically that something is not an F. We will not provide a name for this form because after the next page or two there will be no occasion for explicit reference to it. We regard it as intuitively evident.

With the help of this postulate, any biconditional having one of the four forms displayed here can be inserted in any proof; the following schema shows how, for the first one.

$$
\begin{array}{lll}
\quad\quad 1. & (x)Fx & CP \\
\quad\quad\quad 2. & \sim\sim(\exists x)\sim Fx & IP \\
\quad\quad\quad 3. & (\exists x)\sim Fx & 2,\ DN \\
\checkmark\ \ 4. & \sim Fm & 3,\ EI \\
\checkmark\ \ 5. & Fm & 1,\ UI \\
\quad\quad\quad 6. & \sim(\exists x)\sim Fx & 2\text{–}5,\ IP \\
\quad 7. & (x)Fx \supset \sim(\exists x)\sim Fx & 1\text{–}6,\ CP \\
\checkmark\ \ 8. & \sim(\exists x)\sim Fx & CP \\
\quad\quad\quad 9. & \sim(x)Fx & IP \\
\checkmark 10. & (\exists x)\sim Fx & 9,\ \text{(nameless)} \\
\quad\quad 11. & (x)Fx & 9\text{–}10,\ IP \\
\quad 12. & \sim(\exists x)\sim Fx \supset (x)Fx & 8\text{–}11,\ CP \\
\quad 13. & (x)Fx \equiv \sim(\exists x)\sim Fx & 7,\ 12,\ Conj,\ CC
\end{array}
$$

Similar proof for the other three forms is left as an exercise. With a further appeal to material substitution, any alteration of quantified expressions in accordance with the Q rules of Chapter 5 can be thus reproduced within a formal proof and regarded as a valid inference in the present context.[55] We adopt the policy of making the alterations at once, annotated by the letter Q. Examples are

$$
\begin{array}{lll}
1. & (x)(Fx \supset Gx) & Pr \\
2. & \sim(\exists x) \sim (Fx \supset Gx) & 1,\ Q
\end{array}
$$

$$
\begin{array}{lll}
1. & (x)Fx \supset \sim(\exists x)Gx & Pr \\
2. & (x)Fx \supset (x)\sim Gx & 1,\ S,\ Q
\end{array}
$$

$$
\begin{array}{lll}
1. & \sim(x)(Fx \supset Gx) & Pr \\
2. & (\exists x)(Fx\cdot\sim Gx) & 1,\ Q,\ S,\ CC,\ DN
\end{array}
$$

Manipulations in accordance with the Q distribution principles of Chapter 5 can also be reproduced within formal proofs, without the help of further principles or postulates. Demonstration of this fact is left as an exercise. Because inferences of those kinds are frequently needed in a later context, we also adopt the policy of making them immediately, annotated as *Q-dist*.

---

[55]In showing that certain propositions can be deduced from any premises (or from no premises), we claim also to be showing that they are *logical* truths. Strictly speaking this claim rests on another: The system of proof-construction stated here is *consistent* in the sense that no formal proof can be constructed for an argument that would appear invalid by the methods of Chapter 5. That the system is consistent in this sense can be shown, but the demonstration is not suitable for presentation in this text.

Exercises

1. Assuming the use of (i) all argument forms stated prior to this section, (ii) the adaptation of the Q equivalence principle discussed in this section, and (iii) the nameless form

$$\frac{\sim(x)Fx}{(\exists x)\sim Fx}$$

   show that any proposition having the form of a Q rule biconditional can be inserted into any proof.

2. With assumptions as in Exercise 1, and also granting the immediate use of Q rules, show that any proposition having the form

$$[(x)Fx \cdot (x)Gx] \quad \equiv \quad (x)(Fx \cdot Gx)$$

   or

$$[(\exists x)Fx \text{ v } (\exists x)Gx] \quad \equiv \quad (\exists x)(Fx \text{ v } Gx)$$

   can be inserted into any proof.

3. Show by constructing proofs that the following pairs are equivalent·
   Use universal quantifiers to translate expressions of the form "No F's are G."

   a. No swans are white.
      No white things are swans.

   b. Some swans are white.
      Some white things are swans.

   c. It is not the case that all swans are white.
      Some swans are not white.

   d. It is not the case that no swans are white.
      Some swans are white.

   e. It is not the case that some swans are white.
      No swans are white.

   f. It is not the case that some swans are not white.
      All swans are white.

   g. Something is either a swan or white.
      Something is a swan or something is white.

   h. Some swans are either white or long-necked.
      Some swans are white or some swans are long-necked.

    i.　Every white swan is long-necked.
       It is not the case that some white swans are not long-necked.

    j.　It is not the case that anything white or long-necked is a swan.
       Either some things white are not swans or some things long-necked are not swans.

4. Construct two proofs for each of the following arguments, one using a Q rule and one not.

    a.　All careful teachers prepare before time. Therefore, if anyone does not prepare before time it is not the case that everyone is a careful teacher.

    b.　It is not the case that some careful teachers fail to prepare before time. Therefore, if some teachers fail to prepare before time it is not the case that everyone is careful.

5. Examine the following arguments in the exercises at the end of Section 13, Chapter 5: 1a, 1g, 1i, 1j, 1k, 1l, 1m. For each one construct a proof or show invalidity.

6. Construct proofs or show invalidity for the following:

    a.　This herd has colts but no mares. Therefore, it is not the case that all herds that have colts have mares.

    b.　This herd has no colts. Therefore, all herds that have colts have mares.

    c.　It is not the case that any coat stolen in this restaurant will be paid for by the management. Therefore, some coat will be stolen in this restaurant.

    d.　Either Napoleon or Wellington was a superb tactician. Therefore, someone was a superb tactician.

    e.　All generals know tactics. Either Morgan or Learned did not know tactics. Therefore, there is someone who is not a general.

    f.　Either there are tacticians or there are generals. Hence, Napoleon was either a tactician or a general.

    g.　All liberals are northerners or all liberals are intellectuals. Murphy is not an intellectual or he is not a northerner. Hence, it is not the case that everyone is a liberal.

    h.　Everyone is liberal, intellectual, or wise. Therefore, if Donovan is not liberal and there are no intellectuals, then someone is wise.

i. All competent chemists know the safety rules. Some who are not chemists do not know the safety rules. Therefore, everyone is incompetent.

j. All competent chemists know the safety rules. Therefore, either no one who is competent does not know the safety rules or someone is not a chemist.

k. Every human child is a boy or a girl but not both. Alcestis is a human child but not a girl. Xanthippe is a girl. Hence, if Xanthippe is a human child there are girls and boys.

l. All children are girls or all children are boys, but not both. Anna is a child. Therefore, some children are not boys or some children are not girls, and perhaps both.

m. All children are girls or all children are boys, but not both. Anna is a child. Therefore, some children are not boys or some children are not girls, but not both.

n. All men are mortal if and only if some are. All men are virtuous if and only if some are not mortal. There are men. Consequently, all men are mortal or virtuous.

o. There are apples. Therefore, all apples are red if and only if it is not the case that no apples are red.

p. It is not the case that some apples are red. It is not the case that some apples are not red. Therefore, there are no apples.

q. All men are animals. All animals are mortal. It is not the case that some men are mortal. Therefore, there are no men.

r. If all whales are white and some marine animals are white, then all whalers are color blind. Ahab is a whale and not white. Ahab's brother is a white marine animal. If there are whales, then there are whalers. Therefore, someone is color blind.

s. All philosophers are foolish or some are. No philosophers are foolish or else some are not. Therefore, there are both foolish and nonfoolish philosophers.

t. If all machines think, then all thought is mechanical. If all thought is mechanical, then everything mechanical is conscious. Therefore, if all machines think then all machines are conscious.

u. If some machines think, then some thought is mechanical. If some thought is mechanical, then something mechanical is conscious. Hence, if some machines think, then some machines are conscious.

v. Substance 1 is an acid and all acids turn litmus red, provided substance 2 is a base or substance 3 not a carbonate or substance 1 not an acid. Therefore, substance 1 is an acid.

w. No accident not covered under coverage A will be covered under coverage B. Any accident not covered under A or B will be covered under coverage C unless it occurred before the policy went into effect. Hence, if there is an accident not covered under C, then provided every accident is covered under B unless not covered under A, there is an accident covered under A unless it took place before the policy went into effect.

x. If this crime is a felony then it warrants the maximum punishment. This crime is a felony if and only if all felonies are premeditated and involve major sums. This crime was premeditated and involved a major sum. And there are premeditated felonies that involve major sums. Hence, this crime warrants the maximum punishment.

y. Either every IF component is faulty (unless it has been in the storeroom lately), or some IF components are disconnected. If there are any IF components at all, then all of them are connected. Hence, if there are any warmed-up IF components that have not been in the storeroom lately, some IF component is faulty.

z. Any number that divides N, and divides N plus 1, divides 1. If there is a greatest prime, then it divides N. But no prime divides 1. All primes are numbers. Therefore, there is no greatest prime.

7. Add the needed premise in the following enthymeme and construct a proof for the argument: "Any even number has an even square. Any odd number has an odd square. Hence, any number whose square is even or odd is itself even or odd respectively."

8. From the following sets of premises significant conclusions can be drawn if the premises are supplemented with one clearly true addition. Formulate the complete arguments and construct appropriate proofs.

a. Any truth-table row having 1 under P has 1 under the major connective on the left. Similarly for any truth-table row having 0 under P. And any row having 1 under the major connective on the left has 1 under the major connective on the right.

*b. Any report from one of our agents that comes through our channels is in
   the D code unless it is not secret. If document 717 is in the D code,
   then any of our decoders can decipher it. If there are any decoders of
   ours that can decipher it Harrison can. But in fact Harrison is stumped.
   And document 717 is a secret report that came through our channels.

5 • COMPLETENESS OF THE SYSTEM

The system of proof-construction developed in Sections 1–4 is
complete, in the sense that a formal proof can be constructed for any
argument that would turn up valid under the methods of Chapter 5.
It is easy to establish this fact, because every step in the process of
formulating and analyzing test forms for given arguments corresponds
to a stage in the construction of *indirect* formal proofs for the same
arguments. Rather than submit to the tedium of enumerating those
steps and their parallel stages in formal proofs, we indicate the general pattern by consideration of the following deduction:

1.	$(x)(Fx \supset Gx)$	*Pr*
2.	$Fa \vee Fb$	*Pr* /$Ga \vee Gb$
3.	$\sim(Ga \vee Gb)$	*IP*
4.	$(x)(Fx \supset Gx) \cdot (Fa \vee Fb) \cdot \sim(Ga \vee Gb)$	1, 2, 3, *Conj*
5.	$(x)(Fx \supset Gx) \cdot (Fa \vee Fb) \cdot \sim Ga \cdot \sim Gb$	4, *S, DM*
6.	$(x)(Fx \supset Gx) \cdot [(Fa \cdot \sim Ga \cdot \sim Gb) \vee$ $(Fb \cdot \sim Ga \cdot \sim Gb)]$	5, *S, Dist*
7.	$[(x)(Fx \supset Gx) \cdot Fa \cdot \sim Ga \cdot \sim Gb] \vee$ $[(x)(Fx \supset Gx) \cdot Fb \cdot \sim Ga \cdot \sim Gb]$	6, *Dist*
8.	$\sim\sim[(x)(Fx \supset Gx) \cdot Fa \cdot \sim Ga \cdot \sim Gb]$	*IP*
9.	$(x)(Fx \supset Gx) \cdot Fa \cdot \sim Ga \cdot \sim Gb$	8, *DN*
10.	$(x)(Fx \supset Gx)$	9, *Simp*
11.	$Fa \cdot \sim Ga$	9, *Simp*
12.	Fa	11, *Simp*
13.	$Fa \supset Ga$	10, *UI*
✓14.	Ga	12, 13, *MP*
✓15.	$\sim Ga$	11, *Simp*
16.	$\sim[(x)(Fx \supset Gx) \cdot Fa \cdot \sim Ga \cdot \sim Gb]$	9–15, *IP*
17.	$(x)(Fx \supset Gx) \cdot Fb \cdot \sim Ga \cdot \sim Gb$	7, 16, *Dis*
18.	$(x)(Fx \supset Gx)$	17, *Simp*
19.	$Fb \cdot \sim Gb$	17, *Simp*
20.	Fb	19, *Simp*

21. $Fb \supset Gb$		18, *UI*
✓22. Gb		20, 21, *MP*
✓23. $\sim Gb$		19, *Simp*
24. $Ga \vee Gb$		3–23, *IP*

Line 4 contains the corresponding conjunction for the given argument, which is cast into disjunctive normal form in lines 5–7. Both disjuncts in line 7 have the shape of test forms. In line 8 the first disjunct is isolated for treatment, and in lines 8–15 it is seen to be inconsistent; the critical step is an application of *UI* to the universal. If the inconsistency had arisen through the structure of some *particular* proposition, there would also have been some appeal to *EI* in this sequence.[56] In any case, the inconsistency of the first disjunct (of 7) permits the assertion of its denial in line 16 and a consequent turning of attention to the second disjunct set out in 17. In the balance of the proof we see that the latter is also inconsistent, and the conclusion follows. A similar series of maneuvers can be worked out for any other *valid* argument.

It was observed in Section 1 that any argument that appears to be invalid under the methods of Chapter 5 may also be regarded as invalid in the context of this chapter, in which the finitude postulate is dropped. We now see that the same holds for arguments that appear to be *valid* under the methods of Chapter 5. It follows that *the decision procedure of Chapter 5 is reliable even if the relevant universe of objects is infinite.*

We conclude with three remarks: (i) Our system of proof-construction can be naturally applied to arguments symbolized partly with quantifiers and partly with propositional constants; examples are suggested in the exercises following. (ii) The system is *consistent*, in the sense that no proof can be constructed for an argument that would appear invalid under the methods of Chapter 5, but that will not be demonstrated in this text. (iii) The system can be used to establish any logical truth involving quantified expressions, by exhibiting a formal proof for it that assumes no unconditional (that is, nonindented) premises; again, examples are suggested in the exercises.

---

[56]Note that truth-functional inconsistencies, where they exist, can always be demonstrated by the lengthy but systematic routine of Chapter 4, Section 6.

Exercises

1. For the following arguments, construct indirect formal proofs that parallel the analysis of the arguments by the methods of Chapter 5.

   a. $(x)(Fx \supset Gx)$ b. $(x)Fx$ v $(x)Gx$
      $(x)Fx$ $\sim Fa$
      ———————   ———————
      $(x)Gx$ $(x)Gx \cdot Ga$

2. Produce formal proofs for the arguments in Exercises 1a, 1c, 1d, and 1f following Section 14, Chapter 5.

3. Consider these expressions:

   a. $(\exists x)Fx \supset \sim[(x)(Fx \supset Gx) \cdot (x)(Fx \supset \sim Gx)]$

   b. $(\exists x)Fx \supset [(\exists x)(Fx \cdot Gx)$ v $(\exists x)(Fx \cdot \sim Gx)]$

   The first is a formal statement of the fact that corresponding A and E propositions (in the square of opposition) are contraries provided their grammatical subject exists. The second states that under the same condition, corresponding I and O propositions are subcontraries. Prove these, by constructing formal proofs starting from no premises whatever. Express similarly, and prove, that an A proposition implies the corresponding I proposition, and an E · the corresponding O, provided their grammatical subject exists.

4. Show by formal proof that the following are logically true:

   a. $\sim(\exists x)Fx \supset (x)(Fx \supset Gx)$

   b. $\sim(\exists x)Fx \supset \sim(\exists x)(Fx \cdot Gx)$

   c. $[(\exists x)Fx \supset (x)Fx] \equiv [(\exists x)\sim Fx \supset (x)\sim Fx]$

   d. $[(x)Fx$ v $(x)\sim Fx] \equiv [(x)Fx \equiv (\exists x)Fx]$

CHAPTER 7

Categorical Syllogisms and Related Methods

ABSTRACT: Certain fairly simple arguments and propositions may readily be analyzed by other than symbolic means; some historically prominent and still very useful devices for doing so are studied. In Sections 1–3 the verbal operations of *conversion* and *obversion* are developed, and the argument form known as *categorical syllogism,* or simply *syllogism,* is defined and analyzed. In Section 4 a diagrammatic method useful mainly for the treatment of syllogisms is discussed. The chapter may be omitted without loss of continuity.

1 • CONVERSION, OBVERSION, DISTRIBUTIVITY

We now take a respite from our pursuit of ever more complex forms of argument in order to discuss a topic of great historical importance. The idea of analyzing deductive inferences by reducing them to a restricted number of standard forms was first introduced by Aristotle, a Greek biologist and philosopher of the fourth century B.C. During ancient and medieval times the study of deductive form tended to focus on the analysis of two-term propositions of the subject-predicate type, that is, propositions of the kind we have already singled out for special treatment in the square of opposition.[57] The study of these propositions and their relations led to certain concepts and methods of manipulation that were part of the common intellectual equipment of Western scientists, philosophers, and men of letters for centuries. (The square of opposition is itself one of these.) These concepts and techniques are as useful today as they ever were (although that usefulness is quite limited), and they continue to be used and mentioned in a variety of contexts, particularly in philosophy, literature, and law. Accordingly we shall develop them here and demonstrate their use; but we shall regard them as *justified* by reference to the symbolic methods of the previous chapters.

Almost any proposition can be regarded as an instance of the two-term subject-predicate form treated in the square of opposition, although it sometimes requires a great deal of artificiality to make good on this claim. For example, "Trees grow," is easily rendered as "All trees are things-that-grow." With some strain we can think of "Horses are between whales and bats in size," as "All horses are things-smaller-than-whales-and-larger-than-horses."

In any case, the simple subject-predicate form occurs naturally with extraordinary frequency in English, and with some twists and turns we can as it were force it to occur even more often than might otherwise seem to be the case. This is one justification for the preoccupation with that form that pervades the traditional logic of classical antiquity and the middle ages. Our subsequent discussions in this

---

[57]In this chapter the term *predicate* is usually used to refer to the grammatical predicate of a sentence; this is not to be confused with the notion of a predicate as a property applied to an individual object, which we symbolize as Fa or Fx. The two meanings are obviously related but technically distinct.

chapter will be devoted entirely to universal and particular instances of that form; that is, to the four types that appear in the square of opposition, called *A*, *E*, *I*, and *O* (Chapter 5, Section 6).

We note first that the propositions we are considering can be altered by interchange of subject and predicate, a process known as *conversion*. "No *F*'s are *G*," for example, converts to "No *G*'s are *F*." *E* and *I* propositions can be converted without loss or change of meaning, but not *A* or *O*; these claims are easily verified by symbolic treatment. If we agree to confine conversion to *E* and *I* propositions, it is a nonsymbolic method of changing a proposition into another that is logically equivalent to it.

The attempt to convert an *A* proposition (with a tacit claim that the result is equivalent to the original) is a common logical mistake, known as the *fallacy of illicit conversion*. For example, from "All bald men are virile," one may *not* infer that "All virile men are bald." On the other hand, from "No impotent men are bald," one *may* infer that "No bald men are impotent."

Another verbal operation is called *obversion*. It is accomplished as follows: Given a two-term subject-predicate proposition, we can change it from affirmative to negative or vice versa and then change its predicate-term to a corresponding contradictory term. For example, "All *F*'s are *G*," may be shifted from affirmative to negative, giving "No *F*'s are *G*"; then the predicate *G* is replaced by the contradictory term "non-*G*", yielding "No *F*'s are non-*G*."[58] Unlike conversion, obversion always yields an equivalent result, as the reader can confirm for himself. Although other verbal operations are possible, conversion and obversion are the fundamental types from which the others are derived by combination.

In addition to these methods for manipulation of statements, the traditional logic contains a technical conception of great usefulness concerning the logical status of the terms (subject and predicate)

---

[58]Two *terms* are contradictory if one or the other *must* be applied to any appropriate object, but both can*not* be applied. Thus *green* and *non-green* are contradictory terms. By contrast, *green* and *black* are *contrary* terms, because although they cannot *both* be applied to a given object, it is not necessary that one of them be. It should be observed that *green* and *non-green* may be applied to one object if we distinguish parts or aspects of it, but then we would not be dealing with *one* object in an unequivocal sense.

appearing in the propositions under scrutiny. A proposition may involve an assertion about all of the objects denoted by a term, or some of them. In the former case we say that the term is *distributed* in that proposition; in the latter case, *undistributed*. How can we tell whether a given term in a given proposition is distributed or undistributed?

It is easy enough to see that universal propositions (*A* and *E*) make an assertion about the whole of the class of objects denoted by the subject-term. Correspondingly, the particular propositions (*I* and *O*) make an assertion about part of that class. Hence,

(i) The subject of a universal proposition (*A* or *E*) is distributed.

And

(ii) The subject of a particular proposition (*O* or *I*) is undistributed.

Next consider the two affirmative types, "All *F*'s are *G*" and "Some *F*'s are *G*." In both cases it is asserted in effect that some members of of the class of things having the property *G* also have the property *F* (assuming there are *F*'s). But in neither case is any statement implied about all *G*'s. Hence,

(iii) The predicate of an affirmative proposition (*A* or *I*) is undistributed.

Lastly we consider the negative propositions, "No *F*'s are *G*" and "Some *F*'s are not *G*." Both of these state that certain *F*'s (if there are any) exist apart from the entire class of *G*'s. Thus,

(iv) The predicate of a negative proposition (*E* or *O*) is distributed.

The justification for statements (i)–(iv) is admittedly somewhat vague. It is therefore worth noting that (i)–(iv) may themselves be regarded as defining the meaning of distributed and undistributed. The main use of the concept arises in connection with the theory of the categorical syllogism, which follows in a later section.

Exercises

1. Show by some symbolic analysis that conversion of *E* and *I* propositions yields an equivalent result, but not conversion of *A* and *O* propositions.

2. Show by some symbolic analysis that obversion of any proposition (*A*, *E*, *I*, or *O*) yields an equivalent result.

3. Assuming that objects denoted by the predicate of an A proposition exist, such a proposition can be converted and then reduced from universal to particular. This is called *conversion per accidens*. Show that the result of conversion per accidens is logically implied by the original, but not conversely.

4. For each of the following propositions, produce an equivalent expression by obversion, then convert the result (if possible) to produce another equivalent, then obvert again, and so on, until the process is blocked by the fact that A and O cannot be converted to produce an equivalent result.

   a. All men are mortal.

   b. No whales are vertebrates.

   c. Some bats are carnivorous.

   d. Some teachers are not women.

5. Construct formal proofs paralleling the sequential obversions and conversions in Exercise 4.

6. Show that contradictory propositions in the square of opposition have terms of opposite distributivity.

7. Assuming the grammatical subject of propositions in the square of opposition exists, show that whenever one proposition in the square logically implies another, the latter has no more distributed terms than the former.

2 • SYLLOGISMS

Two propositions (from the square of opposition) having one and only one term in common may be taken as the premises of an argument. We may then formulate a conclusion that combines the two terms that appear separately in the premises, the common term disappearing entirely. Such an argument constitutes a peculiarly simple and common pattern known as the *categorical syllogism*, or simply *syllogism*. Examples are

> All animals are mortal.
> All men are animals
> Therefore, all men are mortal.

> Some mortals are not vertebrates.
> All mortals are animals.
> Therefore, some animals are not vertebrates.

Both of these arguments are valid, and in the strict sense the term *syllogism* should be applied only to valid arguments. However, we shall call any argument a syllogism if its form satisfies the conditions specified here, valid or not. Obviously all syllogisms have two premises and three constituent terms.

The traditional logic studied the varieties of valid syllogisms in great detail. In order to facilitate discussion of these arguments certain technical terms are employed: The predicate of the conclusion is called the *major term*, and the premise in which that term appears is the *major premise*. The subject of the conclusion is called the *minor term*, and the premise in which that term appears is called the *minor premise*. The term that is common to the premises but does not appear in the conclusion is called the *middle term*. It is customary to write syllogisms with the major premise first. In the first of the two examples given here, the major term is *mortal*, the minor term is *man*, and the middle term is *animals*. In the second example the major is *vertebrates*, the minor is *animals*, and the middle is *mortals*.

When a syllogism is written in standard form (major premise first) the arrangement of the major, minor, and middle terms produces one of four possible patterns, called *figures*. Taking S for the minor term, P for the major, and M for the middle, the possible arrangements are diagrammed below; they are called the *first figure*, *second figure*, and so on, in the order given:

First figure:	$M-P$
	$\dfrac{S-M}{S-P}$
Second figure:	$P-M$
	$\dfrac{S-M}{S-P}$
Third figure:	$M-P$
	$\dfrac{M-S}{S-P}$
Fourth figure:	$P-M$
	$\dfrac{M-S}{S-P}$

The first example at the beginning of this section is in the first figure, the other in the third figure.

Each constituent proposition in a syllogism is necessarily one of the four types given in the square of opposition. When a syllogism is written in standard form (major premise first), one can identify the type of each proposition and write out the appropriate letters (*A*, *E*, *I*, or *O*) serially from left to right; for instance *AII*, or *EIO*. This sequence of letters is called the *mood* of the syllogism. The first example at the beginning of this section is in the mood *AAA*, the second *OAO*.

In any given figure, each constituent proposition may be any one of the four types; hence, in that figure there are 4x4x4 or 64 possible syllogistic forms. The same holds for each of the four figures, giving a total of 4x64 or 256 possible forms. Obviously the form of a syllogism is completely specified if one states its figure and mood.

Lastly, we note that there are many arguments whose form approaches that of the syllogism, but that are *not* syllogisms. Some can easily be altered so that they *do* exhibit the syllogistic form, some not so easily. For example,

> No birds are invertebrates.
> All sparrows are birds.
> Therefore, all sparrows are vertebrates.

This is not a syllogism because it contains four distinct terms: birds, sparrows, invertebrates, and vertebrates. However, we could obvert the first premise, obtaining the equivalent argument,

> All birds are vertebrates.
> All sparrows are birds.
> Thefore, all sparrows are vertebrates.

This argument is a syllogism.

Another example of familiar type is

> All pines are larger than bushes.
> All cedars are larger than pines.
> Therefore, all cedars are larger than bushes.

This is not a syllogism because it has four terms: pines, cedars, things-larger-than-bushes, and things-larger-than-pines. One way to transform this argument into a syllogism is the following:

> All things larger than things larger than bushes are larger than bushes.
> All cedars are things larger than things larger than bushes.
> Therefore, all cedars are larger than bushes.

Aside from the extreme awkwardness of this, we see that the nerve of the original argument has really been compressed into the major premise of the revision, and hence the revision is not really an adequate representation of the logical mechanism that underlies the original. In a later chapter we shall develop superior methods for the analysis of such arguments.

Exercises

Each of the following arguments is a syllogism. For each one, identify the major, minor, and middle terms, and the figure and mood. Make a record of the figure and mood. Then test for validity. If it is valid, make a note of that fact. If not, try adding as additional premises the assumption that objects *exist* corresponding to the grammatical subjects of the constituent propositions (including the conclusion). Then test for validity again, and record the result.

1. All scholars are students. All teachers are scholars. Hence, all teachers are students.

2. No scholars are students. All teachers are scholars. Hence, no teachers are students.

3. All students are scholars. No teachers are scholars. Hence, some teachers are not students.

4. All students are scholars. All teachers are scholars. Hence, some teachers are students.

5. All scholars are students. No teachers are scholars. Hence, no teachers are students.

6. All scholars are students. Some scholars are teachers. Hence, some teachers are students.

7. All scholars are students. No scholars are teachers. Hence, no teachers are students.

8. All students are scholars. No scholars are teachers. Hence, no teachers are students.

9. All scholars are students. Some scholars are not teachers. Hence, some teachers are not students.

10. No students are scholars. Some teachers are scholars. Hence, some teachers are not students.

11. Some crimes are misdemeanors. All wrongs are misdemeanors. Hence, some wrongs are crimes.

12. All misdemeanors are crimes. Some wrongs are misdemeanors. Hence, some wrongs are crimes.

13. Some misdemeanors are not crimes. All misdemeanors are wrongs. Hence, some wrongs are not crimes.

14. No crimes are misdemeanors. Some misdemeanors are wrongs. Hence, some wrongs are not crimes.

15. No misdemeanors are crimes. Some misdemeanors are wrongs. Hence, some wrongs are not crimes.

16. All misdemeanors are crimes. No wrongs are misdemeanors. Hence, some wrongs are not crimes.

17. Some crimes are not misdemeanors. All wrongs are misdemeanors. Hence, some wrongs are not crimes.

18. All misdemeanors are crimes. Some wrongs are not misdemeanors. Hence, some wrongs are not crimes.

19. Some crimes are misdemeanors. All misdemeanors are wrongs. Hence, some wrongs are crimes.

20. All stars twinkle. Everything that twinkles is far away. Hence, everything far away is a star.

21. All stars twinkle. Nothing that twinkles is far away. Hence, some things that are far away are not stars.

22. All twinkling things are stars. No twinkling things are far away. Hence, some things far away are not stars.

23. Nothing that twinkles is a star. Some things far away twinkle. Hence, some things far away are not stars.

24. All stars twinkle. Nothing far away twinkles. Hence, nothing far away is a star.

25. Everything that twinkles is a star. Everything far away twinkles. Hence, some things far away are stars.

26. No stars twinkle. Everything that twinkles is far away. Hence, some things far away are not stars.

27. No stars twinkle. Everything that twinkles is far away. Hence, nothing far away is a star.

28. All seeds are fruits. Some nuts are not fruits. Hence, some nuts are not seeds.

29. All seeds are fruits. All nuts are fruits. Hence, all nuts are seeds.

30. No seeds are fruits. All nuts are fruits. Hence, no nuts are seeds.

31. No fruits are seeds. All nuts are fruits. Hence, some nuts are not seeds.

32. All seeds are fruits. All fruits are nuts. Hence, some nuts are seeds.

33. Some fruits are seeds. All fruits are nuts. Hence, some nuts are seeds.

34. All fruits are seeds. All fruits are nuts. Hence, some nuts are seeds.

35. All seeds are fruits. Some fruits are nuts. Hence, some nuts are seeds.

36. All fruits are seeds. All fruits are nuts. Hence, all nuts are seeds.

37. Some chordates are vertebrates. All tunicates are chordates. Hence, some tunicates are vertebrates.

38. All vertebrates are chordates. Some chordates are not tunicates. Hence, some tunicates are not vertebrates.

39. All vertebrates are chordates. Some tunicates are chordates. Hence, some tunicates are vertebrates.

40. No vertebrates are chordates. All tunicates are chordates. Hence, some tunicates are not vertebrates.

41. Some chordates are not vertebrates. All tunicates are chordates. Hence, some tunicates are not vertebrates.

42. No chordates are vertebrates. All chordates are tunicates. Hence, no tunicates are vertebrates.

43. Some vertebrates are not chordates. All chordates are tunicates. Hence, some tunicates are not vertebrates.

44. No chordates are vertebrates. All chordates are tunicates. Hence, some tunicates are not vertebrates.

3 • VALID SYLLOGISMS

It is desirable to be able to decide quickly whether or not a given syllogism is valid. One way to accomplish this is to evaluate one by one the 254 syllogistic forms and make a record of those that are valid. A more elegant procedure is to establish certain rules that describe necessary and sufficient conditions for the validity of a syllogism; if the rules are suitably chosen, they may themselves furnish easy-to-use criteria for the rapid evaluation of given syllogisms, and it may also be possible to deduce *from* the rules a list of valid syllogistic forms.

It is possible to state a set of five rules that meets these requirements. Each rule is accompanied by an informal argument showing that it constitutes a necessary condition for validity. It can then be shown that only 24 forms satisfy the conditions laid down in the rules, and that each of them is valid; the rules thus constitute the necessary *and* sufficient conditions for validity. *It is assumed throughout that the subjects of universal propositions exist.*[59]

We first state the rules, and their justifications.

Rule 1: The middle term must be distributed at least once.

For a syllogism is a nexus of three terms: in the premises it is established that all or some of the objects denoted by the major and minor terms are included among or separated from all or some of the objects denoted by the middle term; then, in the conclusion, *because* of their relations to the objects denoted by the middle, one is able to infer some relation between the objects denoted by the major and minor. But suppose the middle term is undistributed in each of the premises. Then the major premise provides, in effect, information about the relation between *some* of the objects denoted by the middle term and the objects (all or some) denoted by the major term. Similarly, the minor premise provides information about the relation between *some* of the objects denoted by the middle term, and the objects (all or some) denoted by the minor term. Under such conditions the middle term cannot furnish a logically adequate ground for establishing a connection between major and minor, for we have no way of knowing whether or not the *same* objects (among those denoted by the middle term) are involved in both premises. Hence, no conclusion can be drawn.

Rule 2: Any term distributed in the conclusion must also be distributed in the premises.

---

[59]A great deal of the so-called traditional logic derives from medieval and late classical sources, and differs in many significant details from the original work of Aristotle. This is also true of the account developed in this chapter.

For if a given term, major or minor, is undistributed in the corresponding premise, then that premise furnishes information about only *some* of the objects denoted by the term. From such information one cannot draw conclusions about *all* of the objects denoted by the term. But this is what would happen if the term were distributed in the conclusion.

Rule 3: If both premises are negative, there can be no conclusion.

For negative premises state that the objects (all or some) denoted by the major and minor terms are *separate* from the objects (all or some) denoted by the middle. From such information, one cannot infer anything about the relations of separation or inclusion between the classes of objects denoted by the major and minor.

Rule 4: If one premise is negative, the conclusion must be negative.

For suppose the major premise is the negative one. Then it expresses a *separation* between the objects (all or some) denoted by the middle term and the objects (all or some) denoted by the major. The other premise, being affirmative, expresses a relation of *inclusion* between the objects (all or some) denoted by the middle term and the objects (all or some) denoted by the minor. If any conclusion can be drawn from such information, it must involve a relation of *exclusion* with regard to the objects denoted by the major and minor terms. But such a relation would be expressed in a negative proposition.

Rule 5: If both premises are affirmative, the conclusion must be affirmative.

Justification for this rule, parallel in style to the previous ones, is left as an exercise.

The justifications we have furnished for these five rules are informal and somewhat vague and lean heavily upon a spatial metaphor. As proofs of logical principles they are alien to the spirit of proof that we have tried to exhibit in this text; consequently, from our point of view they cannot be regarded as ideally satisfactory. Ultimately, the rules rest on the fact that every syllogistic form that violates one or more of the rules can be seen (by other means) to be invalid. We shall not undertake the essentially mechanical task of demonstrating that fact. Assuming it *is* a fact, which it is, it follows that the rules provide easily recognizable *necessary* conditions for validity.

Our next task is to show that only 24 syllogisms satisfy the five rules. Each premise must be one of the four types of propositions, *A*, *E*, *I*, or *O*. Ignoring the question of figure, there are then only 16 possible kinds of premise-sets:

AA, AE, AI, AO,
EA, EE, EI, EO,
IA, IE, II, IO,
OA, OE, OI, OO.

But by Rule 3 we see at once that *EE, EO, OE,* and *OO* cannot yield a valid conclusion. Striking out these combinations, we are left with 12 possible kinds of premise-sets:

AA, AE, AI, AO,
EA, EI,
IA, IE, II, IO,
OA, OI.

To narrow down this field still further we require some additional propositions that can be proved as theorems following from the original five rules. It is convenient to begin by stating a lemma, as follows.

Lemma: The number of distrubuted terms in the premises must exceed the number of distributed terms in the conclusion.

The proof is obvious, from Rules 1 and 2. Now we develop three general theorems.

Theorem 1: If both premises are particular, there can be no conclusion.

Proof: By Rule 3 at least one of the premises must be affirmative. Suppose one is affirmative and one negative. Then the premises contain one distributed term. By the Lemma the conclusion contains no distributed terms. The conclusion is then affirmative. But by Rule 4 a valid syllogism with one negative premise must have a negative conclusion. Next suppose the premises are both affirmative. Then they contain no distributed terms and this violates Rule 1.

Theorem 2: If one premise is particular and one universal, the conclusion must be particular.

Proof: Suppose there were a universal conclusion (validly inferred). Then the conclusion contains at least one distributed term, and by the Lemma the premises contain at least two. But because one premise is particular, it follows that at least one premise must be negative. By Rule 4 the conclusion is therefore negative, and hence contains two distributed terms. Again by the Lemma the premises contain at least three distributed terms. But because one premise is particular, it would follow that both premises are negative, and then by Rule 3 there is no conclusion at all.

Theorem 3: If the major premise is an *I* proposition and the minor an *E* proposition, there can be no conclusion.

Proof is left as an exercise.

Now we return to our list of 12 possible premise-sets. By Theorem 1 we must drop *II*, *IO*, and *OI*. By Theorem 3 we must drop *IE*. This leaves just 8 possibilities:

AA, *AE, AI, AO, EA, EI, IA, OA*.

Now we turn our attention to the kind (*A, E, I,* or *O*) of conclusion that could be validly associated with each of these premise-sets. By Rule 5, *AA* must be followed by an affirmative conclusion. Hence, the premise-set *AA* could appear in one of two possible moods, *AAA* or *AAI*. By Rule 4, *AE* must be followed by a negative conclusion. Hence, the premise-set *AE* could appear in one of two possible moods, *AEE* or *AEO*. By Rule 5 and Theorem 2, *AI* must be followed by *I*, generating the mood *AII*. By Rule 4 and Theorem 2, *AO* must be followed by *O*, generating the mood *AOO*. Similarly it can be shown (the proofs are left as exercises) that *EA* can appear in the mood *EAE* or *EAO*; *EI* must be followed by an *O*, thus generating the mood *EIO*; *IA* must be followed by an *I*, giving the mood *IAI*; and lastly *OA* must be followed by an *O*, giving the mood *OAO*. Collecting these results we thus exhibit eleven possible moods for valid syllogisms:

AAA, AAI, AEE, AEO, AII, AOO,
EAE, EAO, EIO, IAI, OAO.

The form of a syllogism is given by specifying its mood *and* figure; hence, there are now 44 forms of syllogism to consider. But examples of those 44 forms are listed in the exercises following Section 2. From those, it can be seen that just 24 forms are valid (all satisfying the rules), and the remaining 20 are invalid (all violating one or more of the rules). Of the valid forms, there are six moods in each figure, there are three moods that are valid in only one figure, and two moods that are valid in all four figures. We leave it to the reader to verify these claims.

There are some valid syllogisms with particular conclusions where a corresponding universal conclusion could also be inferred; and some with a universal premise where a corresponding particular premise would have sufficed. These are called *weakened* and *strengthened* syllogisms. There are nine of them, two in each of the first three figures, and three in the fourth figure. Of the 24 valid syllogisms, the weakened and strngthened ones, and no others, would be invalid without the assumption that grammatical subjects exist. Verification of these statements is also left as an exercise.

Finally, we note that there are arguments involving *singular* propositions that meet almost all of the criteria for syllogism. Our very first example of a valid argument was one of these:

All men are mortal.
Socrates is a man.
Socrates is mortal.

The' difference between the form of this argument and the form of a syllogism lies only in the fact that some of its propositions are not drawn from the square of opposition but are singular propositions instead. We shall call such cases arguments in *near-syllogistic form.* They may be evaluated by application of the five rules, provided singular propositions are regarded as kinds of universal propositions; this is in any case a plausible view, because a singular proposition makes a statement about all of its subject.

Exercises

1. Provide a verbal justification for Rule 5.

2. Prove Theorem 3.

3. By appeal to the five rules and three theorems, show that the premise-set *EA* cannot be followed (validly) by an *A* or *I* conclusion, that *EI* must be followed by *O, IA* by *I,* and *OA* by *O.*

4. Consult the arguments listed in the exercises following Section 2. Verify that they illustrate the 44 forms mentioned in the text of this section. Also verify that just 24 are valid, and that those and only those satisfy the rules. Violation of Rule 1 is known as the *fallacy of the undistributed middle term;* note which cases involve this fallacy.

5. Verify that the 24 valid forms of syllogism are arranged with respect to figure and mood as claimed in the text.

6. Verify the claims made in the text in regard to weakened and strengthened syllogisms.

7. Show that if singular propositions are treated as particular propositions when applying the rules to arguments in near-syllogistic form, there will be *valid* arguments that violate one or more of the rules.

*8. Formulate a set of revised rules that furnish necessary and sufficient conditions for the validity of a syllogism, *not* assuming that grammatical subjects exist. It will be necessary to show (i) that the weakened and strengthened moods violate the revised rules, (ii) that the remaining 15 forms satisfying the original rules also satisfy the revised rules, and (iii) that the 232 forms violating the original rules also violate the revised rules.

4 • VENN DIAGRAMS

The logical significance of the propositions appearing in the square of opposition can be represented (or at least suggested) by a diagrammatic device called the *Venn diagram* (after its inventor, John Venn). Consider some two-term universal or particular subject-predicate proposition, say "All F's are G." We may imagine a universe of objects each of which possesses or fails to possess the property F. These objects can be represented by points on a plane, or on a sheet of paper. If we draw a circle on the plane and label it F, points within the circle are naturally regarded as objects having the property F, and points outside the circle as objects not having the property F. Similarly, another circle labeled G can be thought of as enclosing all objects having the property G, and excluding all objects not having the property G. If the two circles are drawn to overlap, they will divide the plane into four regions that exhaust the possible combinations of having and not having the properties F and G.

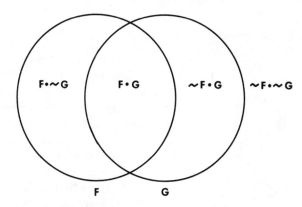

To incorporate in the diagram the logical significance of "All F's are G," we note first that that statement is equivalent to "There is no object that is an F and not a G." This suggests that one of the four regions in the diagram is empty, and we indicate the fact by shading the corresponding area. The fact that one area is shaded here is not meant to convey anything about any of the other areas: *They may or may not contain objects*, but the class of objects that are F's and not G's is empty.

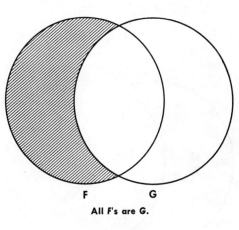

All F's are G.

Similarly, "No F's are G" means there is no object that is an F and a G, and we represent this by shading the overlap. This indicates that the class of objects that are both F's and G's is empty, but nothing is implied with regard to any of the other regions.

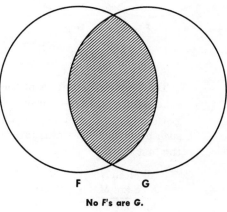

No F's are G.

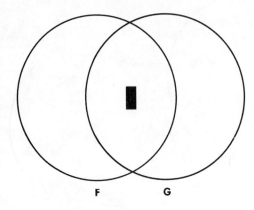

The proposition "Some F's are G" asserts that there *is* an object (one at least) that is both F and G. We may indicate this by placing a bar within the appropriate sector. This bar conveys the idea that at least one object occupies the area in which it appears; no commitment is involved with regard to the existence or nonexistence of objects in other areas.

Some F's are G.

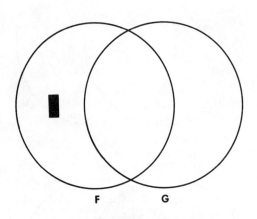

Lastly, we see that "Some F's are not G" is represented by a bar in the region for objects having the property F but not the property G.

Some F's are not G.

The peculiar usefulness of these diagrams rests on their ability to exhibit the inclusion-exclusion relations that are suggested by syllogistic arguments and to provide still another method for evaluating such arguments. We illustrate by considering the syllogism AAA in the first figure:

All M are P.
All S are M.
All S are P.

Because we are here involved with three terms, we draw three overlapping circles, dividing the realm of objects into eight regions. Evidently these regions will represent all the possible combinations of having-or-not-having the properties denoted by the major, minor, and middle terms.

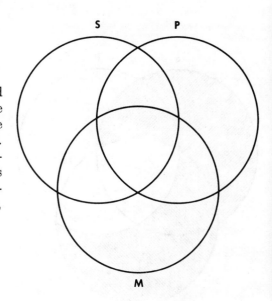

Now to check the syllogism we first consider the circles M and P alone. Referring to the major premise, we make some marks to represent the statement "All M's are P."

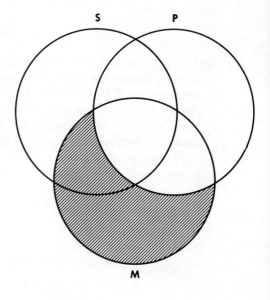

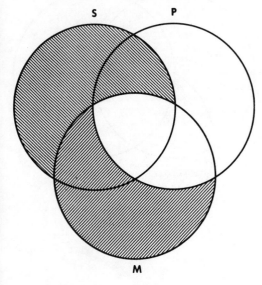

Next, we do the same for the circles M and S, referring to the minor premise.

We have now shown that certain classes are empty. The *conclusion* of the syllogism we are checking asserts that the class of objects that are S and not P is also empty. *But we have already shaded out that area.* Hence, by diagramming the logical significance of the premises, we have implicitly diagrammed the logical significance of the conclusion as well, and the argument must be valid.

Next we consider a case involving particular propositions, say *AOO* in the second figure:

All P are M.
Some S are not M.
Some S are not P.

Again we set out a three-circle array, and incorporate in it the significance of the premises. It is convenient to begin with the minor premise. We want to put a bar in the area of objects that have the property S but not the property M. The trouble is that there are really two such areas, and we may wonder which one to put the bar in. Because we have no information on which to base a decision, we represent our ambiguous condition by letting the bar straddle the two appropriate subregions. This does *not* mean that there are objects in both of the subregions; only that there is at least one object in one of the two regions and, perhaps (for all we know at present), in both.

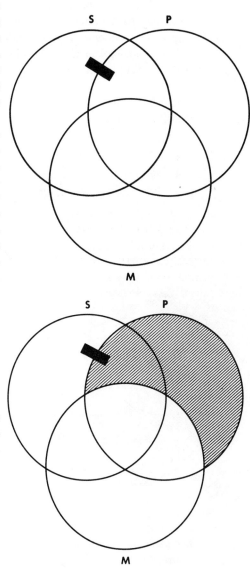

Next, in accordance with the major premise, we shade the area of objects that are P and not M.

337

Because one of the two areas that the bar originally occupied is now seen to be devoid of members, it follows that the bar properly belongs to the other area. But this establishes the conclusion (that some object exists that is S and not P). The possibility of a similar use of the Venn diagrams to demonstrate *in*validity is obvious.

Certain syllogisms are valid only on assumption that objects exist corresponding to some constituent term. For example,

> All M are P.
> All S are M.
> ―――――――
> Some S are P.

Analyzed with Venn diagrams, this will be invalid. We may incorporate the additional premise "There are S's" in the following way:

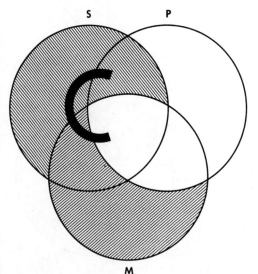

Because the S class is divided into four subregions, the bar is initially placed across all four. But three of those subregions are shaded out (because of the premises), showing that the bar properly belongs in the fourth; this is the area of objects that are both S and P, and because the existence of such objects *is* what the conclusion asserts, the argument is valid.

The same approach can be adopted in other cases requiring existence-assumptions.

In effect, we have extended the method of Venn diagrams to represent a proposition having only one substantive term ("There are S's"). Propositions having three terms can also be represented through a natural extension.

For instance, "All liberal Republicans voted for the bill".

Again, "Some Republicans are conservative or disinterested".

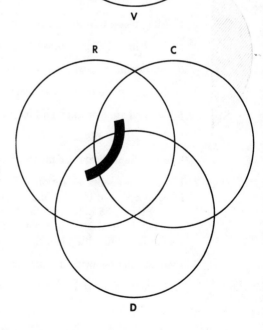

It is possible to represent, in the same way, propositions or arguments involving more than three terms. But the idea is extremely impractical: The figures become hopelessly complex, and logically identical sets of objects have to be spread over spatially separate regions.

Clearly, Venn diagrams can be used to check many arguments other than syllogisms involving one, two, or three terms; a few examples are suggested in the exercises.

Exercises

1. Represent the following propositions with Venn diagrams:

    a. All men are mortal, and there are men.

    b. All men are mortal, and there are mortals.

    c. Apples and oranges are fruits.

    d. Apples and oranges are fruits, and there are fruits.

    e. All apples are fruits and contain seeds.   (three terms)

    f. All apples are fruits and contain seeds, and there are apples.

    g. Some liberal Republicans voted for the bill.   (three terms)

    h. No Republicans who are not liberals voted for the bill.

    i. Some men are mortal and some are not.

    j. All men are mortal and all mortals are men.

   *k. Only some fruits are apples.

   *l. Some Republicans are progressive or conservative, but not both.

2. Refer to the results of Section 3. From each figure of the syllogism choose three moods, one that is valid without any extra existence-assumptions, one that is valid only with the help of some existence-assumption, and one that is invalid with or without existence-assumptions. Verify these results in detail with Venn diagrams.

3. Evaluate the following arguments with Venn diagrams.

    a. All men are mortal. There are men. Hence, there are mortals.

b. No men are mortal. There are mortals. Hence, there are no men.

c. All apples are fruits and contain seeds, and there are apples. Therefore, some fruits contain seeds.

d. Apples and oranges are fruits, and there are fruits. Therefore, some oranges are fruits.

e. All fair teachers give objective examinations. Some teachers are not fair. Therefore, some teachers do not give objective examinations.

f. Only fair teachers give objective examinations. Some teachers are not fair. Therefore, some teachers do not give objective examinations.

g. There are mammals. All warm-blooded mammals are vertebrates. All invertebrate mammals are warm-blooded. Hence, some vertebrates are mammals.

*h. All mammals are vertebrates. All vertebrates are chordates. Some non-chordates are mammals. Therefore, all mammals are warm-blooded.

CHAPTER 8

Complex
Quantificational
Arguments

ABSTRACT: The methods of Chapter 6 are extended to cases in which quantifiers extend over closed propositions, themselves perhaps symbolized with other quantifiers. In Sections 1 and 2 the extension of quantifiers over nonquantified closed propositions is discussed, and the old instantiation and generalization rules are reinterpreted accordingly; in Section 3 certain logical truths— *isolation principles*— relevant to these forms are introduced, and their application to retain use of the decision procedure of Chapter 5 is shown. In Sections 4 and 5 multiple quantification and a consequent reconstruction of instantiation and generalization principles are discussed; a corresponding reinterpretation of the isolation principles permits continued use of the decision procedure, by now terribly burdensome. In Section 6 the new methods are applied to the analysis of relational propositions and arguments; at this level of complexity the decision procedure is no longer available, even as a last resort. In Section 7 some special uses of the relation of *identity* are discussed. In the final section certain general properties of binary relations that are often presupposed in argument are defined. Completeness and consistency are claimed throughout, but not everywhere proved.

1 • QUANTIFICATION OVER CLOSED PROPOSITIONS

It has been our custom when breaking new ground to begin with an argument, for it is the analysis and construction of arguments that concerns us first and last. In keeping with that practice, consider the following:

> If someone cheated, then Adam lied and he (the cheater) went unpunished.
> Someone cheated.
> Therefore, Adam lied and some cheater went unpunished.

This argument is evidently valid; it is of interest to us at present because our earlier techniques do not allow its validity to be demonstrated (that is, reduced to simpler valid forms). The difficulty turns on the first premise, for no symbolic analysis of that proposition we are presently equipped to offer will provide enough detail to permit tracing the inner logic of the argument. Specifically, it appears that the required analysis must have at least the following features:

  (i) It must exhibit the quantificational detail in the antecedent, "someone cheated."

  (ii) It must symbolize as a separate subpart the subproposition "Adam lied."

  (iii) It must, somehow, reflect the fact that the "he" in the consequent refers to the "someone" indefinitely specified in the antecedent.

We begin by proposing the following first approximation:

$$(\exists x)Cx \supset (La \cdot ?).$$

This admittedly incomplete formulation satisfies requirements (i) and (ii); the question mark records our perplexity over the third feature. It is natural to translate "he went unpunished" as Ux, giving,

$$(\exists x)Cx \supset (La \cdot Ux),$$

but then it is not clear that the x in Ux refers to the same x that satisfies the antecedent (if there is one); even worse, the x in Ux does not fall within the scope of a quantifier, thereby violating one of our understandings in regard to the complete formalization of definite propositions.

An immediate suggestion is that we extend the scope of the quantifier to pick up the free x. We would then have,

$(\exists x)[Cx \supset (La \cdot Ux)].$

But now we are faced with new difficulties. In the first place, this expression would be satisfied (and hence rendered true) if there were *one* individual who did not cheat, a condition that evidently fails to do justice to the intention of the original English expression. In fact, we are here confronting a common type of difficulty concerning the term *someone*. It is true enough that the antecedent "someone cheated," when considered in isolation, is properly translated with the aid of an existential quantifier. But the whole proposition we are dealing with is not the kind of truth-functional conditional in which the meanings of the antecedent and consequent are independent of each other. Rather, part of the meaning of the consequent in this case is bound up with the antecedent (because of the *he*), and the whole expression then becomes a *universal* proposition about any individual (any *he*) who happens to cheat. Thus, the correct translation is not

$(\exists x)[Cx \supset (La \cdot Ux)],$

but

$(x)[Cx \supset (La \cdot Ux)].$

There remains yet another difficulty. In this proposition the quantifier extends over a singular subproposition, a state of affairs that we have never met heretofore. But we can meet this difficulty simply by ignoring it: For the significance and accuracy of the final symbolic translation is evident, and there is simply no reason to regard the occurrence of a singular proposition within the scope of a quantifier with suspicion. In effect, then, we have established a new principle governing the formalization of propositions with the aid of quantifiers; namely, *quantifiers may extend over singular propositions*. As another example consider, "It is true of everyone that if Bertrand lied so did he." Obviously this can be represented as $(x)(Lb \supset Lx)$.

Next, let us consider another argument closely related to the first:

If someone cheated, then two members of the class lied and he (the cheater) went unpunished.

Someone cheated.

Therefore, two members of the class lied and some cheater went unpunished.

Like the first, this is valid. And like the first, it will give us some trouble because we do not know how to translate the initial premise. It is exactly like the initial premise of the previous argument, except that the proposition "Two members of the class lied" occurs in place of "Adam lied." Here it is natural and proper to symbolize the former with a propositional constant, say P, and as before we would have

$$(x)[Cx \supset (P \cdot Ux)],$$

where it is clear that P *is* a propositional constant because it is not associated with an individual variable or constant. In effect we have introduced another principle: *Quantifiers may extend over propositional constants.* As another example, take "There is someone such that, if any two people lied, he lied." This can be symbolized as $(\exists x)(P \supset Lx)$.

We regard symbolic expressions such as $(x)[Cx \supset (La \cdot Ux)]$ and $(\exists x)(P \supset Lx)$ as meaningful representations of English propositions that may very well refer to universes containing an infinite number of objects. In this respect they are exactly like expressions such as $(x)(Fx \supset Gx)$ and $(\exists x)(Fx \cdot Gx)$, which contain no closed propositions within the scope of the quantifier. This parallel can be extended to cases where the universe contains, or is assumed to contain, only a finite number of objects. For convenience, let us assume that the universe contains just three objects, a, b, and c. Then we can think of $(\exists x)(P \supset Lx)$ as identical in meaning to

$$(P \supset La) \text{ v } (P \supset Lb) \text{ v } (P \supset Lc),$$

and we can regard $(x)[Cx \supset (La \cdot Ux)]$ as identical to

$$[Ca \supset (La \cdot Ua)] \cdot [Cb \supset (La \cdot Ub)] \cdot [Cc \supset (La \cdot Uc)].$$

It should be obvious that these expressions preserve the sense of the originals under the given assumption.

Exercises

1. Translate the following into symbols, exhibiting as much detail as possible. Translate all subpropositions beginning with the word *the* by means of a single letter (that is, do not attempt to analyze them).

   a. If anything was stolen, the police will come and it will be recovered.

   b. If nothing was stolen, Officer Conners will not come and nothing will be found.

   c. If anything was stolen, Detective Turkle will investigate and it will be found.

   d. Something was stolen, but the police will be here shortly and it will be found.

   e. There is something such that, if this piece of matter is magnetic, then it is, too.

   f. There is something such that, either it is magnetic or sample number 1 is not magnetic.

   g. There is nothing that has the property of being magnetic if and only if sample number 2 is a conductor.

   h. There is nothing that has the property of being magnetic, if and only if sample number 2 is a conductor.

   i. Either the Queen will be annoyed, or someone will go.

   j. There is someone such that, either the Queen will be annoyed or he will go.

   k. Either the Queen will be annoyed, or everyone will go.

   l. It is true of everyone that, either the Queen will be annoyed or he will go.

   m. The party will be a success, and someone will play charades.

   n. There is someone such that, the party will be a success and he will play charades.

   o. The party will be a success, and everyone will play charades.

   p. It is true of everyone that the party will be a success and he will play charades.

    q. There is someone such that, if the ice cubes run out he will be very perturbed.

    r. If the ice cubes run out someone will be very perturbed.

    s. It is true of everyone that, if the ice cubes run out they will be very perturbed.

    t. If the ice cubes run out everyone will be very perturbed.

    u. There is someone such that, if he goes home the restaurant will close.

    v. If everyone goes home the restaurant will close.

    w. It is true of everyone that, if he goes home the restaurant will close.

    x. If someone goes home the restaurant will close.

2. Show that in a universe containing n objects, propositions (i) and (j) in Exercise 1 are logically equivalent.

3. Show that in a universe containing three objects, a, b, and c, propositions (k) and (l) in Exercise 1 above are logically equivalent. Then show that the same holds good of *every* succeeding pair of propositions, all the way to (w) and (x). (It is fairly evident that *these* logical equivalences, when demonstrated for three-member universes, will hold for universes containing any finite number of objects. Proving them for three-member universes cuts down on the busy-work.)

4. Show that in a universe containing three objects, the two arguments stated in the text of this section are valid.

2 • EXTENDED INSTANTIATION AND GENERALIZATION RULES

Prior to this chapter, we have explicitly identified only one kind of symbolic expression as an open proposition (prop); namely, a single predicate letter associated with a (free) variable, or some truth-functional combination of such expressions with the same variable appearing throughout. During the course of formal proofs (or decision-procedure analyses) we sometimes encountered truth-functional combinations of such open propositions along with closed propositions, such as Fx v Ga, or $Fx \cdot P$. Because these expressions are indefinite in meaning, they are themselves open propositions of a complex sort; but we never raised (because we never needed to) questions about the kinds of single closed propositions which might correspond to them.[60] Now, however, we permit and require formalizations in which quantifiers extend over subparts that are themselves genuine (closed) propositions; hence, it is clear that Fx v Ga can be regarded as a prop corresponding to the closed proposition, say, $(x)(Fx$ v $Ga)$, and similarly $Fx \cdot P$ might correspond to, say, $(\exists x)(Fx \cdot P)$.

It follows that we could now take a complex expression such as

(i) $\sim Fx$ v $[P \supset (Gx \cdot Ha)]$,

and regard it as a *single* prop, from which the following substitution instances may be generated:

(ii) $\sim Fa$ v $[P \supset (Ga \cdot Ha)]$,
(iii) $\sim Fb$ v $[P \supset (Gb \cdot Ha)]$, etc.,
(iv) $\sim Fm$ v $[P \supset (Gm \cdot Ha)]$,
(v) $\sim Fn$ v $[P \supset (Gn \cdot Ha)]$, etc.

Each of these could be taken as an *instantiations* of the closed proposition

(vi) $(x)\{\sim Fx$ v $[P \supset (Gx \cdot Ha)]\}$,

and in exact analogy with our earlier practices we could take (i) itself as a kind of universal-instantiation proposition that is true of an arbitrarily chosen individual x if (vi) is true. Furthermore (iv) and (v) can be thought of as existential instantiations of

(vii) $(\exists x)\{\sim Fx$ v $[P \supset (Gx \cdot Ha)]\}$.

It now appears that we can broaden the scope of our earlier rules of *UI* and *EI* to include cases where quantifiers extend over closed propositions. It will then be possible to construct formal proofs for certain valid arguments that contain such propositions, thereby demonstrating the validity of those arguments for possibly infinite universes. As an example, we exhibit a proof for the argument cited at the very beginning of this chapter.

---

[60]We also encountered truth-functional combinations involving more than one variable, such as $Fm \supset Gx$. For the moment we ignore these: They are peculiarly relevant at a later stage, in connection with propositions involving quantifiers that extend over each other.

If someone cheated, then Adam lied and he (the cheater) went unpunished.

Someone cheated.

Therefore, Adam lied and some cheater went unpunished.

1. $(x)[Cx \supset (La \cdot Ux)]$	Pr
2. $(\exists x)Cx$	Pr
3. Cm	2, EI
4. $Cm \supset (La \cdot Um)$	1, UI
5. $La \cdot Um$	3, 4, MP
6. La	5, $Simp$
7. Um	5, $Simp$
8. $Cm \cdot Um$	3, 7, $Conj$
9. $(\exists x)(Cx \cdot Ux)$	8, EG
10. $La \cdot (\exists x)(Cx \cdot Ux)$	6, 9, $Conj$

This proof represents a departure from earlier practices only at step 4, which embodies our now-expanded rule of *UI*. Another example is

There is something such that, if it is not physical then object *a* is immortal.

But nothing is immortal.

Therefore something is physical.

1. $(\exists x)(\sim Px \supset Ia)$	Pr
2. $(x)\sim Ix$	Pr
3. $\sim Pm \supset Ia$	1, EI
4. $\sim Ia$	2, UI
5. Pm	3, 4, MT, DN
6. $(\exists x)Px$	5, EG

Step 3 of this proof embodies our now-expanded rule of *EI*.

It is clear that we can now expand *UG* and *EG* in the same way. For it is just as natural (and logically sound) to pass from *Fx* v *Ga* to $(x)(Fx$ v $Ga)$ as it is to go the other way, assuming of course that the restriction on *UG* is met. Similarly, we may pass from $Fm \cdot P$ to $(\exists x)$ $(Fx \cdot P)$ just as easily as we move from the latter to the former. Both of these extensions (of *UG* and *EG*) are consequences of our expanded notion of a substitution instance. For the original principles of *UG* and *EG* are simply ways of passing from a substitution instance of some prop to a quantificational closure thereof, and the inferences suggested here do nothing more or less than that. We are, therefore, in a position to generalize unquantified expressions by placing quantifiers in front of them (and changing, say, *m* or *a* to *x* if necessary), even if the expressions contain certain closed propositions as subparts. Hence, the following is a proper proof:

If anyone goes home, the restaurant will close.
Therefore, it is true of everyone that, if he goes home the restaurant will close.

1. $(\exists x)Hx \supset R$	Pr	
2. $\sim R$	CP	
3. $\sim(\exists x)Hx$	$1, 2, MT$	
4. $(x)\sim Hx$	$3, Q$	
5. $\sim Hx$	$4, UI$	
6. $\sim R \supset \sim Hx$	$2–5, CP$	
7. $Hx \supset R$	$6, Cont$	
8. $(x)(Hx \supset R)$	$7, UG$	(new)

A final example is

If everyone goes home, the restaurant will close.
Therefore, there is at least one person such that, if he goes home the restaurant will close.

1. $(x)Fx \supset R$	Pr	
2. $\sim R$	CP	
3. $\sim(x)Fx$	$1, 2, MT$	
4. $(\exists x)\sim Fx$	$3, Q$	
5. $\sim Fm$	$4, EI$	
6. $\sim R \supset \sim Fm$	$2–5, CP$	
7. $Fm \supset R$	$6, Cont$	
8. $(\exists x)(Fx \supset R)$	$7, EG$	(new)

We now state formally and precisely our revision of the four instantiation and generalization rules of Chapter 6. Schematically they appear as before, but with some new understandings and restrictions:

UI: $\dfrac{(x)Fx}{Fx}$ $\dfrac{(x)Fx}{Fm}$ $\dfrac{(x)Fx}{Fa}$

EI: $\dfrac{(\exists x)Fx}{Fm}$

UG: $\dfrac{Fx}{(x)Fx}$

EG: $\dfrac{Fa}{(\exists x)Fx}$ $\dfrac{Fm}{(\exists x)Fx}$ $\dfrac{Fx}{(\exists x)Fx}$

It is now *understood* that Fx, Fm, Fa, and so on, are expressions containing one or more predicate letters associated with one or more individual constants, at most *one* distinct variable $(x, m, n, \ldots)$, and any number of propositional constants, the whole being joined by truth-functional connectives; no quantifiers appear *within* these expressions.[61] The particular restrictions on EI and UG stated in Chapter 6 continue as before. We also retain the principle that lower case letters, if altered at all, are all altered uniformly.

These considerations bear upon certain ambiguities in connection with EG. Suppose we take as premise the proposition $Fa \vee Gb$. We could regard this as a statement about a; then EG yields $(\exists x)(Fx \vee Gb)$. Alternatively we could regard it as a statement about b; then EG yields $(\exists x)(Fa \vee Gx)$. Both inferences are equally legitimate. In the first case we shall say that we are generalizing *with respect to* the constant a; in the second case that we are generalizing *with respect to* the constant b. The expression $Fa \cdot (Gb \vee Hc)$ can be generalized existentially in three different ways, *with respect to* any one of the constants appearing in it.

Next suppose we start with $Fa \vee Ga$ as a premise. In analogy with the previous discussion we may be tempted to view this as a statement primarily about the left-hand a; then EG yields $(\exists x)(Fx \vee Ga)$. Alternatively we might want to think of it as a statement about the right-hand a; then we get $(\exists x)(Fa \vee Gx)$. It happens that both in-

---

[61]*Implicit* in this understanding are some peculiar general restrictions. For example, we can apply EG to a statement of the form $Fm \vee P$, getting $(\exists x)(Fx \vee P)$. It is quite possible for a parallel expression, $Fm \vee (x)Gx$, to arise in a line of proof; but we can*not* apply EG to the latter, getting $(\exists x)[Fx \vee (x)Gx]$, for in this case both premise and conclusion contain a prop with an internal quantifier. Again, we can apply UG to a statement of the form $Fx \vee Ga$, getting $(x)(Fx \vee Ga)$. It is quite possible for a parallel expression, $Fx \vee Gm$, to arise in a line of proof; but we can*not* apply UG to the latter, getting $(x)(Fx \vee Gm)$, for both premise and conclusion contain more than one distinct variable. Other examples could be produced.

These implicit restrictions are not obtrusive *at the present stage*, because the inferences they prevent are not needed and would be somewhat unnatural. It may perhaps be felt that the inferences in question are in any case legitimate, and indeed they are; but they issue in forms of symbolic expression that we have not yet had independent reason to produce or discuss, that is, forms with quantifiers extending over other quantifiers, or over distinct variables. Such forms will arise in Section 4; the present discussion is in large measure a preparation for their treatment, and we are therefore reluctant to permit their premature generation. In Section 5 the instantiation and generalization rules will be revised slightly, and these implicit restrictions will disappear of their own accord.

ferences are legitimate, but they violate our rule of uniform alteration of lower case letters. Hence, we do not regard these as legitimate uses of *EG*. The corresponding inferences, if they are needed in a proof, must be established some other way. It happens that all applications of *EG* that violate the rule of uniform alteration yield valid inferences anyway. But such inferences are intuitively unnatural and awkward, symbolically bewildering, and can all be accomplished by some other route, say through *IP*. Consequently, we shall hold to our uniform alteration rule without qualification.

One further ambiguity can arise in connection with *EG*. We regard *P* v *Ga* as a statement about *a*, and by existential generalization with respect to *a* we can produce $(\exists x)(P \text{ v } Gx)$. Again, we may take *Fb* v *Ga* as a statement about *a*, and by existential generalization with respect to *a* produce $(\exists x)(Fb \text{ v } Gx)$. In analogy with these cases one might be tempted to think of *Fx* v *Ga* in the same way, and by existential generalization with respect to *a* produce $(\exists x)(Fx \text{ v } Gx)$. But then we notice that the *x* in *Fx*, which was not at the beginning an object of our attention, has been converted by this process from a free to a bound variable. Or, to put it differently, the free variable in the premise has been converted to a bound variable in the conclusion, even though the generalization process was carried out with respect to *a* rather than with respect to *x*.[62] We characterize this situation by saying that the *x* in *Fx* has been inadvertently *captured*, and we explicitly forbid such occurrences. It happens that many, perhaps most, inadvertent captures through *EG* produce inferences that are in fact valid; but this is not universally true.[63] Where the forbidden inferences *are* valid, there is of course some other way of producing them; for example:

1.	*Fx* v *Ga*	*Pr*
2.	$\sim(\exists x)(Fx \text{ v } Gx)$	*IP*
3.	$(x)\sim(Fx \text{ v } Gx)$	2, *Q*
✓4.	$\sim(Fa \text{ v } Ga)$	3, *UI*
5.	$(x)(Fx \text{ v } Ga)$	1, *UG*
✓6.	*Fa* v *Ga*	5, *UI*
7.	$(\exists x)(Fx \text{ v } Gx)$	2–6, *IP*

---

[62]The latter would have produced $(\exists x)(Fx \text{ v } Ga)$.

[63]Examples of such invalid inferences are available at a later stage; with respect to *UG* the problem does not yet arise, for our present understanding of *UG* does not envision any alteration of lower case letters.

Although inadvertent capture can *at present* arise only in connection with *EG*, we state it as a *general restriction* applying to all instantiation and generalization rules that *free variables must not be inadvertently captured.*

It is important to note that the four rules we are concerned with cannot be derived from the same four rules as stated in Chapter 6, which involved a narrower context. Rather, the rules as stated and employed in that chapter are clearly subcases of the rules as understood in the present chapter. Consequently, and technically speaking, the four argument forms that are called *UI, EI, UG,* and *EG* in this chapter have to be regarded as *new* elementary principles of argument construction, and we take the position that their validity in respect to possibly infinite universes is intuitively evident. To complete the picture we must also add, as an additional postulate, that the argument form

$$\frac{\sim(x)Fx}{(\exists x)\sim Fx}$$

is likewise valid in this new and broader context. For we require this principle or something like it to justify the change-of-quantifier rules (Q rules); it should be apparent that with the aid of this postulate all the Q rules can be established exactly as they were established in Section 4, Chapter 6, for the restricted context of that chapter. In sum, and without further dwelling on details, we take it that *all* manipulations of quantified propositions permitted in Chapter 6 are permitted now as well; Exercise 2 following invites study of the details.

Exercises

1. Employing x as a general variable, m and n as the only particulate variables, and a and b as the only constants, write out all possible inferences by instantiation or generalization (in one step) from each of the following premise lines:

   a. $(x)(Fx \cdot Ga)$

   b. $(x)(Fx \supset P)$

c. $(x)Fx \supset P$

d. $(x)[(Fa \cdot Gb) \supset Fx]$

e. $(\exists x)(Fa \ v \ Gx)$

f. $Fa \ v \ Gb$

g. $Fa \cdot Ga$

h. $Fa \supset Fb$

i. $\sim(Fx \ v \ Ga)$

j. $\sim(Fx \cdot \sim Fm)$

k. $Fx \ v \ Fn$

l. $Fm \supset Fn$

m. $P \ v \ Fa$

n. $P \equiv Fm$

o. $P \cdot Fx$

p. P

Hint: There are 28 in all.

2. Assuming the validity of the instantiation and generalization rules explained in this section, and granting that $(\exists x)\sim Fx$ is validly inferred from $\sim(x)Fx$, show that the Q equivalence principle, the Q rules, and the Q distribution rules can be used now just as they were in Chapter 6. (It may not be necessary to repeat all the proofs, but only to compare them in some systematic way.)

3. Evaluate the following arguments. To establish validity produce a formal proof. Invalidity may be established, as always, by describing some situation in which the premise(s) is (are) true and the conclusion false.

a. It is true of everything that either Socrates is mortal or it is spiritual. Therefore, Socrates is spiritual or Pericles mortal.

b. Everything is material or simple. Therefore, it is true of something that either Socrates is simple or it is material.

c. It is true of everything that either Socrates is mortal or it is spiritual. Hence, something is mortal or spiritual.

d. Socrates is mortal or Pericles is. Hence, there is something that is mortal, or Pericles is mortal.

e. Socrates is mortal or Pericles is. Hence, there is something such that either Pericles is mortal or it is.

f. Socrates is mortal or Pericles is vain. Hence, something is mortal or vain.

g. Socrates is mortal and Pericles is vain. Hence, something is mortal and vain.

h. If anything is physical, then it is true of everything that if materialism is right it is perishable. This apple is physical and materialism is right. Therefore, this apple is perishable.

i. Materialism is a true doctrine. Therefore, it is true of everything that if it is perishable then this apple is perishable.

j. It is true of everything that it is perishable if and only if this apple is not perishable. Therefore, materialism is a true doctrine.

k. It is true of everything that, if materialism is true then it is physical, and if this apple is perishable then it is likewise. Hence, it is true of anything that if materialism is true then it is physical, and it is true of anything that if the apple is perishable then it is also.

l. The same argument as in (k), but with premise and conclusion reversed.

m. The same argument as in (k), but with "something" in place of "everything" and "anything."

n. The same argument as in (m), but with premise and conclusion reversed.

o.–r. The same arguments as in (k)–(n), but with disjunctions in place of the conjunctions.

4. Refer to Exercise 1 at the end of the *previous* section. Propositions 2i–2x constitute eight logically equivalent pairs. Establish these equivalences for possibly infinite universes by constructing formal proofs of the corresponding biconditionals, beginning with no premises at all. (There will be eight rather long proofs.)

3 • ISOLATION PRINCIPLES

It is already clear that any expression containing a quantifier extending over a closed proposition is equivalent to some expression in which no such condition occurs. This follows from a series of logical equivalences that the reader was asked to verify earlier (for finite universes in Exercises 2 and 3 of Section 1, for infinite universes in Exercise 4 of Section 2). The equivalences in question are the following:

$$(x)(P \text{ v } Fx) \equiv [P \text{ v } (x)Fx]$$
$$(\exists x)(P \text{ v } Fx) \equiv [P \text{ v } (\exists x)Fx]$$
$$(x)(P \cdot Fx) \equiv [P \cdot (x)Fx]$$
$$(\exists x)(P \cdot Fx) \equiv [P \cdot (\exists x)Fx]$$
$$(x)(P \supset Fx) \equiv [P \supset (x)Fx]$$
$$(\exists x)(P \supset Fx) \equiv [P \supset (\exists x)Fx]$$
$$(x)(Fx \supset P) \equiv [(\exists x)Fx \supset P]$$
$$(\exists x)(Fx \supset P) \equiv [(x)Fx \supset P]$$

All but the last two are extraordinarily simple, and even those are rather easy to grasp and remember. Together, these logically true biconditionals may be called *isolation principles*, because appeal to some form of them will permit us, always, to isolate closed propositions from quantifiers extending over them.

As an example, let us isolate the closed proposition in

$$(x)[Cx \supset (P \cdot Ux)].$$

The part following the quantifier is a conditional, but neither part of that conditional consists of a closed proposition simply. Hence, we must first convert to conjunctive normal form:

$$(x)[{\sim}Cx \text{ v } (P \cdot Ux)],$$
$$(x)[({\sim}Cx \text{ v } P) \cdot ({\sim}Cx \text{ v } Ux)].$$

By a Q distribution rule, we can split this into

$$(x)({\sim}Cx \text{ v } P) \cdot (x)({\sim}Cx \text{ v } Ux),$$

and then apply an isolation principle to the left-hand conjunct:

$$[(x){\sim}Cx \text{ v } P] \cdot (x)({\sim}Cx \text{ v } Ux).$$

As another example, we can begin with

$$(\exists x)[(P \supset Fx) \cdot (Ga \text{ v } Hx)].$$

Here we must first convert the interior to disjunctive normal form:

$(\exists x)[(\sim P \text{ v } Fx) \cdot (Ga \text{ v } Hx)],$
$(\exists x)[(\sim P \cdot Ga) \text{ v } (\sim P \cdot Hx) \text{ v } (Fx \cdot Ga) \text{ v } (Fx \cdot Hx)].$

Associating the last three disjuncts we can apply an isolation rule to obtain

$(\sim P \cdot Ga) \text{ v } (\exists x)[(\sim P \cdot Hx) \text{ v } (Fx \cdot Ga) \text{ v } (Fx \cdot Hx)].$

By a Q distribution rule this becomes

$(\sim P \cdot Ga) \text{ v } (\exists x)(\sim P \cdot Hx) \text{ v } (\exists x)(Fx \cdot Ga) \text{ v } (\exists x)(Fx \cdot Hx).$

And finally, by further use of an isolation principle, we have

$(\sim P \cdot Ga) \text{ v } [\sim P \cdot (\exists x)Hx] \text{ v } [(\exists x)Fx \cdot Ga] \text{ v } (\exists x)(Fx \cdot Hx).$

We leave it to the reader to convince himself that similar moves will always suffice to transform statements with quantifiers extending over closed propositions to statements that lack this peculiarity. In other words, every proposition of the types we have been discussing is *reducible* to the types treated in Chapters 5 and 6. It follows at once that the decision procedure of Chapter 5 can be applied (after suitable isolations) to arguments that contain quantifiers extending over closed propositions of the types here under consideration. Furthermore, because any biconditional having the form of an isolation principle could be introduced into a formal proof by suitable conditional sequences, the process of isolation can be reflected in formal proofs; hence, the decision procedure when carried out on a valid argument can itself be reproduced in a formal proof, and we see at once that the system of proof construction is complete (compare Chapter 6, Section 5).

It is convenient to appeal to isolation principles directly during the course of formal proofs, annotating such moves with *Is*. For example,

1. $(x)[Fx \cdot (Gx \supset P)]$ *Pr*
2. $(x)Fx \cdot (x)(Gx \supset P)$ 1, *Q-dist*
3. $(x)Fx \cdot [(\exists x)Gx \supset P]$ 2, *S*, *Is*

The motive and justification for using *Is* in this way are the same as the motive and justification for introducing the annotations Q and *Q-dist* in Section 4, Chapter 6.

Exercises

1. Isolate the closed propositions lying within the scope of the quantifiers in the following:

   a. $(x)[P \supset (Fx \text{ v } Ga)]$

   b. $(x)[Px \supset (Fx \text{ v } Ga)]$

   c. $(x)[Px \supset (Fx \cdot Ga)]$

   d. $(x)(Fx \supset Fa)$

   e. $(x)(Fa \supset Fx)$

   f. $(\exists x)(Fx \supset Ga)$

   g. $(\exists x)(Fa \supset Gx)$

   h. $(\exists x)[Fx \cdot Ga \cdot (Hx \supset P)]$

2. Evaluate the following arguments by isolating closed propositions within the scope of quantifiers and then applying the decision procedure of Chapter 5. Also, construct formal proofs for the valid cases, using *Is* where appropriate.

   a. If everyone is strong, Harry is. Hence, it is true of everyone that, if he is strong, so is Harry.

   b. If anyone is strong, Harry is. Hence, it is true of anyone that, if he is strong, so is Harry.

   c. If Harry is strong then everyone is. Hence, it is true of everyone that, if Harry is strong, so is he.

   d. If Harry is strong then someone is. Hence, it is true of someone that, if Harry is strong then he is strong.

   e. Socrates is mortal. Hence, it is true of someone that, if Harry is strong then he is strong.

   f. Socrates is mortal. Hence, it is true of someone that, if he is strong then Harry is strong.

   g. If someone cheated, then Adam lied and he (the cheater) went unpunished. Adam lied but did not cheat. Therefore, someone did not go unpunished.

*h. Someone either cheated or lied. If someone cheated, then Jones lied and he (the cheater) went undetected. If someone lied, then Smith cheated and he (the liar) went undetected. Therefore, someone went undetected and either Smith cheated or Jones lied.

4 • MULTIPLE QUANTIFICATION

Quantifiers, we see, can extend over closed propositions that are singulars or unanalyzed symbolically. Why not permit them to extend over closed propositions that are themselves quantified? Some contexts will require just such devices. For example:

> If anything was taken, then everyone at the party was covering up for the thief and it will never be seen again.
> Something was taken.
> Anyone covering up for a thief is himself guilty.
> Therefore, everyone at the party was guilty.

T: taken
P: person at the party
C: covering up for a thief
S: will be seen again
G: guilty

The conclusion and all premises but the first are

> . . . .
> $(\exists x)Tx$
> $(x)(Cx \supset Gx)$
> _____
> $(x)(Px \supset Gx)$

To approach the first premise let us represent by P the statement "everyone at the party was covering up for the thief." Then we have

$$(x)[Tx \supset (P \cdot \sim Sx)].$$

It is clear that this, although correct, is insufficient to demonstrate the validity of the argument. But P itself is clearly translatable as $(x)(Px \supset Cx)$. Why not insert this for P? We would then have,

$$(x)\{Tx \supset [(x)(Px \supset Cx) \cdot \sim Sx]\}.$$

The only possible objection to this maneuver is that it leaves us with an expression that is symbolically misleading. For we usually think of a quantifier as referring to or indicating the generality of every general variable lying within its scope; whereas, in the last expression here, the first quantifier must be regarded as irrelevant to the significance of the variables lying within the scope of the second quantifier.[64] To avoid this, we shall adopt the policy of allowing *any* lower case letters from the end of the alphabet $(x, y, z, w, \ldots)$ to function as general variables. Then we can render P as, say, $(y)(Py \supset Cy)$, and insert *this* into the first premise:

$$(x)\{Tx \supset [(y)(Py \supset Cy) \cdot \sim Sx]\}.$$

The relation between quantifiers and their corresponding variables is thus kept clear. Naturally this could equally well be written as

$$(y)\{Ty \supset [(x)(Px \supset Cx) \cdot \sim Sy]\}, \quad \text{or}$$
$$(z)\{Tz \supset [(w)(Pw \supset Cw) \cdot \sim Sz]\}.$$

Although the idea of using distinct variables is not absolutely needed for clarity in this instance, it is unmistakably required to translate the following with a maximum of quantificational detail:

> For everyone, there is some woman such that he (or she) can be a league member if and only if she (the woman) was married to one.

To facilitate putting this into symbols we first ignore the beginning phrase. This leaves, "There is some woman such that x can be a league member if and only if she was married to one." In symbols it is

$$(\exists y)[Wy \cdot (Lx \equiv My)].$$

This is in fact an open proposition with free variable x. It is said to hold for everyone, so with the understanding that the variables are confined to people we have

$$(x)(\exists y)[Wy \cdot (Lx \equiv My)].$$

Here the use of distinct variable letters is essential because the variable associated with the first quantifier appears within the scope of

---

[64]A distinction that would be vital if we wished to apply *UI* or *EI* to the expression, as we will in the next section.

the second, a situation by no means unusual.[65] Note also that the expression begins with two adjacent quantifiers, each extending in scope to the end. This, too, is not unusual; to avoid extra use of brackets we lay down the convention that where a quantifier appears immediately to the left of another quantifier, its scope extends just as for as that of the other quantifier.

To clarify the significance of these new kinds of expressions, we exhibit unabbreviated versions of our examples under the assumption that the world contains just two individuals:

$$(x)\{Tx \supset [(y)(Py \supset Cy) \cdot \sim Sx]\}$$
$$\{Ta \supset [(y)(Py \supset Cy) \cdot \sim Sa]\} \cdot \{Tb \supset [(y)(Py \supset Cy) \cdot \sim Sb]\}$$
$$\{Ta \supset [(Pa \supset Ca) \cdot (Pb \supset Cb) \cdot \sim Sa]\} \cdot$$
$$\quad \{Tb \supset [(Pa \supset Ca) \cdot (Pb \supset Cb) \cdot \sim Sb]\}$$

$$(x)(\exists y)[Wy \cdot (Lx \equiv My)]$$
$$\{(\exists y)[Wy \cdot (La \equiv My)]\} \cdot \{(\exists y)[Wy \cdot (Lb \equiv My)]\}$$
$$\{Wa \cdot (La \equiv Ma)] \text{ v } [Wb \cdot (La \equiv Mb)]\} \cdot \{[Wa \cdot (Lb \equiv Ma)] \text{ v }$$
$$\quad [Wb \cdot (Lb \equiv Mb)]\}$$

Such representations often facilitate proofs of *in*validity.

We have in effect adopted the following principles:

A quantifier may extend over *any* closed proposition. And a quantifier may extend over a variable that is associated with a different quantifier *preceding* the former. But in such cases different variable letters must be chosen for each quantifier and its associated variables.

Exercises

1. Put the following into symbols:

   a. There is someone such that, if anyone is unhappy then so is he.

   b. There is someone such that, if everyone is unhappy then so is he.

---

[65]It happens that this proposition *could* be stated without this peculiarity, and indeed without multiple quantification at all; for it is logically equivalent to $[(x)Lx \text{ v } (\exists x)(Wx \cdot \sim Mx)] \cdot [(x)\sim Lx \text{ v } (\exists x)(Wx \cdot Mx)] \cdot (\exists x)Wx$. But the latter is outrageously unnatural and cumbersome. Furthermore, it is hard to see how one could discover or verify the equivalence (see Section 5) without first permitting and manipulating the parent expression.

   c. There is someone who is happy if and only if no one is.

   d. There is someone who is happy, if and only if no one is.

   e. If any Smith keeps up with the Joneses, then some Smiths do not, all Smiths are vindicated, and he (the Smith that keeps up) is to be congratulated.

   f. No Smith keeps up with the Joneses unless all members of the Smith's group condone conformity and he is wealthy besides.

   g. For every man, there is some woman and some child such that he is happy if and only if they are content.

   h. For every proposition there is a proposition that is true if and only if the former is true.

   i. There is something such that, for anything whatever, the former decays if and only if the latter flourishes.

   j. For anything whatever there is something such that the former decays if and only if the latter flourishes.

2. Assuming the world contains just two objects, show that the proposition in Exercise 1c is consistent, and in 1d inconsistent.

3. Assuming the world contains just two objects construct a formal proof for the argument at the beginning of this section.

5 • FURTHER EXTENSION OF INSTANTIATION AND GENERALIZATION

We are now able to expand our instantiation and generalization rules (for the last time) to permit manipulation of the new kinds of propositions that have come into view. The expansion will take place along lines that are thoroughly natural and easily anticipated; only one new restriction (on *UG*) will be found necessary.

First, it is evident that the notion of an open proposition, or a substitution instance thereof, must be broadened to include expressions that may themselves contain quantifiers. For example, Fa v $(x)Fx$ is a substitution instance of Fy v $(x)Fx$, and could be obtained by *UI* from $(y) [Fy$ v $(x)Fx]$. Similarly, $(\exists y)(Fm \equiv Gy)$ is a substitition instance of $(\exists y)(Fx \equiv Gy)$, and could be obtained from $(x)(\exists y)$

$(Fx \equiv Gy)$ by UI. Note in the latter case, the open proposition itself begins with a quantifier that extends to the end:—a characteristic previously confined to closed propositions. The terms used to make distinctions among variables, such as *free*, *bound*, *general*, *particulate*, continue in use as before; but note that a variable may be free even though it is preceded by a quantifier extending over it if the quantifier does not mention that particular letter: x is free in $(\exists y)(Fx \equiv Gy)$.

The rules UI and EI may be used in the usual way, but we must now characterize them in slightly more complex fashion: UI and EI are applied by dropping a quantifier and (if any variable letters are changed at all) changing *all* and *only* the variable letters identical to the one mentioned in the quantifier. Furthermore, where such operations yield open propositions that themselves begin with quantifiers extending to the end, we can apply UI or EI to those expressions as well. An example is

1.	$(x)(\exists y)(Fx \supset Gy)$	Pr
2.	$(\exists y)(Fx \supset Gy)$	1, UI
3.	$Fx \supset Gm$	2, EI

The expression in line 3 is an open proposition obtained from the open (and partially quantified) proposition in line 2.

We are accustomed to changing variable letters with EI and some uses of UI, but we have not heretofore changed letters when using UI to obtain an expression with a free *general* variable. But because we now have a plurality of such variables, it is essential (and obviously legitimate) to permit such change. Otherwise we could not reflect in a formal proof the fact that propositions symbolized with different letters but otherwise identical are equivalent:

1.	$(y)(Fy \supset Gy)$	Pr
2.	$Fx \supset Gx$	1, UI y/x
3.	$(x)(Fx \supset Gx)$	2, UG

Note the new annotational device y/x; it indicates that a change of lower case letters has taken place and tells what the change is. Here it is not really needed, but in some complex contexts it is welcome. Further examples are

1.	$(x)(\exists y)(Fx \supset Hy)$	Pr
2.	$(\exists y)(Fa \supset Hy)$	1, UI x/a

or,

2.	$(\exists y)(Fm \supset Hy)$	1, UI x/m

Again,

1. $(x)[Fa \lor (y)(Gy \equiv Hx)]$	*Pr*
2. $Fa \lor (y)(Gy \equiv Hm)$	1, *EI x/m*
3. $\sim Fa$	*CP*
4. $(y)(Gy \equiv Hm)$	2, 3, *Dis*
5. $Gm \equiv Hm$	4, *UI y/m*
6. $(\exists x)(Gx \equiv Hx)$	5, *EG m/x*
7. $\sim Fa \supset (\exists x)(Gx \equiv Hx)$	3–6, *CP*

The rules *UG* and *EG* may also be used much the same as heretofore, again with the understanding that where a change of lower case letters takes place, one and only one letter is uniformly changed, and it is replaced by *any* general variable that also appears in the new quantifier prefixing the whole expression. Examples are

1. $Fy \lor Gx$	*Pr*
2. $(x)(Fy \lor Gx)$	1, *UG x/x*

or,

2. $(z)(Fy \lor Gz)$	1, *UG x/z*

or,

2. $(y)(Fy \lor Gx)$	1, *UG y/y*

or,

2. $(\exists z)(Fz \lor Gx)$	1, *EG y/z*

Again,

1. $Fm \supset Gy$	*Pr*
2. $(\exists x)(Fx \supset Gy)$	1, *EG m/x*

or,

2. $(\exists z)(Fz \supset Gy)$	1, *EG m/z*

These rules, too, can be applied to expressions containing quantifiers:

1. $Fy \lor Gx$	*Pr*
2. $(y)(Fy \lor Gx)$	1, *UG y/y*
3. $(x)(y)(Fy \lor Gx)$	2, *UG x/x*

1. $Fa \lor (Gm \cdot Hn)$	*Pr*
2. $(\exists x)[Fa \lor (Gx \cdot Hn)]$	1, *EG m/x*
3. $(\exists y)(\exists x)[Fa \lor (Gx \cdot Hy)]$	2, *EG n/y*
4. $(\exists z)(\exists y)(\exists x)[Fz \lor (Gx \cdot Hy)]$	3, *EG a/z*

We continue to specify that variables must not be inadvertently captured. Hence, the following inferences are formally incorrect:

1. $Fy \vee Gx$ Pr
2. $(x)(Fx \vee Gx)$ 1, UG y/x (wrong—the x in Gx inadvertently captured)

1. $(y)(\exists x)(Fy \vee Gx)$ Pr
2. $(\exists x)(Fx \vee Gx)$ 1, UI y/x (wrong—the x in Fx inadvertently captured)

Although these examples happen to be legitimate inferences, the following complete arguments are demonstrably invalid:

1. $(y)(\exists x)(Fy \equiv Gx)$ Pr
2. $(\exists x)(Fy \equiv Gx)$ 1, UI y/y
3. $Fy \equiv Gm$ 2, EI x/m
4. $(\exists y)(Fy \equiv Gy)$ 3, EG m/y (wrong)

1. $(y)(\exists x)(Fy \equiv Gx)$ Pr
2. $(\exists x)(Fx \equiv Gx)$ 2, UI y/x (wrong)

The first shows inadvertent capture in a generalizing step, the second in an instantiation step.[66]

Our old restriction on EI remains unchanged. The old restriction on UG must be slightly recast. Because UG can now be applied to lines containing any free general veriable, and more than one, we now say that UG cannot be applied within the scope of a conditional assumption if the variable with respect to which generalization takes place is free in the first line of the sequence. The correctness of this formulation requires no discussion.

One new restriction on UG appears in the present context. Suppose we have an expression containing a free general variable and an existential quantifier, say,

$$(\exists y)(Fx \equiv Gy).$$

Intuitively this says that arbitrarily chosen x has the property that, for some y, x is an F if and only if y is a G, an assertion presumably

---

[66]The reader can verify that the argument (same in both cases) is invalid by examining the unabbreviated premise and conclusion for a universe of two individuals, or by some other adaptation of Tech 2.

warranted by reference to some prior closed proposition. We can apply *EI* to this expression, yielding

$Fx \equiv Gm$.

This says m is *the* individual (or one of the individuals) having the property that it is a G if and only if arbitrary x is an F. Now for all we know, the exact identity of m may depend upon the particular x that happens to have been chosen initially. Consequently, in assuming as it were that m (when put for y) satisfies the expression $Fx \equiv Gy$, we have produced an expression that cannot be thought of as holding indifferently for any x whatever. Thus, we could not apply *UG* to $Fx \equiv Gm$. The following material is a complete proof for a demonstrably invalid argument that embodies this mistake:[67]

1. $(x)(\exists y)(Fx \equiv Gy)$		*Pr*
2. $(\exists y)(Fx \equiv Gy)$		1, *UI* x/x
3. $Fx \equiv Gm$		2, *EI* y/m
4. $(x)(Fx \equiv Gm)$		3, *UG* x/x (wrong)
5. $(\exists y)(x)(Fx \equiv Gy)$		4, *EG* m/y

We state our restriction formally as follows: *UG* cannot be applied to a line containing a particulate variable if the general variable with respect to which generalization is to be carried out is free in the first line where the particulate variable appears. Thus, to give a more complex example, the following proof could not be executed,

1. $(x)(\exists y)(z)(Fx \text{ v } Gy \text{ v } Hz)$		*Pr*
2. $(\exists y)(z)(Fx \text{ v } Gy \text{ v } Hz)$		1, *UI* x/x
3. $(z)(Fx \text{ v } Gm \text{ v } Hz)$		2, *EI* y/m
4. $Fx \text{ v } Gm \text{ v } Hz$		3, *UI* z/z
5. $(w)(Fw \text{ v } Gm \text{ v } Hz)$		4, *UG* x/w (wrong)

because (i) line 4 contains a particulate variable and (ii) x is free in line 3, where the particulate variable first appears. On the other hand, this proof *could* continue with

5. $(w)(Fx \text{ v } Gm \text{ v } Hw)$		4, *UG* z/w

---

[67] We give it in symbolic form only, because it is difficult to find natural arguments that illustrate the point in this context. Such arguments abound, however, in the next section.

because, although line 4 contains a particulate variable, z is bound in the line where that variable first appears.

There is an instructive analogy between the old and new restrictions on UG, resulting from a similarity between the logical significance of a conditional assumption and a use of EI. In the former case we assume that an *arbitrary* x has a certain property; within the scope of that assumption we are naturally forbidden to infer the same for all x. In the latter case we assume that m has a certain property whose statement involves mention of arbitrary x. Viewed as it were from x's standpoint, this means we assume that the arbitrary x has a certain property whose statement involves mention of m; within the scope of that assumption—that is, in all lines containing m—we are naturally forbidden to infer the same for all x.

We now summarize the final form of our instantiation and generalization rules, including restrictions to prevent inadvertent capture of variables and generation of misleading expressions (that is, one quantifier extending over another with the same variable letter appearing in each). The reader should satisfy himself as to the motives for each restriction. In the following schemata it is understood that a stands for any constant, m for any particulate variable, and x and y for any general variables *not necessarily different*.

UI: $\dfrac{(x)\Phi x}{\Phi y, \text{ or } \Phi m, \text{ or } \Phi a}$

        Remarks: Φx is any expression containing free x; Φy, Φm, and Φa are the same expressions with y, m, or a in place of x throughout.

        Restriction: y, if it differs from x, must not appear bound in Φx.

EI: $\dfrac{(\exists x)\Phi x}{\Phi m}$

        Remarks: Φx is any expression containing free x; Φm is the same expression with m in place of x throughout.

        Restriction: m must not appear in Φx or any prior line of the proof.

UG: $\dfrac{\Phi x}{(y)\Phi y}$

        Remarks: Φx is any expression containing free x; Φy is the same expression with y in place of x throughout.

Restrictions: (i) May not be used if Φx lies within a conditional sequence and x appears free in the first line thereof. (ii) May not be used if Φx contains a particulate variable and x appears free in the first line of the proof containing that particulate variable. (iii) y, if it differs from x, must not appear in Φx.

EG: Φa, or Φm, or Φx

$(\exists y)\Phi y$

Remarks: Φa and Φm are any expressions containing a or m, and Φx is any expression containing free x; Φy is the same expression with y in place of a, m, or x.

Restriction: y must not appear in Φa, nor in Φm, nor in Φx if it differs from x.

We now add, as in Section 2, a postulate to the effect that $\sim(x)\Phi x$ logically implies $(\exists x)\sim\Phi x$. It can then readily be shown that the principles of manipulation for the quantified expressions adopted in Chapter 6, and also in Section 2 of this chapter, continue to hold good in the present context. This also extends to the isolation principles, with the understanding that the x's may be any general variables and the P's any expressions (not necessarily closed propositions) not containing x. Thus, we continue to employ Q equivalence, Q rules, Q distribution rules, and isolation principles, all as before. With the help of these principles it is once again possible to reduce all propositions of the types here considered to the types considered in Chapters 5 and 6. Thus, we still have a decision procedure (although extremely cumbersome); and it can easily be seen that application of the decision procedure to a valid argument corresponds to construction of an indirect formal proof for that argument: Hence, the deduction system is complete. It is not so easy to show that it is consistent; we claim that it is, but no proof is exhibited in this text.

Exercises

1. Construct formal proofs for the following, without using isolation principles.

   a. Fx v Gy (not indented); therefore $(x)(Fx$ v $Gx)$

b. $(x)(\exists y)(Fx \text{ v } Gy)$; therefore $(\exists y)(Fy \text{ v } Gy)$

c. $(\exists x)(y)(Fx \equiv Gy)$; therefore $(y)(\exists x)(Fx \equiv Gy)$

d. $(y)(\exists x)\{Fx \cdot [Fy \supset (z)(Gz \supset \sim Fz)]\}$; therefore $(\exists x)(Fx \cdot \sim Gx)$

e. $(y)(\exists x)(Fx \supset Gy)$; therefore $(x)Fx \supset (x)Gx$

f. $(x)Fx \supset (x)Gx$; therefore $(y)(\exists x)(Fx \supset Gy)$

g. $\sim(\exists x)(y)(Fx \supset Gy)$; therefore $(x)Fx \cdot (\exists x)\sim Gx$

h. $(x)Fx \cdot (\exists x)\sim Gx$; therefore $\sim(\exists x)(y)(Fx \supset Gy)$

i. $(y)(\exists x)(Gy \supset Fx)$; therefore $(\exists x)Gx \supset (\exists x)Fx$

j. $(\exists x)Gx \supset (\exists x)Fx$; therefore $(y)(\exists x)(Gy \supset Fx)$

k. $\sim(\exists x)(y)(Gy \supset Fx)$; therefore $(\exists x)Gx \cdot (x)\sim Fx$

l. $(\exists x)Gx \cdot (x)\sim Fx$; therefore $\sim(\exists x)(y)(Gy \supset Fx)$

2. Check the following proofs and annotate where valid:

a. 1. $(y)(\exists x)(Fx \supset Gy)$ Pr

  2. $(\exists x)(Fx \supset Gy)$

  3. $Fm \supset Gy$

    4. Fm

    5. Gy

    6. $(y)Gy$

  7. $Fm \supset (y)Gy$

  8. $(y)(Fm \supset Gy)$

  9. $(\exists x)(y)(Fx \supset Gy)$

b. 1. $(y)(\exists x)(Gy \supset Fx)$ Pr

  2. $(\exists x)(Gy \supset Fx)$

  3. $Gy \supset Fm$

    4. $(y)Gy$

    5. Gy

    6. Fm

7. $(y)Gy \supset Fm$

8. $(y)(Gy \supset Fm)$

9. $(\exists x)(y)(Gy \supset Fx)$

3. How do you know that establishment of the isolation principles for the context of this section will not violate the new restriction on *UG*?

4. Refer to Exercise 1. Problems (e) and (f) establish a logical equivalence. Verify that equivalence by direct appeal to isolation principles. Do the same for the equivalences established in (g) and (h), (i) and (j), and (k) and (l).

5. Using the results of Exercise 4, apply the decision procedure to the evaluation of the arguments in Exercise 2.

*6. Verify the equivalence asserted to hold in the footnote on p. 362.

7. Construct proofs or show invalidity for the following. (It is often easier to show invalidity by scrutiny of some unabbreviated version than by the decision procedure.)

 a. If anything was taken, then everyone at the party was covering up for the thief and it will never be seen again. Something was taken. Anyone covering up for a thief is himself guilty. Therefore, everyone at the party was guilty.

 b. It is true of everyone that there is some woman such that he (or she) can be a league member if and only if she (the woman) was married to one. Therefore, there is someone who can be a league member if and only if he himself (or she herself) is married to one.

 c. There is a woman such that everyone is happy if and only if she (the woman) is content. Therefore, there is someone who is happy if and only if he himself (or she herself) is content.

 *d. There is a woman such that, all men are happy if and only if she is content. Therefore, there is a woman such that, for any man, that man is happy if and only if she (the woman) is content.

8. Determine which of the following are logically true, with appropriate demonstrations. The symbol Φxy denotes any expression of the types studied in this section, having both free x and free y. The biconditionals, if logically true, represent principles that may conveniently be added to the system of proof-construction. What would you call them?

a. $(x)(y)\Phi xy \equiv (y)(x)\Phi xy$

b. $(\exists x)(\exists y)\Phi xy \equiv (\exists y)(\exists x)\Phi xy$

c. $(\exists x)(y)\Phi xy \supset (y)(\exists x)\Phi xy$

d. $(x)(\exists y)\Phi xy \supset (\exists y)(x)\Phi xy$

6 • RELATIONS

Consider the statement, "John loves Marsha." According to the conventions we have used heretofore, we could define *loving Marsha* as a property attaching to John and write Mj. Similarly we might define *being loved by John* as a property attaching to Marsha and write Jm. In either case the name of one of the individuals involved has been absorbed into a predicate letter, thus obscuring some detail. To retain as much logical detail as possible in the symbolism, we could isolate the relation *loving* as a kind of property that attaches to *two* individuals rather than one. Then we have, for "John loves Marsha," jLm. Terms appropriately symbolized with an upper case letter associated with two or more lower case letters we shall call *relations*. Symbolically it makes no difference how the lower case letters are arranged around an upper case *relation letter*. We could for instance write Ljm instead of jLm, meaning the same thing; but an arrangement once chosen must be retained for obvious reasons. On the other hand the *order* of lower case letters is not a matter of indifference at all; it may be true that jLm but false that mLj—the beginning of many a story.

This new device can be applied equally well to relations involving three or more terms. For example, "Abigail is between Bertrand and Cecil," can be given as $aBbc$; and "The triangle t is bounded by the sides a, b, and c," can be translated as $tBabc$. More to the point, we can construct quantified propositions involving relations. Several examples follow:

Eve loves someone.
xLy: x loves y.
e: Eve
$(\exists x)eLx$

Everyone loves someone.
$(x)(\exists y)xLy$

Everyone has a mother.
xMy: x is the mother of y.
$(x)(\exists y)yMx$

Someone is everyone's mother.[68]
$(\exists x)(y)xMy$

Everyone has parents.
$xyPz$: x and y are the parents of z.
$(x)(\exists y)(\exists z)yzPx$

There are horses' heads.
Hx: x is a horse.
Cx: x is a head.
xBy: x belongs to y.
$(\exists x)[Cx \cdot (\exists y)(Hy \cdot xBy)]$

All horses' heads are animals' heads.
Ax: x is an animal.
$(x)[(\exists y)(Hy \cdot Cx \cdot xBy) \supset (\exists y)(Ay \cdot Cx \cdot xBy)]$

Someone wears a ring on his finger.
Px: x is a person.
Rx: x is a ring.
Fx: x is a finger.
xWy: x is worn on y.
xBy: x belongs to y.
$(\exists x)[Px \cdot (\exists y)(\exists z)(Ry \cdot Fz \cdot yWz \cdot zBx)]$

It is natural to postulate that all of our earlier principles for the interpretation and manipulation of quantified propositions continue to hold unchanged—as indeed they do.[69] A very large number of natural arguments then falls under our techniques of analysis and proof-construction. Some examples follow.

---

[68]The translation here is not *quite* adequate; for, as we shall see, one could infer from this that someone is his own mother, which is clearly not meant. It is not difficult to symbolize the implied qualification that someone is everyone *else's* mother, but we leave this for a later section.

[69]In effect we have already been using quantificational principles with respect to relations; only the relations in question have been defined through predicate letters and truth-functional connectives solely. We now extend the rules to other relations as well. Strictly speaking, we are of course here introducing a whole new set of principles, of which all the previous ones are subcases.

Someone loves everyone.
Therefore, everyone is loved by someone.

1. $(\exists x)(y)xLy$	Pr	$/(x)(\exists y)yLx$
2. $(y)mLy$	1, EI x/m	
3. mLz	2, UI y/z	
4. $(\exists y)yLz$	3, EG m/y	
5. $(x)(\exists y)yLx$	4, UG z/x	

The converse of this argument is evidently invalid. Without our most recent restriction on UG we would be able to construct a straightforward proof for it:

Everyone is loved by someone.
Therefore, someone loves everyone.

1. $(x)(\exists y)yLx$	Pr	$/(\exists x)(y)xLy$
2. $(\exists y)yLz$	1, UI x/z	
3. mLz	2, EI y/m	
4. $(y)mLy$	3, UG z/y (wrong)	
5. $(\exists x)(y)xLy$	4, EG m/x	

Another example is

All beef is meat.
Therefore, beefeaters are meateaters.

Bx: x is beef.
Mx: x is meat.
xEy: x eats y.

1. $(x)(Bx \supset Mx)$	Pr
$\quad /(x)[(\exists y)(By \cdot xEy) \supset (\exists y)(My \cdot xEy)]$	
2. $(\exists y)(By \cdot xEy)$	CP
3. $Bm \cdot xEm$	2, EI
4. $Bm \supset Mm$	1, UI
5. Mm	3, 4, $Simp$, MP
6. $Mm \cdot xEm$	3, 5, $Simp$, $Conj$
7. $(\exists y)(My \cdot xEy)$	6, EG
8. $(\exists y)(By \cdot xEy) \supset (\exists y)(My \cdot xEy)$	2–7, CP
9. $(x)[(\exists y)(By \cdot xEy) \supset (\exists y)(My \cdot xEy)]$	8, UG

Again,

Everyone loves someone who loves him in return.

Therefore, everyone is loved by someone.

1. $(x)(\exists y)(xLy \cdot yLx)$ Pr $/(x)(\exists y)yLx$
2. $(\exists y)(zLy \cdot yLz)$ 1, UI x/z
3. $zLm \cdot mLz$ 2, EI
4. mLz 3, $Simp$
5. $(\exists y)yLz$ 4, EG
6. $(x)(\exists y)yLx$ 5, UG z/x

The change of variables from x to z and back again is not really needed in this proof. Finally, we give an example of an erroneous proof of an invalid argument:

Everyone loves someone.
Therefore, someone loves himself.

1. $(x)(\exists y)xLy$ Pr $/(\exists x)xLx$
2. $(\exists y)xLy$ 1, UI
3. xLm 2, EI
4. $(\exists x)xLx$ 3, EG m/x (wrong)

The last step violates a formal restriction on EG (compare Section 5) and results in inadvertent capture of the first x.[70]

If we were unconvinced of the invalidity of the last argument, how could we demonstrate it? In this case, we need only picture a world of two individuals in which each loves the other but neither loves himself. To be elaborate, the premise would then be

$(aLa \text{ v } aLb) \cdot (bLa \text{ v } bLb),$

and the conclusion,

$aLa \text{ v } bLb;$

then it is easy to assign truth-values making the premise true and the conclusion false. Some such device will hereafter be required in most cases where it is desired to prove invalidity, because *our decision procedure has now been left behind.*

Because we allow expressions of the type $(x)(\exists y)xLy$, where two different variables associated with the same relation letter are separately quantified, complete isolation of quantifiers can no longer be

---

[70]This is a promised example of an *invalid* inference by inadvertent capture through EG. Cf. p. 353 n.

accomplished. Hence, the previous method of reducing complex quantified propositions to simpler types no longer holds good. It can be shown (but not in this text) that no perfectly general decision procedure exists for *all* arguments of the types now in view. It *can* be shown (but again not here) that the proof procedure is complete and consistent.

Finally, it should be noted that the use of relation symbols permits greater delicacy and definiteness in cases that otherwise have to be treated with a certain vagueness. Consider,

> No one who understood economics would say that.
> But John Stuart said that.
> Therefore, John Stuart did not understand economics.

> 1. $(x)(Ux \supset \sim Sx)$ Pr
> 2. Sj Pr
> 3. $Uj \supset \sim Sj$ 1, UI
> 4. $\sim Uj$ 2, 3, DN, MT

Thus analyzed the argument appears valid. But is it? The first premise, after all, should be taken to mean, "Anyone who comes to understand economics would not say that *at a later time*." To symbolize with the time reference explicitly included we propose the following dictionary:

> xUy: x understands economics at time y.
> xSy: x says that at time y.
> xBy: x is before y (in time).
> t: the time at which John Stuart said that.
> j: John Stuart.

Then in symbols the argument is

$$(x)(y)(z)[(xUy \cdot yBz) \supset \sim xSz]$$
$$\underline{jSt}$$
$$(x) \sim jUx$$

This is invalid, as we can see by consideration of its verbal equivalent. But suppose we wish to demonstrate its invalidity by direct examination of the symbolic structure. One straightforward method is to imagine a universe of three entities, j, t, and u, then write out unabbreviated versions of the three propositions and apply truth-functional methods. (This is *not* a decision procedure; an argument that is valid with respect to a universe of three entities might be invalid when considered with respect to a universe of four or more.) It will be found that by taking both *tBu* and *jUu* as true (in words, assuming that John Stuart did understand economics *after* he said that) it will be possible for the premises to be true and the conclusion false.

Although simple in principle this process is very lengthy in execution. It also brings to light a danger. In the symbolic translation given above we have not specified by separate predicate letters that certain individual constants or variables are supposed to be times or persons, because these restrictions are implicitly contained in the definitions of the relation letters. In trying to establish invalidity by the method just sketched we will naturally generate expressions in which the names of times are filled in at places intended only for the names of persons, and conversely. (For example, *tSj*, meaning "The time at which John Stuart said that, said that at the time John Stuart.") Similar expressions could arise with other kinds of related entities in other arguments. It *might* then happen that an argument is erroneously judged to be invalid *only* because some expression of the form *aRb* is assumed to be consistent, and hence possibly true, even though it represents an impossible or nonsensical state of affairs when considered in the light of the verbal meanings associated with it.

One way of avoiding such difficulties is to add supplementary premises that spell out the restrictions implicit in the original dictionary. In the case of the John Stuart argument we might take P for person and T for time and add the following six premises:

Pj
Tt
$(x)(Px \supset \sim Tx)$
$(x)(y)[xUy \supset (Px \cdot Ty)]$
$(x)(y)[xSy \supset (Px \cdot Ty)]$
$(x)(y)[xBy \supset (Tx \cdot Ty)]$

The advantage of such a formulation is that no unwanted combination of individual constants with a relation letter (such as *tSj*) can be supposed true without contradicting the premises. Fortunately, such elaborate supplements are not generally necessary, especially when a proof of *validity* is at stake.[71]

---

[71]In fact, the danger mentioned here is just a further instance of the general principle that symbolic demonstrations of invalidity may be overturned by consideration of previously neglected details of logical structure.

Finally, we note that a further reinterpretation of the argument about John Stuart is possible. The conclusion could be taken to mean, "John Stuart did not understand economics prior to the time he said that." The argument may then be symbolized as

$$(x)(y)(z)[(xUy \cdot yBz) \supset \sim xSz]$$
$$\underline{jSt}$$
$$(x)(xBt \supset \sim jUx)$$

This is valid; proof is left as an exercise.

Exercises

1. Using the dictionary supplied, translate the following into ordinary English:

$$xAy: \quad x \text{ is acquainted with } y.$$
$$Nx: \quad x \text{ is a number.}$$
$$xGy: \quad x \text{ is greater than } y.$$
$$Fx: \quad x \text{ is fire.}$$
$$Sx: \quad x \text{ is smoke.}$$
$$xCy: \quad x \text{ causes } y.$$

 a. $(x)(y)xAy$

 b. $(\exists x)(\exists y)xAy$

 c. $(x)(\exists y)xAy$

 d. $(\exists x)(y)xAy$

 e. $(x)[Nx \supset (\exists y)(Ny \cdot xGy)]$

 f. $(x)[Nx \supset (\exists y)(Ny \cdot yGx)]$

 g. $(\exists y)[Ny \cdot (x)(Nx \supset xGy)]$

 h. $(\exists y)[Ny \cdot (x)(Nx \supset yGx)]$

 i. $(x)[Fx \supset (\exists y)(Sy \cdot xCy)]$

 j. $(\exists x)[Fx \cdot \sim(\exists y)yCx]$

2. Using the dictionary of Exercise 1, translate the following into symbols:

 a. No number is greater than itself.

b. Everything is greater than something.

c. Every number is greater than some number.

d. Everything has a cause.

e. If something is the cause of something, and the latter is again the cause of some (other) thing, then the first is the cause of the last.

f. If anyone is acquainted with someone, then the latter is also acquainted with the former.

g. No number can cause a fire.

h. Only fire can cause smoke.

3. Consider the symbolic translation given in the text for the final (valid) argument about John Stuart. Construct a formal proof.

4. Construct proofs or show invalidity for the following:

a. It is true of anyone that he loves everyone. Therefore, it is true of anyone that he is loved by everyone.

b. It is true of someone that there is someone he loves. Therefore, it is true of someone that there is someone who loves him.

c. Everyone loves someone. Therefore, someone is loved by everyone.

d. Everyone loves someone. Therefore, someone loves everyone.

e. Someone loves everyone. Therefore, everyone is loved by someone.

f. Someone loves everyone. Therefore, everyone loves someone.

g. It is not the case that everyone loves everyone. Therefore, there is someone who does not love someone.

h. It is not the case that there is someone who loves everyone. Therefore, for everyone there is someone who does not love him.

i. It is not the case that there is someone who loves everyone at some time. Therefore, it is true of anyone that there is someone he does not love at any time.

j. It is not the case that there is someone who loves someone at all times. Therefore, it is true of anyone that at some time he does not love anyone.

k. Someone loves everyone. Hence, someone loves himself.

l. Someone loves everyone who loves himself, and no one else. Hence, someone loves himself.

m. Someone loves everyone who loves himself, and no one else. Hence, someone does not love himself.

n. Someone loves everyone who does not love himself, and does not love anyone who does love himself. Hence, someone is Adam's mother.

o. Anything that causes itself is a God. If anything exists that does not cause itself, then there must be something that does cause itself. I do not cause myself. Therefore, there is a God.

p. Causes always precede their effects. The rising of the temperature preceded the speeding up of the reaction. Therefore, the speeding up of the reaction was not the cause of the rising of the temperature.

q. Causes always precede their effects. The rising of the temperature preceded the speeding up of the reaction. Therefore, the rising of the temperature was the cause of the speeding up of the reaction.

r. The eclipse of the sun caused the astronomers to gather on the mountaintop, but it also preceded the latter. Therefore, causes do not always precede their effects.

s. Fire causes smoke. Therefore, where there is smoke there is fire.

t. Fire causes smoke. Therefore, where there is no fire there is no smoke.

u. We eat today what we bought yesterday. We bought meat yesterday. Therefore, we eat meat today.

v. We eat today what we bought yesterday. We bought raw meat yesterday. Therefore, we eat raw meat today.

w. All men are sometimes courageous. Anyone who is courageous at a given time is also trustworthy at that time. Hence, there are times when all men are trustworthy. [Compare Exercise x.]

x. Sometimes all men are courageous. Anyone who is courageous at a given time is also trustworthy at that time. Hence, there are times when all men are trustworthy.

y. If anyone is superior to anyone, then the latter is not superior to the former. Hence, no one can be superior to himself.

z. If anyone is related to someone, then the latter is also related to the former. If anyone is related to someone, and the latter also related to someone, then the first is related to the third. Hence, anyone who is not related to himself has no relatives at all.

7 • IDENTITY

Literally interpreted, the Old Testament seems to say that Adam is everyone's ancestor. We might symbolize this as $(x)aAx$. But then we could infer, by UI, aAa; this is clearly wrong, as no one can be his own ancestor. Obviously we have been too liberal in interpreting the premise; it means that Adam is everyone *else's* ancestor, and to capture this in symbols we have to introduce some character for the notion of otherness, or its opposite, sameness. It is convenient and suggestive to adopt the symbol = for this purpose. Then $b = c$ means b and c are the same individual or b is identical to c. Correspondingly, $b \neq c$ means that b and c are distinct; it may be written alternatively as $\sim(b = c)$. With the help of this symbol we could render the statement from the Old Testament as $(x)(a \neq x \supset aAx)$, and this prevents the preceding puzzling deduction.

The statement "b is identical to c" can be interpreted as a claim that b and c, although distinct symbols, are assigned to the same individual object. Hence, the assertion is partly a statement about the symbols we employ to refer to objects, and this seems to put the identity relation on a slightly different footing from the other relations we have discussed. Because of this feature, the following obvious principle can be added to our system of proof-construction:

If on a line of proof there appears an expression of the form $x = y$ (where x and y are any individual variables or constants), then any prior line available for appeal may be repeated with one or more x's replaced by y's, or conversely, provided such alterations do not change or obscure the relations between quantifiers and variables.

Manipulations in accordance with this principle may be annotated as *Id.*[72]

Many expressions apparently call for direct use of identity:

The author of *Huckleberry Finn* is the author of *Tom Sawyer*.
Twain is the author of *Huckleberry Finn*.
Twain is Clemens.

---

[72]Like the conception of an individual object, the notion of identity is charged with philosophical obscurities. An alternative approach is to understand "x is identical to y" as "For any property F, Fx if and only if Fy." But to formalize the latter and use it in proofs one requires predicate variables and predicate quantifiers, study of which lies beyond the scope of this book.

The phrase "author of *Huckleberry Finn*" is a discription and *"the* author of *Huckleberry Finn"* a definite description. In each of these examples a name or definite description is identified with another name or definite description. Both are ordinarily symbolized with individual constants, and properly so. For instance, consider the argument

> The author of *Huckleberry Finn* is Clemens.
> Clemens is (also) the author of *Tom Sawyer*.
> Therefore, the author of *Huckleberry Finn* is the author of *Tom Sawyer*.

> h: the author of *Huckleberry Finn*
> c: Clemens
> t: the author of *Tom Sawyer*

> 1. $h = c$ *Pr*
> 2. $c = t$ *Pr*
> 3. $h = t$ 1, 2, *Id*

The natural policy of assigning individual constants to definite descriptions cannot be pursued indiscriminately. Take the argument,

> The author of *Huckleberry Finn* lived in New York.
> Therefore, someone wrote *Huckleberry Finn*.

Is this valid? It is if, as seems reasonable, we interpret the definite description as asserting the existence of the described object. Then we can break down the meaning of the definite description into parts with the aid of the following dictionary:

> h: *Huckleberry Finn* (the novel, not its author)
> xWy: x wrote y
> Nx: x lived in New York

For the argument we can now put

$$\frac{(\exists x)(xWh \cdot Nx)}{(\exists x)xWh}$$

for which the proof is trivial.

However, the translation just given for "The author of *Huckleberry Finn* lived in New York" is not quite adequate, because the attempt to exhibit in detail the meaning of the definite description has not succeeded. We can demonstrate this by considering the following argument, which is clearly valid:

> The author of *Huckleberry Finn* lived in New York.
> Shakespeare did not live in New York.
> Therefore, Shakespeare did not write *Huckleberry Finn*.

No formal proof for this can be constructed without symbolizing the idea that there is *only one* author of *Huckleberry Finn*, which is clearly part of the meaning of the definite description. But this work can be accomplished with the identity relation, for saying that *only x* has a certain property is equivalent to saying that anything having that property is identical with x. Hence, with s for Shakespeare, the argument can be symbolized and proved as follows:

1.	$(\exists x)[xWh \cdot Nx \cdot (y)(yWh \supset y = x)]$	*Pr*
2.	$\sim Ns$	*Pr*
3.	$mWh \cdot Nm \cdot (y)(yWh \supset y = m)$	1, *EI, x/m*
4.	$\sim\sim sWh$	*IP*
5.	$sWh \supset s = m$	3, *Simp, UI, y/s*
6.	$s = m$	4, 5, *DN, MP*
✓7.	$\sim Nm$	2, 6, *Id*
✓8.	Nm	3, *Simp*
9.	$\sim sWh$	4–8, *IP*

In summary, we may when necessary interpret definite descriptions of the form "The F is a G" as conjunctions of three statements: (i) There is an F; (ii) nothing else is; and (iii) it is also a G. In symbols it is $(\exists x)[Fx \cdot (y)(Fy \supset y = x) \cdot Gx]$.[73]

The policy of assigning individual constants to proper names must also be pursued with caution, because the latter are not always used for just one individual. Suppose there is a contemporary artist named

---

[73]This interpretation of definite descriptions is due mainly to Bertrand Russell. It is partly motivated by a desire to explain the existence of what appear to be *singular* propositions about *non-existent* individuals. For instance, "The present king of France is bald," understood as having the structure Bk, seems to concede the existence of a present king of France (k) whether true or false, and even to require it in order to be meaningful. On the suggested interpretation, with Kx for "x is a present king of France," the structure is given as $(\exists x)[Kx \cdot (y)(Ky \supset y = x)$ $Bx]$, which asserts the existence of a present king of France but does not presuppose it. Compare Bertrand Russell, *Introduction to Mathematical Philosophy* (London: George Allen & Unwin, Ltd., 1919), chap. 16.

Clemens, and "Clemens is the best tenor in Italy." In analogy with an earlier example, we might then form the following absurd argument:

> The author of *Huckleberry Finn* is Clemens.
> Clemens is the best tenor in Italy.
> Therefore, the author of *Huckleberry Finn* is the best tenor in Italy.

But by using individual constants for Clemens and the definite descriptions, a proof is easily constructed. To avoid suggesting in symbols a uniqueness in the application of names that is not intended in use, one may absorb names into predicate letters. With this dictionary,

> Cx: x is called Clemens
> h: the author of *Huckleberry Finn*
> b: the best tenor in Italy

the argument is symbolized as

$$\frac{\begin{array}{l} Ch \\ Cb \end{array}}{b = h}$$

which is clearly invalid. This method of symbolizing proper names can be made consistent with the other, for if a name *is* understood to be used uniquely, this can be symbolized with the identity sign. For example, if *Clemens* is uniquely used, the preceding argument is valid and can be symbolized and proved as follows:

1.	$Ch \cdot (x)(Cx \supset x = h)$	Pr
2.	Cb	Pr
3.	$Cb \supset b = h$	1, *Simp, UI, x/b*
4.	$b = h$	2, 3, *MP*

Finally, we note that the employment of the identity sign to express uniqueness can be extended in order to symbolize certain numerical propositions. For example, where Bx means "x is an apple in the box," we can translate "There are just two apples in the box," as

$$(\exists x)(\exists y)\{Bx \cdot By \cdot x \neq y \cdot (z)[Bz \supset (z = x \vee z = y)]\};$$

and "There are at least three apples in the box," as

$$(\exists x)(\exists y)(\exists z)(Bx \cdot By \cdot Bz \cdot x \neq y \cdot x \neq z \cdot y \neq z).$$

But these possibilities are of more theoretical than practical importance, because of the length and awkwardness of the resulting symbolic arrays.

Exercises

1. Show with formal proofs that the following are valid:

   a. King Richard is stronger than *anyone* in the tournament. Therefore, King Richard is not in the tournament.   (enthymeme)

   b. King Richard has black armor. King John does not. Therefore, King Richard is not King John.

2. The following arguments are valid. Construct two proofs for each, one assigning constants to definite descriptive phrases, and one not.

   a. Mr. Johnson is a Texan. All Texans are Westerners. The man in my cab is not a Westerner. Hence, the man in my cab is not Mr. Johnson

   b. The author of *Hamlet* is the author of *Lear*. The author of *Hamlet* was a genius. Hence, so was the author of *Lear*.

3. Show invalidity or construct formal proofs for the following:

   a. Shakespeare wrote *Hamlet*. But Christopher Morley is Shakespeare. Therefore, Christopher Morley wrote *Hamlet*.

   b. There is something that Shakespeare wrote. But Shakespeare is Christopher Morley. And Francis Bacon is Shakespeare. Therefore, something written by Francis Bacon was also written by Christopher Morley.

   c. Shakespeare is Christopher Morley. And Christopher Morley is the Earl of Oxford. Therefore, anything written by Shakespeare was written by the Earl of Oxford.

   d. Anyone who wrote *Lear* was a genius. Therefore, the man who wrote *Lear* was a genius.

   e. Anyone who wrote *Lear* was a genius. Therefore, the man who wrote *Lear*, if there was one, was a genius.

   f. The article on the South in today's paper is well written. Nothing written by more than one person is well written. Hence, the man who wrote the article on the South in today's paper is capable of good writing.   (enthymeme)

g. The morning star is Venus. The evening star is Venus. Therefore, the morning star is the evening star.

h. The morning star is Venus. The evening star is Venus. Therefore, any morning star is an evening star.

i. The morning star is called Venus. The evening star is called Venus. Therefore, the morning star is the evening star.

j. The morning star is called Venus. The evening star is called Venus. Therefore, the morning star and the evening star are called by the same name. (Take "x is called Venus" as $xCv \cdot Nv$, where v is a constant and Nx means x is a name.)

k. The only noble king was the sixth-century king of England. Arthur was a king of England, and lived in the sixth century. Hence, Arthur was the only noble king.

l. There were two judges, Tweedledum and Tweedledee, and no others. At least one of the judges was awake at all times. When the muffin man told that horrid lie, Tweedledum was asleep. Therefore, at that moment Tweedledee must have been awake.

*4. With appropriate formal proofs, show that the following are logically equivalent translations of "Shakespeare is the author of *Hamlet*." Note that although each one involves quantifiers, each may be regarded as a complex singular statement about s. Wherever necessary, assume as an additional premise that $(x)(x = x)$.

a. $Hs \cdot (x)(Hx \supset x = s)$

b. $(\exists x)[Hx \cdot (y)(Hy \supset y = x) \cdot x = s]$

c. $(x)(Hx \equiv x = s)$

5. The following arguments are clearly invalid. But, as the proofs show, they can be apparently justified by appeal to *Id*. Discuss the mistakes and/or difficulties here.

a. Clemens is the name given to a famous American author by his parents. Clemens is Twain. Therefore, Twain is the name given to a famous American author by his parents.

1. Nc	Pr
2. $c = t$	Pr
3. Nt	1, 2, *Id*

*b. The safety man intended to tackle the quarterback, and no one else. The quarterback was not the ball carrier. Therefore, the safety man did not intend to tackle the ball carrier.

1.	sIq	Pr
2.	$(x)(sIx \supset q = x)$	Pr
✓3.	$q \neq b$	Pr
4.	$\sim\sim sIb$	IP
5.	sIb	4, DN
6.	$sIb \supset q = b$	2, UI, x/b
✓7.	$q = b$	5, 6, MP
8.	$\sim sIb$	4–7, IP

8 • RELATIONAL ENTHYMEMES

It is characteristic of arguments involving binary relations that certain properties of the relations themselves, although clearly understood, are left unstated. For instance,

A is greater than B.
B is greater than C.
Therefore, A is greater than C.

This is formally invalid without the expressed statement that the relation "greater than" is *transitive*. By this we mean that if any three entities fall under the relation in such a way that one is related thereby to the second, and the second to the third, then the first is similarly related to the third. In symbols, we say that a relation R is *transitive* if and only if the following is true:

$$(x)(y)(z)[(xRy \cdot yRz) \supset xRz].$$

Evidently the addition of such a statement for "greater than" to the preceding argument would render it formally valid. Some relations are *intransitive*; we shall say that a relation R is *intransitive* if and only if it is true that

$$(x)(y)(z)[(xRy \cdot yRz) \supset \sim xRz].$$

Example: "twice as great as".

Finally, we note that the quantified expressions we have produced to define the qualities transitivity and intransitivity are not contradictory. A relation R may be neither, in which case we say it is *nontransitive; nontransitivity* for R is defined by the truth of the following:

$$(\exists x)(\exists y)(\exists z)(xRy \cdot yRz \cdot xRz) \cdot (\exists x)(\exists y)(\exists z)(xRy \cdot yRz \cdot \sim xRz).$$

Example: "loves".

A second commonly unexpressed property of binary relations is *symmetry*. A relation R is *symmetrical* if and only if,

$$(x)(y)(xRy \supset yRx).$$

Example: "sibling of".

A relation R is *asymmetrical* if and only if,

$$(x)(y)(xRy \supset \sim yRx).$$

Example: "greater than".

Finally, if neither of the preceding holds for a relation, we say it is *nonsymmetrical;* that is, a relation R is nonsymmetrical if and only if,

$$(\exists x)(\exists y)(xRy \cdot yRx) \cdot (\exists x)(\exists y)(xRy \cdot \sim yRx).$$

Example: "sister of".

A third property of binary relations is *reflexivity*. A relation R is *reflexive* if and only if,

$$(x)xRx.$$

Example: "equal to".

Similarly a relation R is *irreflexive* if and only if,

$$(x)\sim xRx.$$

Example: "greater than".

And finally a relation R is *nonreflexive* if and only if,

$$(\exists x)xRx \cdot (\exists x)\sim xRx.$$

Example: "loves".

The exercises furnish examples of enthymemes that presuppose one or another of these properties, and of invalid arguments that have an air of validity precisely because of such presuppositions vaguely or erroneously implied.

This terminates our survey of deductive forms; it has not been exhaustive. In Appendix C some directions for further inquiry are suggested. It has often been maintained that deductive logic is an established science, in the sense that its elementary principles are firmly understood and immune to criticism. It is a philosophical question whether this is true of deductive logic, or of any science.

Exercises

1. Classify the following relations with regard to transitivity, symmetry, and reflexivity. In some cases there may be legitimate differences of interpretation.

   a. equal to

   b. prior to

   c. listens to

   d. causes

   e. logically implies

   f. divides evenly

   g. son of

   h. married to

   i. points to

   j. due north of

2. According to the symbolic definitions of transitivity and intransitivity, could a relation be both? Could a relation be symmetrical and asymmetrical? Reflexive and irreflexive?

*3. Where M is for *male* and P for *parent of*, the statement "a is the half-brother of b" can be rendered as

$$Ma \cdot (\exists x)(xPa \cdot xPb) \cdot (\exists x)(xPa \cdot \sim xPb) \cdot (\exists x)(\sim xPa \cdot xPb).$$

Classify as in Exercise 1 the relation *half-brother of* and justify the results by reference to the symbolic definitions of transitivity, symmetry, and so on.

4. Suppose a binary relation R applies universally; that is $(x)(\exists y)(xRy \vee yRx)$. Show that if R is transitive and symmetrical it must be reflexive.

5. Construct proofs or show invalidity for the following, adding statements about the properties of the relations involved where appropriate.

   a. John is Mary's sibling. Therefore, Mary is John's sibling.

   b. John is Mary's brother. Therefore, Mary is John's brother.

   c. John is not greater than himself.

   d. John is equal in size to Mary, and Mary is equal to George. Therefore, George is equal to John.

   e. John is George's brother. George is Harry's brother. Therefore, John is Harry's brother.

   f. John is George's brother. George is Harriet's brother. Therefore, John is Harriet's brother.

   g. A causes B. B causes C. Therefore, A causes C.

   h. A is the immediate cause of B. B is the immediate cause of C. Therefore, A is the immediate cause of C.

   i. Mannfried is the fastest man in the group. Halloway and Smythe are both in the group, and Halloway is faster than Smythe. Therefore, Mannfried is faster than Smythe.

   j. Mannfried is the fastest man in the group. Smythe is in the group. Therefore, Mannfried is faster than Smythe, and Smythe is not faster than Mannfried.

   k. Plato's philosophy is different from Aristotle's, and Aristotle's is different from Plotinus'. Therefore, Plato's philosophy is different from Plotinus'.

   l. Jones is related to someone who is related to Smith. Therefore, Smith is related to Jones.

   m. A and B are siblings-in-law (that is, each is brother-in-law or sister-in-law to the other). B and C are siblings-in-law. Therefore, A and C are siblings-in-law.

n. Cain and Abel belong to the same race, but Cain and Jacob do not. Therefore, Jacob and Abel do not belong to the same race.

o. Cain and Abel share a secret, but Cain and Jacob do not. Therefore, Jacob and Abel do not share a secret.

p. The murder was prior to the ringing of the bell, but not prior to the backfire. Hence, the ringing of the bell was not prior to the backfire.

q. *A* is not the immediate cause of *B*, nor is *B* the immediate cause of *A*. But *B* is the immediate cause of *C*. Therefore, *A* is the immediate cause of *C*. [Compare Exercise r.]

r. The murder was simultaneous with the ringing of the bell (that is, neither preceded the other), but the ringing of the bell preceded the backfire. Hence, the murder preceded the backfire.

s. Every man is smarter than some woman. And there is some woman who is smarter than every child. Therefore, every man is smarter than every child.

t. There is some woman such that every man is smarter than she. And there is some woman who is smarter than every child. Therefore, every man is smarter than every child.

u. Every man is smarter than Jane, and Jane is smarter than every child. Therefore, every man is smarter than every child.

v. Eric is always stronger than Hans. Hans is always stronger than Rolfe. Therefore, Eric is always stronger than Rolfe.

w. Eric is sometimes stronger than Hans. Hans is sometimes stronger than Rolfe. Therefore, Eric is sometimes stronger than Rolfe.

*x. Any Turk is sometimes stronger than Hans. Hans is always stronger than Rolfe. Therefore, there are times when any Turk is stronger than Rolfe.

*y. There are times when any Turk is stronger than Hans. Hans is always stronger than Rolfe. Therefore, there are times when any Turk is stronger than Rolfe.

*z. There are times when all comedies are more pleasing than any tragedy. Some tragedies are always more pleasing than some melodramas. Therefore, there are times when any comedy is more pleasing than certain melodramas.

APPENDIXES

APPENDIX A • REDUNDANCY OF MATERIAL SUBSTITUTION

We have to show that anything provable with the help of material substitution is provable without that principle, and without use of conditional or indirect proof. Suppose we have an atom or molecule P imbedded in some context, and a biconditional holding between P and some other atom or molecule Q:

1. $(\ldots P \ldots)$
2. $P \equiv Q$

We must obtain $(\ldots Q \ldots)$; that is, a proposition identical to line 1 but having Q in place of P. We assume that P occurs only once, or that only one occurrence of P is to be replaced by Q, and it is marked with some special auxiliary sign.

We first convert line 1 into conjunctive normal form (see Chapter 4), taking P as a single unit. This is accomplished through successive appeals to DM, DN, and $Dist$; hence, each step is reversible. We then have a series of conjuncts that is split by $Simp$ onto separate lines. Those conjuncts not containing P we ignore for the moment. Consider those that have one occurrence of P; they will have the form $R_i \vee P$, or $R_i \vee {\sim}P$, where R_i is the balance of the i-th such conjunct. Suppose the form is $R_i \vee P$. Then on successive lines we can put ${\sim}R_i \supset P$, $P \supset Q$ (from line 2), ${\sim}R_i \supset Q$, and finally $R_i \vee Q$. If the form is $R_i \vee {\sim}P$, a similar series of moves will yield $R_i \vee {\sim}Q$. We do this for every conjunct containing one occurrence of P. Those containing more than one such occurrence are similarly transformed by repetitions of the process. Eventually every original conjunct containing P will have generated another just like it but with Q in place of P.

Finally, we collect all the transformed conjuncts, along with the ones that never contained P to start with, and reassemble them by $Conj$. The processes of the original conversion to conjunctive normal form are then repeated in reverse, and we are back to line 1 with Q in place of P. If line 1 contains more than a single occurrence of P, and substitution in more than one such occurrence is desired, repetition of the same procedure will suffice.

APPENDIX B • THE NEED FOR CONDITIONAL PROOF

The inference principles available at the end of Section 13 of Chapter 3 do not suffice for establishing (by formal proof) the validity of this argument:

$$\frac{P \supset Q}{P \supset (P \cdot Q)}$$

A demonstration of this fact can be given in three stages:

I. Given any argument for which there is a proof by means of the principles mentioned here, we can show that there is also a proof for the same argument employing a smaller group of principles, called the *slender set*. II. By means of numerical matrices something like truth tables we define an abstract property of symbolic expressions and show that that property is hereditary with respect to the slender set; that is, if a group of premises has the property in question, then any propositions deducible from those premises by the slender set will also have the property. III. Lastly, we show that $P \supset Q$ has this property, whereas $P \supset (P \cdot Q)$ does not. We now sketch these stages successively.

I. We imagine an arbitrarily chosen argument, expressed so that the signs ∇ and $\equiv$ do not appear in the premises or conclusion, and for which there exists a formal proof. If that proof contains any appeal to material substitution we can write another proof without such appeal (by Appendix A). And this new proof can if necessary be revised to eliminate all occurrences of ∇ and $\equiv$, because no inference rules operate on propositions containing those signs except material substitution and the two CC rules for their introduction or elimination.

It can then be shown that the proof can be further revised to employ the following principles and no others:

MP	Logical substitution
Simp	*Com* ⎫
Conj	*Ass* ⎬ — {conjunctive forms only}
Hyp	*Dist* — {$[P \cdot (Q \text{ v } R)] \equiv [(P \cdot Q) \text{ v } (P \cdot R)]$ only }
Add	*DN*
	Taut
	DM — {both}
	CC — {$(P \supset Q) \equiv (\sim P \text{ v } Q)$ only }

We take this list as the slender set. Shorter and equally adequate lists may be produced, but the adequacy of this particular one is easily shown. The general procedure has been illustrated in connection with discussions of redundancy in Chapter 3, and we omit details. The result of this final revision we call the *revised proof*.

II. Assume that number-values 0, 1, or 2 are assigned to atoms in a symbolic expression, and number-values for molecular groups are determined as functions of the number-values of their constituent atoms. This is simply a generalization of the idea employed in ordinary truth tables, using three different numbers instead of two. The number-functions that determine the number-values of molecules are defined in the following tables:

A	B	~A	A·B	A v B	A ⊃ B
2	2	0	2	2	2
2	1	0	1	2	1
2	0	0	0	2	0
1	2	1	1	2	2
1	1	1	1	1	1
1	0	1	0	1	1
0	2	2	0	2	2
0	1	2	0	1	2
0	0	2	0	0	2

Note that the value of $(A \cdot B)$ is the lesser of the values given to A and B, whereas the value of $(A \vee B)$ is the greater.

Now we construct an array exhibiting all possible combinations of number-values for arguments of the form MP:

P	/	P	⊃	Q	//	Q
2			2	2		2
2			1	1		1
2			0	0		0
1			2	2		2
1			1	1		1
1			1	0		0
0			2	2		2
0			2	1		1
0			2	0		0

It appears that in any row in which all the premises have number-value 2, the conclusion has the same value. That result can easily be proved for all other inferences in accordance with the slender set.

It can also be shown that substitutions in accordance with equivalence principles in the slender set produce *no* change in the number-value patterns of the molecules in question.

III. We have now shown (in outline) that if there exists any proof running from $P \supset Q$ to $P \supset (P \cdot Q)$, there is a corresponding revised proof; and if there is an assignment of number-values to the atoms under which the premise has number-value 2, the conclusion (and all intermediate steps of the revised proof) will also have number-value 2. It remains only to show that there is an assignment of number-values under which $(P \supset Q)$ is 2 and $P \supset (P \cdot Q)$ is not:

P	⊃	Q	/	P	⊃	(P	·	Q)
1	2	2		1	1	1	1	2

This completes the demonstration.

Evidently the role played here by 2 is analogous to the role played by 1 in our regular truth tables. But note that the simple logical truth $(P \vee {\sim}P)$ does *not* have value 2 throughout:

P	v	~	P
2	2	0	2
1	1	1	1
0	2	2	0

This suggests that the additional proof-capability attained through *CP* could also be attained if we permitted the insertion of logical truths of the form $(P \vee {\sim}P)$. Indeed this is the case, as we can prove briefly: A formal deduction for any valid propositional argument is easily produced if the argument's corresponding conditional can be inserted into the proof. But the latter is a logical truth, and when expressed in conjunctive normal form it will consist of a series of conjuncts each having the shape $(P \vee {\sim}P \vee R)$. If we are permitted to introduce expressions of the form $(P \vee {\sim}P)$, then each conjunct can be inserted into the proof (with the help of *Add*), and the group can be collected by *Conj* and then transformed into the corresponding conditional. It thus appears that the addition of conditional proof to the system of Section 13, Chapter 3, is equivalent to the addition of a rule permitting the introduction of logical truths.

APPENDIX C • SUPPLEMENTS AND COMPLEMENTS

In the following paragraphs there are listed a series of problems and topics that are related to the subject matter of this book by natural lines of development and the names of a few textbooks frequently employed to initiate the corresponding studies. Extensive bibliographic materials for logic and related matters are available in almost any college or university library, in most public libraries, and in the *Journal of Symbolic Logic.*

The survey of deductive forms in the foregoing text is evidently not complete. For example, there are numerous arguments that require the quantification of properties, such as,

> John and Jim are alike in every way.
> John has red hair.
> Therefore, Jim has red hair.

Again, some arguments demand consideration of properties of properties, or properties of properties of properties, and so on, such as,

> All of John's visible properties are desirable.
> Hair color is a visible property.
> John has red hair.
> Therefore, red hair is desirable.

To formalize such arguments along the lines pursued in this text, one requires symbols and conventions for the quantification of properties and for the translation of statements involving properties of properties, and so on, as well as rules for drawing inferences from such expressions. It can be shown that such extended systems cannot be both complete and consistent; that is, they cannot be such as to permit the construction of proofs for all valid arguments, unless they also permit the construction of proofs for some invalid arguments.

Completeness and consistency are themselves properties *of* logical systems, highly desirable for obvious reasons; another is the existence of a decision procedure for the types of arguments to which a method of proof-construction is applied. When considering such properties the logical systems themselves become objects of attention, without regard to their intended employment. Some of the methods developed in this text have been examined in that way, but not exhaustively.

Further study of these abstract properties practically requires the *axiomatization* of the logical systems involved. Roughly, this means that only a few principles or rules are chosen as axioms, and it is then shown that all of the principles that occur in the finished system can be regarded as repeated applications of the axioms. Small steps in the direction of axiomatic reconstruction are visible in this book, notably in Section 4 of Chapter 6, in scattered discussions of redundancy, and in Appendixes A and B. Axiomatization not only facilitates the study of a system's general properties; it also clarifies its structure and limits, and aids in the formulation and comparison of alternatives.

There are some deductive arguments that are paradoxical, in the sense that a contradiction is apparently deducible from logically true or otherwise unexceptionable premises. The oldest known example concerns a man who says, "I am lying." If true, it seems to follow that this is false; and if false, true. Paradoxes occur in a wide range of contexts, including mathematics; their proper classification and solution are matters of contemporary disagreement. But discussion of the paradoxes is considerably facilitated by consideration of extended and axiomatized logical systems. Such systems also figure prominently in discussions of the relation between logic and mathematics.

Generally, the greatest difficulties arise in connection with propositions that make reference (perhaps implicitly) to what are obviously conceptual entities. For instance, statements may refer to entities or circumstances that are known to be non-factual, or possibly so. (Compare the discussions of material implication in Chapter 2 and of vacuous truths in Chapter 5.) Again, statements may refer to a person's beliefs or intentions. (Compare Exercise 5 following Section 7, Chapter 8.) Finally, propositions may refer to *other* propositions, in order to assert something about their status *as* propositions. Under this heading we may place those propositions that assign truth-functional relations to (other) propositions; in general, we know how to approach such cases. Propositions may also assign *probability-values* to (other) propositions; the study of such cases is part of inductive logic. Finally, and commonly, there are propositions in which the concepts of *necessity*, *possibility*, and *impossibility* are applied to (other) propositions; these are frequently called *modal* propositions and the arguments in which they appear *modal* arguments. Here is an example of a modal argument:

> It is necessarily true that if Kant was a bachelor then he was unmarried.
> Kant was a bachelor.
> Therefore, it is necessarily true that Kant was unmarried.

If we interpret a necessarily true proposition as one that cannot conceivably or possibly be false, we see that this argument is invalid (true premises and false conclusion). Note also that if the phrase "it is necessarily true that" is erased in both occurrences, the result would be a valid argument. This suggests (rightly) that there is no simple way to extend the conventions and principles developed in this book to the analysis of modal arguments; supplementary methods are needed.

Axiomatic development, systems with higher-level predicates, completeness, consistency, decision procedures, paradoxes, modal arguments:—all of these are parts of what is usually termed advanced symbolic logic. Studies in this area can be conveniently initiated in many texts, among which the following are often used.

> Church, Alonzo, *Introduction to Mathematical Logic*. Princeton, N. J.: Princeton University Press, 1956.
>
> Copi, Irving, *Symbolic Logic*. New York: The Macmillan Company, 1954.
>
> Lewis, C. I. and Langford, C. H., *Symbolic Logic*. New York: The Century Company, 1932. Paperback reprint (2nd ed. rev.): Dover.
>
> Quine, Willard Van O., *Mathematical Logic*. 2nd ed. rev. Cambridge: Harvard University Press, 1951. Paperback reprint: Harper & Row, Publishers, Inc.

The Lewis and Langford volume, although considerably older than the others, is the only one in this list containing an extensive treatment of modal arguments.

Deductive logic has been here defined as the study of necessary inference. The study of probable inference, or inductive logic, has close ties with deductive logic, but also with statistical theory and with the philosophy of science. Also, logic of either kind is related in complex and sometimes obscure ways to language, mathematics, and empirical science. Finally, like all disciplines, logic has a history, and a cluster of philosophical problems associated with it. The following are widely respected for their illuminating surveys of those topics:

Angell, Richard B., *Reasoning and Logic*. New York: Appleton-Century-Crofts, 1964.

Cohen, Morris R. and Nagel, Ernest, *An Introduction to Logic and Scientific Method*. New York: Harcourt, Brace and Company, 1934.

Copi, Irving, *Introduction to Logic*. New York: The Macmillan Company, 1961.

Eaton, Ralph M., *General Logic*. New York: Charles Scribner's Sons, 1931. Paperback reprint: Charles Scribner's Sons.

These and other general textbooks also contain introductory treatments of deductive logic, each from a somewhat different perspective. Thus, they put the subject that has been the exclusive preoccupation of this book into its wider context of human interests and activities.

INDEX

Format by Jeanne Ray Juster
Set in Monotype Modern 8A
Composed by Trade Composition, Inc.
Printed by The Murray Printing Company
Bound by The Haddon Craftsmen, Inc.
HARPER & ROW, PUBLISHERS, INCORPORATED